To Brian Fenton

with best wishes

Tony Judge

Sept '01

The Force of Persuasion

Tony Judge

PF The Police Federation
15 Langley Road, Surbiton, Surrey KT6 6LP

First published in Great Britain in 1994 by
THE POLICE FEDERATION
15 Langley Road
Surbiton, Surrey KT6 6LP

ISBN 0 - 901786 - 04 - 7

Typeset by the Police Federation Printing Department
Printed in Great Britain by
Butler & Tanner Ltd, Frome

Distributed by
Avon Direct Mail
PO Box 1, Portishead, Bristol BS20 9EG

Index

Foreword

Shortly before the Golden Jubilee conference of the Police Federation in 1969, Dick Pamplin and Reg Gale asked me to write its history. Time was short and *The first fifty years* could do little more than cover the main events of that period. I have always wanted to write in more detail about the early years, and to place the Federation in its proper context as an essential part of police history.

The first book appeared at the same time as the late Gerry Reynolds MP and I published *The night the police went on strike*, which dealt with the short life of the police union and its tragic climax in 1919, so *The first fifty years* did not cover this important episode, which shaped the form in which the Federation was created by Parliament. This book remedies that omission.

I have related the Federation's story to contemporary events and the evolution of the police service. After all, 1994 is not only the 75th anniversary of the Federation, but of the foundation of the national police service. This book appears just as the most fundamental changes to the system created in 1919 are about (for better or worse), to happen. I have also been able to devote more attention to the slow and often difficult expansion of the role of women officers.

It was twenty five years ago, just after the Golden Jubilee, that the Federation began to fulfil its other role as the voice of the police service. It has now taken its rightful place as a negotiating body and a part of police policy making. In attempting to keep up with the vast range of topics on the Federation's 'public' agenda in recent years, I must apologise to readers for having to switch so abruptly, on many occasions, from these to domestic issues and back again.

I have relied on my own recollection of events and on the Federation's extensive records. The facts, so far as I can see, have been faithfully recorded. The opinions, and the historical interpretation of those events, are my own.

I hope that non-police readers will find these pages increasing their understanding of the unique world of policing. A lot of nonsense is spoken today about 'police culture'. The police service, despite the Sheehy report, is a very special vocation and at its best, its comradeship and fierce professional pride serve police and people very well. The Federation, while fiercely defending the rights of its members and constantly striving to improve their status, has never lost sight of the principles which make the service truly special.

I dedicated *The first fifty years* to the pioneers who sacrificed their own careers to serve their comrades, when to do so invited victimisation from the authorities. Those days have gone for good, and today's Federation leaders are full time professionals, well trained and competent. But the modern police officer still owes a lot to the dedication of those who laid the foundations and built the Federation into what it is today, and this history is respectfully dedicated to them all.

Tony Judge, Surbiton, 1994

ONE

John Syme's body

The Police Federation of England and Wales was born on 14 July 1919, when the report of the Committee of Inquiry into the Police Service was published as a White Paper. On the same day, the Government published the Police Bill, which received its Second Reading in the House of Commons just three days later.

The cause of such haste was the Government's determination to banish trades unionism from the police service. It was almost a year since the National Union of Police and Prison Officers had called a sudden and successful strike among the London police. For two days, almost every constable and sergeant in the capital had refused duty in support of the union's demands for a substantial wage rise; a pension for police widows; recognition of the union, and; reinstatement of police officers who had been dismissed for belonging to it.

The strike, which occurred at a crucial stage of the First World War, shocked the country and required the Prime Minister, David Lloyd George, to intervene personally. The Commissioner of the Metropolitan Police, Sir Edward Henry, had resisted the idea of a police trade union for years, and when a Metropolitan Police Union was formed in 1913, instigated by a former inspector, John Syme, he informed the force that no police officer could belong to it, on pain of instant dismissal.

John Syme was dismissed from the Metropolitan Police in 1910. He had protested against an adverse report by his superiors which had resulted in a compulsory transfer. In a letter to the Commissioner which gave his side of the incident, he made allegations against two senior officers, saying that their treatment of subordinates at Gerald Road police station in Pimlico was tyrannical. He was charged with making false allegations and reduced to the rank of station sergeant. His appeal to the Commissioner was dismissed. He tried to appeal to the Home Secretary, but was informed that the Commissioner's decision was final, whereupon he wrote again to the Commissioner to say that he intended to put his case to a Member of Parliament in the hope that the matter would be raised in the House of Commons. This was construed as a further disciplinary offence, and Syme was summarily dismissed.

From then until his death 35 years later, John Syme fought a long campaign for justice. His constant allegations of corruption and tyranny in the Scotland Yard hierarchy brought him into conflict with the authorities. He was prosecuted and imprisoned for a criminal libel against Sir Edward Henry, and again for trying to persuade policemen not to join the armed services during the war. In later years he was often arrested for throwing stones through the windows of Number Ten Downing Street. In prison, he would go on hunger strike and was subjected to the torture of forcible feeding. In 1931, a Government inquiry concluded that the original disciplinary decision against Syme was wrong, and he was granted a pension, backdated to 1910, but this came too late to save his health, and he continued his lone campaign for a full apology.

The union which Syme founded in 1913 never consisted of more than a handful of members whilst he was its leader. In the face of constant harassment by the force, it was obliged to hold meetings in secret, and its members kept in touch with each other by leaving messages in newsagents shops. During the war, union meetings were sometimes raided by officers of the Special Branch and any officer caught in the net was dismissed and called up for service in the trenches. Some became conscientious objectors and went to prison rather than wear army uniforms.

It was during one of Syme's absences in prison that the other members of the union concluded that they would never make progress under his leadership. As late as April 1917, there were only 47 paid-up members. Syme was not interested in pursuing the normal trade union aims of better working conditions. To him, the union was a rallying point for other police victims of 'officialdom'. The members decided to dismiss Syme from the secretary's post, and new officers were elected. They set to work to persuade prominent politicians and trades union leaders to take up their cause, and press Sir Edward Henry to recognise the union. The Commissioner had the same answer to all the public men who approached him; there would be no union in the Metropolitan Police.

As the war continued, police officers were experiencing real hardships. Their wages fell below the levels of other workers while inflation reduced the value of their wages. They were required to work many hours of unpaid overtime to make up for the absence of thousands of colleagues who had joined the armed forces, and their weekly rest day, the right to which had only been secured a few years earlier, was suspended. Any man who complained was informed that he could always join the Army and take his chance in the trenches, but wartime regulations forbade officers from resigning to take other jobs, such as better paid work in munitions factories.

When it became known that the union had turned from attacking the force leadership to campaigning for the men's interests, its membership began to increase, in spite of the risk of dismissal. Union activists began to take the message to other forces, and the name was changed from Metropolitan Police Union to National Union of Police and Prison Officers. The union attempted to lessen fears among the chief officers by inserting a new 'no strike' clause in its constitution. Although by 1918 actual membership remained small, the union contained a nucleus of dedicated men with the ability to organise their colleagues. This was to prove invaluable when the strike came.

The end of August 1918 was the moment chosen by the union leaders to deliver an ultimatum to the Commissioner. Whether by accident or intention, this caught Scotland Yard and the Home Office totally unprepared. The Commissioner and the Permanent Under Secretary had left London on holiday. The Acting Commissioner took the union's letter round to the Home Office and discussed it with the Home Secretary. On being assured that the threat need not be taken

seriously, Sir George Cave left London on his summer holiday.
There had been some talk among senior officers of dissatisfaction in the force, but a meeting of all the superintendents
had assured the chief officers that there was no support for
the illegal union. This information was passed to the Home
Office by Henry, who was anxious to secure a widows'
pension scheme and thought that the delay over this was a
major reason for discontent in the force.

The spark that started the strike was the dismissal of a
union official, PC Tommy Thiel. The Chief Constable of
Manchester had complained to Henry that Thiel had been
trying to organise a union branch in that force. On the 27th
August, the Union executive sent its ultimatum, saying that
unless its demands were met by midnight on the 29th August,
it would suspend its 'no strike' rule and the authorities would
be responsible for any situation that might arise.

When no reply had been received by the deadline, union
officials toured London police stations on their bicycles,
calling out the night shift, and by the next morning it was
clear that the vast majority of uniformed constables and
sergeants due to parade had obeyed the union's instructions.
The next day, thousands more did not turn up for duty and
the streets of the capital were devoid of police.

The strike had a number of immediate consequences. Lloyd
George and his cabinet colleagues were obliged to meet the
strike leaders in Downing Street on the morning of the 31st
August. To spare their own embarrassment and that of the
force hierarchy, they insisted that they were receiving the
delegation as representatives of the men, not as the union
executive, for this, said the Home Secretary, Sir George Cave,
'Would be recognition'. The demands on pay and a widows'
pension were conceded in full, and the Prime Minister agreed
that officers who had been dismissed for union activity would
be reinstated.

The demand for a substantial pay increase was the principal
reason for the success of the strike. The men had been driven
to refusing duty by their inability to live on their pay. When
war broke out in August 1914 a constable was paid thirty
shillings weekly on joining the Metropolitan Police, and he
had the prospect of reaching two pounds a week after twenty

years' service. A labourer in London could expect to earn twenty two shillings, and a skilled engineering fitter about thirty eight shillings. The police enjoyed benefits which were exceptional among working class occupations; a pension; paid annual leave; job security and either a free house or an allowance towards the cost of rented accommodation (in London this was two shillings weekly). Most large police forces paid rates akin to the Metropolitan, but wages in small and rural forces were considerably lower. Here, it was traditional to equate the wage of a constable with the going rate for agricultural labourers, and there was no shortage of men willing to work for that.

It was not long before wartime inflation, coupled with the acute shortage of labour as volunteers flocked to answer Lord Kitchener's call - *Your country needs you* - saw earnings in other jobs outstrip police pay. By 1917 the average wage of a labourer in London was 48s 9d, whilst the skilled fitter could expect 67s 4d. The top rate constable, even with wartime cost of living bonuses, was getting only 48s, plus 1s 6d for each child. Many policemen had got into debt to shopkeepers. The Desborough Committee saw the typical household budgets of police families when they conducted their Inquiry in 1919, they were shocked to discover that real poverty existed in many country policemen's households.

The pay issue was settled almost as soon as the Downing Street meeting commenced. The pensionable pay of a top rate constable was increased from 40s to 53s, plus 12s war bonus.

But the key issue to both sides was union recognition. Lloyd George had no intention of allowing a body which was to him little different from the workers and soldiers Soviets which had swept away the Russian establishment only a year before, to gain a permanent foothold in the British police, but he was anxious to end the strike before serious disorder broke out in London. The strike leaders, advised by the TUC and some Labour members of Parliament, knew that it was now or never. For a brief moment they held the initiative, and if they agreed to end the strike without getting the union recognised, their main objective would not have been secured.

Lloyd George made an offer which took the Government to the brink of recognition without actually granting it. He told Charles Duncan MP, the secretary of the Workers' Union who acted as an intermediary in bringing the strike leaders and the government together; that the men could have an organisation to speak for them; 'Whether it is to be the union or an internal body is something to be decided.' He agreed that the ban on union membership in the Metropolitan Police and other forces would be lifted, and there would be no objection to the men joining the union so long as it agreed not to interfere with the discipline of the police force. This formula was sufficient to get the negotiations going. The union pressed Lloyd George to concede recognition, but he pointed out that this was wartime, and normal trade union bargaining arrangements would not be appropriate when the service was on a war footing. He promised that 'in the meantime', there would be some kind of organisation to allow grievances to be ventilated.

When the union leaders emerged from Downing Street, they told the great crowd of strikers who had waited outside, that they had won a total victory, but a carefully worded Home Office press statement set out the Government's position on recognition. It reiterated Lloyd George's view that there could be no recognition 'in wartime' and his fear that allowing the police, 'a semi-military force', to have a union, was too akin to the 1917 Revolution, and he 'would not have a repetition in this country of what had happened in Russia.' It was ludicrous to compare the ordinary constables and sergeants who had been forced to strike for a living wage, but had conducted themselves with great good humour while waiting for the results of the meeting, with the murderers of the Russian royal family. But as Lloyd George said years later, when talking about the strike to a policeman in the Houses of Parliament; 'This country was nearer to Bolshevism that night than at any time in our history'.

As the triumphant strike leaders were holding a victory rally on Tower Hill, after marching from Downing Street, the man who was to lead the Government's counter attack against

Bolshevism in the police service was entering Number Ten through the back entrance. This was General Sir Nevil Macready, at that time the 56 years old Adjutant General to the Forces. He was Lloyd George's choice of successor to Sir Edward Henry, who had promptly resigned following the Prime Minister's capitulation, as he saw it, to the mutineers.

Macready was a leader of men and a martinet. His career had been marked by frequent clashes with authority, military and political. He had argued with the previous Prime Minister, Herbert Asquith, over the executions of the leaders of the Easter rebellion in Ireland, and more recently with Parliament over his refusal to allow a Select Committee to investigate his department at the War Office.

In 1910 Macready had been appointed by the Home Secretary, Winston Churchill, to command detachments of the Metropolitan Police and the army which were dispatched to the strike bound coalfields in South Wales. The clashes between police, troops and miners at Tonypandy and Penycraig are still part of the folklore of the Labour movement. Macready, as he recorded in his memoirs, gained a great respect for the Metropolitan Police during this time, and thought them much superior to the local police, whose senior officers felt obliged to support the mine owners. He was not annoyed, for example, when a strike committee allowed the pompous and incompetent chief constable of Glamorgan, a Captain Lindsay, to be lowered to the bottom of the mineshaft, to order strikers who were occupying the coalface to come to the surface, but once the chief's party alighted, the cage was winched to the surface and they stayed marooned overnight.

When Macready met the Prime Minister, he at first refused Lloyd George's offer of the Commissionership, because he wanted to play his part in the creation of the new 'Model Army' which many professional soldiers knew must emerge from the carnage of the trenches, a catastrophe caused by the generals who were stuck in the time warp of the Empire and the dominance of cavalry. But the Premier, encouraged by Churchill, insisted that it was the General's duty to 're-store the discipline of the police.' The argument, according to Macready's account, lasted for two hours but eventually he gave in.

Macready's first look at the situation at Scotland Yard appalled him. He found that the hierarchy was completely out of touch with the force, and that many men in high positions were incompetent. They were quickly removed. The General brought in trusted Army colleagues to fill the vacant posts, and sought and found able police officers who were quickly promoted. The district chief constables were turned out of their cosy offices at Scotland Yard and dispatched to the areas they were supposed to be in charge of. Macready told them that from now on they were to be his 'eyes and ears.' He wanted to know what was happening, and what the men were thinking.

The union leaders immediately dismissed Macready as a typically stiff necked military brasshat, but he made a big impression on the force by visiting stations and talking to the men, something that Henry had never done in his long reign at Scotland Yard. The force also welcomed his reforms, including the abolition of some irksome regulations and a pernicious 'fines' system which meant that men were punished for trivial offences out of all proportion to their 'crimes'.

Macready did not require more than a cursory examination of the state of the force to understand why the unthinkable, a strike of Metropolitan Police officers, had occurred. He was shocked to learn that experienced police officers with large families to keep were taking home less than shopgirls and women working in Woolwich Arsenal filling cartridge cases. The force's medical officers were writing certificates to confirm that some officers on the sick list were suffering from malnutrition. All this had been kept from the ageing Henry, who pottered around nursing his pet scheme, the widows pension, oblivious of the fact that some of his men were going hungry because they did not earn enough to feed their children and themselves. Yet on many occasions sympathetic MPs had asked questions in the House of Commons about the low state of pay and morale in the force, and the Home Secretary had given procrastinating answers, accepting Henry's assurance that talk of discontent was just the work of union troublemakers. There was no mystery about the sudden success of the illegal union; without a recognised body to speak for them, the men had chosen to follow those who spoke out on their behalf.

Within days of taking command, Macready called a meeting of representatives of every division at which he set out his plans for a representative body to act on behalf of constables and sergeants. There was, said Macready, a need for the police to have their own association for ensuring that grievances were heard, but if this was done, a trade union was not needed. This angered the union leaders, but it was clear from the outset that Macready was against any form of trades unionism in the police force.

Soon afterwards, at a meeting between Macready, the Home Secretary and the union leaders, it was agreed that dismissed union activists would be taken back in the force, and that the men were free to join the union. This agreement was one that Macready had no qualms about breaking immediately. Several of the men concerned had refused to serve in the Army after being dismissed from the police, and had been sentenced by courts martial to terms in military prisons. He told the force that he did not want as policemen, men who would not fight for their country.

The agreement stated that the union would keep out of the 'regulation and discipline of the service' and not induce police officers to withold their services. If this condition was breached, members of the force might be called upon to sever their connection with the union.

The meeting agreed on the form that the new representative board would take. Constables, sergeants and inspectors at every station were to elect one man to represent all of them. The board was to be entirely independent of any outside body, and would have direct access to the Commissioner. When the first elections took place, all the union officials secured election and the board consisted of one inspector, five sergeants and twenty five constables. This was not at all the result Macready had intended or expected. He had seriously underestimated the great support in the force for the heroes of the strike. When the results were announced, the Commissioner stated that fresh elections would be held in a few months time, at which the three ranks would each elect their own boards. Thus was born the principle of rank representation which has persisted to the present day.

The union leadership maintained that the representative board was no more than a stop-gap body, pending full recognition of the union once the war was over. Just a month after the first board was elected, came the armistice of 11th November. But, as the nation rejoiced and looked forward to the years of peace, General Macready was quite determined that the union would be destroyed within a very short time, and he was planning to ensure that its' destruction would come about largely through the union's own actions. And time was to prove him right.

TWO

The union has to go

'If the police of Manchester or Liverpool or Glasgow go wrong today,' General Macready told the Desborough Committee in 1919, 'it would be very uncomfortable for those particular towns, but it would not shake the Empire. If the Metropolitan Police go wrong, it will.'

Police forces outside London had taken no part in the dramatic Metropolitan Police strike, and the service was amazed and excited by the event. Chief constables were shaken. In a few forces, one or two individuals had been involved with London union members in attempts to form branches, but these had all been suppressed by the chief officers. The latter were not at all pleased when at the end of September 1918, the Home Office issued a circular, drawing attention to the new scales of pay which had been part of the strike settlement, and hinting that provincial forces should follow suit. The circular spelt out the Home Office view on union membership, which coincided with the formula agreed in the Metropolitan Police. Chief constables saw this as interference, and while they felt they had no choice but to allow men to join the union, they urged them not to do so, saying that the forces could have representative boards on the Metropolitan pattern. The chief constable of Birmingham, Colonel Rafter, told his force that the ban on union membership would stay, but this did not dissuade hundreds of Birmingham officers from joining it.

The provincial officers were eager to join the union. Within weeks its paid-up membership reached 40,000, almost the total strength of uniform constables and sergeants at that time, when forces were depleted by the calls of military service and the gaps were being filled by thousands of special constables. Almost all forces had seen their pay increased as a direct result of the strike, and it was hoped that the union would, at long last, be able to do something about conditions in the forces outside London, where chief constables had ruled without challenge ever since their forces were formed.

The leading figure in the union was PC James Marston, a 43 years old Norfolk man who had fifteen years' service. He had been the chief spokesman during the strike. Macready despised Marston, whom he ridiculed in his memoirs as a dim witted yokel, unable to express his ideas clearly and incapable of understanding plain English. At that time, the rank and file found no difficulty in understanding what Marston said. He was a bluntly spoken and obdurate man, who distrusted all senior officers and was convinced that Macready was the union's sworn enemy, as indeed he was. Marston's main failing was his overbearing and dictatorial manner, which in the end was to alienate him from his supporters. He regarded the union as his own creation, even though he had come to it quite lately, and was determined to maintain his own powerful position as chairman of the executive committee.

A far more significant and competent leader than any of the group which had planned and lead the strike soon emerged. This was Sergeant Jack Hayes, who was elected to the post of General Secretary at the union's first and only national conference. Born in Wolverhampton, Hayes was 32 years old when he took office. Macready saw at once that he was a different proposition from Marston. When Hayes told the Commissioner that he was about to leave the force to become the full time general secretary at £500 a year, Macready advised him not to do so, saying that if the union collapsed, as he believed it would, he would be left in the lurch, while if he stayed in the force his future was assured. Hayes answered that his mind was made up, and the new post would allow him to take part in politics. He was destined to be the Labour MP for Edge Hill in Liverpool for two brief spells between the wars, when he became known as the Policeman's MP.

The Government remained nervous about the reliability of the police service. Macready was pleased when the ineffectual Home Secretary, Sir George Cave was replaced by a politician more attuned to the Commissioner's views of what needed to be done. Edward Shortt KC, Liberal MP for Newcastle West, kept in daily contact with the Commissioner, and approved the plans he was making to deal with any threat of further disruption in the force These included arrangements to call on the army garrisons stationed in London, and the widespread use of special constables. In the City of London, for example, the Honourable Artillery Company, at Macready's suggestion, raised a company of Special Constables against the possibility of a strike in the City Police. The HAC Specials are active in the City today. The General was not impressed with Sir William Nott Bower, the City Commissioner, and later wrote that the existence of this separate force in the heart of the capital was an unwarranted anachronism, which made it difficult for him to make complete plans to deal with the union. If he had his way, Macready wrote, he would abolish it and retain a small force of about fifty to deal with ceremonial duties at the Guildhall.

The General never had any doubt that there would soon be a decisive showdown between himself and the union. He did not hide his contempt for members of the union dominated representative board, which may have been his creation but was certainly not his creature. Attending the first meeting of the board in October 1918, Macready told them that he was aware that pressure was being exerted on men who had not joined the union, and he warned that he would not tolerate intimidation. The union leaders were equally dismissive of the Commissioner. They were confident that the great majority of the Metropolitan Police backed them. When the time was right, they planned a repeat of the first operation, when the authorities would cave in rather than risk another strike. Some of the more moderate union members doubted this, but knowing Marston's way with opposition, they kept their views to themselves.

Macready was not content merely to frustrate and crush the union. He saw the strike and the union as manifestations of the malaise which had afflicted the entire service for years. He invited all the other chief constables to a secret conference in London, where he urged them to consider the advantages of improved national police organisation and liaison between forces. He suggested that there should be more Home Office inspectors, keeping in constant touch with all forces, and suggested that for the first time, the Home Office should have a specific police department. These ideas were not received with enthusiasm by his listeners, who were almost all long serving police officers or men with far more police experience than Macready. They were not ready to see the Metropolitan Commissioner taking a leading role in the national affairs of the service, and the idea of a national force, answerable to the Home Secretary, was unthinkable. After this meeting, the Commissioner wrote to the Home Secretary, setting out his strategy;

> 'I do not think the main body of the force will be led away a second time, but it is just possible that a few hot-heads may attempt a strike, and if so, it must be smashed once and for all time, otherwise I do not think that you will ever have any peace with the police of this country. I am making my plans known only to two or three people (for I do not trust many people here). They consist very shortly in carrying out the work with those men who remain staunch, with special constables and the military. I am of course paying attention to such things as telephones, power stations etc. If anything of this kind happens, there will be no time for talk at the Cabinet. Therefore, I suggest that the line to take with the men should simply be the sack and no reinstatement.'

On Christmas Eve 1918, in his final act as Home Secretary, Cave gave orders that a draft Bill should be prepared, to be enacted immediately in the event of a strike, which would place the police under military-style discipline in the event of any emergency. Presumably, and with the all too recent example of what happened to mutineers in France in mind, this would have given Macready the right to shoot strikers! In the event, the Bill was never activated.

In January 1919, the union organised a national rally in the Albert Hall. Over 5,000 police from all over Britain and

Ireland attended, but it turned out to be far from the triumphant celebration the organisers had intended. Already the union was beginning to tear itself apart as provincial officers fought with the strongly entrenched Metropolitan leaders for at least a share of power. For the first time, rank and file members learned of dissension among the executive members. One well known leader had resigned after a row with Marston. A second, who was widely respected, had been accused of being a spy for Macready and dismissed from office. This was Ernest Harrison, a former constable who, during the war, had wrested the union from John Syme and turned it into the body which organised the strike. He had been dismissed by Henry and sent to a military prison for refusing to serve in the Army. Macready had offered him reinstatement if he would join the Military Police for a period, and when Marston heard of this, Harrison was regarded as a traitor to the union.

The atmosphere of the meeting became ugly when Marston was unable to give satisfactory answers to critics who wanted to see the accounts and accused him of trying to run the union on his own. It emerged that there was a backlog of 800 unanswered letters. There were scuffles between some northern members and Marston's supporters. As they left for home, many members would have been concerned about the disturbing state of the union's organisation.

The rank and file union members had further cause for doubt soon after the Albert Hall meeting. At a Government sponsored conference of all trade unions and employers' organisations; the National Industrial Conference, presided over by Mr Lloyd George, Marston made a speech which acknowledged that in the past, the Government and police commanders had been guilty of 'deliberate and persistent misdirection of the police in times of labour troubles.' He went on; 'Henceforth, the government must not use the police force as a tool against any other sections of the nation'. Macready was furious because, through the ignorance of a Ministry of Labour official, the police union had been given credentials to attend the conference. This, he said, was tantamount to granting it recognition.

The Government stated that it would approve the report

of the National Industrial Conference, which proposed the setting up of a National Industrial Council. Marston had impressed the other trades unionists at the Conference, so much so that they elected him as a member of the Joint Committee of Unions and Management, along with leading Labour figures including Arthur Henderson and Margaret Bondfield, both future cabinet ministers. Moreover, the trades union side pressed the Government representatives at the conference on the question of recognising the police union. After all, its general secretary was now a full member of the Government's own Industrial Council. Sir Robert Horne, the Minister of Labour, gave the union side an assurance that the government accepted the NIC in total, which suggested that he and his officials were either unaware, or uncaring, of the problem this created for the Home Office.

Marston described himself as a marxist. At a Labour demonstration in Hyde Park in February 1919, he told the crowd that in Ireland armed police were suppressing the people and he expected they would soon be called upon to do the same in England. All this was carefully noted by Special Branch observers who were reporting to Macready on everything the union was doing. He knew that most police officers would be shocked by Marston's remarks, and a number of union branches, reading reports of these meetings, protested to HQ.

Mr Shortt, the new Home Secretary, was totally behind Macready. In February 1919, he told Parliament that the Government had decided to appoint a Committee of Inquiry, chaired by Lord Desborough, to inquire into police conditions. Among the other members were two Labour MPs, one of whom was a trade union general secretary, and a Liberal MP, Sir James Remnant, who had championed the police cause for a long time. The Committee's terms of reference were;

> 'to consider and report whether any and what changes should be made in the method of recruiting for, the conditions of service of, and the rates of pay, pensions, and allowances of the police forces of England, Wales and Scotland.'

In London the new Commissioner was stamping his personality on the force. He introduced a number of small welfare improvements, while cracking down on lax discipline. Some men were sacked for offences which would not have been dealt with quite so harshly in the past — such as being off their beats and drinking on duty. The union saw this as a further example of the General's 'Prussianism'.

It was not long before there was a total breakdown of relations between Macready and the representative board. He had been careful to demonstate that improvements could be achieved through negotiations. The split shift system, by which the men's working day could be spread over sixteen hours and involve two return journeys, was abolished. A better promotion system was brought in, and the Victorian oil lamps carried at night were replaced with electric torches. But mostly the board made demands which he rejected, ridiculed or ignored. Finally, after an argument about overtime entitlements, Macready exploded when he read the contents of a letter sent to him by the Board. He marched to the room where the members were in session, and told them they had gone too far. Within days he published a force order;

> 'The Commissioner, judging from his experience during the past six months, is of the opinion that it is impossible that the discipline necessary to the efficiency of the force can be maintained if the interests of superior officers are placed in the hands of the lower ranks.'

Macready, fully supported by Shortt, went on to state that the first board was now abolished, and elections would be held to elect three separate boards for constables, sergeants, and inspectors. The union immediately rejected this decision. Marston sent a circular to all divisions, saying that the force 'will not take part in any way in the election of representatives under the scheme put forward by the police authorities.'

One union official, Constable Spackman, was dismissed from the force for writing 'No action' on the official notice giving details of the election arrangements. He was singled out to provoke the union, and show that Sir Nevil would not tolerate dissent.

On the 18th March, the War Cabinet discussed the trouble in the Metropolitan Police. It was decided that the time had come to make it clear that the union would never receive recognition, and Macready immediately published the decision to the force.

For once, the union showed some subtlety when reacting to the not unexpected news. Jack Hayes pointed out that the deadlock was between the Commissioner and the representative board, not the union. The Downing Street agreement had stated that the recognition question would be dealt with in peacetime, so it was not for the War Cabinet to make the decision. He would have been encouraged if he had known that the Minister of Labour, to the annoyance of the Home Office, had presented the War Cabinet with a paper outlining the circumstances in which the police union might be recognised. In those days, cabinet papers did not find their way to the press.

The union decided to hold a demonstration in Trafalgar Square on the 3rd of May, to protest against the decision to withhold recognition. Because of the Trafalgar Square Act 1844, Hayes had to apply to the Commissioner for permission to hold the rally in the square. Much amused, Macready not only agreed, but on the day he was among the crowd of more than 5,000 which gathered in front of Nelson's Column to hear speaker after speaker condemn his tyrannical rule. The crowd had marched along the embankment and up Whitehall, headed by brass bands and the banners of the police union. As the marchers passed the traffic refuge at the end of Whitehall, opposite Admiralty Arch, many of them recognised the frock coated, disdainful Commissioner staring at them contemptuously. Some of the senior officers on duty that Sunday afternoon, already deeply embarrassed about the nature of the gathering, were worried that some hotheads might attack Sir Nevil, but none dared to suggest to him that he should not be there. He heard Constable Jack Zollner, an executive member from the City of London police, forecast that Macready would be out of office 'within a week'.

Later in the same month, the union organised a national

ballot of its membership. The voting paper asked each man if he was prepared, if necessary, to strike in support of the recognition of the union and an immediate and substantial increase in pay. The Commissioner could not have been reassured about the metal of the provincial chief constables when he learned that many had actually assisted the union to organise the ballot, allowing posters and ballot boxes in police stations. Some of the chief constables of the largest forces told Shortt that they could not guarantee that their men would not strike. The City of London Commissioner had made arrangements with the army to send detachments of mounted soldiers to each police station as soon as trouble broke out, and he published this information in force orders. Macready, exercising strict secrecy, had made exactly the same arrangements in respect of ninety pivotal stations throughout London, and was furious that Sir Edward Nott Bower had shown his hand in this way.

The union declared that in the ballot, 44,000 members had said they were prepared to strike, against 4,000 who were not. Marston thought that Lloyd George, who was attending the Versailles peace conference, might yet intervene and a friendly MP sought to obtain Shortt's permission for Marston and Hayes to fly to Paris to see him. This plan was vetoed by Macready. Lloyd George, in any case, had no intention of getting involved again. He sent a message direct to Macready;

'... ... the police force is so essential to the stability of social order that at all hazards we must take steps to ensure that we have a body of men at the disposal of the state who can be relied upon. That we cannot command at the present moment as long as you have thousands of men who are under contract to disobey the authorities at the behest of an outside committee.'

While Marston and a majority of the executive of the union felt that a strike was now the union's only chance of gaining recognition, Jack Hayes and some of the newly elected provincial members of the executive were opposed to one. Hayes argued that the conditions had changed in favour of the authorities. The men were better paid, and thanks to

Macready, the force was prepared to smash a strike in London. He did not believe that there would be anything like the membership support they had enjoyed the previous year. At a tense meeting of the executive committee, held on the same day as a second mass rally in Hyde Park, there was a narrow majority against an immediate strike.

A crowd estimated at almost twenty thousand was present in Hyde Park on the 1st of June, listening to the speeches. It soon became clear that the union was split over the strike question, with some speakers making bitter attacks on the 'fainthearts' who had held back from challenging the Government a second time.

Just a few days later, Shortt told the House of Commons that the Government intended to legislate to prevent police officers belonging to a trade union. Looking ahead to the report of the Desborough Committee, he said the police would have an internal body, and then they would be asked to leave the union.

The police union was represented at the 1919 annual conference of the Labour Party, which met at Southport just after Shortt's announcement. The conference gave unanimous backing to a motion submitted by the union, demanding immediate full recognition But it was a blow to the union that James Sexton, one of the trades unionists on the Desborough Committee, was saying;

> 'I find myself unable to subscribe to the formation of a Police Union on the same lines as the ordinary trade union or, in fact the affiliation of a police union with any industrial organisation.'

The Report of the Desborough Committee was published on the 14th of July. It proposed that constables should be paid £3.10s a week on joining, rising to £4.10s after 10 years' service. There were to be two further increases, subject to efficiency, after 17 and 22 years service, bringing the top pay of a constable to £4.14s. There were *pro rata* increases for other ranks, and for the first time in police history, common rates of pay would apply throughout Great Britain. Desborough stated in his Report;

'... ... we have attempted to appraise ... ... the services rendered by the police to the community, the standard of qualifications required and the rate of remuneration which seems to us reasonable and proper in all the circumstances and likely to attract recruits of the right stamp ... ... we are satisfied that a policeman has responsibilities and obligations which are peculiar to his calling and distinguish him from other public servants ... ... and we consider the police entitled to special consideration in regard to their rate of pay and pension.'

The report contained more good news. The pay increase was back dated to the 1st April, which meant that the men could expect four months' back pay. The Home Secretary announced that the recommendations were acceptable to the Government, and boosted morale in the service by announcing that every man would receive £10 back pay without delay. By conceding such an increase so quickly, the government had shot the union's fox, and the shrewder activists, Hayes among them, knew it.

The Desborough Report made no direct reference to the police union, but the Committee's proposals for a Police Federation confirmed that the union would never be recognised and that police officers would no longer be allowed to join it. Desborough proposed that the new body should consist of separate boards for constables, sergeants and inspectors in every force (there was to be no repetition of the constable dominated board first elected in the Metropolitan). The boards could act together as joint boards in matters of common interest. There was to be a central conference of each rank once a year, at which the delegates would elect a central committee to make representations to the Home Secretary and the police authorities. There would be a separate Federation for Scotland.

The publication of the Police Bill at the same time as the Desborough Report, and its immediate introduction into the House of Commons, caught its few opponents unready to mount an effective opposition to the provisions to set up the Police Federation and force policemen to choose between the union and their jobs. A Labour MP, Jack Jones of the General Workers union, declared in Parliament;

> 'The Government is mistaken if they imagine that we are going to stand idly by while they make it known that workmen, because the police are workmen, may not belong to a certain trade union, and that if they do belong to it the Government are going to bring the whole power of the state against them. They are raising an issue which is not going to end with the introduction of this Bill.'

But in the event, the Labour party and the trade union movement was indeed about to 'stand idly by' while the Government rushed the Bill through Parliament in a few days.The Police Act 1919 received the Royal Assent before the end of the month, and there was to be no assistance for the union when the final act of the drama was played out immediately afterwards.

THREE

The lost cause

T he Police Bill received the Royal Assent on the 30th July 1919. Macready and Shortt were relieved that the legislative procedure had occupied less than two weeks. The Bill had encountered no real opposition. The coalition government had an overwhelming majority in the House of Commons, and the speed with which the Bill was rushed through did not allow the handful of Labour MPs who were appalled at the legal destruction of a trade union, any chance of mounting an effective protest. The general view in Parliament and the country was that a group of dangerous revolutionaries was trying to take over the police, and they must be stopped. With a general election in the offing, Labour leaders had no intention of pursuing a hopeless cause.

In effect, the new Act outlawed the National Union of Police and Prison Officers. Serving officers who belonged to the union were required to resign their membership within a month, or disqualify themselves from being members of the force. Henceforth, police officers could not belong to a trade union or any body which sought to concern itself with the government of the police force. It became a criminal offence, punishable with two years' imprisonment, to seek to cause disaffection in the force.

The union executive met at its Bishopsgate office in the City on the same day that the Police Bill completed its Parliamentary passage. The leaders had to choose between capitulation and fighting for survival. Most of the London members were determined to call a strike. They were supported by some provincial members, especially two delegates from Liverpool, PCs Holliday and Smithwick. Conditions in Liverpool were especially bad and the mood of the force was heavily in favour of striking. So keen to call the men out were Holliday and Smithwick that they left the executive meeting at noon in order to catch a train home and organise things on Merseyside. They were confident that the executive would vote for a strike. It would have occurred to those executive members who were so anxious to strike, that for them, there was nothing to lose. Their union activities had singled them out as agitators and trouble makers, none could look forward to a worthwhile future in the police service. For those opposed to a strike, the prospect of being involved with the new Federation was certainly more attractive than the grim realities of life without work.

Hayes and most of the provincial members argued against a strike. The chief spokesman for the moderates was Sergeant Thomas of Bristol, who had already persuaded the members of that force to change their views, originally in favour of striking. Delegates from Sheffield and Manchester, PCs Barthorpe and Fox, said that their forces would not give it much support, in spite of Barthorpe's attempts to persuade the Sheffield men to come out. Fox was personally opposed to a strike.

Hayes pointed out that the Desborough pay scales, and the back pay, had transformed the feelings of the service. The previous August, the Government had been taken by surprise, now it was ready for any emergency. Moreover, Parliament had passed the Police Act, so the Government had a huge mandate to remove the union from the police service. Most men would see it as an act of madness to go on strike now, and probably put an end to their employment in the police. He felt that their best course, indeed their only course, was to accept that the Federation was now in being and the union would have to close down. The men still supported their leaders, he said, and they could continue to fight for them through the new body.

Marston would have nothing to do with such defeatism, and suggested that any union man wanting to accept the authorities' creation, the Federation, was betraying the membership. Marston and his supporters clung to the 'mandate' of the big membership vote in June in support of a strike. That had been about union recognition as well as pay, and Marston claimed that the members would stand by the union. The moderates told him that what applied in early June was no longer applicable, but he was past listening.

Hayes persuaded the executive to make one more attempt to negotiate with Lloyd George. He wrote a letter to the Premier, asking that those provisions of the Bill which concerned the union should be held in abeyance until he had discussed the issue with the executive. The letter claimed that Lloyd George had promised that the police would have the right to remain members of their own union, and ended; 'I cannot too earnestly impress upon you, Sir, the grave nature of the present situation.'

The letter was sent to Downing Street by hand, and within an hour the messenger was back with the news that Lloyd George was not at home and a private secretary would deal with the letter. Marston called for a decision as to whether to strike or not.

When the vote was taken, the members were evenly divided. Unwilling to exercise his casting vote, Marston proposed that a deputation wait outside Number Ten until the Premier returned at midnight. As Lloyd George got out of the car, Marston and Hayes stepped forward and asked him at least to listen to what they had to say. He brushed them aside. The executive digested this rebuff and continued in session until it was almost daylight. Finally, they decided that a strike should be called as from 10pm that night (31st July). There is no record of how the executive voted, but unless the moderates had already walked out, it must have been close. The union's strike manifesto was published on the front page of the Labour paper, the *Daily Herald*. In it, the union members were told;

> 'You must act or lose your freedom for ever ... ... the members of the executive committee have already withdrawn their services and are prepared to sacrifice all for the cause, being assured that the members they represent will fight for justice and liberty.'

For the rest of the day, both the union and Macready were busy making dispositions. The plans which Macready had laid so carefully were put into effect. Every senior officer was on duty, stiffening the sinews of the middle ranking officers, and encouraging constables and sergeants to stay loyal. The message from the Yard was uncompromising; any man who went out on strike was finished with the police force.

For the strike organisers, it was a case of bad news following closely upon bad news. They too had made plans for this day, but now one after the other trusted officials who had been assigned key roles in bringing out stations, admitted that they would not even be striking themselves. While George Lansbury, the editor of the *Daily Herald*, was writing an editorial which anticipated a great victory for the union, Hayes and Marston must have realised that Macready had won even before the skirmish had started. As the 10pm deadline approached, it became clear to the union leaders and General Macready that this time there would be no massive walk out from London police stations. Marston was stunned to find that the men were being advised by their union representatives not to strike. Several union officials, including Constable Albert Goodsall at New Malden, who was to become the national secretary of the Police Federation some years hence, tore up their union cards on hearing of the decision to strike.

At 10pm on the 31st July, the station sergeant at Loughton police station telephoned his superintendent, as instructed. He reported that only one man had notified the station that he was on strike - Constable James Marston. The union chairman was presiding over an enthusiastic rally in central London, declaring that its victory was certain. But many in the large audience at the Faringdon Road Memorial Hall were not even policemen. Outside, London's police were quietly getting on with their duties.

Macready issued a special Order to the force in the early hours of the 1st August. This stated that up to midnight, only 240 men in 17 divisions had joined the strike. The order warned;

> "It must be clearly and distinctly understood that every police officer who withdraws himself from duty will forthwith be summarily dismissed from the

force and thereby forfeit all pension rights and other benefits.'

In all, 1,100 Metropolitan Police officers joined the strike over the course of the next week, about five per cent of the strength. Even though the strike was clearly a failure, several hundred men went on strike even when they knew the cause was hopeless. Some came back from leave and reported themselves on strike. They had given a pledge to support the union, and were ready to lose their jobs to honour their word. With the exception of some Liverpool men who took advantage of the opportunity to return to work on the first day of the strike (one, PC George Smith, rose to become chief constable of Liverpool), not a single striker was ever reinstated.

The Labour and trade union movement was forced to see an affiliated union outlawed by an Act of Parliament. Some prominent MPs and activists such as Harry Pollitt, the future Communist leader, tried to encourage sympathy strikes, but rank and file trades unionists felt no sense of solidarity with striking policemen. Too many had bitter memories of past clashes between police and workers on strike.

Many of the 2,000 plus policemen who were sacked during the strike, faced years of unemployment afterwards. Some were the victims of employers' blacklists. Marston and other London union leaders could only find work with ARCOS, the All Russia Co-operative Society, which imported Soviet goods into Britain. In the anti-communist hysteria of the twenties, it was raided by the Special Branch and forced to close, putting the ex-policemen out of work for a second time. Some strikers were reduced to taking up collections outside London police stations when the officers drew their weekly pay. Among those who stayed at work there was some sympathy for the sacked men, but the Police Federation refused to support requests for their reinstatement.

Only on Merseyside and in Birmingham did union members respond in strength to the call to strike. In Birmingham, about 120 men came out. There was no disorder and all the strikers could do was hold meetings in the Bull Ring, the traditional Birmingham meeting place in the city centre. Local unions and the Labour Party provided speakers at these rallies, but this was the limit of their assistance. In Liverpool, almost half the total strength of the city force came out. Many strikers may have believed the assurances of Smithwick and Holliday that London had come out "to a man". When they realised that the claims being made in the *Daily Herald* bore no relation to the truth, some strikers quietly returned to duty, taking advantage of the amnesty offered by the watch committee that men who went back before midnight on the 1st August would be reinstated.

The Liverpool mob took full advantage of the absence of so many police. For two days and nights, rioters and looters roamed the London Road and Scotland Road area. Shop windows were stripped, and the remaining police, reinforced by middle class citizens who had been sworn in as special constables, fought a long and vicious battle. The Lord Mayor got the Government to order the troops who were garrisoned in the area to come to the aid of the civil power. Tanks were drawn up outside St George's Hall. When a mob attempted to loot a bonded liquor warehouse on the docks, a bullet from a soldier's rifle killed one of the looters. The situation became so tense that the battleship *HMS Valiant* and two destroyers were despatched from Scapa Flow, making full steam for Liverpool. When they arrived at the pier head, Royal Marines joined police and troops in house by house searches of the slums of Liverpool and Birkenhead, looking for stolen goods and making arrests. For many years afterwards, the three dramatic days of the police strike, referred to always as "The Loot", were recalled by those who took part, either as looters or defenders of law and order.

The union, cut off from its membership and with no money coming in, collapsed before Christmas 1919. The leaders who had organised the strike committees in London, existed for a while on strike pay but this was soon exhausted. The defiant promises of eventual victory turned to bitter attacks on the Labour and trades union leaders who had done nothing to help, and on the union members who had stayed on duty. Within a few weeks, there was no one left to listen. For more than 2,000 former policemen who had struck for the right to belong to their union, the future offered nothing but unemployment.

In 1924, the first Labour Government, which did not have a Parliamentary majority, was faced with the need to do something about successive resolutions of the party's conference, calling for the reinstatement of the strikers. The Home Secretary, unable to implement the Party's hasty pledges, set up a committee, which reported that the men were in the wrong and could not be taken back. There was one small sop to the sacked men, their wives could, if they made personal application, have their husband's pension contributions returned to them.

FOUR

A new beginning

When the first central conference of the Police Federation was held at the Methodist Central Hall in London in November 1919, the strike was already fading from public memory. In the meantime, every force had elected local branch boards and nominated delegates to attend the conference. Many had, in the brief period after the first strike, been union activists. Now they were keen to see the new Federation succeed. It was to these men that the delegates turned for leadership. The great majority of those who assembled in London had no conception of what the Federation was all about. Desborough had set out the framework of the new organisation in his report;

> 'It appears to us that if the pensionable pay and various other conditions are to be fixed for the police service as a whole, as we consider they should be, it is essential that means should be provided at the same time to enable the police, as well as the police authorities, to submit their views through their chosen representatives to the central authority with regard to any changes of pay and other matters affecting the service as a whole ... ...
>
> ... ... any system for this purpose should provide for;
>
> (a) a local representative body for the ranks of inspector, sergeant and constable in each force ... ... and the representatives of the various ranks might, by agreement, meet together to discuss matters affecting the force as a whole;

(b) a conference of representatives from each of the three ranks, meeting perhaps once a year, each force to be represented;

(c) a central committee consisting of representaives of the Metropolitan Police, county police and borough police in equal proportions, elected by the conference of representatives from among their number. This central committee might meet with the representatives of the chief constables, the superintendents and police authorities on the basis of a round table conference presided over by a representative of the Home Office to consider questions affecting the police service as a whole."

The Desborough Committee was careful to specify that the new organisation must be 'confined to serving members of the police. Questions of discipline and promotion, except questions of general principle, should be excluded from its scope.'

The police service that was beginning to emerge from a traumatic year was facing the most significant changes in the ninety years' history of professional policing in England and Wales (Scotland had known police forces for some thirty years longer). Until the Police Act, only the Metropolitan came under the direct control of the Home Secretary.

No fewer than 186 police forces operated in England and Wales at this time. Some were ridiculously small; Tiverton in Devon had just 11 men, Congleton in Cheshire 13, and Clitheroe in Lancashire, 15. Forty forces had fewer than 50 officers each. There were 57 county forces, with 18,000 men. Prior to the Police Act 1919, these were subject to limited Home Office controls. The Home Secretary approved the appointment of county chief constables, and had a say in the numbers of officers employed. There were 128 city and borough police forces, which were wholly controlled by the watch committees of the city or borough councils. They appointed the chief constables and decided the strength of the force.

The cost of each force was met from a combination of local revenue and central taxation. Finally, there was the City of

London Police, which received no government grant, and had 1100 members.

The Desborough Committee recognised that the very substantial pay increases which they had recommended, and the Government had accepted, would thrust a large financial burden on every police force. They therefore proposed that each force should receive a direct grant, equal to at least half the cost of the force, including pensions.

In addition to the pay proposals, the main recommendations of the Desborough Committee, all of which were embodied in the new Police Act were;

- standardisation of pay, allowances, pensions and conditions of service throughout Great Britain;

- pay (for constables and sergeants) would in future be fixed by the Home Secretary and the Scottish Secretary, after consultation with the police authorities and the Police Federation, through the new Police Council;

- police housing would in future be provided free of rent and rates, and other officers would be paid a rent allowance in lieu of free housing;

- a standard eight hour working day would apply to all forces;

- overtime would be compensated by time off, or paid for where time off could not be granted;

- CID officers would receive detective duty and plain clothes allowances;

- all ranks would be entitled to retire on pension after 25 years service, when the pension would amount to one half of annual pay, rising to two thirds after 30 years' service. This scale was optional for serving members, some of whom had the right to a maximum pension after 26 years' service;

- a national representative body (the Police Federation) for the police.

There remained a large number of lesser matters to be considered by the Committee in a more leisurely manner. It had completed its main task in four months, and had given the Government the opportunity to put the police house back in order.

The delegates who assembled at Central Hall on the 17th November 1919, were mostly strangers to one another. The difference in policing experience was just as vast. Some of the men from the remote rural areas had been untouched by the upheavals of the previous year. Some police authorities had held out against Home Office advice to adopt the pay scales agreed after the first strike, and already these authorities were protesting against the 'nationalisation' of the police, and being compelled to pay the police at rates which were far greater than local conditions required. In Dorset for example, the rate for recruits was 32 shillings a week, which included a 12 shillings 'war bonus'. Now a Dorset constable would start at 70 shillings a week, three times the going rate for a farm labourer.

The Home Office sent top officials to conduct proceedings until each separate rank conference had elected its central committee and chairman. The two Inspectors of Constabulary, Major General Atcherley and Captain Tommason presided over the constables' and sergeants' conferences, and Mr Arthur Dixon, the head of the newly formed police department and secretary to the Desborough Committee, took charge of the inspectors. Tommason and Dixon had a simple task, but it took the constables more than three hours to complete the business of electing a chairman. He was James Farley of the Metropolitan. The sergeants chose Alfred Thomas of Bristol, and the inspectors chose Chief Inspector Faulkner of the Metropolitan. The proceedings appear to have been amicable, by way of a vote of thanks to Major General Atcherley, the constables sang 'For he's a jolly good fellow.'

Having elected their chairmen, the separate conferences went on to choose central committee members and discuss some of the topics which had been submitted for debate by the newly elected branch boards. Motions which called for new regulations to govern promotion and discipline in every force were ruled out of order in the constables' conference, in case they breached the prohibition on Federation involvement with these matters. After the conference, one delegate wrote to the Police Review to complain that the constables conference had not discussed the key issues which were concerning the membership. The conference did debate the question of compulsory retirement after 26 years' service. Delegates were aggrieved that men would now have to serve for 30 years' to benefit from the Desborough pension scales.

After completing their separate business, the three conferences came together for the first joint conference. The delegates chose Constable Farley as chairman, and he became the first chairman of the Joint Central Committee. Of the proceedings at this first meeting which brought all the federated ranks together, another correspondent wrote in the *Police Review*;

> 'At no time during the joint meeting was there any exhibition of rank. Each member, whether constable, sergeant or inspector, felt that he was there for the welfare of the police as a whole.'

James Farley was only 30 years old when chosen to be the first joint chairman. He had six years' service and before joining the police had worked in engineering in his native Leicestershire. Farley had been a union official, but when the second strike was called, he persuaded his colleagues at Brockley to stay on duty.

The first joint central committee secretary was Station Sergeant Johnson of the Metropolitan. A Yorkshireman, Johnson was an official police shorthand writer and taught the subject at the London Working Men's College. Within a year, he had left the Committee and his place as secretary was taken by Inspector Ernest Dalton of Leeds, whose own term was to be short lived. Within a few months, he was promoted to Superintendent.

Another former union man to be elected to the constables' central committee was George Fox, aged 34. He had served in Manchester City Police for 13 years, broken by a brief spell in the Ceylon European Police. It was Fox who persuaded the union branch in Manchester not to support the strike. He was just beginning to make his mark as a national figure in the Federation when he was promoted to sergeant and had to leave the Committee. He died only a few months later. Harry Collins, who became the first secretary of the constables' committee, was a clerk in the office of the chief constable of Birmingham. Alfred Thomas was chosen to be the chairman of the sergeants' committee. He had been a Bristol policeman for 23 years, and was a well known Wesleyan preacher in Bristol.

The first Federation Conference revealed a host of problems in the provinces. Many forces had not yet implemented the pay scales recommended in the Desborough Committee's report. It would be some months before the Police Council met for the first time, to begin drawing up standard conditions of service in Police Regulations. Until then, there was no means of compelling the recalcitrant police authorities to increase pay to the new rates. Many police authorities, particularly those responsible for rural forces, were angry at the decision to standardise conditions. They had never experienced problems in filling their forces with recruits willing to work for slightly more than the prevailing wages in agriculture, and they saw no reason to pay men in sleepy villages the same wages as a London policeman. In East Anglia, for example, the Desborough Scale was almost three times the previous pay of a constable, and even in Manchester and Glasgow it represented a doubling of the local rate. This was to be a constant complaint of local authority spokesmen for years, and besides the complaints from the shires, feelings were strong among councillors in some urban areas, where the police had suddenly overtaken the wages paid in mining, shipbuilding and manufacturing.

Other matters which were discussed at the first Conference included the granting of a right of appeal to members of county police forces against disciplinary punishments imposed by chief constables. Members of borough forces had a right to appeal to the watch committees, but it was not until 1927 that an Act of Parliament gave all officers a right of appeal to the Home Secretary against dismissals or reductions in rank. (In 1964, officers were given the right to appeal to the Home Office against all disciplinary findings, and the watch committees lost their powers over disciplinary matters, except in the case of chief officer ranks.)

The first Conference called for standard promotion examinations, with an examinations board to oversee recruiting and promotion standards. This was a radical approach at a time when promotion in many forces depended entirely on the whims of chief officers. Here too, it was to take until 1958 before the objective set out in 1919 was achieved.

Immediately after the Conference, the officials of the first Joint Central Committee walked around the corner from Central Hall to the Home Office in Whitehall. They were shown in to Mr Arthur Dixon's office. They presented Dixon with the resolutions passed by the Conference, and he assured them that Mr Shortt would give them careful consideration. Dixon and the Federation officers must have contrasted these grave courtesies with the drama of a year before, when Home Office officials and even Cabinet ministers were bending over backwards to placate the triumphant leaders of the now defunct union. The Home Office officials and chief constables were just as pleased to note the changed circumstances now facing the service. The new Home Secretary had been decisive, the Police Act was on the Statute Book, and the revolutionary threat had disappeared. After the failure of the second strike, the humorous magazine *Punch* had a cartoon of Mr Punch chatting to a London Bobby. 'Stands Robert where he did?' Mr Punch was asking. 'Good. I thought for one moment that my idol had feet of clay.'

The natural order of things had been restored.

FIVE

The 'Goose Club'

W hen the delegates to the first Conference, armed with
third class railway warrants, boarded trains back to
their forces, the newly appointed national committee
members had the chance to take stock. What they found was
discouraging.

Not one official had been granted any duty time to carry
out Federation business. The national body existed in name
only, there was no office, not even a telephone, and no staff
to type letters, take minutes, and circulate documents.

The Home Office had allocated a small sum to each central
committee, to cover the cost of postage and sundry items.
The Police Act laid down that attendance at authorised
meetings of the Federation could be in duty time, and
members of branch boards and central committees received
the prescribed rates for travelling to and from meetings,
overnight lodging where necessary and for meals taken in
transit.

As a deliberate act of policy, the Federation was prohibited
from collecting contributions or subscriptions from its membership, which consisted nominally of every member of the
service below the rank of superintendent. The government
felt that if the Federation had funds of its own, it would not
be long before it was taken over by the same brand of trouble
makers who had controlled the union. But Home Office
officials and chief constables appreciated as well, that the
possession of its own resources would enable the Federation
to become more effective and influential than the authorities
intended it to be. It was to be nearly forty years before the
Federation was permitted to raise voluntary contributions
from the membership, and even then the uses to which the

money could be put were strictly circumscribed by police regulations.

Some of the earliest correspondence sent out by the secretary of the Joint Central Committee, Station Sergeant Johnson, survives in the archives of the Federation. The letters are hand written. Johnson and his successors in the twenties and thirties were expected to carry out their Federation duties in their own time, working either from their police stations or their homes. It was to be years before a typewriter appeared, and it took eleven years, and several disillusioned secretaries, before the Home Office at last agreed that there was a case for a full time secretary.

This was the representative body which Parliament had decided was enough to avert further unrest in the police, while exorcising the last threads of trades unionism from the service. The pattern of separate central committees for each rank was repeated in the local arrangements. The central committees were allowed to hold meetings six times a year, and the boards could meet once a quarter. The Act said that meetings could last for a day, but in all save the largest forces one afternoon was deemed sufficient to transact the business. In some of the smaller forces, every inspector and chief inspector was automatically a member of the inspectors' board and attended meetings of the joint branch board. As these were, for the most part, the disciplinarians who ran the forces, and occasioned most of the local discontent among constables that the branch board was supposed to alleviate, little was achieved that would persuade the lowest rank that the Federation was a better proposition than the union. It was noticeable that in most of the small forces, the chairman of the joint branch board was an inspector or chief inspector. They were not chosen because of their dedication to the Police Federation, but because it was deemed to be the correct thing to do, and in the hope, rather than expectation, that their rank would carry some weight when making representations to the chief constable. The Federation was derided in many forces as 'the goose club', a contemptuous nickname it had been awarded by the union during that body's brief fight for survival.

When the first annual elections became due in the autumn

of 1920, many of those elected for the first time a year earlier decided not to stand again, and in some forces there were no candidates in some divisions. This was hardly surprising when some members of the constables' board found themselves branded as trouble makers, or parade room lawyers, if they were considered too vocal in making representations. It soon became clear that an active interest in the Police Federation was hardly a means of gaining promotion. An enthusiastic branch board representative would soon find himself being transferred to another division, thus losing his position on the board, while his family also suffered through the compulsory move to another part of the force area, with all the domestic disruption that a transfer entailed.

In contrast, the meetings of the Joint Central Committee found all ranks working in harmony. The members came from different forces, and there was no disciplinary relationship between, say, a county inspector and a London constable. They were both members of the Joint Central Committee. It was a different matter when the force joint branch boards met. The constables could bring their members' complaints and proposals for improved conditions to joint meetings, but invariably these were vetoed by the combined votes of the inspectors and sergeants, who feared the reaction of senior officers. When a resolution was respectfully forwarded to the chief constable, his reply would take a long time, and in most cases was a curt refusal. Once the dramatic happenings of 1918 and 1919 had begun to recede from memory, it became clear that as far as the rank and file were concerned, little had changed in their daily experience of life in the police forces.

They were better paid, without question. Desborough had boosted the pay of the police far above the generality of wages, and the policeman was now ahead of the miner, the engineer and the train driver as the wage pace setter. With his relative job security and expectation of retiring early with a good pension, he was considered to be the aristocrat of the working class. He was now on a par, in terms of income, with shop managers and bank clerks, and in some cases he was better off than most white collar employees, because he had job security and could look forward to a pension. The policeman's good fortune was resented by other workers, and many police authority members felt the same way about it.

The sudden transformation brought about by Desborough had burst upon the service like a high explosive shell. Besides the large pay increase, there was now a Police Federation and a Police Council; standard conditions of service would apply, laid down by statutory regulations. To the majority of police authority members, standardisation was just a staging post along the road to nationalisation of the police, and once they had recovered from the shock of events, their spokesmen made loud and pointed protests. The country gentry who formed the county police committees found common ground with the socialist councillors in the industrial cities. The attitude of the latter was recalled in vivid terms some forty years later, when the chairman of the Sunderland Watch Committee, Alderman Jake Hoy, gave evidence to the Royal Commission on the Police 1960;

> 'I remember,' he said, 'being in the thick of industrial wage negotiations at that time - what an upheaval there was in trade union circles at the very big uplift which the police got. It took a very long time for the general body of industrial workers to get up into that category which was enjoyed by the police for some considerable time. I remember only too well and I have very bitter memories of the inter-war years.'

It was with men like Alderman Hoy, the trade union official, fiercely resenting the new found affluence of the police, that the Federation had to contend when they sought to improve conditions of service. Labour councillors, whose sympathies were with manual workers and who tended to see the police as the obedient servants of the bosses, were quite ready to make common cause with Tory council leaders in the shires and cities, almost all of whom were opposed to the increased central government control of the police service resulting from the Police Act.

This enabled the local authority representatives to present a united front when the first meeting of the new Police Council was held at the Home Office in July 1920. The Home Secretary, Edward Shortt, took the chair. The Police Federation representatives were pleased to note at least one friendly face among the councils' delegation — Sir Francis Blake, a member of the Desborough Committee and chairman of Northumberland County Council, but they were soon to learn that Alderman Willis Bund of Worcestershire was the man to reckon with, and he was determined that no more public largesse should be bestowed on a police force he considered to be grossly overpaid.

Neither the Home Office officials nor the councillors were pleased when the Police Federation began the meeting by presenting a resolution, asking that the Desborough pay scales should be updated to reflect the rise in the cost of living, which had gone up from 110 points in April 1919 to 150. A sub-committee was appointed to consider how pay should be revised in the future. On this first occasion, the Police Council acted with a speed that was to be noticeably absent from its future meetings. The sub-committee met on the same day, and submitted its report to the full council the following morning. It proposed the setting up of a permanent committee, on the lines of the Whitley Councils that had been established for the civil service during the war. The committee would make recommendations on pay to the Home Secretary.

The pay committee produced its first report a month later, and it was controversial. Although the vast majority of police authorities had stated that they were against any adjustment of police pay, the committee had agreed that the rapid rise in the cost of living index justified a temporary increase, in the form of a special bonus. If this upset the local authorities, there was also a shock for most of the provincial police. The committee was proposing a sliding scale for the bonus, with the London and large city forces getting twelve shillings a week and rural forces only three shillings and fourpence. In supporting this proposal, the Federation was seen by its provincial members to be undermining the national rate of pay established by Desborough.

At this first meeting, which lasted for four days, the Police Council spent many hours examining the Home Office draft of the first Police Regulations, governing every aspect of conditions of service. These standardised, among other things; the qualifications for appointment to forces; the number of ranks in a force; hours of duty; annual and weekly leave; the promotion system; and disciplinary procedures. A Federation proposal that would have given officers the right to appeal to a Tribunal against a chief constable's disciplinary punishment was rejected because it required legislation.

The establishment of common conditions of service by the middle of 1920 marked the completion of the biggest change in police organisation in the history of the service. However, its constitutional implications appeared to be greater than the impact on the ordinary police officer. Police forces were still run on military lines. The county forces were commanded by ex-Army officers who found a chief constable's billet a congenial means of existence in civilian life. The pay was modest, but the position carried status in the county, enabling chief officers and their ladies to take their place in local society. Many rode to hounds, and shot and fished with the gentry, and most used police constables as grooms and house servants. These gentlemen chiefs bore the burden of police responsibility lightly, being content to leave most matters in the hands of the deputies, who were career police officers risen from the ranks. The deputy chief constable was all powerful, and many were strict disciplinarians, feared by the lower ranks.

The borough forces had career policemen as their chief constables. These men were more rough hewn than the county chiefs (who emphasised the social chasm between them and the borough chiefs by having their own county chief constables' club). The borough chiefs had got to the top through the support of the watch committee chairmen, all powerful councillors who exercised considerable patronage and could make or break the careers of policemen, whom they regarded as council employees.

The life of a county policeman went on after 1919 very much as it had before. The men lived in police houses, often with an office attached for the benefit of the public. Constables' wives, who were not allowed to go out to work, were required to attend to any matters that arose while their husbands were out on their beats. If the cell was occupied by a prisoner waiting to appear before the magistrates, the

wife was obliged to cook his meals. In 1920, following complaints that some police authorities failed to reimburse
constables for the full cost of meals which their wives cooked
for prisoners, the Federation asked the Home Office to
impose a standard menu and allowance. As he usually did
with such resolutions, the Home Secretary replied that this
was a matter for each authority to decide upon.

A county officer was forbidden to leave his station on his
weekly rest day unless he had ensured that a constable on
a neighbouring beat would cover for him, and he had
informed his superiors where he could be found in an
emergency. Thanks to Desborough, the house now came free
of rent and rates, but an officer had no say as to where he
served, and could be moved at a few days' notice to a distant
part of the county, with his furniture being moved by himself
and his colleagues. It was not unusual for a county policeman's wife to say, on his retirement, that they had lived in
more than twenty homes during his police service. Most
forces operated a policy of frequent moves for village
constables, because the hierarchy thought that if an officer
became popular with the locals, he would lose his zeal for
prosecuting offenders, especially poachers. A policeman's
children went through a succession of schools and their
education suffered accordingly. The new Police Regulations
might state that the normal working day should be eight
hours, but a village policeman was expected to work on a
24-hour responsibility. There was no payment for overtime
(a word that did not figure in a county chief constable's
vocabulary) and time off for extra work was unheard of.

The borough man was a little better off, in the sense that
the job did not make so many demands on his domestic life.
Very few married officers lived in police property, and once
their shift was over, they could enjoy their leisure. But the
restrictions on private life were still there. Wives could not
have a job without the chief constable's permission. All police
officers had to get permission before marrying, and this was
only granted after the intended bride's character and that
of her relations had been checked. All forces had a bar against
an officer marrying until he had completed at least five years'
service.

In every force, the men had real grievances. The Desborough Committee had listened to many policemen during its inquiry, and they all told of the hardships of policing. Housing was a major problem. A Home Office official, Mr J B Simpson, told the Inquiry that borough policemen, unlike county officers, were not provided with police accommodation and had to pay rent out of their wages. Jack Hayes, the union secretary, told Desborough that Metropolitan officers were required to live close to their stations, and often this meant living in insalubrious areas where housing conditions were bad, and neighbours were hostile to police and their families. Chief Inspector Duckworth of Liverpool told Desborough that there was a 'housing famine' in that city. Men were paying high rents for poor quality rooms.

Constable George Strangeways of Newcastle upon Tyne police, who was to become one of the most respected national figures of the Federation, told Desborough that unmarried officers, amounting to almost half the strength of the force, were obliged to live in police barracks; 'devoid of all furniture - merely a bed, bare floors and walls coloured similar to the workhouse'. Strangeways said that the force's promotion system was a main cause of complaint. Men who started their careers as clerks in the chief's office rose rapidly through the ranks, whilst operational constables had to wait for years for their first promotion. Representatives of Leeds City Police told a similar story to the Committee. Inspector Dalton said the watch committee was better at finding excuses for bad conditions than improving them.

The rent allowances paid in the boroughs did not cover the rents, which were higher than they had been for years. When branch boards asked chief constables for increases in rent allowance to cover reasonable expenditure on housing, the invariable reply was that the watch committee considered that the men were being paid enough as it was.

Sickness was another matter which caused discontent. Nearly all forces had regulations which required men reporting sick to obtain a certificate from the police surgeon, not their own doctor. Men were not encouraged to be off sick for long and were subject to frequent visits from sergeants and inspectors to make sure they were not malingering. Some forces, including Bristol, disallowed periods of sickness when calculating pensionable service. Men reporting sick were sometimes obliged to go to the station and wait for hours until the police doctor examined them, and decide whether or not they were unfit for duty. Desborough abolished the deductions from pay which most forces had imposed on officers who were off duty through illness, but the treatment of sick officers continued in many forces to be oppressive and vindictive.

When the Joint Central Committee, early in 1920, complained to the Home Office that some forces kept records of the number of offences reported by each constable, and said that officers were put under undue pressure to submit summonses against offenders, the Home Office replied that their inquiries showed that, except in one unspecified case, the returns were not used in any improper way. The Joint Central Committee members knew better. Probationers were often told that their appointments would not be confirmed unless they submitted more summons reports.

The Committee complained that the chief constable of West Sussex had forbidden his officers to enter licensed premises when they were off duty. The Home Office replied that the chief constable had been told that if he wished to retain this order, it should be embodied in the discipline code for the force and referred to him for approval, when he would bear the Committee's views in mind. In fact, although there was supposed to be standardisation of restrictions on the off duty lives of policemen, local conditions continued to apply in many forces.

The Joint Central Committee did what it could to help branch boards to secure local improvements, but the chief constables knew that they could expect to be supported by the Inspectors of Constabulary and the Home Office. The branch boards were fulfilling the function intended for them, to be a safety valve to allow the men to voice their complaints, but not to bring about real change, still less to be allowed to interfere with the way chief constables and senior officers ran their forces.

It was not long before the members of the national committee felt obliged to tell the Home Secretary that the new Federation was in danger of foundering through apathy and disappointment. In 1921, the Joint Central Committee passed a resolution which set out their complaint;

> 'That the success which has attended many of the representations of this committee on matters connected with the welfare and efficiency of the police service has been so small that we are forced to the opinion that sufficient regard is not given to our resolutions.'

At this time, the British economy was in crisis. The Government decided that public expenditure had to be drastically reduced,and the Geddes Committee was appointed to wield the axe. Its first report called for major economies in the public sector, and when it was announced that Geddes was to scrutinise the police service, the Federation knew that a serious attack on the Desborough pay scales was inevitable.

When the committee produced its report on the police in February 1922, it was quite as bad as had been feared. On pay, it recommended cuts for provincial forces, but not for the Metropolitan, because it was 'generally accepted that work in the Metropolis justifies a special rate of remuneration'. If it had been adopted, this proposal would have killed off a cornerstone of the Desborough Report, common pay scales throughout Great Britain.

It was the good luck of the service that Edward Shortt was still the Home Secretary when the 'Geddes Axe' fell upon the police. He sent for the Federation leaders and told them that he understood the importance they attached to a national rate of pay. They could avoid permanent pay cuts by agreeing to economies in other spheres, he said, and gave them details of a Home Office plan which entailed;

- a cut in rent allowances and abolition of tax rebates on them;
- a 'levy' of two and a half per cent on pay;

- reductions in some allowances;
- overtime to become payable after 9 hours duty instead of 8.

The Home Office assured the Committee that the pay levy would be temporary, probably of just a year's duration. An alternative had been considered, to double the policeman's pension contribution to 5 per cent of pay. This had been rejected as being too permanent.

The Joint Central Committee knew it had to agree to the package, in order to save the national rate of pay. The leadership came under attack from branch boards for accepting what was seen as a savage attack on living standards. It must have hurt the Committee members to find that one of their harshest critics was Inspector Thomas of Bristol, one of the original union stalwarts and a former JCC member. In the *Police Review*, Thomas complained;

'The Home Secretary pulled the wool over their eyes. ... ... they seem to have fallen into line with the cheerfulness of ready debtors. While our antagonists have been marshaling their forces for a trial of strength, what have the JCC done? We can answer, 'Nothing'.'

Stung by such empty rhetoric, and the flood of protest from branch boards, the JCC set out its case in a circular sent to branch boards, many of whom agreed with Thomas;

'We were assured that the government must effect economies or be faced with financial disaster. We were told that they had decided that the police must bear a share of the burden. We were faced with the alternative that it would only be by finding some other means of obtaining the money that we could hope to maintain our existing scales of pensionable pay.'

The Committee went on to stress the realities of the Federation's lack of any industrial muscle;

'We are subject to great and important limitations within our constitution, within the terms of which we are bound. We may make representations, and having made them to the best of our ability we must leave them to the authorities for decision. When we have exhausted every means available within our constitution the authorities may still decide against us.'

This put the Federation's status accurately and starkly, but in fact, the boards which had heaped criticism on the JCC ought to have been congratulating it. The local authority spokesmen, the 'antagonists' whom Thomas had said were marshaling their forces, were unhappy with the outcome of the Geddes exercise. They had urged Geddes to sever the knot that tied provincial police pay to the Metropolitan, and had they succeeded the consequences for most provincial forces would have been far worse than the effects of the 'temporary deductions' deal.

In the early summer of 1923, the police authorities went to the Home Office to complain to Shortt that the police were being overpaid at a time when unemployment was rising and most workers were suffering pay cuts. Shortt, with reluctance, agreed to reappoint the Desborough Committee to consider what changes, if any, were necessary to police pay.

This caused consternation in the service, but in March 1924 Lord Desborough and his colleagues reported that too short a time had passed, following their original report, to talk about revising the pay scales;

'... ... it must be unsettling to any service to have frequent revisions of their rates of pay. We are of the opinion that this is not an opportune moment for disturbing an arrangement come to so recently.'

This reprieve helped to cushion the impact of the Government's decision to continue with the two and a half per cent pay levy for a second year, but the deduction still rankled, and the JCC decided to seek its repeal when the Police Council met in March 1924. After the chairman, Constable

George Strangeways, had outlined the Federation's complaint, the delegation was rebuked by Sir John Anderson, the Permanent Under-Secretary. The police, he implied, should thank their lucky stars. In securing the Desborough scale when they did, he told them, the police had been fortunate in getting in on the crest of a wave. Sir John reminded them that in the summer of 1919 the country had been expecting a long period of post war prosperity. Now, five years later, they were in the grip of recession, with millions out of work. Compared to the plight of others, the police had nothing to complain about. It was a line which would be employed against the Federation on many occasions during the inter-war years, whenever it attempted to secure any improvements in pay or conditions.

In March 1925, it was the Home Secretary himself, Sir William Joynson-Hicks, who decided the fate of the levy. He told the Police Council that he had discussed it with the Chancellor of the Exchequer, Winston Churchill, and they had decided that the deduction should be made permanent in the form of a 5 per cent pension contribution. Churchill, said the Home Secretary, had wanted an even higher contribution towards a pension he considered to be very generous. Thus encouraged, the local authority associations at once sought a higher contribution. The county councils demanded seven and a half per cent. Strangeways again voiced the Federation's consternation. He pointed out that policemen still felt aggrieved because, following Desborough, they were now required to serve for 30 years for full pension, instead of 26 years.

The issue quickly developed into the first full scale dispute between the Federation and the official components of the Police Council. To resolve it, the Home Secretary appointed yet another committee, this time under Lord Lee, to examine the question of continuing the temporary deductions or increasing the pension contribution. Either way, the policeman was not going to see any of the deductions back in his pocket, so there was little surprise or reaction when Lee supported the contribution being doubled to 5 per cent.

SIX

The trouble with women

The doubling of the pensions contribution rankled with the police, but they had to accept the decision. In any case, public opinion would not have supported any form of protest. The police were seen as well paid and lucky to be in a secure pensionable job. Rank and file officers saw the decision as proof of the ineffectiveness of the Police Federation. The body had achieved nothing in its first few years and now there were signs that the Desborough standards might not last much longer. The mood among county officers might have been gloomier still if they had known that Winston Churchill, the Chancellor of the Exchequer, had suggested in Cabinet that the pay of rural officers ought to be less than those working in the cities. Fortunately for them, the Home Secretary had persuaded the Cabinet that this was not a good idea.

The Federation leaders were anxious to pursue some of the objectives which had been agreed at successive annual conferences. The only forum in which this was possible was the Police Council, and for five years from 1925 to 1930 the Home Office declined to call a meeting because it was not considered there was a need for one. Just one major improvement in conditions was secured in this period, the Police (Appeals) Act of 1927 gave all officers who had been dismissed or required to resign by a disciplinary decision, a right of appeal to the Home Secretary. The measure was a major disappointment to the Federation, because it excluded appeals from other severe punishments, and an appellant would be able to be legally represented at an appeal only if the chief constable, as respondent, chose to appear through counsel. In practice, most appeals were decided on the basis of written submissions and only rarely was a tribunal appointed.

Pay was back on the agenda in 1927, and once again there was a proposal to reduce the cost of the service. The odd thing was, that the Federation and the rest of the service knew nothing about it. The Home Secretary appointed a Committee under Lord Chalmers to examine whether new entrants should be paid at a lower rate. There was no public announcement of the Committee's appointment, nor of its conclusion that new entrants should be paid at fifty-five shillings a week on joining, (a reduction of fifteen shillings) and seventy five shillings after ten years (as against ninety five shillings). There is no record of the reasons which prompted the Home Secretary to take no action on the Report, and its existence was not disclosed until 1931, when the May Committee was examining the question again.

The principal reason for the Federation's inability to make progress was that it had been established by the authorities, who intended that it should never become another police union and a threat to discipline. It had no money and no full time officials. Even the elected national officers were given virtually no facilities to perform their functions. One JCC chairman of the twenties, Constable Jack Branthwaite of the Metropolitan, was stationed at Devonport Dockyard (the force used to police all the naval dockyards). Branthwaite was expected to complete a tour of night duty before catching the London train to attend a meeting, returning to Plymouth the same evening. Members of the national committee were given third class railway warrants to travel to the six statutory meetings each year, plus the regulation expenses for meals and accommodation. All the members found themselves out of pocket after a JCC meeting.

In 1928 a point was reached where it seemed that the Federation was about to collapse. The JCC Secretary, Station Sergeant Berry of the Metropolitan, resigned because he found it impossible to do the work on top of his full time police duties. No member of the Committee was prepared to take over. A deputation was sent to the Home Office to see Mr Arthur Dixon, the official who had been most involved in establishing the Federation in 1919. He was sympathetic, and arranged for the annual grant to be increased to £300, to cover all the JCC's expenditure on postage and stationery. He also persuaded Berry to stay on by promising that while he could not be given full time status, he would have 'every facility' to do his Federation work.

The Police Council was at last recalled in 1930, to discuss a Home Office proposal to establish a Police College. This was the brainchild of Arthur Dixon, the head of the police department, who was aware of a feeling among politicians that some recent scandals involving the police pointed to poor leadership. In the nineteen twenties, it was revealed that police officers in London had taken substantial bribes from the operators of night clubs, in order that a blind eye would be turned to breaches of the licensing laws. In 1929, the arrest of a prominent man, Sir Leo Money, for alleged indecency with a young woman in Hyde Park became a *cause celebre* and lead directly to a Royal Commission on police powers. The Commission reported in 1930 and called for improved training arrangements, including regional schools run under the auspices of the large forces. In a comment on leadership of the forces, the Commission said it was imperative that the Service should encourage the entry of 'at least a proportion' of men 'whose attainments qualify them for positions of considerable responsibility.' This required the introduction of a system that would provide for the rapid advancement of 'outstanding young men.' The Commission bluntly rejected prevailing police sentiment, that all chief constables and senior officers should come through the ranks;

> 'Long experience and good service in the lower ranks are not the only, nor even the most important, qualifications for the higher posts. It would be inimical to the public interest to limit the appointments to the higher posts to those who had joined the service as constables. Such posts should be filled by the best men available, irrespective of the source whence they are drawn.'

The scheme submitted to the Police Council in 1930 went some way towards meeting the Royal Commission's views.

The Home Secretary in the Labour Government was J R Clynes, who within a year would join his leader, Ramsay MacDonald in a National Government. For a Labour politician, and a trades unionist, Clynes held surprisingly elitist views on the appointment of police commanders. He told the Police Council that the current system of filling the highest ranks in the service was unsatisfactory;

> 'Some people say that it should be possible to find within the police service all the candidates required for appointment to the highest ranks. Others say it is not possible because the experience afforded by service in the lower ranks does not afford the experience, training and outlook a chief officer should have. Personally, I think there is much justification for both views.'

Clynes added that the 'right personality' was more important than knowledge of police procedure. He told the Council that the service was not developing as it should do. Far too little was known of technical and other developments in police work elsewhere and far too little advantage was taken of such developments in other countries.

The proposed college, said Clynes, would provide a resident two year course covering police duties and general studies including opportunities to travel abroad. The College would also be a centre for research. Entry would be by a qualifying examination open to the service, with limitations on age and length of service. Those who passed the examination would face a selection board. Each course would consist of about 50 officers. All officers who completed the course would be promoted to inspector and be posted to force headquarters as staff inspectors. After a few years, it would be a requirement for appointment to chief officer posts (and possibly to Superintendent) that a candidate should have completed the College course.

The chairman of the JCC, Staff Sergeant George Strangeways of Newcastle, said that he regarded the training of recruits as of more importance than that of future chief constables. If higher posts were going to be given to men of comparatively short service because they had been to the College, he said, there would be a sense of unfairness to others. In spite of this, Strangeways said he would support the plan, provided it was confined to serving officers.

A committee was appointed to develop the College scheme and a year later the Police Council endorsed its conclusions, in spite of some opposition. In the interval, Strangeways had left the JCC on promotion. The new JCC chairman, Sergeant Tommy Holmes of Durham, said that the scheme could not provide the right sort of training but it would be a short cut to the top for a favoured few. The Inspectors' Central Committee registered its total opposition, which was understandable because no current inspectors would be eligible for the course, and all stood to be excluded from higher posts.

The local authorities baulked at the expense. The report of the Police Council committee said that the cost of the College might be deemed high, considering the small number of students, but it was small compared with the £20 million that the police service cost the country each year. Nevertheless, it was abandoned immediately because of the 1931 economic crisis, although the service had certainly not heard the last of a police college.

The same meeting of the Police Council considered another matter arising from the Report of the 1929 Royal Commission, which had urged the employment of more policewomen in all forces. Although women were employed in uniform during the 1914-18 war, their numbers had been reduced since then, mainly because of economy cuts in all forces, and also because of the general hostility of policemen, and in particular chief constables. The Federation opposed policewomen on two grounds; police work was a man's job, and every woman employed as a constable was taking work away from a man, and a family breadwinner. Sir John Anderson asked for the views of the Council members and found them virtually unanimous in opposing the Royal Commission's proposal. Alderman Maxwell of Liverpool said that there was a limited area of police work which women might perform, but this did not require police powers. His colleague, Alderman Millican of Newcastle said that women were not usefully employed in uniform and should not be attested as constables. The chief constables of Cardiff and Middles-brough said that it was better to employ police matrons and probation officers than to recruit women as constables. Sir Francis Blake of Northumberland, who had served on the Desborough Committee, was also opposed to policewomen. Alderman Wyles of Coventry said his force had employed women in the past but they had not been satisfactory. Constable Albert Goodsall, for the Federation, said that policewomen in London had 'a tendency to find immorality where it did not exist, and so to get into difficulties from which the men had to extricate them.' Only Sir Leonard Dunning, the Inspector of Constabulary, acknowledged that there was a role for women in the service, but even so, he considered it 'immaterial' whether they wore uniform and were sworn in as constables. Sir John Anderson undertook to convey these negative opinions to the Home Secretary, but implied that the issue could not be left where it was. The few policewomen in service in a number of forces had powerful friends in Parliament, including the formidable Lady Astor.

When the Police Council met again, in July 1931, the formidable Miss Dorothy Peto, staff officer of the 50 strong policewomen branch in the Metropolitan, was among those present. She was there to argue the case for more women in the service.Her own position reflected the ambivalence of the service towards women. Miss Peto had served in a number of forces before being asked to take on her present job. She regarded it as equivalent to a superintendent, but had to accept the 'staff officer' title and was not allowed to wear a uniform. She was attested as a Constable, but only because she had insisted on it, and she was regarded officially as a member of the civil staff. Her appointment had been made on a probationary basis - 'to see if it worked out'.

The Home Office tabled a set of new police regulations concerning policewomen for the Police Council to consider. Sir John Anderson said that in spite of the hostility which the Council had demonstrated the year before, it was apparent that a section of public opinion wanted to see women in the police. These included many Members of Parliament, church leaders, and other establishment figures. The regulations established the women's conditions of service, but it would remain a matter for chief constables as to whether they served in a force.

The regulations provided that only single women could be appointed, between the ages of 22 and 35, and must be at least 5'4" tall. Women employed on patrol duty would have a seven hours tour of duty, against eight hours for men. The Home Office proposed that they should be paid on a lower scale, as recommended some years earlier by the Baird Committee.* In spite of Miss Peto's objections, the Council voted to reduce the recommended scales of pay by ten shillings weekly, which meant that a women would start at fifty shillings a week, compared with seventy shillings for a man.

The discussion became more heated when the Council turned to the duties on which women could be employed. Sergeant Holmes declared that women were incapable of performing beat duty. Nor, he said, should they be used on moral preventative work, since the police were not concerned with public morals.

Holmes said that if policewomen took statements from women or children in sexual cases, this should be under the supervision of the male officer in the case. It was precisely this point which had brought about the 1929 Royal Commission. After accusations had been made in Parliament about the arrest of Sir Leo Money in Hyde Park, two senior detectives were appointed to look into the case. They took the young woman who had been with Sir Leo from the office where she worked as a typist and brought her to Scotland Yard in a way that amounted to an arrest. There, after ordering the policewoman who had chaperoned her to leave the room, they grilled her for an hour to try to back up the tale told in court by the arresting officers, which the magistrate had thrown out. As soon as MPs learned of this, uproar ensued, it was seen by the Government and the Opposition as a gross breach of Parliamentary privilege. The

---

* Sir John Baird MP, a junior Home Office minister, was the chairman of a Departmental Committee appointed in 1920 to examine the question of women police. The JCC evidence to the Committee underlined its total opposition to women officers. The Committee was unanimously in favour, saying 'there is not only scope, but an urgent need, for the employment of policewomen.' Most forces ignored the Report, and elsewhere the women were the first to go when financial cuts were required during the 1920s.

result was the appointment of the Royal Commission. Yet here was the Chairman of the Police Federation still insisting that policewomen could only deal with women witnesses under male supervision, and being backed up in that view by the chief constables and police authorities.

This was too much for Miss Peto. She said that the women officers in the Metropolitan exercised a vital role in helping women and girls who might otherwise be destined to be prostitutes. Colonel Malcolm, the chief constable of Cheshire, said that women were weaker than men, and to employ them on duties which might expose them to injury would have serious consequences for police pensions. Miss Peto said that Metropolitan policewomen made arrests in the streets, and there had been no cases of serious injury. That, retorted Constable Goodsall, was because there was always a male officer on hand to assist the women.

The council voted to delete 'patrol duty' from the tasks which women might undertake, but the recommendation did not bind the Home Office. General Sir William Atcherley, the Inspector of Constabulary, said that women could be employed on the care or custody of women and children, watching over females who had attempted suicide, and searching female prisoners. These duties did not require police powers and could be performed equally well by police matrons. Sir William said that women could also perform patrol duties and undertake clerical and detective work.

Writing her memoirs in 1970, Miss Peto recalled what, for her and women officers, was a historic meeting of the Police Council;

> 'It was held in the big conference room of the Home Office. Most of the members present smoked, and all the long mullioned windows overlooking Downing Street were tightly closed. I hope I may have made some other useful contribution to the discussion, but my sole recollection is of rising to my feet at about half time, when the room had long reached that airless and smoke-filled condition which men seem to find essential to their deliberations, and saying, 'Gentlemen, what about an open window?' We got it - and the Women Police Regulations into the bargain!'

In fact, Miss Peto remained in the service until the end of the 1939-45 war, in which hundreds of women, regulars and auxiliaries, played a major role in all police forces. It was thanks to her and a small band of able and determined women that the whole idea of having female officers was not quietly interred between the wars. In time, the opposition of the service, even of the Police Federation, was overcome, but each grudging concession followed years of debate and frustrating disappointments for the advocates of women police.

Another matter before the Police Council in 1930, was the Federation's request to be allowed to raise a general purposes fund. The JCC realised that the organisation would never make progress while it was denied any funds of its own. It stressed the importance of establishing a fund which would provide legal assistance for officers subject to civil actions for damages. Sir John Anderson said that the main objection to such a fund was that it might find the Federation interfering in disciplinary matters, but he suggested that a committee be appointed to examine the proposal. This was accepted, and the Committee proposed that police authorities should be encouraged to support officers involved in litigation, and the officer should be able to appeal to the Home Secretary if the authority refused to support him.

The Joint Central Committee was alarmed by a proposal in the Road Traffic Bill which was before Parliament at the time, that would have allowed chief officers to employ traffic wardens instead of police officers. The matter was put on the Police Council agenda. Sir John Anderson said that a conference had taken place at which representatives of chief officers and police authorities had agreed that any 'guides' employed on such duties should either be supplied by the RAC, or be police pensioners. He said that such guides were employed only in one or two coastal forces during the summer months, and the strengths of police forces was not affected.

When Station Sergeant Berry retired in 1931, the JCC again found itself unable to appoint a secretary. After further discussions with Arthur Dixon, the Home Office agreed that in future the post would be full time, and Constable Albert Goodsall of the Metropolitan was appointed. For the first time, the Federation had a fully experienced secretary. Goodsall was the only survivor of the Police Union activists and had built up the Metropolitan branch board, a far more effective body than the national committee. He was an effective negotiator, strongly opinionated and impatient of any opposition from inside the Federation.

At the 1931 Police Council, there was some concern about police pensions. The Government Actuary had examined the scheme, and his conclusions were alarming. Arthur Dixon told the Council that the cost of pensions was rapidly increasing. The causes were the Desborough pay scale; the widow's pension, and the increases in the size of police forces resulting from the introduction of a weekly day off some twenty years earlier. The Actuary had reported that eventually the cost of pensions would amount to more than 50 per cent of the men's pay bill, at which point the 5 per cent contribution from the police would amount to less than 10 per cent of the cost of pensions. The main problem, said Dixon, was that pensions were paid out of current income because there was no fund. The current cost of pensions was £4 million a year and was expected to rise to £7 million by the year 1960, without taking account of inflation. As usual, the Council set up a committee to consider the establishment of a police pensions fund.

Within a few weeks of this meeting, the Police Council was again in session at the Home Office, and this time it met in an atmosphere of crisis which was to become the Federation's biggest test so far.

SEVEN

A time for sacrifice

A National Government and a new Home Secretary, the Liberal MP Sir Herbert Samuel, were in office when the Police Council met in August 1931, immediately after the dramatic events which had forced Ramsay Mac-Donald to break from his Labour colleagues and form an all party administration.

Samuel said that he regretted that his first task was to tell them that the pay of the police had to be cut as a contribution to the nation's rescue from the edge of bankruptcy. The situation demanded sacrifices from all classes of the community. The Home Secretary reminded the Council that the pay of the police had not been reduced in the post war period, in line with the fall in living costs, whereas all other public servants had seen their pay reduced over the years. In 1919, a constable's starting pay had been fixed by Desborough at seventy shillings a week, and no provision had been made for cost of living adjustments. The position now, said Samuel, was that a civil servant who was earning the same as a police recruit in 1919 had seen his wage fall to 51s 7d, and after the cuts now being imposed, it would be 49s 11d. Constables and sergeants were now receiving a pound a week more at the top of the scale, than their civil service counterparts. The police should remember, also, that they had job security and the prospect of a generous pension.

Samuel did not say that the reason why police pay had not been scaled down with the cost of living index was not that the service had been given special treatment, but it was unique in having its pay prescribed in statutory regulations, which did not include provision for such adjustment. However, he was correct to point out that the police had seen the purchasing power of their pay rise since 1919. The May Committee on public expenditure had recommended that police pay should be reduced by twelve and a half per cent, to be achieved by an immediate reduction of six and a quarter per cent, and another a year hence. The Committee said that because of the fall in the cost of living since 1919, they would have been justified in recommending a cut of 25 per cent.

The Government hoped to save £1 million from police costs in the first year and £2 million in the next. Samuel offered one crumb to his disconsolate police listeners, he would consider alternative ways of achieving such savings if the Council could think of them.

There was little that the Federation leaders could say to counter the demand for sacrifice. Holmes did his best, arguing that the May Committee had been forced to work at great speed and had made its proposals for the police in ignorance of the real situation. He suggested that there was scope for savings in administration, rather than taking all the money out of pay. Albert Goodsall recalled that the Desborough scales had not been based solely on the cost of living, other factors had been considered. He reminded the Home Secretary that the police had suffered a permanent reduction through the pension contribution, and what was supposed to have been a one year reduction in rent allowance had extended to three years.

For the county councils, Mr S Taylor JP of Lancashire said they would favour reducing the pay of new entrants but felt that serving officers should not suffer a cut. The chief constable of Cheshire, Colonel Malcolm said that any cuts should be in the form of deductions from pay, rather than reductions in the scales themselves, to preserve officers' pension rights. Alderman Sennington of Bristol was totally opposed to the cuts, saying that to reduce the wages of the community was to cut purchasing power and add to unemployment. The Desborough scales had benefited the service and the public and the Alderman warned that another crisis in the police service could be the result of such drastic cuts as those proposed.

The Police Council adjourned for a week to allow for consultations. When it resumed, Samuel was even more insistent that the cuts must be ratified. He pointed out that the police had been given special treatment, because alone in the public service, their deductions had been phased over two years. The local authority associations told the Home Secretary that, with reluctance, they had fallen into line.

Holmes warned that the effect on morale would be very bad, as members would see the cuts as a demonstration of the weakness of their Federation. He was supported in this view by the Superintendents' Association. Samuel observed that relations between the police and the public would not be improved if the unemployed saw the police being exempted from the call to make sacrifices. He was prepared to make one major concession, the cuts would not be from pensionable pay, as the May Committee had proposed.

There was a sharp disagreement over another proposal of the May Committee, that police due to retire on pension should be compelled to continue to serve. Samuel said he would not implement this proposal. He also rejected two other ideas of May's: that the right to retire on a pension of half pay after 25 years should be ended, and no officer should be allowed to retire before the age of 50.

The Federation and other speakers were concerned about the introduction of a lower pay scale for new entrants. Sir John Anderson said this was an interim measure pending a full inquiry into the pay of recruits.

Shortly after the Police Council meeting, the Government decided that cuts in public service pay would be limited to ten per cent, but this did little to curb the growing anger of policemen, who felt that account should have been taken of the previous deduction.*

Goodsall and Holmes proved to be effective leaders during this difficult period, and for the first time the men were able to identify with the Federation as the champion of their interests. Packed meetings were held up and down the country, with prominent politicians opposed to the cuts appearing on the platform. Close to 10,000 policemen attended a protest rally at the Albert Hall in London. The campaign had no affect on the National Government, which had been returned

---

*The economy cuts lasted longer than the two years' intended originally. One half was restored in September 1934, and the remainder a year later.

at the 1931 General Election with the biggest ever majority. One of the many Labour casualties was Jack Hayes, the ex-Union secretary and 'Bobbies' MP'.

In 1932, yet another Committee, under Sir George Higgins, reported on the pay of new entrants and recommended a reduced scale, which became known as 'Scale B'. This provided for a new starting rate of sixty shillings a week, and it would take twelve years instead of ten for men on the new scale to reach top pay.

The cuts left the service with a deep sense of grievance. The men had not reacted as some had feared, and followed the lead of the naval 'mutineers' who had demonstrated against their pay cuts, but their anger with the Government was real enough. The Federation leaders, for the first time, went on the attack. The 1932 Report of the Joint Central Committee contained none of the fulsome tributes to Home Secretaries and officials of previous years. Instead, Goodsall told the members;

> 'there has been attack after attack upon the police service ever since the Desborough Committee reported and we fail to find any concern on the part of the Government for our welfare .... we must remind the Government that it was the intolerable conditions that prevailed before Desborough that caused the trouble in 1918.'

Looking back over the years to the events of 1931, it is striking to note how the Federation leaders, and to some extent chief officers, appeared to be insulated against the reality of the crisis that faced the country. As Sir John Anderson had reminded them a few years earlier, the police enjoyed an unprecedented lead over the pay and conditions of what, after all, was a fast diminishing national workforce. In the first stage of the cuts, the top pay of a constable on 90 shillings a week was cut by 5 shillings. It was rather ludicrous that Inspector George Mynors of Nottingham could assure the Police Council that the constables of his force faced real hardship and could not afford to lose one penny of their pay. The plight of the unemployed, and the real poverty of millions, were never mentioned by police speakers in the hours of talks at the Home Office. Perhaps this was only to be expected. Twelve years earlier, the Government had forced the police out of contact with the labour movement, and in consequence the Federation had operated as if in a vacuum, cocooned from strikes and lay-offs, and any threat of unemployment. Faced by demands to accept the need for sacrifice, the Federation leaders could see only a threat to the precious Desborough standards.

If Goodsall and his JCC colleagues thought they had come through a year of trial in 1931, more problems were soon to confront them. One man had decided that the Federation was getting too big for its police boots. He was Marshal of the Royal Air Force the Lord Trenchard, Commissioner of Police of the Metropolis, who was not a man to tolerate dissent. He took over the force as the Federation's protest campaign was at its height, and was shocked and annoyed to find that an organisation resembling a trade union represented the lower ranks and was challenging Government policy in this fashion.

Lord Trenchard succeeded Viscount Byng, the elderly and very sick war hero whose term at Scotland Yard had been ineffective and marred by scandal. Byng had been popular with the force, probably because he was content to be a figurehead and appeared at ceremonial parades and visits to stations as a father figure, keenly interested in the welfare of the men. Byng's term had not been marked by any significant developments, but the Force had figured in a number of well publicised cases, one of which resulted in the 1929 Royal Commission, and its public standing was lower than it had been since the time of the Ripper murders in Whitechapel and the labour riots of that period.

Sir Herbert Samuel knew that the Metropolitan Police was in great need of a motivator at its head. Trenchard, who had worked minor miracles in building up the RAF, was the natural choice, but like General Macready some years earlier, he did not want the job. He allowed himself to be persuaded to go to the Yard, but only after extracting a promise that he could go back to the RAF if the threat of war returned, as he was convinced it would. Trenchard described himself as an old man in a hurry, and expected to stay in the post for a maximum of four years.

What Trenchard found at the Yard appalled him. The force seemed to be hidebound by its past. Modern technology had passed it by. Macready had purged a moribund hierarchy, but most of the senior officers Trenchard encountered ten years later, failed to impress him. He decided that drastic measures were needed, and began to make plans. These did not include taking the Police Federation into his confidence. He was sure that the Metropolitan Branch Board, under Goodsall's leadership, would oppose and seek to obstruct any reforms he initiated, and accordingly he intended to cut it down to size.

In January 1932, Trenchard sent for Goodsall and Sergeant 'Rocky' Knight, the chairman of the board. It was a strange, strained and short meeting. Afterwards, a shocked Goodsall sent a full report to the national chairman, Tommy Holmes.

'We found the Commissioner accompanied by Sir Trevor Bingham (Deputy Commissioner), his aide-de-camp, his personal secretary and his private secretary. He read a long typewritten statement dealing with Open Meetings which commenced as follows; "My attention has been drawn to the fact that the Police Federation held an Open Meeting at Manchester to protest against the economy cuts".

'He then went on to say that the meeting had been held at the Albert Hall and every facility afforded, but to continue with such meetings was getting away from the whole idea originally intended and approved by the Home Office. People were invited on to the platform and they made speeches and the object of the meetings was being misconstrued, and people would think we were becoming agitators. We had the proper machinery through which we could express the views of the men, and he would not permit us to take part in any future meetings which had for their object a protest against the economy cuts.

'It was explained by us that the Metropolitan Police did not arrange the meeting, and the Metropolitan Police could not prevent provincial forces holding such

meetings, and if the Joint Central Committee desired
to take part therein, we were part and parcel of the
Police Federation and it was a matter for the Home
Office and not for any one police authority. It was also
explained that if the Joint Central Committee decided
to accept future invitations, as members of the Joint
Central Committee, we should attend.

'He replied to me personally, saying; 'You are the
secretary of the Joint Central Committee and must
advise your committee'. I said that it was a difficult
matter to advise on and I was, after all, only a member
of the committee and could not attempt to advise them
on such an important matter.'

The idea of Goodsall not being able to 'advise' the JCC
on any matter would have struck Holmes as odd. Goodsall
was an autocrat and the JCC invariably did what he wanted.

Trenchard told Goodsall that he had seen the Home Secretary to express his concern about the next mass meeting,
which had been arranged to take place in Portsmouth. The
Home Secretary, on Trenchard's advice, had rescinded his
earlier permission for this meeting. Goodsall protested that
the meeting had been arranged by the Portsmouth Joint
Branch Board, not him. Trenchard said that he was not
prepared to argue with him, and that the chief constable of
Durham was at that moment informing Holmes that the
meeting had been banned. In fact, when Holmes saw his chief
officer, he was informed that so far as he, the chief constable,
was aware, there was no objection to Holmes's attendance
at Portsmouth or at a later meeting in Newcastle, provided
the events were not advertised as 'protest' meetings. On
learning this, Goodsall wrote to the Home Office to ask what
was the position with regard to meetings. The Home Office
replied to say that his letter 'would be considered'. It appeared
that Sir Herbert Samuel was unwilling to commit himself
and risk a public row about the ban. Goodsall wrote to
Trenchard to ask for clarification and the Commissioner
confirmed that meetings could not be held without the
Minister's authority. Trenchard said that his meeting with

Goodsall had been intended as 'a friendly warning' and he added;

> 'I wish to tell you, as officers of this force and import-
> ant members of the Federation, that open meetings
> of protest must cease altogether as far as the Federa-
> tion and its associated bodies are concerned.'

Goodsall interpreted this as a blanket ban on all open meetings of the Federation. Apart from the annual conference in
London each November, the Federation would have no
opportunity of speaking to its membership directly. It had
no funds to contact them in writing, and the open meetings
had been a valuable way of keeping in touch with forces.
Goodsall wrote to the Home Office again, and this time he
received a reply which confirmed that the open meetings had
been banned. The letter from Sir Ernley Blackwell, the under
secretary, said;

> 'The Secretary of State has come to the conclusion
> that no useful purpose is likely to be served by the
> holding of further open meetings in present circum-
> stances. It is clear that, at the present time, no open
> meeting could be held without the economy measures
> now in force becoming the main subject of discussion;
> the policy adopted by the Joint Central Committee has
> been explained on more than one occasion and must
> be fully understood throughout the police service. The
> Secretary of State does not feel justified in giving
> permission for the holding of open meetings merely
> or mainly for the purpose of voicing protests against
> measures which have been taken by the Government,
> with the sanction of Parliament, after ample oppor-
> tunity had been accorded to all branches of the police
> service to submit their representations on the subject.'

Nor did the Federation find any support for open meetings
when, at a Police Council meeting in October 1932, they
asked for the ban to be lifted. Superintendent RJ Smith of
Nottinghamshire said that open meetings were a drain on

manpower. If a Federation meeting which had been scheduled in London had been allowed to go ahead, he said, the
Midlands police would have been depleted by half their
strength This at least suggested that the Federation was
strongly supported in its opposition to the cuts, whatever
Superintendent Smith thought. Mr C Morley, the chief
constable of Durham (and Holmes's chief officer), said the
county chief constables considered such meetings were
contrary to the Police Act and should never be allowed. This
ignored the fact that whenever they had been held, county
chief constables were on the platform with other guests.

The Government, and especially the Home Office, had
been surprised by the vehemence of the Federation's
opposition to the economy cuts, although there had been no
suggestion of taking the protests beyond angry words. The
man who had signed the Home Office letter to Goodsall, Sir
Ernley Blackwell, would have recalled the dramatic days in
1918 when he had been the only senior civil servant on duty
at the Home Office when the Metropolitan went on strike.
The letter reflected the anxiety of the authorities that the
open meetings would be used to incite another strike. Nothing
was further from the thoughts of the Federation leadership,
but officialdom had a long memory.

EIGHT

Trenchard's high flyers

T he Police Federation made more progress in the Metropolitan Police during its formative years than it did in
the provincial forces. There were a number of reasons
for this. The Police Union had also been most successful in
London, and there had always been a certain irreverence for
rank amongst London officers, in marked contrast to the firm
discipline exercised in the provinces. The branch boards were
able to hold more meetings, and their members to keep in
day to day contact with each other, whereas provincial
Federationists had few opportunities of this kind. The Federation was represented on a number of police charity committees, particularly the Metropolitan Police Orphanage, where
eight Federation officials attended a board of management
committee meeting every week. All this meant that the office
holders of branch boards in the Metropolitan, with their
various commitments, were employed virtually full time on
representative duties. Albert Goodsall, for instance, combined
the secretaryships of the constables branch board and the
joint executive committee, as well as being the national
secretary of the Constables' and Joint Central Committees,
a combined power base which made him the most powerful
figure in the Federation.

It was unfortunate for the Federation that Lord Trenchard
formed an instant dislike of Albert Goodsall. In the Army,
and during his eleven years as the 'Father' of the Royal Air
Force, no subordinate had ever questioned, still less contradicted, one of his orders. Yet here was this blunt spoken
constable prepared to stand up to his commander-in -chief
and challenge his instructions. What irked Trenchard was
that, although his first instinct was to sack the man for gross

insubordination, Goodsall had been careful to stay within the strict limitations of the 1919 Police Act. So long as he did so, the Act protected him. As for Goodsall, he hated Trenchard and the mutual animosity of the two men was to colour the clash that soon came.

Trenchard was not impressed by the way in which the force hierarchy had been dealing with the Federation. A few weeks before Trenchard's appointment, Goodsall had protested angrily to the Acting Commissioner, Sir Trevor Bingham, about 'interference' from some area senior officers with the Federation's divisional meetings at which resolutions of protest against the pay cuts were being passed. One divisional commander had instructed a shorthand writer to attend and make a note of the speeches. Bingham reprimanded two senior officers for their actions, and assured Goodsall that the divisional meetings had his full approval. He 'appreciated that good work was being done by the Joint Executive Committee in arranging such meetings'. Trenchard, when he learned of the incident, made it clear to his senior officers that such kid glove treatment of the Federation was to cease forthwith.

Not all the hierarchy was as accommodating to the Federation as Sir Trevor Bingham. Mr H D Morgan, a district chief constable, was the chairman of the Orphanage Board of Managers. He wanted to reduce the Federation's representation from eight members to three, and hold monthly meetings instead of weekly. Goodsall would not agree, because it was his members' whose subscriptions kept the Orphanage going. When Lord Trenchard arrived, Morgan referred the dispute to him. Trenchard commented that it would be better to sell the place and give the money direct to the children's mothers. However, the issue was to bolster the little surprise he had in store for the Federation.

One of Trenchard's first decisions was to revive the Special Constabulary. As he anticipated, the Federation protested. There was much rank and file antipathy towards the Special Constabulary. It sprang from the war years, when so many regular officers were recalled to the armed forces and their places were taken by special constables, some of whom, the men felt, ought to have been in the trenches themselves.

Coming at a time when police pay was being cut and recruitment frozen, the revival of the Special Constabulary was seen in the force as an attempt to get policing on the cheap. The real reason, which Trenchard kept to himself, was that in the event of the pay protests boiling over into another strike, he was making contingency plans and, as with Macready in 1919, the Specials were a vital part of them. When Goodsall conveyed the Federation's views about the Specials to the Commissioner, Trenchard cut him off in mid-sentence. 'I am not concerned with the views of anyone on this matter,' he said. 'I am responsible for efficiency and I will not be dictated to by anyone.' Even so, Goodsall refused to be cowed. He told Trenchard that we was merely reporting what the men were thinking. Of course, if he did not wish to know the opinion of the force, then said Goodsall, he would refrain from telling him. What this exchange did for Trenchard's legendary temper is not minuted.

Goodsall decided that he should take his problems with Trenchard outside the force. He conveyed a resolution passed by the joint executive committee, of which he was the secretary, to the secretary of the JCC (himself) asking that it be forwarded to the Home Secretary. The resolution dealt with 'dissatisfaction' in the Metropolitan Police. What Goodsall hoped to gain from bringing the national committee into the dispute is hard to discover. The branch board could have approached the Home Secretary itself, as he was the police authority for the Metropolitan Police. Goodsall knew that Sir Herbert Samuel would reject the resolution out of hand. Its wording, and the lengthy memorandum which accompanied it, simply demonstrated that the board was implacable in its opposition to the Commissioner's policies. Goodsall had delivered a powerful weapon to his enemy, and Trenchard knew how to exploit it. He told Arthur Dixon at the Home Office of everything that had passed between himself and the Federation, and even suggested that the Metropolitan branch board wanted to 'get its hands on the provident fund in order to finance a strike.' This, at a time of unrest in the Royal Navy, did not sound so far fetched to worried officials in Whitehall.

Dixon, who regarded himself as the friend and mentor of

the Federation, sent for Goodsall, whom he had known for years. Referring to the 'dissatisfaction' resolution he asked sadly, 'Where are we heading for?'. Goodsall told Dixon that the work of the branch boards had been made 'unpleasant' by Trenchard's bullying attitude towards the board. Dixon was concerned at the obvious signs of strain that Goodsall was showing, and advised him accordingly. 'You are in need of a holiday,' he said, 'and must have one. You will return refreshed. There may be bigger things ahead and we shall require cool heads and clear brains.' Dixon knew better than anyone that there were indeed 'bigger things ahead'.

Dixon's kindly advice went unheeded. Goodsall was convinced that Trenchard was out to destroy the Federation in London and he was not capable of delegating his duties to others. It was not long before Goodsall was summoned to Dixon's office again, and this time the conversation was less friendly. The election defeat of Jack Hayes had meant that there was no direct liaison between the Federation and Parliament. Goodsall expected that he would need sympathisers in the House but Holmes was anxious that the Secretary did nothing to upset the Home Office. Goodsall therefore wrote to Dixon to ask if there would be any objection to his approaching MPs on matters affecting conditions of service. Dixon said that he regarded this as a blatant attempt to by-pass the proper channels, and to undermine the Government on police matters. If this was what the Federation was going to do, he told Goodsall, then there was no good purpose in his interesting himself, as he always had done, in the success of the Federation.

As Trenchard's biographer, Andrew Boyle, recalled in his book, *Trenchard*, throughout 1932 the Commissioner was preparing the ground for the reforms he had decided upon. One of his allies was King George the Fifth, who had been kept fully informed by Trenchard himself. The King was so alarmed by Trenchard's description of the malignancy of the Federation that his private secretary, Lord Stanfordham, noted in his diary that His Majesty wondered how 'such a Bolshevist organisation' came to exist in the force.

When he came to Scotland Yard, the Commissioner had brought with him, by arrangement with the Home Secretary and the Air Ministry, some of his RAF staff officers. He set them to work on plans to rejuvenate a force he considered to be hopelessly out of date and unfitted for its task. He also recruited a small group of able young men, just down from Oxbridge, and added them to the team. Among them were Joseph Simpson, a future Commissioner, and Eric St Johnston, who became the Chief Inspector of Constabulary in the Sixties.

Early in 1933, Lord Trenchard published his Annual Report for 1932. It caused a sensation inside and outside the force. The police had heard many rumours that major changes were afoot but Trenchard had insisted on total security and there was no leak of the report. It began with a strong attack on the bedrock principle of promoting only men who had 'served their time' as constables;

'On coming to Scotland Yard, I was very surprised to find that the very great improvements in the status and pay of the police after the Desborough Committee's report had not led to much change in the type of man entering the service. A good deal had been heard about university graduates and young men with a public school education joining the police, but in fact the number of such recruits has been, until quite recently, altogether negligible. The entrance examination remains of the same rudimentary character that was deemed sufficient in the days when police duty was very different from what it is today, and when the facilities for education were much less .... the number of candidates accepted who have not carried their education beyond the elementary stage has remained much the same and constitutes between eighty and ninety per cent of the total.

'Hitherto there has been a rigid adherence to the 1829 plan of Sir Robert Peel under which all positions up to and including the rank of superintendent are filled by promotion from below. Such a rule was no doubt essential in the early days, but that an organisation of the size and complexity of the Metropolitan Police should have carried on for so long officered entirely by men from who little more was demanded at the start than that they should have a good character and a satisfactory physique is very remarkable ... ... it seems to me no longer possible to shirk the problem of how to secure a steady supply of the best brains from every available source.'

This prefaced Trenchard's description of the scheme he was putting forward for a Metropolitan Police College. Although he is credited with the concept, once again its progenitor was Arthur Dixon. He had been very disappointed when the national college scheme had been abandoned two years earlier. Soon after Trenchard's appointment, Dixon had dined with him at his club, where His Lordship had expressed his contempt for most of the senior officers at Scotland Yard. Dixon had seized the chance to suggest a college for the Metropolitan Police. He knew that Trenchard would grasp the opportunity and that Herbert Samuel would support it. Moreover, given Trenchard's attitude towards the Federation and promotion from the ranks, this scheme did not have to be inhibited by the need to avoid any suggestion of an 'officer class'. An 'officer class' was exactly what Trenchard wanted to create.

There were to be three avenues of entry to the College. The first was by an open examination; the second was to have a university degree or similar qualification; the third was for serving sergeants or constables aged under 28, who would be selected by a board. Those candidates chosen from outside the service would have to complete 12 months as constables before commencing the two years' course at Hendon. On passing out, they would be posted to stations as Junior Station Inspectors, a new rank.

In an incidental step, Trenchard stated that the new JSI's would not be members of the Federation, and that current sub-divisional and chief inspectors would be taken out of it as well. He wrote that it was not necessary for such officers to belong an organisation which had been set up to ventilate the grievances and views of the junior ranks.

Another significant change announced in the Commissioner's report was the lowering of the age of compulsory retirement for superintendents and senior officers, from 60 to 57 years. This was intended to clear some of the 'dead wood' and ensure that there was room at the top for the Hendon graduates in a few years' time. This was the one Trenchard reform which survived into the modern era, in spite of many attempts by Metropolitan senior officers to change it.

It was not only the quality of senior officers that concerned Trenchard. He had formed a poor opinion of the calibre of many constables. Too many, he believed, were simply uniform carriers, with no interest in, or hope of, promotion. Such men were working without enthusiasm until they could retire on pension. Trenchard knew that his scheme for potential senior officers would limit the opportunities of other officers still further. His solution was novel, and in its way even more radical than the college plan. He announced that a proportion of recruits would in future join under a short service scheme. They would serve for ten years, after which they would leave with a gratuity. They would not be offered a further engagement. This, he said, would reduce the average age of the constable grade. It would also improve the status of those who joined as career officers, and give them a greater chance of promotion above the lowest rank. It would also cut the police pension bill.

Anticipating that Goodsall would campaign against these innovations, Trenchard devoted a long section of the report to an attack on the Federation. He said that the Metropolitan branch board members attended 480 meetings in 1932, and this figure excluded meetings of the force charities. The Commissioner went on to accuse the Board of deliberately stirring up discontent in the force. Notices had been displayed in police stations containing 'untrue and insubordinate' statements which could not be tolerated in a disciplined service. Trenchard said it had never been intended that the Federation should become a 'legalised and subsidised machine for fomenting discontent and stimulating resistance to Government decisions'. The Report implied that the Federation had been behind unpleasant incidents involving regular officers and Specials when the latter had turned out to help police the unemployed demonstrations in 1932.

The Commissioner's Report had the affect that Trenchard

intended. Most newspapers accepted his strictures on the Federation (which hardly anyone outside the police had even heard of) at face value. Shorn of the right to hold membership meetings, the Board had no opportunity of countering the criticisms. On the day of publication, Goodsall telephoned Holmes in Durham and they agreed to make an immediate approach to the Home Secretary. In a letter to Goodsall, Holmes wrote;

> 'If Lord Trenchard's proposals are acted upon, it is the end of all representation. We shall seriously have to consider whether we can carry on at all. I think we must seek permission to make public our side of the case. The Commissioner's report has received wide publicity. The matter will presumably come before Parliament and our request for permission to interview MPs *(which had angered Dixon)* is more apposite than ever.'

Sir Herbert Samuel received Holmes and Goodsall at the Home Office, but rejected their request for permission to issue a press statement, defending the Federation's reputation. Samuel gave both men a strong warning that they must not enter into public controversy. Goodsall was inclined to ignore this gagging order, but Holmes was not a career Federationist He was an inspector with expectations of promotion (he reached the rank of superintendent and served in MI5 during World War 11). At the next JCC meeting, a resolution of strong protest against Trenchard's report was passed, and in the usual way Goodsall sent it to the two weekly papers, *Police Review* and *Police Chronicle*. Holmes feared that this contravened Samuel's instructions, and gave orders that it must not be published. The West Sussex branch board sent a resolution of protest to the Home Office. An angry Arthur Dixon rang the chief constable to object to its terms, and the board was forced to respectfully apply for permission to withdraw the offending item.

A decade earlier, another dynamic Metropolitan Commissioner, Sir Nevil Macready, had found himself at odds with the lower ranks. He had called them together and appealed, over the heads of the police union leaders, for their support. He got it. Trenchard decided that he too would address the men, and called a meeting in the Queens Hall. When he arrived, some two thousand officers were present, and the air was blue with smoke. The Commissioner strode on to the stage and barked, 'Clear the hall. Open the windows. Come back in five minutes when I can breathe.' When the meeting resumed, he made no attempt to explain his policies. He was content to warn the men that he would dismiss anyone found talking to the press and to give them a lecture on their general attitudes. The force had cheered Macready. They listened to Trenchard in total silence.

What Trenchard had not foreseen was the opposition that his schemes would arouse in the rest of the service. With the Federation silenced, any dissent in the Metropolitan itself was suppressed, although most senior officers were angered by his poor opinion of the existing leadership of the force, and outraged by the lower retirement ages, which would bring their careers to an end. Provincial chief constables were not inhibited by the bullying tactics of the Commissioner, and most spoke out against the idea of accelerated promotion and short service constables. Even some of the retired military officers among the county chief constables condemned Trenchard's plans.

Jack Hayes, although out of Parliament, still had friends on both sides of the House. He sent a detailed memorandum to every MP, setting out the Federation's views, and explaining that the body had been forbidden to write to them. It made no difference. The Government's huge majority ensured that the Metropolitan Police Bill went through without a hitch.

In retrospect, it is fair to say that the Hendon Police College scheme was at least a partial success. About 200 students took the course between 1934 and the outbreak of war in 1939. Of these, a majority were serving constables before the scheme began. When the war came, most of these young men joined the armed forces and many did not return to the police afterwards. By the late 1960s, a bare majority of provincial chief officers were Hendon graduates, and the highest posts at Scotland Yard were all occupied by former students. As it happened, it was during their regime that the deep seated and institutionalised corruption in the CID was exposed by the press. It was left to Robert Mark, the ex-grammar school boy whose higher police training consisted of three weeks at the national police college, to cleanse the force of the villains in its midst. One consequence of Hendon was that after the war, police authorities saw no need to appoint outsiders as chief constables, and relevant police service became a requisite qualification for such posts. The college closed in 1939 and the Labour Government of 1945 refused to reopen it, in spite of the protests of Lord Trenchard, speaking in the House of Lords.

The short service scheme was a failure. Many of the men who joined it remained in the Metropolitan Police for a very short time, and then transferred to provincial forces which were only too pleased to have recruits who did not need to be trained.

Trenchard considered that with the implementation of his 'reforms' he had discharged his responsibilities as Commissioner. Hitler and the Nazis were in power and threatening to make war. The Government had allowed the RAF to run down to a dangerous level. While still Commissioner, Trenchard spoke in a House of Lords debate and launched a withering attack on the Government's defence policies. The incongruousness of his position was obvious, and within a short time he resigned. He was succeeded by another RAF man, Air Marshal Sir Philip Game, who quietly dropped the short service scheme. But the Metropolitan Police, and the service, would remember Trenchard for many years to come.

There is a story that during the war Trenchard was in Whitehall on the morning after an air raid. Police and troops were dealing with an unexploded bomb. Trenchard recognised the superintendent in charge as a Hendon graduate and stepped over a barrier rope guarded by a constable, to march up to the hole in the ground. The superintendent was alarmed. 'Please get back, sir,' he said, 'It's a live one.' 'Funny that the constable didn't try to stop me,' said Trenchard. 'Perhaps he knew who you were, sir,' said the superintendent.

NINE

At war with Hitler (and Morrison)

T he excitement and tension of the campaign against the pay cuts and the disagreements with Lord Trenchard had made life interesting for the Police Federation leaders, but a quieter time followed. In 1932, there had been some concern among members of the smallest borough forces when a Parliamentary Select Committee proposed that the 15 forces which served populations under thirty thousand should be merged with their county neighbours. There were then 181 forces in England and Wales. Fourteen had less than 25 members, the smallest being Tiverton in Devonshire, with just eleven officers. Only 15 forces had more than 500 officers. For the Home Office, Arthur Dixon said that the main arguments in favour of force mergers were: increased efficiency, and cost savings. The case for retaining the small forces was that local feeling strongly favoured their retention. Dixon reminded the Committee that Desborough had said in 1919 that the multiplicity of small forces hampered crime detection. The Home Office view, said Dixon, was that with some exceptions, such as Oxford and Cambridge, the smallest forces should be merged as soon as the necessary legislation could be passed. He advised that the medium sized forces, serving populations below 75,000, should also be merged whenever convenient occasions arose, such as the retirement of a chief constable.

The Police Federation gave evidence to the Select Committee. It was firmly on the side of the small forces, arguing that men joined a force with the object of serving in it throughout their service. Holmes and Goodsall told the Committee that the members of a force that was merged with another should be safeguarded against compulsory transfer.

The Government decided that the Select Committee's report would not be acted upon straight away, preferring to wait until there was a need for a new Police Act.

The Federation was anxious to improve the widows' pension scheme. Since 1921 the widow of a police officer had been paid a flat rate pension of £30 a year (£40 for inspectors' widows). This could be supplemented by children's allowances from police charities, such as the Gurney Fund, but most police widows lived in near poverty. The younger widows were slightly better off than those whose husbands died before 1918. They had no pensions.

The Federation pressed the authorities to do something about police widows. Goodsall reminded the Home Office and the police authorities that pensions contributions had been doubled since 1918, and there had been no increase in benefits. The employers were sympathetic when the matter was raised at a meeting of the Police Council in 1935 and there was much optimism that something would be done. This proved unfounded. The Home Office did not call another meeting of the Council until March 1939, and just before it met, Goodsall was informed that the Government would concede an increased pension for widows, but only if the members agreed to a further increase in their pension contribution.

When the Council discussed the issue, the prospect of an increase for the widows disappeared in a welter of recriminations. The Home Office tabled a memorandum which called for an increase in contributions from 5 to 7 per cent, and suggested that the rising cost of the scheme could be reduced by extending the period of service for maximum pension beyond thirty years.

The likelihood of another war with Germany was in everyone's thoughts as the Thirties went on. The 1939 Police Council met at a time when it was dawning on the public that the Prime Minister, Neville Chamberlain, had not after all brought back permanent peace from his Munich meeting with Hitler a few months before. Police forces were getting ready to meet the extra demands that war would put upon the service. Forces had always recruited mainly from the armed forces, and there were thousands of officers who knew that they would be recalled to the colours as soon as the war started. Many were recalled throughout the summer. The recalled men were replaced by members of the First Police Reserve, a body of retired policemen who had been held in readiness.

As soon as war was declared, in September 1939, the Police and Firemen (War Service) Act was introduced, as one of many emergency measures the Government had prepared. It suspended the right of police to retire on pension, unless the chief officer consented. The police were included in the category of 'reserved' occupations, which meant that they could not volunteer for the armed forces. The men who had been called up as reservists could count their military service towards their police pensions, and police authorities were told that they could, if they wished, make up the difference between army and police pay, and all but a handful of authorities did so.

Wartime policing was very different from normal times. The police had to enforce a wide range of regulations, from ensuring that citizens carried gas masks and observed the black-out at night, to looking out for black marketeers and military deserters, and keeping track of aliens. They were required to work extended hours of overtime, as well as undertaking unpaid fire watching duties at police premises. The period of the 'phoney' war, from September 1939 to the dramatic German breakthrough in the late spring of 1940, gave the service an opportunity to train the thousands of reserves and special constables and operate on as near to a normal footing as possible. All this changed after Dunkirk, when Britain became the front line. Before the war in Europe ended in 1945, hundreds of police were killed, and many more injured, in air raids.

The Federation did its best to carry on. The first consequence of the war was the cancellation of its Annual Conference in 1939, but in August 1940, the Police Council met at the Home Office. Bearing in mind the state of the war, with the Battle of Britain raging in the skies above southern England and an invasion expected at any time, the fact that a meeting could take place in London to discuss the pay and conditions of the police, says something about the nation's determination to carry on with its daily life. More than once during the proceedings, the air raid sirens sounded and the delegates adjourned to the shelters in the Home Office cellars.

One of the main items was police pay. In 1937 the Federation had submitted its first ever claim for an increase in pay. It was based on a general increase in duties and responsibilities since 1919, especially traffic duties. The Home Office did not respond until the 1940 Police Council meeting, when it said that police officers would be treated in the same way as civil servants, and receive temporary bonuses to offset wartime inflation. The bonus, five shillings a week, was paid to constables, but not to sergeants, inspectors and above, because their earnings were over £5 a week.

The Federation was pressing for the abolition of 'Scale B' pay. Although a large proportion of the men recruited since its introduction in 1933 were now in the fighting forces, the existence of two scales of pay among constables was a source of growing dissatisfaction. The grievance was emphasised by the fact that some of the war reserve officers were getting more pay than the Scale B men. The Federation argued that all police were performing many extra hours of unpaid duty and the circumstances of the financial crisis of the early Thirties no longer applied. There was support for this view from the local authorities and the chief constables, but the Home Office was unsympathetic. Sir Alexander Maxwell, the permanent under-secretary, said it was all very well for the members of the Police Council to say that it was time to rectify a grievance; that argument could be applied to everyone in the country who happened to have a grievance. However, the Home Office did concede an additional three shillings a week, on top of the war bonus, to compensate constables for the extra hours. The sergeants got four shillings, and the inspectors nothing. It was also agreed that officers who had been kept in the service when they were qualified for pension would receive a special payment. This was not an unqualified benefit, because the supplement took most officers above the £5 mark, so they lost the war bonus.

The Home Secretary in the coalition government headed by Winston Churchill was Herbert Morrison, a Labour member who had been a highly successful leader of the London County Council. Morrison was the son of a Metropolitan policeman, but he soon became deeply unpopular because of his autocratic manner when dealing with the Federation. He had no sympathy with the claim for the abolition of 'Scale B' pay. He was disliked by many patriotic policemen because he had been a conscientious objector during the First World War. Those who despised him for this ignored the malformed foot which would have kept him out of the Army in any case.

In March 1941, Morrison appointed a committee under Lord Snell to examine the question of widows' pensions. The Committee was asked to consider the three options put forward in a report on the pensions scheme by the Government Actuary. These were; to increase pensionable service from 30 years to 33; to increase contributions from 5 to 7 per cent; to allow members to surrender part of their pension entitlement to provide increased benefits for their widows. All three propositions were anathema to the Federation, which believed that the widows' pension should be increased without any additional contributions from the men.

The Snell Committee reported in September 1941. It recommended that the widows of constables and sergeants should have their pension increased from £30 to £52 a year, and that inspectors' widows should get £70. In return, the men's contribution should be raised to 7 per cent.

When the Police Council met in May 1942 to consider the Snell Report, the chairman of the Joint Central Committee, Inspector George Strangeways of Newcastle, shocked his colleagues by declaring that he was in favour of accepting it. He told the Council that the majority of inspectors were in favour of accepting the Report, and the opposition from the Federation was unrepresentative of the views of his rank. All the other Federation delegates to the Police Council were opposed, and Goodsall was furious with Strangeways. The chairman was a greatly admired figure in Federation circles. He had served as chairman of the JCC in all three ranks, and when he relinquished the post in 1926, on promotion to sergeant, he was given the unique honour of a service testimonial.

The remainder of the Joint Central Committee was meeting in London while the Police Council was in session and as soon as the Council adjourned, Goodsall and the other members of the delegation went back to the JCC to report. Strangeways found that he had only one supporter, Inspector Middlewood of Durham, and the JCC passed an immediate vote of censure upon him. When his own Inspectors' Committee followed suit at its next meeting, Strangeways resigned. The internal row overshadowed the real issue. The widows did not get their increased pension.

Wartime inflation caused the pay bonuses to be increased early in 1941. The constables got ten shillings, sergeants five, and for the first time the inspectors got a war duty allowance of four shillings. Whilst this would have helped with domestic budgets, the morale of the service was being affected by a range of grievances, some more important than others.

The Home Office had relaxed the rule that officers must be fully qualified by examination before being promoted, and the Federation alleged that there had been cases of blatant favouritism in some forces, with qualified men being passed over. Some chief constables decided that the payment of the war bonuses meant that they did not have to allow time off to compensate for overtime. The Home Office agreed, when approached by the Federation about this, to advise chiefs that any duty in excess of twelve hours a day, should be compensated by time off when conditions allowed.

In 1943 twenty two small forces, mainly in the south east, were merged into surrounding county forces for the duration of the war. The Federation protested because this had been done without any consultation, and as a result men were now serving under different conditions. Herbert Morrison reminded the JCC that he was not required to consult them about any action taken under wartime regulations.

As the war went on, police were allowed to volunteer for aircrew duties with the RAF, but in general the service was still a reserved occupation. This meant that policemen could not be called up for military service, but neither could they leave for other jobs, which were paying much higher wages than the police could command. The Annual Reports of the JCC began to dwell upon the morale question. When Morrison attended the Federation Conference in October 1942, the chairman of the JCC, Inspector Trigg of Cardiff, referred to a number of issues which were causing discontent. Morrison, addressing the delegates, was arrogant and scornful, dismissing what he termed the 'charter of grievances'. He insisted that Scale B pay must remain, and told the delegates that they were lucky that the pay of all police had not been cut in 1933.

When Quintin Hogg, then a young Conservative MP, questioned Morrison in Parliament about discontent in the police, the Home Secretary was equally scathing about the Federation's attitude. In a debate on police force amalgamations, he returned to the attack; 'I went to the Police Federation Conference where they had a long string of troubles and they were not too forthcoming on most of them.' The Home Secretary's attitude would have reminded Goodsall and the JCC of the clashes with Trenchard. The military autocrat, Trenchard, and the ex-pacifist bureaucrat, Morrison, had found one thing in common, their antipathy towards the Police Federation.

When the JCC sent Morrison a strongly worded resolution asking for a change in the negotiating machinery, including the right to arbitration on some matters, in view of the 'ineffectiveness' of the existing system, the Home Secretary retorted that he supposed by 'ineffective' the Federation meant that they did not get all that they asked for. In his view, the Federation had secured benefits for the service by way of the current system. If there was dissatisfaction, he said, it might be due to the Federation's inability or unwillingness to acquaint the membership with the reasons for decisions on pay and allowances.

Each year brought increases in the amounts paid as war bonuses. It did not please sergeants and inspectors that the amounts granted to constables brought the total pay of the lowest rank to almost the same level as themselves. This was because the higher allowances went to public servants on the lowest scales. The increases were decided by the civil service negotiators and passed on automatically to the police, a procedure which annoyed Goodsall, who saw that the bonus system prevented any discussions in the Police Council on the Federation's demand for more pensionable pay.

Throughout the war, Goodsall worked unceasingly to keep the Federation alive. It was not an easy task and he had little assistance. He worked from a small room in New Malden Police Station, with one shorthand typist as the sole staff. She was paid by the Home Office as the Federation was still not allowed to have funds.

Somewhat to the Committee's surprise, Morrison agreed in 1944 to permit an open meeting to be held in Manchester. It was 13 years since they had been banned. The meeting at least gave the wider membership an opportunity to meet the Federation leaders, who were virtually unknown to anyone but Conference delegates.

The Committee members were convinced that the Federation was unlikely to make real progress on conditions of service until the right to arbitration was conceded. Goodsall and other members had met and discussed the issue with W. J. Brown, the independent MP for Rugby who was also the leader of the civil service negotiators. After the initial request for arbitration rights had been rejected by the Home Office, the Committee even suggested that a special Parliamentary seat should be created for serving or retired policemen, who would speak for the service. It sounded a naive suggestion, but the creation of life peers some twenty years later gave opportunities for experts in many walks of life to be heard at Westminster.

The success of the allied landings on D Day and the realisation that the end of the war was in sight turned the Committee's thoughts to the future. In its annual report for 1944, Goodsall anticipated another Committee on the lines of Desborough, to look at all conditions of service. If such a body were to be appointed, he wrote, 'the Police Federation is ready to prove its claim for vastly improved conditions.'

The conviction that only a second independent inquiry would help the police had been strengthened by a fraught meeting at the Home Office in September 1944, when Morrison had summoned the entire Committee to lecture them on their responsibilities as he saw them. The JCC had forwarded yet another lengthy memorandum of complaints, this time asserting that the police had been unfairly discriminated against. The memorandum instanced widows' pensions, Scale B pay, and the failure to respond to the pay claim, as examples of grievances which had gone unremedied.

Morrison told the Committee that he was not sure they had the right approach to their duties as representatives. They clung unreasonably to requests that could not be granted. If the rank and file at Conference pressed for things that could not be achieved, he said, the JCC must suppress the undeserving or the impracticable. When the Home Office rejected a request, it was the duty of the JCC to explain to the membership why something had been rejected, not to attack the Home Secretary's decision. Morrison added that the Federation was wrong to want formal arbitration. It would be a mistake to tighten up the informal proceedings of the Police Council by dividing the authorities from the employees.

Inspector Trigg, the Committee chairman, gave what reply he could. The Federation felt that they had a good case and that they had not had justice, he said. It was inevitable that they would go on pressing their demands.

Early in 1945, the Police Council negotiated the first increase in the pensionable pay of the police since 1919, but the new scales were a bitter disappointment to the Federation leaders and the membership. The Federation had startled the Home Office and the police authorities by demanding a new scale for constables starting at £5.10s, rising to £7.10s after eight years' service. Sir Alexander Maxwell was horrified. The Home Office was proposing a new scale of £4.6s rising to £5.15s after 15 years. Sir Alexander said that the Federation was making exhorbitant demands and doing a disservice to its members. The rest of the Council agreed that the Home Office offer was inadequate, but the police authorities and the chief constables said the Federation was asking for too much. The meeting broke up without agreement. When it resumed two months later, Herbert Morrison was in the chair. The Home Office proposal was now slightly higher, £4.10s on appointment rising to £5.17s after ten years. Morrison pointed out that the new scale abolished Scale B pay, which ought to satisfy the Federation. He condemned the Federation's claim, and said it should have more regard for the rate payers. It would impair relations with the public if people thought that police pay was too high. The Home Secretary emphasised that this was the final offer and would have to be accepted.

When the new scales were announced, the police realised, that with the ending of their war bonuses, the top rate constable would be just six shillings a week better off. Expressing its disappointment with the pay award, the Joint Central Committee told the members that it was clear that 'Desborough' was dead. Goodsall argued that the new scales had been based on Scale B, not the Desborough scale.

The end of the war in Europe brought about the end of the coalition government and, to the general pleasure of the police service, Herbert Morrison left the Home Office. Following the Labour victory in the 1945 election, James Chuter Ede became Home Secretary. Where Morrison had been antagonistic, Ede was conciliatory and courteous. Here was a man whom the Federation was prepared to take on trust.

TEN

The problems of peace

A wartime phrase that survived in the language when peace came, was 'normal service will be resumed as soon as possible.' In 1944, in an attempt to ensure that this would be the case with the police, the Home Office set up a Police Post-war Committee, charged with examining all aspects of police organisation. The Committee consisted of Home Office officials and 21 chief constables, and one Superintendent. The Police Federation was omitted, presumably on the grounds that the future of the service did not concern it. The Federation's exclusion might have had something to do with its relationship with Herbert Morrison and senior Home Office officials. The Home Office did not see any necessity for the presence of local authority representatives on the committee. Its terms of reference were; to examine police organisation, training and promotion, buildings, amenities and welfare.

In its first report, published in June 1946, the Committee dealt with the higher training of police officers. It endorsed the idea of a national police college, which should offer short courses to inspectors and senior officers. There would be a six months' course for sergeants about to be promoted to inspector; and one of three months for superintendents. The Committee recommended, that when sufficient college trained candidates were available, no man should be appointed inspector until he had completed the course. The Committee was anxious to ensure that the new national college would not be regarded by the rank and file as a resurrection of Trenchard's Hendon scheme. The Committee said that it had been urged upon them that the service should adopt the officer training system of the armed forces, because it was necessary to give outstanding men 'a thorough and broad police education while they are still young enough to derive benefit from it, i.e., while they are still in the rank of constable.' It had also been suggested that entry to the college should be by selection from among officers with more than five years' service who had passed a competitive examination. The Committee said that this would involve judging a man's fitness for high rank by an assessment of his potentialities, rather than on the record of his actual achievements on the job. The Committee concluded that it was;

> 'against the provision of officer training before a man has shown by his service in the ranks of constable and sergeant that his abilities as a practical policeman justify his being placed in the field of selection for further advancement.'

Thus it endorsed the traditional view that the higher ranks of the police service should be selected on the basis of practical experience. The service attached more importance to policemanship than leadership in its choice of senior officers, taking it for granted that these two diverse qualities would somehow both be present in a future chief constable. Of the chief constables and HMIs on the Committee who endorsed the principle that experience at the bottom was necessary for the men who got to the top, something like a half had gone straight from the army into chief constables posts. Among the members, incidentally, was Sir Philip Game, Trenchard's successor at Scotland Yard.

In 1947 the Government published a White Paper setting out its plans for a national police college, which endorsed the ideas of the Post-war Committee, except that the local authorities were granted greater representation on the governing body. The White Paper stated;

> 'The (Post-war) Committee make it clear, however, that they do not wish their proposal (for a junior course limited to sergeants) to be regarded as the last word on the subject, and the question of providing a course open to young constables should be reviewed in the

light of experience. They emphasise that the proposal which they will make will be likely to succeed only if police authorities and chief officers of police send to the College a proportion of outstanding young officers.'

In this, the Home Office and the chief officers who served on the Post-war Committee were to be disappointed. The college began its life in a disused camp for wartime munitions workers at Ryton on Dunsmore near Coventry. In its first ten years, it became clear that many chief officers were not giving effect to the idea that the College would train mostly young sergeants who were destined to reach higher rank at a relatively early stage. Some, who openly voiced their disdain for the college and the whole idea of higher police training, made a point of sending the men they had no intention of selecting for higher rank. It was the attitudes and actions of such chief officers that was to lead to more radical developments at the college some years later. One future chief officer who attended the college for a three weeks course during these early years (his one and only experience of higher police training) went on to become perhaps the outstanding Commissioner of the Metropolitan Police. Of his brief encounter with Ryton, Sir Robert Mark said in his memoirs that the only thing he learnt there was how to fill in an application form for a higher post in another force, as 'most of the directing staff were doing little else'.

The Second Report of the Police Post-war Committee dealt with the way the police were organised. It concluded that the historic beat system was still the best means of policing. The Committee said; 'In our view the present system (of police organisation) is essentially sound, and we consider that the principles to be followed in the post-war police service should be in the main those that have been followed hitherto.'

The Committee frowned on the system, still common in many forces, of requiring constables to follow a fixed route when patrolling their beats. This was very convenient for supervising officers who 'would know at all times exactly where each constable ought to be and when any particular premises were due to be examined'. However, the routes taken by beat officers became well known to criminals, who simply waited for the constable to pass before breaking into property. Moreover, fixed beat working was monotonous and discouraged individual resource and initiative. The Committee asserted that the disadvantages of fixed beats were so widely known that 'this system has been virtually abandoned'. This writer joined the service some eight years later, and it was not abandoned in his force until the arrival of an enlightened chief constable in 1959.

The Post-war Committee gave a succinct description of everyday policing in the middle of the twentieth century;

'The main distinction in beat work is between town and country beats, that is to say between the beat for which one constable resident on the beat is responsible throughout the 24 hours (and which is therefore only patrolled for the 8 hours in the 24) and the beat which is patrolled throughout the 24 hours by constables working in shifts.

'The country constable has less ready access to specialised services and equipment than the town constable, and in the day-time therefore it is his duty, besides carrying out his routine patrol, to attend to such matters as crime enquiries, coroner's officer work, and diseases of animals; and in view of his more personal relationship to the public he is often expected to give advice and assistance on subjects that are not strictly police work.

'The town constable, in day-time, is mainly occupied in keeping order and checking offences in streets and public places, controlling traffic and dealing with accidents, and answering miscellaneous inquiries from the public. At night, the town policeman's duty is to ensure the security of premises, deterring would-be thieves in his presence, examining shops and houses to see that they are secure, and stopping and questioning persons who may be in possession of stolen property or housebreaking implements. The country constable at night has fewer premises to examine and supervise (though some country houses are extremely vulnerable) but he has to look out for poachers and poultry thieves and outbreaks of fire.'

The Committee pointed out that the standard of police cover varied considerably throughout the country. This was because the service was made up of so many forces which differed in size and the provision of resources. The service had been built up in piecemeal fashion to meet local needs, there had been no regard to setting a general standard of cover. The Committee admitted that it had sought and failed to come up with a formula by which such a standard could be established. In the years to come, others would also seek and fail to find the elusive yardstick of policing standards. The Post-war Committee was dismissive of 'mechanised beats'. In the United States, forces had supplied patrol officers with cars 'in which they make a tour of the beat first rapidly and then slowly, then very slowly. The constable remains in his car the whole time until he comes across some incident requiring his attention.' The Committee said that this method 'almost completely dispenses with trying property at night and also diminishes that contact with the public which is so useful to the police and to the public.' It added; 'Even if all the cars were fitted with wireless apparatus, this method would not be suitable for adoption in this country.' The era of the Panda car was still some way off.

The Committee went on to consider the position of women in the post-war service. It referred to the attitude of the Police Federation, which; 'has always been opposed on principle to the employment of women, largely, it appears, on the ground that the work that they do can be better done by policemen, or by voluntary organisations in touch with the police.' Recently, the Federation had expressed the fear that if more women were employed, there would be fewer opportunities to keep disabled policemen in the service. The Committee noted that although policewomen were *ipso facto* members of the Federation, it had always opposed their exercise of the rights of membership. If the Federation persisted in this attitude, it would be necessary to give the women their own organisation (a threat which was to bring about a swift change of heart among the members of the all male JCC). Not that there were any feminists (or women, for that matter) on the Post-war Committee. When discussing the duties that women could perform, it plumped for dealing with women and children, moral welfare, clerical and communications work, and under cover duties. The Committee said that women should be given as wide a range of police experience as possible, because 'it is clearly undesirable that they should be mainly or exclusively employed in dealing with the more sordid type of police work coming under the general definition of sexual offences.' They added that many of the duties of men and women officers were not interchangeable, and it was obvious that 'the police service must remain preponderantly a masculine service.' Therefore, there must be a separate establishment and career structure for policewomen.

The Post-war Committee commented at some length on what appeared to be a vexed question linked to policewomen: where did police work end and moral welfare begin? It noted that many acts of immorality were not illegal and the police should not concern themselves, as a general rule, in such matters. However, it was only right that the police 'should make use of their experience of humanity and its failings to try to prevent men and women (especially young persons) drifting through moral and physical depravity into a life of crime.' Having said this, the Committee added that while it was proper in wartime that policewomen should take a broad view of their functions and undertake moral welfare work, in peacetime they should concentrate on police duty and not set themselves up as moral censors.

The Post-war Committee members were pleased to note, that while they were examining the role of women in the service, the regulation which required that policewomen must be unmarried had been repealed. They said the previous requirement, that a woman must resign on marriage, was wasteful of valuable experience, and thought that a married woman could, with her experience of life, be better placed to gain the confidence of another woman than a single colleague.

The Committee thought it appropriate that women officers should be directly responsible to male superior officers during their day to day duties, with senior women officers taking care of their welfare, training and so on. The question of whether senior women officers could supervise male officers did not arise.

An illuminating picture of working conditions which had prevailed until the war, and still obtained in some forces, was contained the report of a Police Council committee which was appointed in 1946 to examine local conditions of service. It found that most forces had retained the condition that a constable could not marry without the permission of the chief officer. Some forces required a constable to produce character references for his bride to be, and in some a constable had to prove that his financial position was sufficient to support a wife (who was not permitted to go out to work). The report said that there was no justification for any restriction on an officer's right to marry.

In some county forces officers were not allowed to leave their beats on their rest days, and in some borough forces they had to obtain permission if they intended to leave the borough on rest days. Other rules said that a constable had to leave particulars of his whereabouts and the expected time of his return, if he intended to be away from his home or lodgings. The Committee reminded chief officers that a constable was off duty when he had completed his eight hours and should be free to enjoy his leisure as he thought fit. The report noted that in one force a rule prohibited constables who were in licensed premises in their free time, from sitting down. Another banned its officers from going into pubs, on or off duty. The Committee thought it was reasonable to forbid officers from drinking in pubs when on duty and in uniform. They recommended that forces should be as liberal as possible, but advised that a country constable should not make a habit of patronising one particular pub which he had the duty of supervising when he was on duty.

Other rules in existence in some forces required constables to seek permission if they wished to take legal action in a private matter. Others stipulated that a constable who wished to resign early in his service must pay compensation to the police authority in respect of the cost of his training and uniform.

While expressing surprise that such antideluvian attitudes survived in a modern police service, the Committee was not inclined to be critical. Even the rules about marriage, it said, had been prompted in the first place by the anxiety of chief officers to look after the welfare of their men. The Committee stressed that it had found relatively few causes for real complaint about local conditions of service, but recommended that all forces should conform to a set of standard conditions of service. However, a Federation member on the Committee might have held a less sanguine view of the way some chief officers exercised control over the private lives of their men and their families.

The most pressing problem facing the service in the immediate post-war period was manpower. Out of a pre-war strength of 60,000, more than 16,000 police joined the armed forces during the war. More than half the wartime strength consisted of war reserves, full time special constables, and men who had been retained past pension age. These left the service as soon as the wartime regulations were ended. Of the 13000 auxiliaries in the Metropolitan Police, 10000 had gone by Christmas 1945. The armed forces were demobilising men as quickly as possible, and those wishing to return to the police had some priority, but it soon became clear that a sizeable proportion of former policemen had no wish to return to the force. They knew that the 1945 pay settlement meant that the service had lost its lead over most other occupations, but there were other reasons which decided them against resuming their careers in the police. Many policemen had achieved commissioned or senior NCO rank in the armed forces, and did not intend going back to the status of constables. Others shared the general mood of returning servicemen, that they had experienced enough military discipline to last for a lifetime, and police forces were still run on autocratic lines. Nevertheless, some 7,000 demobilised servicemen rejoined the police in 1946. One major factor in the decision of many to rejoin, was that their families had continued to live in police houses while they were in the armed forces. Others felt an obligation to forces which had made up their wages during the war.

The Annual Report of the Inspectors of Constabulary for 1946 gave a cheerful description of the process of resettlement;

'... ... while the return to civilian life after a service one is not an easy matter in any walk of life, in returning to a disciplined service like the police the human difficulties were intensified. Many police officers had obtained rank and distinction in one of the fighting services, and to revert to subordinate positions, to submit to the essential discipline, and to perform irksome duties which must inevitably arise, called for strength of character on the part of the returning men which was not simple, and considerable patience and sympathetic understanding were necessary on the part of chief constables and their senior officers. 'How would the men settle down?' was a question asked with some concern. It can be reported with satisfaction and pleasure that generally speaking these young officers have resumed police careers in a creditable manner.'

Between the wars, the service had found no difficulty in recruiting men of the required calibre. The service offered benefits that were not obtainable in most other jobs; good pay, job security, free housing and a pension payable from an early age. In the immediate post war period, Britain believed that the heady promise of 'full employment in a free society' had actually arrived. Mass unemployment was to be a thing of the past, and the police service would now have to compete in a totally changed labour market. It soon became apparent that the service was not in a position to compete for men of the calibre it had recruited without difficulty before the war.

At first glance, the recruiting position looked healthy. In 1946 the service recruited 9,046 men, including the 7,000 returning servicemen, but the net gain was just 770, as 8,270 officers left in that year, mostly men who had been kept in the force because of the war. The service was not used to having large numbers of officers resigning before pension.

The 1946 HMI's report expressed concern, citing low pay as a major factor.

Housing was a huge problem. Some police authorities managed to secure a small allocation of newly built council houses for police use. The local authorities had embarked on a massive building programme to replace the many thousands of homes destroyed by enemy action. Their priorities were concerned with the homeless and the thousands of young couples living in overcrowded conditions with relatives. Most councils took the view that it was for the police forces to find tied accommodation for their officers. For some years after the war, police families had to put up with the same housing problems as the rest of the population. The housing shortage was a huge handicap for the forces which were becoming desperate for recruits, and the capital grants for house building which the Home Office was able to secure from the Treasury were wholly inadequate to meet the need. Officers found that the supply of rented accommodation had almost dried up, and what there was commanded rents that were well above the allowances in payment.

The Third Report of the Police Post-war Committee concentrated on welfare matters, with emphasis on police housing. It drew up specifications for new police houses, which in keeping with the times, deemed inspectors worthy of better accommodation for their families than would be available (when finance, building materials and labour became available) to constables and sergeants. Dwellings designed for occupation by Mr and Mrs Superintendent were proportionately more opulent, but all such plans were limited because of strict Government controls on house building, which limited the size of a dwelling to 1000 square feet, well below the Post-war Committee's wish to build houses for constables and sergeants of 1,180 square feet.

In 1944, the Home Office urged police authorities to give priority to the housing requirements of the service once the war was over. It warned that all police authorities would need to provide housing, whereas before the war very few of the city and borough forces had felt it necessary to do so, because there was a plentiful supply of rented property, and new housing was available for sale at prices that police officers could afford. The Home Office suggested that authorities should get to work at once on acquiring sites, enlisting the co-operation of housing authorities, and where possible buying vacant houses, some of which could be converted into flats. Police authorities which tried to buy houses found that market prices were far above the values placed on them by the District Valuers, and they were not allowed to pay more.

The police housing situation was exacerbated because normal recruiting had been suspended for six years and the service was trying to recruit many thousands of men in very quick time. Most recruits were ex-servicemen (National Service requirements ruled out the recruitment of most young single men). The recruits were mostly married with young children, and many had been attracted to the police simply because it looked like a good opportunity to jump the long housing queue. The days were gone when every force could pick and choose from among dozens of keen applicants for the few vacancies that arose through retirements. Although no force admitted it, standards were lowered simply to get a few more uniformed officers on the streets. It was an expensive stratagem, as the wastage rate among recruits continued to rise.

Progress on police housing was painfully slow. By July 1948, three years after the end of the war, the Home Office had approved tenders for a total of 1300 houses, of which only 400 had been completed. One problem was the supply of materials. Britain did not have the foreign currency to buy enough timber for all its housing needs, and steel was in just as short supply. There was a huge shortage of bricks. In 1947, the situation was bad enough for the Home Office to say that for the time being no building tenders could be approved.

The Metropolitan Police had built extensively in the Thirties, providing new section houses for single men, and these were a boon to the force in its time of dire manpower shortage, but now the force had to embark on building and buying houses for married officers. Lord Trenchard had foreseen the need for decent married quarters and had planned a programme of 800 houses and flats a year, but the section houses for single men were given priority. As a result, the force had only about a thousand married quarters, nowhere near-enough the number required. None of the local authorities in the capital could help the force with its housing problem. London had been devastated by the blitz and the later rocket raids, and the priority was to replace the many thousands of dwellings that had been destroyed or damaged. Some of the section houses were having to be used as emergency married quarters.

Complaints about housing figured prominently in the matters dealt with by branch boards. With so many men having to live in overcrowded conditions with relations, or pay exorbitant rents for substandard flats, this was inevitable. Forces attempted to allocate police housing according to priorities, but there were frequent complaints of favouritism when a house was given to one officer and not to any of the others.

In its post war planning, the service had estimated that about 10,000 recruits would be needed in the first two years of peace. It had been decided to train recruits on a regional basis, and surplus premises were earmarked as the new district training centres. The Home Office was anxious that recruits should not be taken on in numbers that were too large for the service's training resources, but it soon became clear that this was not going to be the problem. Of those who joined, many left after only a few months. The service was unused to men resigning in large numbers, but this was to become an endemic problem over the next thirty years. As the gap between authorised strengths and actual numbers grew, forces began lowering their entry standards. Height requirements were lowered in all but a few forces, the City of London adhering to its insistence on six foot tall recruits while the surrounding Metropolitan managed with a 5' 8" rule.

It was no surprise, therefore, that pay was on the agenda once again when the Police Council met in September 1946. The Home Office now realised that it had miscalculated badly. The new rates were agreed very quickly, and they reflected the need to get more police as soon as possible. The constables scale was increased to £5.5s, rising to £6.12s after ten years. Long service increments brought the constables' maximum to £7. There was a condition attached to the rise;

the new rates were to last for three years, during which time there would be a comprehensive review of police conditions of service.

The Federation leaders were convinced that they had done well. Goodsall told the council that the deal would promote 'contentment and efficiency in the service'. The negotiators might have been pleased, but it soon became evident that the service was not. The Commissioner of the Metropolitan Police, in his annual report for 1947, showed how the pay deal had failed to improve the situation. Over a quarter of the first post war recruits, brought in during 1946, had resigned before the end of 1947. The stated reasons for resignation were pay, housing, family problems, and the higher paid jobs on offer elsewhere. The Metropolitan was over 4,000 officers short of its establishment of 20,000.

The Labour Government was busy implementing the welfare state. The police, who had enjoyed free medical treatment and sick pay as part of their conditions of service, were not pleased at having to pay contributions to a state scheme which brought them no additional benefits, any payments made from national insurance to a policeman would be deducted from his salary or police pension. The Federation urged the Government to allow the police service to be opted out — but this was contrary to the concept of a universal scheme. It was decided that the police pension contribution should be reduced by twopence a week to take account of the industrial injury benefit of the national insurance scheme. When the state superannuation scheme commenced in 1948, the police were given the option of paying the full police pension contribution (5 per cent less twopence a week) and thus qualify for the state retirement pension at age 65, in addition to their police pension, or to have a further deduction of one shilling each week from their pension contribution, and forego the state pension. New entrants had no choice, their pension contribution became 5 per cent less one shilling and twopence a week. If the intention of this arrangement had been to exclude the police from the state pension scheme, it failed to do so. The police pension contribution was not adjusted on subsequent occasions when national insurance contributions were raised, so that when they reached state pension age, retired police officers had their state pensions reduced only by the amount of that pension in 1948. Police officers have remained eligible for the basic state pension, but have been opted out of subsequent 'earnings related' state schemes.

In July 1947, Goodsall tried to persuade the Police Council that it had been a mistake to impose a three year standstill on police pay. He said that there was widespread dissatisfaction with the levels of pay, but the chief constables disagreed with this view. The chiefs attached more importance to the need to keep to the agreement, and their spokesmen rebuked the Federation for wanting to reopen the question.

There was better news for the service when the Police Council met again in September 1947. Pay was not on the agenda, but the authorities agreed to reimburse police officers for income tax levied on rent allowance. This removed a long standing grievance, going back to the cuts made by the Geddes Committee in 1922. The purpose of rent allowance was to reimburse the expenditure of officers who were not provided with police accommodation. The authorities agreed with the Federation that it was, therefore, inequitable to deduct income tax from an allowance which reimbursed actual expenditure. As the Inland Revenue insisted that rent allowance was a taxable emolument, reimbursement was made by way of a taxable compensatory grant.

The service also had some reason to be pleased with the Report of a Police Council Committee on Rent Allowance in 1948. This recommended that the allowance should be increased to a maximum of thirty shillings a week in the provinces and thirty five shillings in London. The increase did something to assist the men to meet the increasingly high rents being charged in most towns, but they still had to find money out of their own pockets to meet a charge that, after all, the authorities should have been meeting in full. Worst off were the small number of police in the towns who were owner occupiers. The Report recognised that many such officers had been forced to buy houses because of the shortage of rented property. It recommended that the allowance paid to them should be based on 125 per cent of the Inland Revenue's 'Schedule A' assessment of the rental value of the member's house. This amounted to a notional rentable value of the dwelling, on which income tax was levied. This unpopular form of taxation was ended some years later. The report recommended that single men living in lodgings or at home should be paid one half of the maximum limit rent allowance for the force.

Faced with pressure from the membership, the Federation tried again to break the three year pay freeze when the Police Council met in March 1948. This time the other components were sympathetic, but outside factors were working against a police pay rise. An economic crisis was building up, and a Government White Paper on incomes preached firm restraint. Chuter Ede said he saw no prospect of a police pay increase being brought forward, but promised to expedite the appointment of the promised Committee of Inquiry.

In May, Ede told Parliament that the Committee would be headed by Lord Oaksey, who had been the British judge at the Nuremburg trial of the German leaders. The other members were a woman magistrate, two trades unionists, a law professor, and a former chairman of an employers' federation.

The Oaksey Committee was to be the climax of Albert Goodsall's career. He had been working on the Federation's submission for nearly two years, and was quietly convinced that an independent body would restore the police to the top of the wages tree. But within a week of Ede's announcement, Goodsall became seriously ill and was in hospital for the next two months. The Committee members were appalled. Such had been Goodsall's dominance over the Federation for so many years, that none felt able to take over the reins if the unthinkable happened, and someone else had to present the evidence to Oaksey.

Goodsall, still desperately sick, returned to the office in New Malden in July and worked long hours putting the finishing touches to the evidence. On the 3rd of August he appeared before the Committee, accompanied by the JCC chairman, Inspector Bert Mobbs of Worcestershire. He performed well, and along with Mobbs and other members of the JCC, made a good impression. The next day, he had an appointment with the Metropolitan Police chief medical officer, who examined him and declared that he was unfit for further service. The JCC immediately asked that his sick leave should be extended until he had completed the Oaksey evidence. With some hesitation on the part of the force, this was agreed. Goodsall carried on at the office, but while at work on the 30th August, he collapsed.

Mobbs and the acting secretary, Alec Hamilton of the Metropolitan, went to the Home Office on the 8th September, to ask that Goodsall should be kept in the service at least until the November Conference, so that he could continue to deal with Oaksey. By this time, they must have known that the secretary would not be returning to duty. The purpose of the request at this stage was to give Goodsall encouragement, but the Home Office officials were unable to give an immediate reply. The next day, the JCC members received the news they dreaded. Albert Goodsall was dead.

ELEVEN

Oaksey gives an 'Irishman's rise'

Goodsall was 58, and had been in the service for thirty eight years. He was long past the age of compulsory retirement for a constable, but had been granted annual extensions of service because of the pending Committee of Inquiry. Now the Joint Central Committee had cause to regret allowing Goodsall to persuade them that he was indispensable. In truth, he had run the Federation for almost twenty years as a one man band, content to let successive chairmen of the JCC take the plaudits for speeches at open meetings and the annual conference, but keeping a firm grip on the policies and deeds of the Committee. He was able to do this because his knowledge was unrivalled, and he was careful to impart to the Committee and the membership only those things he wished them to know. The Committee held him in awe and he did not tolerate fools. If a JCC member spoke out of turn, his days on the Committee were numbered, as he had demonstrated even with a Chairman of the calibre of Strangeways.

Goodsall's single mindedness and combative style did not endear him to chief officers and the police authorities, but Sir Arthur Dixon was at the Home Office during all the years that Goodsall was JCC secretary, and the two men respected and understood one another. That the Federation survived long enough to face Oaksey thirty years after its inception, was largely due to the different but complementary qualities of these two men from such widely different backgrounds - Goodsall the Cockney constable and Dixon, the Oxbridge educated civil service mandarin.

The choice of a new JCC secretary was made easier by the immediate action of Constable Tom Doody of Manchester.

Doody, a devoted Goodsall disciple, was the nominal assistant secretary. He was also the secretary of the Constables Central Committee and the Manchester branch board, and he had no wish to move to London, where he would be away from his family and his electoral base (JCC members were dependent upon being elected to their branch boards every year, and being appointed as Conference delegates so that they could stand for re-election to the Committee). Doody wrote to the chairman, Mobbs, to say that he did not wish to succeed Goodsall, adding that Alec Hamilton was the only man for the post, a view shared by the rest of the Committee.

Alec Hamilton was a Scot who had served in the Metropolitan Police for just over 20 years. He had been active in the Federation for most of that time and had worked with Goodsall. In many ways, Alec Hamilton was a younger edition of Goodsall, and soon established the same total command of the Committee as his mentor had enjoyed.

The Federation asked Oaksey to set a new scale for constables of £7, rising to £9.10s. after 10 years, and for sergeants £11, rising to £12.15s. For once, Goodsall had not been able to ensure that all three rank committees stayed together on the pay issue, and the inspectors insisted on submitting their own evidence to Oaksey. They wanted the current scale of £475 to £515 after four years, changed to a starting rate of £700 and 'increments that should reflect the status of the inspector'. They said that Desborough had enabled inspectors to 'live up to their status as Officers of the police service' but now they could not, although an inspector was 'expected to mix with persons of standing.'

Whether the Inspectors memorandum had any affect on Oaksey's findings on pay is debatable, but by submitting a claim that failed to take account of the aspirations of sergeants, the Inspectors had weakened the Federation's overall position.

The local authorities' evidence to Oaksey contained no comfort for the Federation. The County Councils' Association said there was no case for an immediate increase in pay. They proposed instead that the annual increments be increased from three shillings to four, provided there was no increase of the maximum scale for each rank. The CCA said that account should be taken of the monetary value of free housing and a pension. The Association wanted the pension contribution to be raised from 5 per cent of pay to 12 per cent. It also objected to the reimbursement of income tax on rent allowance, through the compensatory grant.

The Association of Municipal Corporations was rather more generous, probably because it was the urban forces that were facing the worst of the manpower problems. The AMC agreed that some increase in pay was justified, because the police had lost ground from their pre-war position.

In April 1949, the Oaksey Committee published its Report on pay. Its findings were a shattering blow to police expectations. The constables were to get £330 a year on starting, rising to £420 after 22 years' service. The sergeants scale would be £445, rising to £485 after four years, and the inspectors £530, rising to £575 after three years. This meant that the recruit got an increase of £1.2s a week, and a man with ten years' service got £1.3s. The general reaction was that the rises had not been worth the prolonged wait since 1946.

The Committee recommended that policewomen should receive 90 per cent of the men's scales. The Federation had recommended 80 per cent for the women, but admitted that the JCC was divided on the question of what was the appropriate level of pay for a woman.

Oaksey started from the premise that the Desborough Committee had been right in 1919 when saying that a policeman 'has responsibilities and obligations which are peculiar to his calling and distinguish him from other public servants.' This entitled him to special consideration in regard to pay and pension. Oaksey said;

> 'We entirely agree with these observations. The policeman's responsibilities are essentially unchanged; but they are now exercised in a wider field. Legislation since 1919 has added to his duties and increased their complexity ... ... The organisation and technique of modern criminals, their use of cars, and their increased tendency to carry firearms, have all added to the difficulties and dangers attached to preventing

crime and capturing criminals. Moreover the police have had to deal with a much wider cross section of the public since motor traffic regulations, the liquor licensing laws, rationing and controls have brought increased chances of wrong-doing to even the well-intentioned and the well-to-do.

'Since 1919 there has been a notable spread of educational facilities and they are to be extended in the near future. A police service which has to deal with a better educated public must itself be properly equipped for its task. Some concern has rightly been expressed to us lest the rise in general educational standards should not be adequately represented among the recruits to the police service. So far the spread of knowledge has not lightened the policeman's task: in fact it has added to his responsibilities. Some of the problems which face the police in the performance of their duties at the present time may be only temporary and may eventually disappear. But we are convinced that police responsibilities are more exacting now than they were when the Desborough Committee reported in 1919 and are not likely to become less; and we have had this at the forefront of our minds in all our enquiries into police emoluments.'

Policemen reading these early paragraphs in the very long report must have been gratified. But their hopes were soon dashed in subsequent passages. Oaksey turned to the 'value' of police emoluments;

'The representatives of the men were inclined to base their comparisons and claims upon their pay alone and, in our view, to underestimate the value of the various subsidiary emoluments. Representatives of the Home Office on the other hand, impressed upon us the relatively high value of the 'concealed' emoluments.'

The Home Office had told the Committee that when the estimated value of pension, free quarters or rent allowance, boot allowance and uniform, was added to the basic pay of a recruit of £5.5s. weekly the 'true' value of his pay package was £7.19s.5d. At the top of the inspectors scale, £9.17s. 6d. weekly, it was £18.1s.1d. It was this calculation, above every other aspect of the Oaksey report on the pay question, which angered the service. They felt they had been the victims of the 'three card trick'. To tell constables with take home pay well under £5 a week that they were actually receiving the equivalent of £8 a week was beyond their comprehension.

Oaksey summarised the case that had been put for higher pay as follows;

(a) that police remuneration, relative to that in industry, was now much below the level at which it was placed in 1919;

(b) that while police responsibilities were *sui generis* and could not be closely compared with those of other occupations, general comparisons with occupations which involve shorter hours and increased pay for night work and week-end duty as a regular feature indicated that the police were underpaid;

(c) that certain solid advantages over other occupations which the police had in the period between the wars - security of tenure, holidays with pay, free medical and dental treatment and a generous pension scheme - had disappeared now that there was full employment and the whole community was under the wing of national insurance, and;

(d) that the responsibilities of the police had increased because their duty now involved dealing with problems of greater complexity, with criminals who were better equipped, and with people drawn from a wider range than ever before.

In justification of its award, the Oaksey Committee sought to show that the fall in the comparative standing of the policeman's pay since 1919 was much less than had been claimed. They said that Desborough had based his report to some extent at least upon a comparison of wages in certain other occupations. The Ministry of Labour had traced the wage rates of seven of these, and found that whereas in 1919 Desborough had placed the police at 78 per cent above the average of those occupations, now they were 66 per cent higher. 'Taking into account the great increase in the absolute amount of pay and emoluments, the advantage over these other occupations has not greatly decreased.'

The Committee did agree that, when comparisons were made with other occupations which required shift and weekend working, the police had not fared well since 1939. They were still on a six day week of 48 hours, whereas other occupations which worked a 48 hour week in 1939 had now reduced as low as 40 hours in some cases, with no decrease in pay.

Oaksey said it was essential that members of police forces should be contented and free from financial worry, and feel that they were fairly treated, having regard to the hardships and responsibilities of their jobs. The difficulty was to value those responsibilities fairly in terms of pay and other emoluments. They had considered paying allowances for shift work and concluded that the best solution was a 'steady inclusive wage' They had also considered whether there should be uniformity of pay throughout the country, and had decided that this should continue. The rent allowance system, based on local costs, brought about a degree of differentiation. They had rejected the idea that rent allowances and free housing should be consolidated into pay.

The Committee was clearly concerned about the cost of police pensions. They reported that they had thought about diverting some of the money spent on pensions into pay, because a disproportionate part of the policeman's remuneration was reserved for his retirement. This came relatively early, when a policeman could find other work for up to 15 years. They said;

'We should have liked to recommend a change in the structure of police remuneration which would recognise that the police participate in the national insurance scheme and would give a greater increase

in pay than we now recommend, at the cost of some
reduction in the scale of retirement pensions. We have
regretfully come to the conclusion that this would be
impracticable ... ... and our recommendations on pay
are conditioned by the realisation that the police have
more generous retirement pension rights than most,
if not all, other members of the community.'

In other words, besides paying contributions towards their
pensions, police officers would henceforth be paying for them
in the shape of a pay package that was less than it would
have been, but for the pension!

If the men were disappointed by the size of the Oaksey
increases, they were even more upset by a proposal of the
Committee, which the Government accepted, that in future
an officer's pension would be based on the average pay he
had received in his final three years' service. This meant that
if a serving officer at the end of his 30 years' spell, wanted
to get the full benefit of the Oaksey award in his pension,
he would have to serve for three more years. The Committee
was concerned to retain men who had completed 25 years'
service and were eligible to retire on half pay. If averaging
were not applied, they would have been able to retire
immediately on the Oaksey scale, and draw £210 a year.
Averaging meant that immediate retirement would give them
a pension based on the previous scale, £182 a year. After
three years', when they had completed 28 years' service, their
pension would increase (taking account of the additional
service as well as the Oaksey rates) to £252 a year. Oaksey
accepted that men due to retire would be 'disappointed', but
said 'it would not be right for policemen to secure a
substantial improvement in their pensions as a result of our
proposals except in return for some period of service under
the conditions which we recommend.' To which the
Federation retorted that these men had not had a pay rise
for three years, while waiting for the outcome of the
Committee's inquiry. The proposal was even harsher on the
men who had completed thirty years' service. If they wanted
to retire on a 'two thirds' pension of £282 a year instead of
the pre-Oaksey rate of £243, the three years' additional

service would reduce their earnings capacity in the labour market. Indeed, many men decided that averaging was not worth the candle, when they could leave on the old pension and get a job paying more than Oaksey was offering the police.

The Joint Central Committee's verdict was scathing and bitter. Writing his first Annual Report in 1949, Alec Hamilton said;

> 'Only the most incurable optimist could claim that the new pay scales and other recommendations are likely to attract and retain recruits of the quality and in the numbers that are necessary ... ... the soundest reason for not rejecting the Oaksey Report was the simple and tragic fact that the lower ranks could not afford to turn down any proposals that would put extra money into their pay packets.'

Retention was the purpose of the averaging proposal. The Committee had been told by the Home Office that the manpower position was very serious, and that many officers who had qualified for a pension, or were coming up to it, were just waiting for the Committee's report, so that they could retire on an enhanced pension. Of the existing strength of about 50,000, there were 7,000 who could go on pension immediately. 'If any considerable proportion of them retired during the next few months,' said Oaksey, 'it would be a serious embarrassment to an already undermanned service.' The Committee added that 'averaging' over final years of service was common elsewhere in the public sector, and there was no reason why the police should be exempt. The proposal infuriated police opinion, and averaging was likened by many to 'the Irishman's rise'.

The legal position was that serving officers were protected by law from any change affecting their pensions entitlements. The Government got round this, at Oaksey's suggestion, by requiring that every officer signed an agreement that he would accept averaging. Those who did not agree, stayed on the pre-Oaksey scales of pay. The service described this as blackmail, but individual officers had little choice. Only those who were due to go at once could afford not to sign the Oaksey ultimatum. Just one man, Constable Leonard Jackson of Leeds, refused to sign and for the remaining 12 years of his service, he was paid at the pre-Oaksey rates, foregoing all subsequent pay increases. When he retired in 1960, the Home Office agreed to let the Leeds police authority give Jackson an *ex-gratia* payment and his pension was based on the current pay scales.

Another Oaksey proposal, seemingly insignificant at the time, was to be the cause of major dissension in the Federation. To compensate for the higher cost of living in the capital, constables and sergeants in London were given an allowance of £10 a year. London inspectors and chief inspectors were given a pensionable pay lead over the proinces of £25 to £40 a year, to take account of greater responsibilities. The proposals caused an immediate split on the JCC, with several provincial members voting against the recommendation, and the London members insisting that the allowance was insufficient.

Besides pay, the Oaksey Committee dealt with other parts of the pay and emoluments package. They recommended a number of improvements to the police pensions scheme, saying that when manpower permitted, officers should have the opportunity to retire on a reduced pension after 20 years' service. Widows pensions were improved, as were childrens allowances.

On overtime, the Committee was firmly of the view that the basis of compensation should be time off rather than payment, because 'the police working week is long and strenuous'. Time off should be granted at the rate of time and a third, and payment should be made only if time off could not be given. At the time inspectors in England and Wales received time off for overtime but could not be paid if time off was not granted. Scottish inspectors were paid in such circumstances. Oaksey thought payment for overtime could not be reconciled with the status of an inspector and recommended that all inspectors' compensation should be by way of time off. Compensation for lower ranks, for working on a rest day or public holiday should be time off at the rate of time and a half, with payment if time off could not be granted within three months.

Overtime among detectives was a particular problem. Oaksey considered whether detectives should have higher pay, rank for rank, than uniformed officers. He concluded that detective duty was different from, not more valuable than, other police work; 'If there is a difference in quality between the two groups it is because the CID can be more thoroughly 'pruned', with the result that only the more efficient members are retained.' Detectives on 'outside' duty were paid a detective allowance. A detective, said Oaksey, was more or less a 'free-lance' who decided for himself how he did his work and how long it took him. For this reason, it was not feasible to pay CID officers for overtime.

The Committee rejected the view of the Federation and the Scottish Home Department, that detectives should be compensated in the same way as uniform staff. It accepted that most detectives worked long hours, which could be due to under staffing but was equally caused by the nature of their duties. The Committee therefore recommended that outside detectives should be paid a detective duty allowance, to compensate for overtime, of £30 a year for constables, £36 a year for sergeants, and £42 a year for inspectors. As, on the rare occasions that qualified for payment, uniform constables received four shillings an hour, this meant that CID constables were being compensated for 150 hours overtime a year, or three hours a week.

The Committee dealt with rent allowance at length, and concluded that there was no need to change the system. Again, however, they rebuked the Federation for failing to recognise that rent allowance was 'a substantial emolument which places the policeman in a very favourable position compared with most other members of the community.' Annual leave had been increased at the end of 1945 by six days all round, the first increase since 1920. A constable now got 18 days a year, and a chief inspector 21 days. The Committee did not recommend any change, but hoped that more men could be granted annual leave in the summer months. It was only in 1945 that the police had been granted the right to take leave on the six public holidays each year.

Turning its attention to welfare matters, the Committee devoted a large section of the report to the deplorable state of police canteens in the Metropolitan Police. Most canteens could not supply substantial meals to the men, and the whole operation recorded a substantial 'loss', amounting to £100,000 a year during the war, a situation which had attracted much criticism from the Public Accounts Committee of the House of Commons. This, in turn, had inhibited those in charge of the canteens from improving the service. The state of some canteens was so bad that the Force Medical Officer had called in the Ministry of Health. The Ministry reported that the standards of cooking, service, cleanliness and hygiene, and the quality of the poorly paid and understaffed canteen workers, was very low. The Ministry said that many of the problems of the canteen service would be alleviated if the starting times of the shifts were changed, and it also recommended that in the interests of the health of the officers, they should remain on the same shift for a minimum of one month at a time. Oaksey made recommendations for improving the canteens, but in the economic climate which prevailed for some years afterwards, very little was done to improve matters.

Oaksey was critical of the poor provision made in many police stations for men to eat their refreshments during meal breaks He said thought should be given to the provision of mobile canteens, and the more extended use of police boxes. Finally on the subject of food, he pointed out that most officers took sandwiches to work when no canteen was available, and the food rations did not allow for this, especially cheese, which was the most satisfactory sandwich filler to give the men the energy they needed. As a result, the cheese ration of the police was increased.

When the Police Council met to consider the Oaksey Report in May 1949, the Federation and the chief constables told Chuter Ede, the Home Secretary, that the service was bitterly disappointed. Ede said there was no opportunity for debating the report. The Government was prepared to accept the recommended pay increases, in spite of the White Paper which had been issued, limiting rises to other workers, but the report would have to be taken as a whole. The Commissioner, Sir Harold Scott said that the averaging proposal would cause promotion to stagnate. Herbert Mobbs, the JCC chairman, raised the legal question, and the Home Office replied that no officer would be forced to accept averaging - the Regulations would simply provide for individuals to 'opt for averaging and the increased rates of pay'! The Federation and the police service was left to reflect on the irony of a situation which saw a Labour Government treating a group of employees in a fashion that none of the trade unions, which had become so powerful in post war Britain, would countenance for one minute.

This unhappy episode made the remainder of the business on Oaksey's agenda; considering the future of representative and negotiating machinery, all the more important. The Constables Central Committee took a very different view from the Sergeants and Inspectors on the future of the Police Federation. In discussions before the evidence to Oaksey on representative organisations and negotiating machinery was submitted, the constables could not persuade the rest of the JCC to their viewpoint, and decided to submit separate evidence.

In essence this called for the Federation to become a free association, which would be virtually a trade union. It would embrace all the ranks and membership would be voluntary. The association would be financed entirely by subscriptions. The Constables estimated that it would cost £15,000 a year to run a free association, but they aimed to raise £25,000 annually to allow for expansion. The free association would have complete freedom to decide on its own constitution, except that it would not be able to affiliate to another body, and the prohibition on striking would remain in force. The sergeants and inspectors opposed the free association concept, because they believed it would be dominated by the constables.

Alec Hamilton, the new JCC secretary, was the constables' spokesman when the Federation gave oral evidence to Oaksey on representative organisations. He said that the case for a free association was based on the Federation's experiences since 1919. He said that these had included; lack of consultation; failure to respond to representations; and problems over the Federation's role in discipline cases. Oaksey rejected the idea of a free association, principally because it would be constable controlled. The Committee said that the Federation should continue more or less in its current form, as the sole representative body. However, Oaksey agreed with the Federation that it was now sufficiently mature to have funds of its own, and recommended that it should be allowed to collect voluntary subscriptions from its members. The Committee said that police funds should continue to meet a substantial part of the Federation's running costs, including the expense of meetings of the central committees and conference. This was because;

> 'it is an advantage to the authorities for the men to have an efficient representative organisation and this, combined with our view that the police cannot be allowed freedom to set up machinery entirely of their own choice, leads us to conclude that the police fund should bear some of the cost.'

Oaksey added that public funds should continue to meet the cost of the JCC secretary, who should be paid as an inspector, and provide reasonable time for the chairmen and secretaries of branch boards to carry out their Federation duties.

There was still a lingering fear among chief constables and the Home Office that the Federation might misuse funds to bring about a repetition of the situation that existed in 1919. Oaksey sought to meet these reservations by attaching conditions to the setting up of a fund. It had to be entirely voluntary and no pressure must be placed on members to join it. Non-subscribers would continue to be members although of course they could not benefit from the funds. There must be no contributions from outside sources and the funds must not be used for political purposes, or to assist members on criminal or disciplinary charges. The contributions should be collected by way of pay roll deductions. The rules governing the funds would be subject to the approval of the Home Secretary.

Oaksey also considered the question of representation of policewomen. The Federation told Oaksey that they should have full membership. Oaksey thought it would not be enough simply to absorb the women into membership, and recommended that they should have their own electoral structure to ensure they were included on branch boards and central committees.

The most important and lasting recommendations of Oaksey concerned negotiating machinery. Here, the Committee sided with the Police Federation and against the local authorities in favouring a system akin to the Whitley Councils of the civil service. The Home Office had come round to believing that the advisory nature of the Police Council was no longer appropriate to wage bargaining. Between the wars, when virtually no one was getting a pay increase, the unsuitability of the Council as a bargaining forum was not exposed, but the two occasions since the war when it had dealt with police wages had shown up the problems. The Home Office relied on the Treasury for the line to take, the local authorities saw police pay solely in the context of local government relativities and the affect on the rates; the police were divided, with a large gap between the aspirations of the Federation and the views of the chief constables. In the end, the Council could do no more than allow the Secretary of State to 'take the views' of all the components of the Council.

Oaksey accepted that the Federation had a point in its criticisms of the Police Council, and said that the problem was, that it was called upon to perform some functions which could only be carried out by a properly constituted negotiating body, with recourse to arbitration. The Committee proposed that the police should have a special arbitration tribunal, saying it was not in the public interest that the service should be part of the national arrangements.

The new Police Council for Great Britain recommended by Oaksey, would have two main functions; the 'negotiable' subjects of pay, allowances, annual leave, hours of duty, and so on, and pensions, which were 'non-negotiable' because the cost of the scheme was met in the main by the Treasury.

Therefore, there could be no right to go to arbitration on a pensions matter.

Oaksey said that an agreement of the Council, including an arbitration decision, would be binding on all parties, subject to the overriding authority of Parliament. This meant that the Secretary of State had the right to reject or amend an agreement, but as changes in conditions were embodied in police regulations, the last word would lie with the House of Commons.

The new Police Council would consist on an 'official' side, comprising of the Home Office and the police authorities, and a 'staff' side, consisting of all the service associations from England and Wales, and Scotland. There would be three panels, to deal with matters affecting the federated ranks, the superintendents, and the chief officers. Oaksey also recommended that there should be three independent members, appointed by the Lord Chancellor, one of whom should preside at the meetings. The Committee intended that these 'three wise men' would form an arbitration tribunal in the event of disagreement.

The existing Police Councils for England and Wales, and for Scotland, would continue to deal with such matters as training and discipline, recruitment and promotion, said Oaksey, but they would be called 'advisory boards'. Because there would be a delay before the necessary legislation could be passed, the statutory councils would have to meet to ratify the decisions taken by the new negotiating body.

Oaksey called for an extended role for branch boards, with board secretaries being given reasonable duty time to carry out their tasks, and personal, rather than written, representation to chief constables.

When the Police Council met in 1950 to discuss these further aspects of Oaksey, the chairman of the JCC, Sergeant Haydn Griffiths of Mid Wales, was concerned that the Home Office would have too much control over the Federation's funds. Chuter Ede assured him that there would be full consultation, but the Home Secretary was doubtful if non-subscribers could co-exist with fund members in the same body. Griffiths was sure that there would be no problems, but Alec Hamilton, for the constables, shared Ede's doubts.

As if the disappointing outcome of the long awaited Oaksey Inquiry was not sufficient to depress police morale, a further blow came in the shape of some shabby treatment of police who had joined the police after wartime military service. The Government had agreed that men and women who had entered the civil service following demobilisation would be able to count their war service towards their pensions. In Parliament, the Minister responsible for the enabling Bill had stated that the concession would also apply to the police. There were immediate objections from the local authorities, who feared that all their employees would have to be included, and the Government rescinded the promise. This was an issue the Federation raised with Oaksey. True to form, he rejected the idea.

Police dissatisfaction over pay soon built up after Oaksey, and in November 1950 the Federation was back at the Police Council, demanding an increase. The proposal annoyed the Home Office, for whom Sir Frank Newsam, the Under Secretary, said that the Federation would have to await the inception of the new machinery. Alderman Hoy of Sunderland referred to the Government restrictions on pay increases, and said the Federation was doing a disservice to the country by demanding a pay rise at this time.

In June 1951, when the Police Council met again, the Federation was angered because there was still no sign of the new body. This time the Federation's pay claim could not be fobbed off, if only because every other union was pressing ahead with claims and making deals. The Home Office suggested that three independent persons should be appointed to hear the Federation's claim, and the authorities' response, at a special meeting of the Council. The chairman would be a distinguished lawyer, Sir Malcolm Trustram Eve KC. If the police and the employers could not agree, the idea was that the three wise men would make a decision.

The special meeting took place the following month. The Federation proposed an increase of thirty nine shillings a week for the constables. The inspectors once again decided to go it alone, asking for £800 a year and the abolition of the London inspectors' lead established by Oaksey. The Home

Office and the police authorities proposed a flat rate increase of £40 a year.

It was up to Sir Malcolm and his colleagues to make a decision. The constables were awarded £70 a year, bringing the maximum up from £420 to £490. Sergeants were awarded £100, taking them to £585, and the inspectors maximum went up £115 to £690. The award left the police side feeling far more satisfied with the outcome of the first ever arbitration case than the employers. Trustram Eve said that he and his colleagues would have upheld the official side's offer if the only issue was to update the Oaksey scales, but there was now a chronic shortage of police and a substantial award was needed to attract recruits and retain men in the service. By implication, the arbiters were saying that Oaksey had got the pay badly wrong.

The enthusiastic reception of the award by the service was just as important as the actual increase. The rank and file felt, for the first time, that their Federation had actually won something. The Federation members were not at all upset when they heard Alderman Hoy say, when the Council met to rubber stamp the award, that he still felt that £40 would have been sufficient. The employers were not to know it, but they were destined to suffer further rebuffs over the next few years.

TWELVE

Mr Callaghan lends a hand

The beginning of the Fifties found the Federation in a more optimistic mood than at any time since its inception three decades earlier. According to the JCC's Annual Report for 1951, the munificence of the three wise men headed by Sir Malcolm Trustram Eve had brought about a transformation in the police service. It said;

> 'Almost overnight the whole of the service changed from one that was thoroughly dissatisfied with its working conditions to one that was reasonably satisfied and content ... ... this has been reflected in the outlook of the members who realise that the pay increases and change of status imply greater responsibility on each individual ... ... Members are taking a keener pride in their work and now feel confident that the service has the backing and support of the community as a whole ... ...'

Whatever the award had done for police morale, there was evidence to show that it had brought about a marked improvement in the manpower situation. Trustram Eve's decision to give the police a higher increase to stimulate recruitment and retention appeared to have done the trick. In eighteen months following the award, police strength in England and Wales went up by nearly 5000 men and women to 66000. Not only were more people recruited, but the rise was big enough to persuade men who would otherwise have left on pension to remain and get the award in their pensions by 'averaging' over the three years. However, industry was booming and the rise in the cost of living, and consequently the wages index, had rapidly overtaken the boost in police pay from Trustram Eve. Significantly, police numbers began to drop again in the summer of 1953.

One consequence of Oaksey's proposals on representation was that the pay negotiations leading to the Trustram Eve award were the first at which a policewoman represented the interests of her colleagues. The machinery for electing a woman to each of the three central committees was not in place, so an emergency meeting of chairwomen and secretaries of the eight district conferences of policewomen, and their Scottish counterparts, together with six Metropolitan policewomen, met in London in July 1951 and chose Sergeant W Barker of the Metropolitan, who was instructed by the assembled women to press the case for equal pay. If she did so, no action was taken.

The JCC's 1951 report also revealed that the local authorities had tried, shortly before the crucial meeting of the Police Council, to renege on the agreement to appoint the 'three wise men'. Ede had overcome their objections by simply appointing Sir Malcolm as Chairman of the Police Council and instructing him to report his findings directly to the Home Secretary.

One exception to the general harmony of the service was the growing dissension caused by the award of a London Allowance to constables and sergeants, and a pensionable pay lead to London inspectors. The JCC reported that every decision on the subject had been taken by a majority vote, with the London members isolated from their provincial colleagues. The former wanted the allowance increased, the rest wanted it abolished. The provincial side was annoyed because the Metropolitan branch board had approached the Home Secretary, as their police authority, asking for the question of the allowance to be placed on the agenda of the Police Council. The Home Office asked the JCC if they wished to discuss the allowance in that forum, and the committee had voted not to do so. The Metropolitan board wrote to the JCC asking it to raise the issue of an increase in the allowance at the next Police Council meeting, and asking as well that they should not oppose it. Again by a majority, both requests were rejected.

It is fair to say that the provincial opposition to the London Allowance was not motivated by jealousy. All agreed that the amount of money involved was too small to make any difference, but the provincial members were opposed to any increase because they knew that this would lead to similar demands from undermanned provincial forces. If granted, such differentiation would, they felt, spell the end of the national rate of pay. It was in London and the large cities that the manpower shortage was acute, and the fear was that they would get the future pay increases, while the county officers would fall behind. During the 'Trustram Eve' pay talks at the Police Council, the London members raised the issue of the London Allowance, but Sir Malcolm ruled that it was outside his terms of reference.

Another group with a grumble was the owner occupiers. They were unhappy with rent allowances which averaged only about half the amounts paid to members in rented property, because their allowance was based on the 'Schedule A' tax formula. The JCC had little sympathy with them, suggesting that they were rather privileged to be able to live in their own homes. They said;

> '... ... whilst owner occupiers may contend that they receive less than their colleagues who are tenants, they cannot dispute that in normal cases all their outgoings are actually covered and, further, that it is quite irrelevant and unreasonable to introduce into these calculations such factors as the purchase price and mortgage repayments.'

The 1951 Annual Report told members that the Police Council was considering the possibility of allowing retiring officers to commute part of their pensions in return for a lump sum, based on their age at retirement. The JCC was not too keen on the idea, because a similar scheme operating in the Royal Navy showed that men retiring at 55 and commuting, found that the loss of pension exceeded the lump sum payment after 11 years, but this was before account was taken of the tax free status of the lump sum, and the interest that could be earned on it. The majority of the service was

The executive of the National Union of Police and Prison Officers in April 1919. The president, PC James Marston is fourth from left on front row, and on his left is Sgt. Jack Hayes, the secretary, who became known as the "Bobbies MP."

At each Federation conference in November, delegates marched past the Cenotaph in Whitehall, and the Home Secretary laid a wreath. *(Left to right):* Sgt Haydn Griffiths (chairman of the JCC), Major Gwyllam Lloyd George, MP (Home Secretary), PC Arthur Evans (JCC secretary).

The JCC deputation which met the Home Secretary in 1957 to discuss public concern about the police. *(Left to right):* Sgt Jim Murray (Metropolitan) Insp Arthur Bleach (East Sussex) Sgt Charles White (Bedfordshire, Chairman) and PC Arthur Evans (Kent, Secretary).

James Callaghan (MP) was the Federation's first Parliamentary adviser and worked closely with Arthur Evans *(right)*. Also pictured *(left)* is Insp. Sydney Vass (Metropolitan) chairman in 1958.

Reg Gale (JCC chairman), presents the Home Secretary, James Callaghan, with the Federation Bowl at the official opening of the Surbiton HQ in 1969. Les Male looks on.

Alec Hamilton took over as JCC secretary after Goodsall's sudden death in 1949, and put the Federation's case to the Oaksey Committee.

Reg Webb (Metropolitan) was an effective chairman who strengthened the Federation's links with Government.

JCC Secretary Dick Pamplin *(left)* escorts Home Secretary Roy Jenkins to the conference hall at Blackpool in 1976.

Reg Gale was the first chairman to become well known to the public.

Scarborough 1977: a tense Merlyn Rees ploughs through his speech, received by the audience in total silence.

Federation members show off the *Daily Mail* headline as they arrive at the Scarborough conference.

Rees is booed and jostled as he leaves the hall.

Joe Martucci. His blunt aggression
took the Home Office by surprise.

Unofficial action: "Police Wives' Support Groups"
backed the 1977 pay fight, with a march and rally in
Trafalgar Square, and a mass lobby of Parliament *(right)*.

Lord Justice Scarman's report on the 1981 riots put much of the blame on "insensitive" young constables.

(Right): Brixton 1981. Police lacked effective protective equipment.

Handsworth, Birmingham: the morning after the rioting.

Leslie Curtis has a joke with Home Secretary Leon Brittan at Scarborough in 1983, but Brittan's economy axe was soon to fall.

The miners' strike: over 6000 police went into the coalfields during the bitter conflict.

growing to like the idea of commutation, in spite of what the JCC members thought of it.

The Committee was much more enthusiastic about another policy which had been endorsed by the annual conference - compulsory retirement. In its evidence to Oaksey, the Federation had asked that all officers should be compulsorily retired on completion of 30 years' service, when they would be entitled to the maximum pension. The proposal might have sounded a little odd, coming from the Federation, because Goodsall had been in the service for 38 years when he died in office, but perhaps in this, too, he was a law to himself. Oaksey rejected the suggestion, but suggested that the lower compulsory retirement ages for senior officers and superintendents in the Metropolitan Police, which Trenchard had introduced, might be applied to other forces, in order to increase the promotion flow. The JCC thought this was worth a try, and the 1950 annual Conference called for the compulsory retirement age of all ranks up to chief superintendent to be 55. The idea was to stimulate promotion. It would have had a marked affect on promotions to inspector and above, where officers could serve until they were sixty years old. The Home Secretary told the JCC that he was not prepared to raise the matter with the Police Council, but there was nothing to prevent them doing so.

The delay in setting up the new negotiating machinery was beginning to cause concern. A Police Council committee had been charged with working out the details of the new body and issued its Report in 1952. This outlined the rules and scope of the Federation's voluntary funds. It went on to outline the constitution of the new Police Council for Great Britain. The principal variation from Oaksey was the omission of the three independent members. Although this had worked to the total satisfaction of the police side in 1951, the Federation persisted in its opposition, and the local authorities opposed the inclusion of independent members. Instead it was agreed that there would be an independent chairman of the Police Council for Great Britain, who would act as a conciliator when necessary. In addition, there would be a Police Arbitration Tribunal, whose members would be appointed by the Prime Minister.

1952 was a landmark year in the emancipation of police-women. A constable, sergeant and inspector were elected at the annual conference to represent women officers on the Joint Central Committee. Because the Government could not find time for legislation they could not vote at meetings except on funds matters and were styled 'advisers'.

The first meeting of the Police Council for Great Britain was held at the London offices of the local authorities' conditions of service bureau in Belgrave Square, London, on the 26th November 1953. For the time being, the new body had to act on a non-statutory basis, pending the passing of legislation (of which there was little prospect in the near future). The first joint secretaries of the new Council were Mr Edward Bishop, a vastly experienced negotiator who dealt with all local authority staffs, including teachers, and Alec Hamilton, the JCC secretary who had no experience of collective bargaining.

The first item of business was a pay claim for an increase of 15 per cent in the pay of the federated ranks, superintendents and chief officers. There had been prior discussions between the three service associations, something unique in itself and indicative of the change which Oaksey had brought about. The chief constables, or at least those who understood what was happening in the area of conditions of service, accepted that they were to be part of the new staff side, not adjuncts of the employers in such matters. There would be no more of the business of inspectors submitting their own claim and complicating the aims of other ranks, while the superintendents and chief officers understood that their pay depended on the outcome of the bargaining for lower ranks.

In response to the claim, the official side made an offer of 8 per cent. In further discussions, agreement was reached whereby constables received £45 a year, equivalent to 9 per cent, and sergeants and inspectors got £50 and £55 respectively. In addition, and on a majority vote, the staff side accepted an offer to double the London Allowance to £20.

As a first exercise in collective bargaining, both sides felt the outcome was satisfactory. Trustram Eve's award in 1951, with its 'manning-up' element, had given a more substantial lead over the Oaksey scales. The new agreement meant that

police pay had risen above Oaksey by 30 per cent, while in
the same period the cost of living index had risen by 26 per
cent and the wages index by nearly 27 per cent. The police
were ahead of the game, but only just. The manpower
situation was made sharply worse when 400 men left the
force in August 1954, significantly the third anniversary of
the Trustram Eve award. By August 1955, the overall
strength of the service had declined by more than a thousand
officers, to just over 65,000.

There was a row within the Federation because the negotiators had agreed to the increase in the London Allowance.
A member of the Joint Central Committee, Tom Doody,
recalled challenging the JCC chairman when the police
members of the Council were considering the official side's
offer. Haydn Griffiths said; 'Look at the bloody fog outside.
Isn't it worth twenty quid a year for working in a dump like
London?' By this time, the argument over London pay was
driving a deep wedge between the provincial and London
members of the JCC and the Federation as a whole. The
solidarity and friendship which had been a feature of the
Federation throughout its existence was being destroyed by
mutual recriminations, and the issue was colouring attitudes
to all other matters. Provincial members who were considered
to be 'soft' on the issue, or personally friendly towards the
London members, were taken on one side and reminded
where their loyalties should lie.

The new negotiating body had an early success when
agreement was reached, in April 1955, to reduce the standard
working week from 48 hours a week to 44. In effect, this
meant that members became entitled to one day off one week,
and two days off the next. The undermanned forces were
unable to allow the additional time off, and as a result members began to enjoy regular overtime payment. The shortened
working week, coupled with the payment of overtime in many
forces, acted as a spur to recruitment, however, and helped
to stem a damaging hemorrhage of experienced men.

1955 was also notable in Federation history as the year
when the voluntary funds came into existence, six years after
the Oaksey report. The initial subscription was threepence
a week, and the JCC was gratified that all but a handful of

police officers immediately agreed to pay contributions. Within a few months, more than 99 per cent of the potential membership had signed up to the funds.

One of the first actions of the JCC, when funds started to flow in, was to acquire the professional expertise that would allow the Federation to begin to match the formidable machine at Belgrave Square, where the local authority negoiators had a professional team of vast experience. Hamilton discussed the matter with a number of politicians and trades union leaders of his acquaintance, notably Douglas Houghton, a Labour MP who had spent a lifetime with the civil service unions, and had been secretary of the Inland Revenue Staff Federation. Houghton suggested that the Labour MP for South East Cardiff, James Callaghan, who had once worked under Houghton at the IRSF, might be interested. Callaghan, at 43, was regarded as one of the most promising younger members of the Parliamentary Labour Party, and had held a junior post in the Ministry of Transport in the last months of the Attlee Government. Hamilton saw that his greatest value to the Federation would lie in his close knowledge of how to conduct negotiations in the public sector. The Federation was not looking for a paid spokesman in the Commons, and it is noteworthy that Callaghan, although he exercised considerable influence on the Federation's behalf at Westminster, spoke in the House on police matters only rarely, in what became a nine year stint as the Federation's consultant and adviser.

Hamilton and the chairman, Haydn Griffiths, met Callaghan in June 1955 and immediately they concluded that he was the man they were looking for. Callaghan was invited to attend the next meeting of the JCC, in Oxford, where he impressed the Committee with his depth of trade union experience and his outgoing personality.

Callaghan and the JCC members got on well together, and one reason for this was that he came from the same background as they did. He was the son of a naval rating, a former scholarship boy at Portsmouth Grammar School who had left at 16 because his widowed mother needed to be supported. He had experienced the same lifestyles as policemen and his upbringing had taught him the same values. In common with many policemen, he had fought in the war, starting off in the Royal Navy as an ordinary seaman and ending up as a Sub-Lieutenant. Policemen felt at ease with James Callaghan, who was destined to be the first man in history to hold four of the great offices of State, including Prime Minister.

The appointment of a Labour MP raised eyebrows in the service, particularly among chief officers. It was even said, that in this first action taken after the inception of voluntary subscriptions, the Federation appeared to be confirming the fears of those who had forecast it would become a trade union and drift to the left. Most serving officers could not recall the time when Jack Hayes, the former secretary of the Police Union, had been a Labour MP and an unpaid spokesman for the policeman's interests. Even the chief constables of the Thirties, Conservatives to a man, had not objected when forces took collections on pay parades to meet Hayes's election expenses in Liverpool. Fears about party political links with the Federation were not held in Parliamentary and Government circles. The Home Secretary, Gwilym Lloyd George, extended a cordial welcome to Callaghan following his appointment. Hamilton had been careful to keep the Home Office informed and knew there was no objection in that quarter.

When the question of a fee arose at the JCC meeting which confirmed his appointment, Callaghan suggested that they should wait until they saw how much work was involved, and what was his worth to them. The opportunity to demonstrate both came at once, because the Federation was in the middle of pay negotiations which were going badly. The staff side had asked that the starting pay of a constable should be increased from £445 to £570, rising to £700 after 15 years. It was a staggering claim by the standard of previous awards, but reflected the wages spiral that was taking place outside the service. The employers responded with an offer to increase the starting pay by £5, with maximum pay going up to just £600 after 20 years. It was a disdainful, almost contemptuous offer, which virtually invited the police to try their luck with the newly appointed Police Arbitration Tribunal.

In September 1955, the Tribunal met for the first time to

hear submissions from both sides. James Callaghan lead the staff side team, and proved himself a superior advocate to the official side's negotiators. The Tribunal awarded a new scale to constables, giving them a rise of £30 on appointment, with another £50 a year after two years, and five further increments up to a new maximum of £640 after 15 years. It was a clever award. By rejigging the incremental scale, the arbiters gave the constables the maximum satisfaction at the least cost. Overall, the award meant that a constable's top pay was now 52 per cent above Oaksey, while the cost of living had risen by only 35 per cent and the wages index by 40 per cent. Mr Callaghan was well on the way to earning his fee, whatever that was to be.

The first arrangement between Callaghan and the JCC was in the nature of a gentleman's agreement. It stipulated that the Consultant was being appointed as a negotiator, to assist in the preparation of claims and to present them at the Police Council. It also discouraged him from speaking in the House on police matters, except with the prior knowledge of the Committee. The fee was not made public, but was related to the starting pay of the constable.

There were two features of the arbitration award that interested the service. The Tribunal had referred to the common scales of pay for each rank that existed in the service, adding;

> 'We have felt compelled, since neither side has raised the question of the propriety of altering this arrangement, to assume for the purposes of our award that it will continue. We are, however, of the opinion that a review of the arrangement should be undertaken now, so that any modifications of it which may be desirable can be embodied in the terms of any future settlement of police rates of pay.'

The message was unmistakable, and thus encouraged by the arbitration body, the Metropolitan branch board renewed its campaign for the claims of the London forces to be supported by the national committee. The provincial members, although disconcerted by this turn of events, were equally resolved not to give way on the bedrock adherence to the national rate of pay.

The Tribunal's second point was universally popular with the service. They drew attention to the absence of any legal power to back date their award. The two sides had registered disagreement in July, the Tribunal sat in September, but their award was not published until the middle of December. It noted that there was sympathy in the official side for the staff side's view that the award should be retrospective. The Tribunal was saying that before the next pay award, the law should be changed to permit retrospective rewards.

James Callaghan thought there was a good chance that retrospection could be achieved on this occasion. He organised support from Members of Parliament on both sides of the Commons, and branch boards were encouraged to see their local Members and enlist their backing. The campaign was highly successful. After at first saying that nothing could be done, Gwilym Lloyd George realised that if Callaghan, with cross party support, put a motion to the House in favour of making the award retrospective, such was the support in Parliament that the Government might be defeated. He therefore gave way with grace, and introduced an enabling measure to cover this and future awards. The award was back dated to the 8th September, the date of the Arbitration meeting. When 68000 policemen and women found the back pay in their envelopes, they knew that they had the Federation and James Callaghan to thank for it.

The new Police Council had made an auspicious beginning, and there was more to come. It was agreed that police officers should have the right to commute up to a sixth of their pension entitlement into a tax free lump sum. The scheme was restricted to those retiring after 30 years' service or on medical grounds. However, each officer wishing to commute had to satisfy the force medical officer that he had a 'normal' life expectancy. Some were refused commutation on this basis, and pressure grew to have the scheme amended to include all retirements on full and medical pension. This was conceded, but the lump sums were reduced to take account of the fact that 'bad risk' officers could commute. The amount of pension which could be commuted was increased from a sixth to a quarter, the maximum permitted by the Inland Revenue. More than one branch board representative had the sad experience of helping an officer on the point of death to sign a commutation application so that his widow would benefit.

In 1955, the Council agreed that the pensions of police widows should be increased to one third of their husband's pension entitlement. This was a major advance on the position of existing widows (to whom the new scheme did not apply), but was conditional on serving officers exercising an option to join the new scheme, the cost of which was to be met equally between the police authorities and the men. New entrants would have no such option, their pension contribution would go up from five per cent to six and a quarter per cent. Serving members who wanted to ensure that their widows qualified for the new pension also had to increase their contribution, and 'buy in' back service, either by paying enhanced contributions or taking an abated pension when they retired. Men with more than 20 years service could not serve long enough to 'buy in' their back service by the contribution route, and had to settle for a reduced pension.

The scheme represented a reasonable deal, but many older officers felt that the cost of joining was prohibitive. Others, with memories of the arguments over whether the police should contribute their share of such a scheme, which had led to the resignation of George Strangeways, felt that the JCC should not have changed policy. A substantial proportion of officers decided to stay out of the scheme, and in the years to come, many a newly bereaved police widow got a shock when she discovered that her late husband's action had left her with the pittance of a flat rate pension from the police.

Alec Hamilton, the JCC secretary, was meanwhile making good use of the Federation's new found financial freedom. For years he had operated from two rented rooms above a shop in Camden High Street, north London, with just one young assistant, Miss Jean Chaffé, who had succeeded the long serving Miss Edith Caines as the secretary and shorthand typist in 1953. Now, new staff were gradually employed and some modern office equipment was purchased.

One of the uses to which the voluntary funds could be put

was assisting members in the pursuit of civil claims for damages following accidents on duty. Hamilton chose an old established firm of solicitors, Ludlow Head and Walter, who were the successors of the former solicitors to the Metropolitan Police, as the Federation's lawyers. Unfortunately, the firm was both old established and old fashioned, and quite unable to cope with the volume of work which began to flow in from the Federation. Within a short time, the manner in which the claims were being dealt with gave rise to complaints from the members and, acting on the recommendation of James Callaghan, the Federation took its business in 1959 to Russell, Jones and Walker, a very small law firm which specialised in trade union work, notably for the iron and steel workers union, in whose headquarters in Grays Inn Road they rented two small offices. Neither the Federation officers who met John Walker, the senior partner, or the solicitors themselves, realised that this was the beginning of many years association, during which the firm would expand into one of the country's leading accident claims specialists. John Walker became a trusted adviser to a succession of Federation leaders. The success of the solicitors in securing damages for injured officers was another boost for the Federation. Previously, if an officer was injured on duty, he relied on the force solicitors to secure proper compensation, which was rarely achieved. It had been almost unheard of for a police officer to sue the police authorities.

In 1956, Hamilton decided to retire after 28 years service. He had advanced the Federation's status and effectiveness during his eight years in office, and his monument was the establishment of collective bargaining and arbitration, something he had advocated and fought for over many years. Thanks to the funds, the JCC was able to retain his experience and expertise by employing him as a civilian assistant at the office. Hamilton had hoped and expected that another Metropolitan officer, Sergeant Eric Hall, would be appointed secretary in his place. Normally, this would have been done. Hall was able and experienced, but another Metropolitan officer, Constable George Gale, felt that he had at least an equal claim to the post and he insisted in standing for election against Hall. The election took place when the anti-Metropolitan faction among the provincial members was strong, and this group supported a third candidate, Constable Arthur Evans, a relatively new JCC member from Kent. In the election, the split between the two Metropolitan contenders, and the support of at least one Metropolitan member, Inspector Sidney Vass, allowed the outsider, Evans, to top the poll.

Arthur Evans was 40 years old and had been in the service for nine years He had spent most of the war years in a German prison camp, and was the first 'post-war' man to hold national office in the Federation. He may have arrived in the Federation's key post by something of an accident, but he was by far the best candidate of the three and destined to play a seminal role in the momentous events that were to follow in a short time. Before that, he had to overcome the hostility of the 'old guard' on the JCC who looked upon him as a Johnnie-come-lately who had usurped a post that rightly belonged to a more experienced man. Evans turned out to be a tough character who was more than capable of holding his own, and soon came to be accepted in the same way that his predecessors, Goodsall and Hamilton had been. However, his refusal to concede an inch to the claims of the London branch boards made them regard him as an implacable opponent.

Apart from the potentially damaging split over London pay, the organisation which Evans took over from Hamilton was in better condition than ever before. The successes of the new Police Council, the impact made by James Callaghan, and the campaign to win retrospection on the pay award, had shown the membership, that the Federation, which had hardly touched the lives of ordinary officers in past years, had at last got itself some teeth. It had travelled beyond dependence on the goodwill of Home Secretaries and police authorities. It was now at the negotiating table and capable of influencing events. Ironically, much of the credit for this was due to Lord Oaksey and his colleagues. They had got the pay wrong, but they had given the service viable bargaining machinery, and now the Federation was playing in the major league.

THIRTEEN

A family quarrel

The London Allowance dominated the Federation's 1956 Conference. One incident symbolised the damage it was doing to the organisation. Every November, the Home Secretary made the short journey from the Home Office in Whitehall to the Methodist Central Hall in Westminster to address the Federation Conference. It was the high point of the Federation year, although in truth the occasion was normally marked by an exchange of platitudes, in which the Home Secretary assured the assembled police officers that he and the Government were on their side. Just before the 1956 Conference, Haydn Griffiths was promoted to inspector, and his position as chairman had been taken by Inspector Bert Beavitt of Kent. Griffiths was at Conference as an inspector delegate from his force, Mid-Wales. As Beavitt and Evans waited on the steps of Central Hall to greet Gwilym Lloyd George, the Home Secretary, they did not know that a 'coup' was taking place in the conference hall. It had been expected that Conference would automatically appoint Beavitt and Evans as Conference chairman and secretary respectively, but when nominations were called for, a Metropolitan delegate moved that Griffiths, a popular figure whose personal relationships with the Metropolitan members were excellent, should take the chair. Griffiths accepted nomination and in the vote that followed, defeated Beavitt. Evans defeated Eric Hall, whom he had beaten for the JCC secretary's post. When Beavitt and Evans escorted Lloyd George into the hall it was to find Griffiths occupying the chairman's seat on the platform.

Griffiths was a charismatic figure, a superb public speaker in the Welsh tradition, and vastly experienced. Beavitt was a pedestrian figure and a poor speaker. But he was the Chairman of the JCC. There was no doubt that the majority of the Conference delegates thought that Griffiths should resume his career as the national Chairman, a view that was not shared by the majority of the JCC members. After Conference, harsh words were spoken in the committee. Griffiths explained that he felt, having been chairman for all but a few weeks of the year, he was entitled to make the address to the Home Secretary, which suggested he considered the chairman's post was his by right. The critics attacked him for having kept silent about his intention to accept nomination as Conference chairman. They noted that he had carefully prepared his speech to Lloyd George, suggesting that there was a deep laid plan to take over the Conference chairmanship, and then oust Beavitt as JCC chairman. When it became clear that only the Metropolitan members supported his action, Griffiths resigned from the Committee. He went on to become a Superintendent and the deputy chief constable of his small force.

The Metropolitan branch board decided in 1956 that the non-pensionable London Allowance should be replaced by a London rate of pay. They argued that civil servants in London were paid at higher rates than provincial counterparts, and that pensionable London Weighting was common in the private sector. These views found no sympathy among the provincial members.

The London members maintained that a London rate of pay would be additional to a national rate and would take account of the cost of travel to and from work incurred by London officers. They asked the JCC to agree to the matter being discussed by the Police Council, and when this was rejected they informed Evans that a direct approach would be made to the Home Secretary, as the police authority for the Metropolitan, to ask him to put the issue on the Police Council's agenda. They would 'inform the Home Secretary that the Board is ready to accept the implications of the references to differentiation' in the comments made by the arbitration tribunal in 1955. The board agreed not to take such unilateral action while a national pay claim was pending, after James Callaghan had warned them they could easily sabotage the staff side's case.

The pay claim submitted by the staff side was for a general increase of seven and a half per cent. The official side responded by saying they saw no need for a further increase of pay so soon after the previous award. The claim was referred to arbitration, and the hearing took place early in 1957. On this occasion, the official side paid a compliment to James Callaghan's formidable negotiating skills by briefing a leading barrister, Gerald Gardiner QC, who was to become Lord Chancellor in the 1964 Labour Government. The way in which Callaghan had outshone the official side's vastly experienced chief negotiator had surprised the local authorities and the Home Office, and they were determined that he would not do so a second time.

The Tribunal was impressed by evidence of a marked increase in recruits since its last award. Gardiner spoke of training centres that were full to capacity, with recruits having to sleep in libraries; 'There has never been anything like this in the whole of the force.' He also pointed out that the police were benefiting from the overtime being paid as a result of the 44 hour basic week. Gardiner said that the Tribunal had been over generous in its previous award, which was partly due to the fact that the official side had agreed with the staff side that the pay should be increased. It would, he said, be 'disastrous' if the Tribunal were now to make an award that would enable the police forces to reach their authorised strengths within a year. The service would be unable to cope with such an influx of recruits.

The outcome was an increase of three per cent all round. Callaghan, writing in the Federation's new occasional journal, the *Newsletter* called the award disappointing. It fell short of the rise in the cost of living since the last increase, and Callaghan said that the arbiters had been over influenced by low settlements in other occupations during 1956, whereas the 1957 pattern of increases was higher. He predicted that the manpower situation would quickly get worse, and the Federation would be back at the pay table in the near future.

Callaghan was not satisfied with the new Police Council. It was still functioning on a non-statutory basis and there was no sign of a new Police Bill which would enable it to become 'legitimate'. Callaghan felt that the local authority influence had become too dominant in the attitude of the official side towards police conditions of service. It irked him that the official side had refused to concede that the police deserved any increase, while the civil service unions had just negotiated with the Government for a general increase which gave their members a much larger increase than the arbitration tribunal had awarded the police. Callaghan blamed the local authority members on the official side for this. In a speech to a Federation open meeting at Taunton in July 1957, he spelt out some of the problems;

'Since this negotiating machinery came into existence less than four years ago the Police Federation can feel, for the first time since it was established in 1919, that it has become an effective instrument to express the democratic decisions of the membership. However, although we have won this position by persistent representation, we still only enjoy the right on sufferance. The fact that I am standing on the platform this evening could be challenged because I have no right to remain here if authority became awkward and took umbrage. There are many things which the Joint Central Committee are doing which are not strictly within the terms of the Police Act 1919, but which are being done with the tacit assent of the Home Office. This is unsatisfactory. Suppose we offended against the canons of good taste? Suppose the administration bared its teeth? Everyone of these facilities can be swept away! Therefore, one of the first tasks we must undertake is to make the existing machinery statutory and legal. Until we have done that, we are not secure.

'Now we have got the machine, we have not got a complete understanding on our side of the best way to work it, nor is the official side free from blame. There is still too much on their part of the attitude of receiving us as our superiors, rather than of negotiating as one of two equal sides to a discussion.

We suffer because there are so many elements of the official side that we do not get from them a common approach to our national problems. In the light of my experience I am not over-impressed when at an open meeting the Mayor tells us how good we are, or the chairman of the standing joint committee makes rousing speeches about how splendid we all are, and that they are willing to do all they can to help. The trouble is, that their representatives, when they arrive in London at the negotiating table, do not seem to have heard these speeches ... ... My belief is that the municipal authorities are concerned far less with the intrinsic merits of the police case than with the possible repercussions a concession may have upon other employees for whom they are responsible. This makes our task doubly difficult. We have 126 employers. Some of the larger ones are most active in ensuring that the watch committee's views are known to the negotiators, but at the other extreme we have men with an extremely limited and narrow horizon who bring to the task of settling the conditions of 70,000 policemen an experience culled merely from their observation of the work of the village constable.

'I have formed the opinion after two years in this work that we need men of wide vision and experience on the employers' side, otherwise they are going to ruin local government in Britain if they have no understanding of the concept of a national service. This is extremely serious. It is a gloomy prospect for us that the worst body of employers in Britain is to be found in the town halls.'

Callaghan was becoming convinced that the official side, with its secretariat entrenched in the local authority negotiating set-up in Belgrave Square, would never be the vehicle for restoring the police to the place in the wages league they had secured from Desborough. He and Evans thought the Federation's best hope lay in securing another independent inquiry, but the time was not yet opportune.

One major success on the negotiating front in 1957 concerned rent allowance. Besides increasing the maximum limits that could be paid in forces, it gave a new deal to the owner occupiers. The link between their 'Schedule A' valuations and the allowance was ended. Instead, the District Valuers in each area would examine every owner occupier's home and assess its rental value on the open market. This sum would be paid to the owner occupier, subject to the maximum limit of the force. The agreement represented a major improvement for the owner occupiers, and lead to many more officers in city and borough forces buying their homes. This option was still not open to the county officers, who were obliged to occupy police premises.

The improvement in rent allowance was cited by the majority of the JCC as a good reason for refusing the Metropolitan's claim for a London rate. The maximum limit in London was the highest in the country. After the JCC had accepted the report of a sub-committee it had appointed to examine the issue, and which failed to reconcile the opposing views, the Metropolitan board made its direct approach to the Home Secretary, now R A Butler. He agreed to refer the matter to the Police Council, which annoyed the provincial JCC members. Evans led a deputation to the Home Office to protest, but was told that the Home Secretary had acted in his capacity as the police authority of the Metropolitan Police. Sir Charles Cunningham, the Permanent under-secretary, pointed out that Butler was not expressing a view as to the merits of the London claim. It was obvious to Evans, however, that the Home Office would prefer to pay a little more in London than have to pay the whole of the police service. The Metropolitan members accused Evans of deceit because he and Beavitt had gone to the Home Office without letting the Metropolitan know. He had also upset them by using the *Newsletter* to publish an article attacking their actions, while refusing to allow them to reply. In his article, Evans claimed that the Metropolitan Board's actions could only result in a damaging split which would enable the authorities to play off one party against another. He said that the 'misguided behaviour of a few of the members' of the Board would bring the Federation into disrepute and tarnish the memory of their 'far sighted and nationally minded' predecessors, including Goodsall. He appealed 'in their memory' to the Metropolitan members to 'cast off this partisanship and obsession with sectional interests'. The Federation, he said, was at the crossroads;

> '... ... either we go forward together united, or we divide into relatively weak, ineffective and competitive sectional bodies.'

The extravagant language used by Evans to describe the actions of the Metropolitan Board hardly constituted a genuine attempt at reconciliation and unity, and in fact the article served only to polarise views among Federation activists. As for the official side of the Police Council, they were more likely, if they thought about the matter at all, to wonder what all the fuss was about.

Bert Beavitt resigned from the JCC on his promotion early in 1958 and was succeeded by Inspector Sidney Vass, a Metropolitan member. Vass was a friend of Evans, and although he thought there should be a London lead (which already applied to the inspector ranks) he was strongly committed to preserving the unity of the Federation. This stance did not endear him to the Metropolitan constables and sergeants.

Pay was on the Police Council agenda again in 1958. The 1957 arbitration award of three per cent had turned out to be well below the going rate for pay rises in the country. In January the staff side submitted a claim for a general increase of ten per cent. The official side asked for three months to consider it, and when the Police Council met again in April, they asked for a further three months delay. This was rejected by the staff side and for the third time the arbitration tribunal was called in. It awarded four per cent, which they explained would have been five per cent but for the increase in rent allowances which had been negotiated in 1957. One of the arbiters, in a minority report, said that he would have awarded a higher starting rate to recruits aged 22 and over. This time, Callaghan was fairly pleased with the award. He pointed out to the membership that the Government was trying to restrict public sector pay increases to three per cent or less.

Away from the pay arena, the Federation was quietly pressing for changes in other areas. For many years it had called for standardised promotion examinations. The standard of local examinations varied considerably, and gave rise to suspicions of favouritism in promotions. Since the end of World War II, the Metropolitan Police had operated a system of competitive examinations for promotions to the ranks of sergeants and inspectors. The force was able to anticipate with reasonable accuracy the number of promotion vacancies that would occur in the following year. Candidates in the promotion examinations for constables and sergeants could, by achieving the percentage of marks required, ensure that they were promoted in that year. The only stipulation was, that candidates wishing to be promoted through the competitive system required a certificate from their divisional commanders saying that they were suitable to hold the higher rank. A tenth of all vacancies were reserved for officers who achieved the qualifying standard, but did not reach the competitive mark. The provincial forces preferred to treat the promotion examination as simply a qualifying standard, leaving actual promotions to the discretion of senior officers. In some borough and city forces, local councillors on watch committees insisted on selecting officers for promotion themselves. It was a pernicious system regarded with deep suspicion by most police officers, especially those who did not benefit from it There were allegations of nepotism, and of undue influence by masonic or religious interests. The supporters of a national examination system thought that these local abuses would be less likely to occur than when the examination was controlled by each separate force.

A Police Examinations Board was appointed, consisting of members of the Civil Service Commission and the Police Council, to conduct standardised examinations for all forces except the Metropolitan Police, whose members were highly satisfied with the competitive system. Such was the enthusiasm for the national system that in 1958, the first year in which the national examinations were held, it was estimated that 4,000 constables would sit. In the event, more than 9,000 did so. However, enthusiasm for the new system soon waned when the first results were published, and it was revealed that only about 10 per cent of candidates for promotion to sergeant had passed the examination One problem was that there were five separate papers in the police duty part of the examination, and candidates for promotion to sergeant were required to achieve the pass mark of 50 per cent in each paper. Besides police duties, candidates were examined in educational subjects, but some years later this was dropped, mainly because its usefulness was questioned.

One of the ways in which many police forces, especially the Metropolitan, had sought to overcome the post-war shortage of manpower was to set up police cadet schemes. The intention was that service as a cadet would bridge the gap between a youngster leaving school at sixteen and joining the police at 19. The schemes had been given impetus when the Government agreed that a police cadet could be exempted from national service, and then when the call-up was abandoned altogether. At first the service regarded the cadets simply as uniformed office boys rather than potential constables. The Metropolitan was among the first forces to recognise that they needed to be trained properly, and established a cadet corps at the Hendon training centre. The idea was to give the boys (girls were admitted at a later date) further education and an induction course in which they learned about the police service. Much of their time was spent on community service and adventure training, because it was felt that they should not be too closely associated with operational policing until nearer the time of their joining the force as constables. When the manpower problems became acute in later years, the cadets schemes continued to supply forces with a stream of recruits.

The Federation was unhappy about police cadets when they first appeared, but in 1959 the JCC changed its policy, mainly because so many former cadets were now serving as constables and the committee agreed that 'they tended to be drawn from the type of young men whom the Federation should welcome into the service', as Evans wrote in the *Newsletter*. However, the Federation remained opposed to cadets being allowed to accompany constables on the beat, pointing out that they lacked police powers and that a constable had enough to do without having to worry about the safety of an 'encumbrance'. The Federation informed the Home Office that it was opposed to cadets being employed on outside duties, because they were not protected by the pension regulations, and in particular, it objected to a cadet being used instead of a policeman as an observer in a police car.

Another cause for concern was evidence of the increasing use of special constables as a means of filling gaps in the regular ranks. The Federation suspected that in some rural forces, there was a deliberate policy of using specials rather than recruit additional constables. The Federation had never been comfortable with the concept of the Special Constabulary. They maintained that all the legislation covering the subject stipulated that specials could be used only in times of emergency. It accepted that they could be employed occasionally on police duties as a form of training for such an emergency, but not as a permanent addition to police strengths.

It was not only the Federation which had sought to put strict limits on the use of specials. The Police Post-war Committee had insisted that no special should perform duty until he had been trained and been out on the beat at least six times in the company of a regular constable. Moreover, said the Post-war Committee, it was not necessary to use a special for more than one tour of duty every two months, just to retain his interest. The commandants of the specials, when consulted by the committee, said that special constables should perform between ten and twelve duties a year.

By the Fifties, specials were performing regular duties in many forces. In seaside towns they were out every day dealing with parked cars. Elsewhere they turned out in force at football matches and country shows, creating a popular view among the regulars that the forces used specials rather than give them much needed overtime pay. The Federation claimed that specials were used on a regular basis on telephone switchboards, in control rooms and as observers in cars. It reported that one individual in a borough force has performed 500 hours duty in the previous year. The Federation complained to the Home Office that there was widespread abuse, 'bordering on illegality', of the Special Constabulary, and asked that their duties be limited to six tours of duty, each lasting two hours, every year. The Home Office adhered to the view that the deployment of the specials was a matter for the chief constable of each force to decide upon.

Towards the end of the Fifties, doubts began to surface about police integrity. By the standards of subsequent scandals, the cases which gave rise to public unease were trivial. In Brighton, an inspector and a sergeant in the CID were charged with conspiring to pervert the course of justice.When the case was heard at the Old Bailey, their chief constable was in the dock with them. It was alleged that they had enjoyed hospitality from a prominent local bookmaker and showed him favour over the granting of a licence. The trial created a sensation, not only because the police had enjoyed for many years the image of being totally free of corruption, but because Brighton still enjoyed a risqué reputation. It added spice to the lurid press reports that the meetings between the bookmaker and the defendants took place in a nightclub called *The bucket of blood*. The jury convicted the CID men, and they received a surprisingly heavy sentence of five years imprisonment. The chief constable was acquitted, although the judge when sentencing the detectives said they had not had the leadership they were entitled to expect from him. The Brighton watch committee took the judge's hint and promptly dismissed the chief without a hearing, and he sued them successfully for wrongful dismissal. Other chief constables were not so lucky. The chief of another small force, Worcester, was jailed for embezzling police club funds, and the deputy chief constable of Norwich was sacked for an extra-marital affair. In the remote Welsh county of Cardiganshire, a Home Office inquiry was held after allegations were made against the chief by local councillors. In the report of the QC who held the Inquiry, the chief was censured for not taking action when told that an inspector had spent a night in a hotel with a woman who was not his wife. Social attitudes in Britain might be changing slowly, but even in the Fifties, a policeman who was named as the 'guilty party' in a divorce involving adultery, risked being charged with the disciplinary offence of bringing discredit on the police force. The private lives of police officers were expected to conform to conventional morality and it was a frequent complaint among them that this extended at times to members of their families.

In another celebrated incident, two Scottish officers in Thurso were accused of having boxed the ears of a youth. The local MP made a strong speech in the House of Commons and persuaded the Government to set up an Inquiry under the Tribunals of Evidence (Inquiry) Act. This concluded that the officers had probably assaulted the youth, but they had been sorely provoked by him. The expense of the Inquiry fell upon the local ratepayers, most of whom supported the policemen, and at the next election the voters elected a new Member of Parliament. In Nottingham, the watch committee suspended the somewhat eccentric and elderly chief constable, Captain Athlestan Popkess, when he refused to show them a report on alleged corruption among staff of the city council (they were forced to reinstate him very quickly). There was another Parliamentary row when police were alleged to have assaulted a man named Podola who had been arrested following the murder of a London policeman. Articles in some newspapers alleged that Metropolitan officers were taking bribes from street bookmakers and prostitutes.

These incidents were discussed when the JCCs of the Scottish and the England and Wales Federations held their biennial meeting at Bournemouth in June 1959. Callaghan told the meeting that there was growing unease in Parliament about relations between the police and the public, and the accountability of the police. He thought that such concern could be the two Federations' opportunity to press for the appointment of an independent inquiry into policing, with pay and conditions forming part of the terms of reference. He felt, however, that this was still a long term objective. It was only ten years since the Oaksey Committee had examined pay, and history suggested that inquiries of this kind did not occur at lesser intervals than twenty years. The Federations would do well, Callaghan advised them, to secure an independent inquiry within five years. In the meantime, he suggested that the Federations should be seen to be concerned about the apparent deterioration in public support for the police, and be more open in their approach to public relations.

Hitherto, the Federation had taken no part in public relations, sharing the widespread police suspicion of the press. Evans was the first JCC secretary to see that the press could be useful allies of the Federation. In July, he wrote to R A Butler, the Home Secretary, saying that the Federation was disturbed by recent allegations, and asked him to receive a deputation. In the House of Commons, Callaghan asked Butler if he would receive the deputation, and Butler said he would be 'very glad' to do so. The Federation issued its first ever press release;

'The Joint Central Committee of the Police Federation has asked the Secretary of State to receive a deputation regarding comments that have been made in the Houses of Parliament, in the press and on the radio, which suggest that the traditional good relationship between the police and the public has deteriorated. If it is a fact that the public is losing confidence in the police, it is the urgent wish of the Police Federation that this confidence should be restored.

'There are a few black sheep in every service and the police service is no exception, but the Police Federation is greatly disturbed at the way in which these few black sheep have been used in recent months to weaken the good relationship which has always existed between the police and the public. It is our view that many of the allegations of rough treatment and corruption are false and malicious, but the Police Federation will not condone the action of any member of the police service who is guilty of these offences.

'The deputation will stress to the Secretary of State the difficulties experienced by the police in enforcing legislation approved by Parliament but with which the public is out of sympathy, eg., street betting, gaming, the liquor licensing laws and many of the regulations concerning road traffic.'

Butler received the deputation at the Home Office in September. It was led by the new chairman, Sergeant Charles White of Bedfordshire. Butler agreed with the Federation that betting and prostitution were particular problem areas, and promised that these were being looked into. After the meeting Evans was interviewed on television, the first occasion on which the Federation had been featured by the media, and there was favourable press comment.

As to traffic, the deputation pointed out that the rapid growth of vehicle ownership had placed a huge burden on police resources in towns. Many beat officers spent their entire daytime shifts dealing with illegally parked cars. It was mundane work, and it caused friction between the police and motorists. The deputation urged Butler not to deal with the problem through a Corps of Traffic Wardens, as was being suggested, because this would only deflect hostility away from the police and on to itself. The answer was to provide more off street parking.

In March 1959, another JCC deputation saw a junior Minister at the Home Office, and afterwards wrote to R A Butler;

> '... ... the members of the Police Federation are firmly opposed to any form of auxiliary body in the police service whose duties would be concerned with any aspect of traffic control. It is maintained that the establishment of such a body is not necessary and that all forms of traffic control should continue to be performed by police officers. Having regard to the functions of such a body as published in the national press, the members of the Federation are convinced that there would be no saving of public money and a greater burden would be placed on the police service.'

It was not long, however, before the first traffic wardens began to take the burden of street parking away from the police in central London, a development which was widely welcomed by the constables who had been forced to perform the task for so long. The Federation might be worried that the wardens could be the forerunners of a separate traffic police, but the beat officers welcomed the opportunity to get back to dealing with crime.

The General Election of 1959 resulted in the return of the Conservative Government with a greatly increased majority. This had not been expected in the pre-election period, and the JCC had anticipated that James Callaghan would leave the Federation to take office in a Labour Government under his close friend Hugh Gaitskell. In fact, Callaghan had only just held on in his Cardiff constituency and the outcome of the election had greatly depressed him. He had spent eight years on the Opposition front bench and now doubted if Labour would ever return to power, a thought that was shared by many political commentators of the time. At the November 1959 meeting of the JCC in London, there was a discussion about the consultant's future, and it emerged that Callaghan was thinking of leaving politics altogether. These were not the days when leading Labour politicians were snapped up by commerce and the City of London on leaving the House, and Callaghan was entirely dependant on his modest Parliamentary salary and the fee from the Federation. Now he told the Committee that if it could be arranged, he was ready to become the full time Secretary of the staff side, at an appropriate salary. It was agreed that this possibility should be explored with the other police associations and the Home Office, and that meanwhile Callaghan should be given a contract which made provision for superannuation. Nothing emerged from the tentative approaches to the Home Office over Callaghan's future, and he quickly found a new enthusiasm for politics which led him, eventually, to Downing Street.

That meeting of the JCC in November 1959 ranks as one of the most significant in Federation history. Callaghan was able to tell them, in confidence, that the long hoped for independent inquiry into police pay was not, after all, at least five years away. It was almost certainly imminent.

FOURTEEN

Waiting for Willink

On a December morning in 1958 a Metropolitan Police traffic officer, Constable 'Buster' Eastmond, stopped a car being driven in Putney and accused the driver, who was the well known comedy actor, Brian Rix, of exceeding the speed limit. The incident was witnessed by another driver, a senior civil servant named Garratt, who stopped his vehicle and spoke to Mr Rix. An altercation ensued between PC Eastmond and Mr Garratt which ended with Mr Garratt either falling or being pushed over a garden hedge. Mr Garratt was arrested and taken to the police station, where the station sergeant refused to accept Eastmond's charge of obstruction. Mr Garratt then sued PC Eastmond for assault and on the advice of the police solicitor, the matter was settled out of court with a payment to Mr Garratt of three hundred pounds.

The matter did not end there, because the manager of the Whitehall Theatre, where Mr Rix was appearing at the time, was a Labour MP, George Jeger. He and Mr Rix did not understand why the Metropolitan Police could pay compensation to Mr Garratt and yet take no disciplinary action against PC Eastmond. In making the offer to Mr Garratt, the force had denied liability. The incident received a lot of press coverage, no doubt because of the involvement of Brian Rix. A Parliamentary question to Mr Butler, the Home Secretary, failed to satisfy the Opposition. On the 18th November, 1959, they moved a censure motion in the House, regretting the Home Secretary's failure to explain the payment of £300.

The Eastmond affair was the opportunity for which Callaghan and Evans had been waiting. The Opposition was intent on making it an issue of confidence in the Government, and Callaghan was quite happy to see his party colleagues putting this kind of pressure on Butler. A few days before the Commons debate, he had met Butler privately and told him that if, as was being reported, the Government was minded to have an Inquiry into the police, the service would be disappointed if its terms of reference did not include pay and conditions. He told Butler that police morale was low and the main cause of dissatisfaction was low pay. Callaghan and Evans had already seen R E Griffiths, the secretary of the official side of the Police Council. In a tongue in cheek approach, Callaghan told Griffiths that the Federation wanted an independent examination of police pay, and invited the local authorities to support the idea. Griffiths, of course, was totally opposed to an outside inquiry, saying it would be seen as a slur on the local authorities.

In his reply to the censure debate, Butler announced that he had decided to appoint a Royal Commission on the Police. Its terms of reference would be;

'To review the constitutional position of the police throughout Great Britain, the arrangements for their control and administration and, in particular, to consider;

(1) the constitution and functions of local police authorities;

(2) the status and accountability of members of police forces, including chief officers of police;

(3) the relationship of the police with the public and the means of ensuring that complaints by the public against the police are effectively dealt with.'

There was no mention of pay in Butler's announcement to the House. Evans wrote at once to the Home Secretary to express the Federation's disappointment and to ask him to receive a deputation. Callaghan saw the Parliamentary under-secretary, David Renton, and pressed the same view. On the 30th November, Butler asked Callaghan to see him at the Home Office and told him that after consultation with the Cabinet he was going to add pay to the Commission's terms of reference. Callaghan urged him to request the Commission to deal with pay before the other terms of reference. On the 16th December, Prime Minister Harold Macmillan told the House that Sir Henry Willink, a former Minister of Health, would be the chairman of the Commission. Of the other members Alistair Hetherington was the editor of *The Guardian* and Sir Ian Jacob had just retired as Director General of the BBC. Lord Geddes was a former President of the TUC, and Dr A L Goodhart was Master of University College, Oxford. There were two MPs and two local government representatives. Macmillan announced that the Commission would be asked to consider;

> 'the broad principles which should govern the remuneration of the constable, having regard to the nature and extent of police duties and responsibilities and the need to attract and retain an adequate number of recruits with the proper qualifications'.

Asked by the Labour spokesman on Home Affairs, Patrick Gordon Walker, if the Commission would deal firstly with the pay question, Macmillan replied that this was a 'valuable suggestion' and it might well be that the Commission would divide its work in this way. Given such guidance, Sir Henry Willink decided to deal with the pay question before tackling the original remit.

Callaghan told the membership, through the *Newsletter* that the Federation could look back on the recent past with pride. It had made all the running on the pay issue, without any help from the other service associations and in the face of opposition from the official side. Now, he said, it was for the Federation to prepare its evidence;

> 'We have been presented with an opportunity that will probably not recur during the career of the latest joined probationer in the police service. What we do, and the results that flow from it, may determine the status and levels of pay of the police officer for the next twenty years.'

Immediately following the appointment of the Royal Commission, the Joint Central Committee set to work on preparing its evidence. A small team was assembled under the direction of Evans and Callaghan. Five JCC members visited forces throughout the country to collect information about the current state of the service. At the JCC office in Camden Town, a young Oxford graduate was brought in to undertake research. He was recruited by Callaghan and introduced by him as probably the outstanding Oxford student of his generation. His name was Peter Jay, who was engaged to marry Callaghan's daughter Margaret. Years later, Callaghan would appoint his son-in-law Ambassador to the United States.

The lengthy memorandum was submitted by both Federations. It was written by Callaghan and Evans, along with Jim Murray, a Metropolitan sergeant. It opened with a reminder to the Commission that forty years earlier, the Desborough Committee had put the constable at the pinnacle of the earnings league, so that between the wars he had enjoyed a substantial lead over other occupations. That had been eroded by the war, and the Oaksey Committee, meeting against the background of a a wage freeze and a financial crisis, had failed to restore the lost ground. As a result, the pay of the police had been devalued in recent years, and was the main cause of the endemic manpower problems of the service.

The current position was that the constable earned £9.15s.6d a week on appointment, rising to a maximum of £13.6s.5d a week. This compared with an average weekly wage in all manufacturing industries of £14.1s.3d. A constable with five years' service, who had probably passed his promotion examination, could reckon that the average worker in almost any occupation would be getting more pay than he was. The comparison between the police constable and average earnings was bad enough, but it was far worse when the pay of workers in the top earning industries was examined. It could not be right, said the Federation, that an engineering fitter should be getting more pay than a police inspector who was carrying a heavy responsibility supervising a substantial number of men.

The Federation went on to say;

> 'By definition, a policeman is above average in charac-
> ter, ability and intelligence and we would, therefore,
> expect to find him in the upper earnings bracket. To
> the extent that this is true, the table we have quoted
> in the Ministry of Labour Gazette does not reveal the
> degree to which the policeman's pay has declined
> relatively to other workers. Such a situation would
> have been inconceivable 25 years ago. The Federations
> submit that the Royal Commission need not look any
> further to discover the cause of the discontent among
> serving police officers, the constant drain of trained
> manpower from the service, and the difficulties in
> finding sufficient recruits of the right standard to fill
> police establishments.'

As to the cause of this 'dramatic decline', the Federations
said the rot had set in during the war when earnings rose
in industry but not in the police. This had continued since
the war. Oaksey had been wrong to over estimate the value
of police 'perks', such as free housing or rent allowances, and
pensions. Many other workers now enjoyed fringe benefits,
including holidays with pay and occupational pensions, and
in a period of near to full employment, job security was no
longer a recruiting sergeant for the police.

After giving the Commission a short outline of the roles
of constable, sergeants, and the inspector ranks, the Federations turned to women police, of whom there were 2,700
serving in Britain. England and Wales forces had removed
the marriage bar in 1946 but Scotland retained it. The
Federations acknowledged that women had become an
integral part of the service, but their still ambivalent attitude
towards them is revealed in this passage;

> 'It should be mentioned that women in many forces
> have had to fill the gaps caused by the shortage of male
> constables, and in consequence have gained experi-
> ence and opportunities which might not otherwise
> have been given to them.'

As to their pay, the Federations said that the 90 per cent principle should be retained.

The memorandum claimed that the educational standard of recruits in the hard pressed forces had been lowered. The official career handbook, discussing educational requirements, told prospective applicants;

> 'If you can spell, write legibly and do simple arithmetic, you have nothing to worry about.'

The Federations commented acidly;

> 'We are faced with a situation which allows a candidate to find entry into the police service by a process which can only be described as 'descending the ladder of educational attainment'.'

They pointed out that a low standard of entry threatened the retention of the principle that the future leaders of the service must come through the ranks. The Wynn Parry Committee, examining the prison service, had made it clear that there was not enough talent in the lower ranks of that service to fill the governor grades. The Federations recommended that all candidates should be required to pass a common entrance test. On crime, the Federations showed that serious offences had more than doubled since the pre-war era, to a point where in 1958 there were 626,000. They quoted with approval the views of Lord Chief Justice Parker in the House of Lords. He had said that in case after case, prisoners were asking for batches of other offences to be considered. This only confirmed, said the Lord Chief Justice, that crime paid. The Federations added;

> 'We regard it as a grave reflection on the state of law and order that in Britain today, any would be offender has a 50:50 chance of getting off scot free.'

Not surprisingly, the Federations argued that the presence of more beat officers would cut crime, citing a recent experiment in Harlem in New York City, where a fourfold increase in street patrols had cut crime by over 50 per cent in ten weeks, and detection rates had soared. In Britain, the Federations said, many town beats were left uncovered day after day. The service was using cars as a substitute for foot patrolling, not to supplement the man on the beat. They cited the jewellery quarter of Birmingham, where before the war there had been 25 foot beats, fully manned day and night. There were now only 9 beats, and cover could only be maintained by requiring officers to work 12 hour shifts.

The Federations went on to make their own pay proposals to the Commission. After examining the changes in fixing and changing pay rates in other public services, they said that all these changes had occurred in the recent past, in consequence of the general rise in living standards in the community. It was essential that the police should share in that rise. The pay of public servants had to be linked to changes in wage rates generally, otherwise they would be increasingly left behind. There was a social reason for this, police satisfaction with their lot, and an economic reason, because wages had to be fixed at a level sufficient to recruit enough people to allow the police service to do its job.

The Federations argued that the pay of the constable should be uplifted to a point between 40 and 45 per cent above the average earnings of manual workers;

> '... ... at this level of pay, the country could reckon to hold experienced men and could recruit an adequate number of new men of the necessary standard. There is little doubt that such a rate of pay, adequate in itself and reflecting the responsibilities of the constable, would also make him feel that his social status had been recognised.'

The memorandum argued that the tie between economic position and social status was important. It was also reciprocal, because if the status of the constable was raised, the men would feel that their job was highly valued and they would prize it. Morale and service to the public would benefit. The total benefits, it said, would be incalculable;

'In the Federations' view, it is well worth paying a higher price to secure an impartial, fearless, enforcement of law and order, the prevention of crime, and the protection of the private citizen. The fundamental question before the Royal Commission is this: what is the price the nation is prepared to pay for its police service? Because it will surely get the degree of protection it pays for.'

In summary, the Federations' case to the Royal Commission was;

(1) Police pay should be uplifted and maintained at between 40 and 45 per cent over the average weekly pay of manual workers;

(2) The Index of wage rates for male workers should be reviewed each year, and if it moved up by more than two and a half per cent there would be an automatic adjustment of police pay. Every third year, it would be open to the staff or official side of the Police Council to ask for a review of the pay structure;

(3) National rates of pay should be maintained, and the London allowance and the pensionable lead of London inspectors should be discontinued;

(4) The differentials of the ranks above constable should not be less than those fixed by Desborough;

(5) Central Government should bear a higher cost of the police in the ratio of 2 to 1.

Translated into cash terms, the Federations' proposals meant that the maximum of the constable's pay scale should go up to £1,000 a year. It was a breathtaking demand, and predictably it infuriated the local authorities. But Callaghan attached immense psychological importance to the idea of the £1,000 a year constable. Desborough had made him 'a £5 a week man', then the accepted epitome of success. Now people talked about 'the £1,000 a year man' in the same way, and the aim of the Federations was to reclaim the high ground.

It was not only the police authorities who baulked at the Federations' pay ambitions. The chief officers had been drawing up their own memorandum, and when Callaghan discovered that they would be proposing a much lower scale, he was furious. With Evans in tow, he went to Wolverhampton to confront the chief constable, Norman Goodchild, who had drawn up the chief constables' evidence. When Goodchild confirmed that the rumour was correct, Callaghan was not averse to a little bit of blackmail. 'If you go ahead,' he warned Goodchild, 'and the Commission gives us less than we have asked for, I shall stump the country blaming the chief constables.' The threat was sufficient. While all the arguments in the chief constables' memorandum argued for a lesser amount, they fell into line with the Federations when it came to suggesting figures.

The most virulent opposition to the Federations' claim came, as expected, from the Association of Municipal Corporations, which represented most of the city and borough police authorities and was dominated by Labour. Whereas the police associations presented virtually a united front before the Commission, the local authorities were fragmented and divided. Not only did the various local authority associations insist on presenting separate and conflicting evidence and proposals, many county councils submitted their own memoranda, some of which bordered upon the eccentric. The official side's professional negotiators, who understood the complexities of wage bargaining and could have warned the Commission of the possible repercussions in the public sector of being generous to the police, never got the chance to counter the police case. It was a good example of the vanity of elected councillors overshadowing the experience and expertise of their officials.

The Home Office, although it was represented on the Police Council as part of the official side, followed tradition and submitted a factual statement to the Commission, without expressing an opinion on the merits of the issues, although they annoyed the Federations by repeating their attempt to put monetary values on housing provision and pensions, as they had done to such telling effect with Oaksey. This time the Home Office said, that when account was taken of rent allowance, the value of boot allowance and the free uniform, plus a notional pension value of 26 per cent of pay, the recruit starting at £510 a year had a package worth £728, and the constable on the top of the scale, £695, was getting the equivalent of £991. According to the Home Office, the top rate PC was already a £1,000 a year man.

The Association of Municipal Corporations dismissed out of hand the Federation's view that the constable should be restored to the position he was in after Desborough. What mattered was whether the rate of pay was sufficient to ensure the supply of enough constables to preserve order. The bulk of the manpower deficiency was in the Metropolitan and Birmingham and Liverpool. Elsewhere, it was small. There was no cause for concern. Recruiting was generally satisfactory. The service lost a lot of men each month on pension, and perhaps the answer was to offer inducements to men qualified for pension to soldier on for a few more years. The Commission, said the AMC, should accept that the Police Council was quite capable of settling the appropriate rate of pay for the police, and that supply and demand should be the main criterias for so doing.

The Association's spokesman before the Royal Commission was Alderman Jake Hoy of Sunderland, who was the chairman of the official side of the Police Council. He proved to be a powerful witness in support of the Federations, because of his obdurate refusal, in the face of persistent and increasingly exasperated questioning from the members of the Commission, to acknowledge that there was anything in the nature of a problem about police manpower and pay. The Alderman, a former official of the Durham Mineworkers Union, became increasingly agitated in the face of this inquisition, and finally his patience snapped;

'The Desborough Committee decided to give the police a very big uplift and I remember being in the thick of the industrial wages negotiations at that time - what an upheaval there was in trade union circles at the very big uplift which the police got ... ... the general body of industrial workers from 1921 to 1945 could not get within anything like measurable distance of the wages and conditions being enjoyed by the police. I have read the Federation memorandum. It is all very ancient history. Where they make comparisons with heavy industries, such as ship building, coal mining and heavy engineering, you deal with men who are very highly skilled, who earn very big money and work a tremendous amount of overtime. I do not blame the Police Federation for submitting these figures but they leave a lot to be desired. I am the last man in the world to say that a policeman should not be well paid for the responsibilities he carries, but I question very much whether the police ought to enjoy a standard of living in excess of that of the general body of the public he is called upon to serve. If you allow the Police Federation to leapfrog too far ahead of industrial workers, you would be aggravating the general industrial position. If we were to give the large advancement which has been asked by the Federation, I think that a skilled man, semi-skilled man, skilled labourer and unskilled labourer would take a very poor view indeed.'

Members of the Joint Central Committee, sitting in the public seats at the hearing and listening to the Alderman venting all this resentment, realised that he was making their case for them. After this, the Commission knew that it would have to recommend a specific rate of pay, rather than give general guidance to a Police Council in which Mr Alderman Hoy held influence.

The evidence of the County Councils Association concentrated on the 'true' value of the constable's pay;

'The intrinsic value of the constable's overall remuneration has never been sufficiently obvious to public or police, and while emoluments continue to form so substantial a proportion of remuneration, it never will be. Whatever views may be held on the right level of remuneration there can be no doubt that its inadequate 'presentation' militates against recruitment, fosters public misunderstanding, and obscures its apparent value even to the constable himself.'

The Association reminded the Commission that policemen retired with between 25 and 30 years service with pensions and went straight into other employment, while other employees were still working towards their pensions. It pointed out that the Phillips Committee on the Problems of the Provision for Old Age (Cmnd. 9333) had even urged the Government to raise the minimum age for the National Insurance retirement pension to 68 years for men and 65 for women. The Association said that the Commission should take a leaf out of Oaksey and attach to any pay award a condition that the minimum pension age in the police should be 55 years. It said a young constable would prefer an increase in his wage to earlier retirement, even if this meant that his pension would be deferred by ten years. If this did not find favour with the Commission, they might consider additional, but non-pensionable, pay for constables who continued to serve after 30 years' service.

The county councils suggested that rent allowances should be consolidated into pay, as had been done in the fire service some years earlier. This would mean that the 'true' rates of police pay could be shown more clearly. They added that the recent Police Council agreement on reduced weekly hours had been the equivalent of a 9 per cent pay increase.

Other proposals put forward from the CCA were to apply special rates of pay in the undermanned forces, and to offer higher starting pay to mature entrants. The Association was also in favour of incentives to attract better educated recruits;

'It is clear that there is, at a quite early stage, a clearly defined division of constables between those destined for promotion and those who are not. It is essential that there should be a greater increase in the number of the first mentioned class since it would seem that, for the ordinary duties of a constable, nothing more than existing requirements need be insisted upon.'

The Association said that the service had to compete with industry and other services for youngsters with educational qualifications and was presently failing to do so It suggested a 'substantial plus' on the constable's starting pay should be offered to recruits with a GCE pass in 5 subjects at ordinary level.

The evidence submitted by the Treasury was the one which worried Callaghan the most, all the more so because it was the Treasury witnesses who gave evidence at the final public hearing in July. After all the pleadings of the service and the protestations of the local authorities that all was well, the Treasury evidence was devoid of rhetoric and sentiment. It was the Government line on wage restraint, and it advocated the strict application of market forces to police pay.

The test of any pay structure, said the Treasury, was whether it was sufficient, but not more than sufficient, to attract and retain the staff required to do the job. It noted with approval that the recent Grigg Report on the pay of the armed services had paid particular attention to 'conditions' rather than pay as such, and had consolidated such benefits as housing and food into the pay of servicemen. The Treasury view was that benefits in kind, such as the police rent allowance, should also be consolidated.

The Treasury rejected the idea of a 'quasi-moral' criteria for fixing pay. No service had a 'right' to a particular relativity with other employments, or because it was believed by its members, or even society as a whole, to be superior to other employments in status and repute, etc. It added;

> 'Even in the most essential of public services, if for any reason he had to pay employees £2,000 a year, the citizen might well be content to have fewer than if he got them at £1,000.'

As to the right level of police establishments, the Treasury said that before the war an increase simply meant less unemployment in the community, whereas now it would mean less employment and output from industry. Hence the need for greater mechanisation because it reduced the need for more manpower, and made the service use what there was, more economically.

The Treasury argued that there were plenty of people in the population who met the criteria of 'the right type of man' (everyone still thought in terms of the constable as a male, even though the memorandum was written by a woman, Mrs E M Abbott CBE, a Third Secretary to the Treasury and in her own words: 'Two from the top in the Treasury');

> 'Granted that police have to be distinctly above average in many qualities, there are a great many people who are. In this respect the police are much more 'normal' than (say) University and scientific staffs and some highly skilled crafts, where there are fairly absolute limitations on the numbers of men with particular qualities available, or who could be made available by income differentials.'

The Treasury's solution to any perceived problem of recruitment, was for the service to reduce entry standards;

> 'It may have been possible in the days of mass unemployment to set minimum standards for a secure job which were above those strictly necessary for its competent performance; it is not possible nowadays. By the same token, it is important in present conditions not to be perfectionist in the application of standards. No public service can be immunised from those pressures which, under conditions of high employment, produce a general shortage of staff of optimum quality; and everyone must be expected to accept some shortage of the best type of recruit and some dilution of quality.'

From the point of view of economy, there was everything to be said for making efforts to keep men on as long as possible, and for not using them on duties which others could do for less pay, such as traffic wardens and typists.

The Federations and the service associations had urged the Commission to make 'fair comparisons' of the constable's pay with other occupations. The Treasury dealt with this at length, and made suggestions which, in the event, the Commission was to follow to a great extent. It accepted that the principle had just been adopted following the report of the Royal Commission on the Civil Service - the Priestley Commission (Cmnd 9613), but said that this could be done in the civil service with its hundreds of different grades, because fair comparisons could be made with the same or similar jobs in the private sector. Therefore, market forces - recruitment and wastage - amounted to no more than a useful check on the assessment of civil service pay. But in general the Treasury regarded 'fair comparison' only as a subsidiary technique for guessing the amount that was needed to remedy a recruitment problem.

The Treasury agreed that there was no occupation which could be compared with the police *as a job*. Therefore, the problem had to be approached in a different way. The pay of the policeman should not be compared with that of men doing similar *jobs* but with similar *men*. There were plenty of men with similar qualities to those required by policemen, so the Commission should find out what *they* were earning. After all, they and their successors in the next generation, were the field from which the service would recruit. It did not follow, however, that because the men were roughly the same whatever their occupations, they would all be getting the same pay. Their work would vary in its nature, and require different pay to attract workers. The technique of comparing the pay of the constable with those of other similar men was that which was used by the Pilkington Commission on the pay of doctors and dentists.

The memorandum went on to warn the Royal Commission of the dangers of awarding the police a pay increase that was designed to remedy a labour shortage quickly. A large increase might well attract some men who would not otherwise come forward - men who would need special inducements. But it would be inordinately expensive to pay the whole force at the rate needed to get these very marginal recruits, and very awkward not to. Even if the expense was regarded at the start as a short term necessity, it would be difficult to keep it temporary. The only solution to this dilemma, said the Treasury, was one it admitted to be not an attractive idea - a once for all payment to be withdrawn when the back-log of recruits had been secured.

The Treasury queried whether the national rate of pay was appropriate for the police. It would require the Commission to increase police pay across the board. If a national rate of pay existed in a service, the dilemma was that it was set at a level high enough to attract and retain men in most areas but not in others. The Treasury saw 'no harm and some good' in regional differentiation where it was necessary for recruitment, but such incentives should be on a non-permanent basis, because conditions in areas could change in the future.

On this point, the Federation had been happy to solve its internal arguments over the London Allowance by allowing the branch boards of the two London forces to submit independent evidence to the Royal Commission, with both sides agreeing that they would abide by the outcome. It was a happy and fortuitous solution to a dispute which could well have seen the Federation splitting in two.

By the summer of 1960 the Commission had completed its public hearings and there followed an anxious summer and autumn for the service, while it awaited the verdict. This came in November, and the Interim Report of the Willink Commission (Cmnd 1222) created an immediate sensation.

FIFTEEN

The thousand a year man

'The maintenance of law and order ranks with national defence as a primary task of government. It is an essential condition of a nation's survival and happiness. We do not think that anyone acquainted with the facts can be satisfied with the state of law and order in Britain in 1960. The criminal statistics give a broad indication of social malaise, of failure by society to curb irresponsibility and deal effectively with growing lawlessness ... ... Society has, in our opinion, a duty not to leave untried any measure which may lead not only to the detection, but above all to the prevention of crime.'

With these words, the Royal Commission explained why it had decided to deal with the pay issue before its other terms of reference, and why it was going beyond its instructions by recommending a specific scale of pay for the constable, rather than delineating 'the broad principles' which should govern his pay. The Report went on;

'The evidence we have heard and the information we have obtained in the course of our visits convince us that police pay is not at present inadequate either to inspire in the police and the community a sense of fair treatment, or to attract to the service as a whole, and retain in it, enough recruits of the right standard. Hence the effect of our recommendation about pay is to improve the level of remuneration.'

The Commission described the manpower position as 'grave'. The shortage affected nearly half the population. The service was short of 13,000 men on existing establishments, and strength had declined during the year that the Commission had been sitting. The beat system, the foundation of policing, had largely broken down. There were towns where only two or three policemen were on the streets at any one time. When Commission members visited Coventry there were only three constables on beat duties, and they were probationers. The Commission found that the problem was not so much recruitment as premature wastage.

The starting point for assessing pay, the Commission said, should be police morale. Pay must be recognised by the police themselves and the public as fair and reasonable. It was not possible to have fair comparisons, as with the civil service, and the Treasury approach of supply and demand was rejected.

The answer, said the Commission, was to devise a formula for fixing pay, which would take account of what had happened to police pay since the war. The formula they were proposing was explained as follows;

'A.   We take as our starting point the minimum or standard time rates of wages paid to skilled workers in a wide range of industries. These are men employed in trades for which an apprenticeship is required and may be regarded, in the Treasury's phrase, as 'men with comparable qualities in other occupations'. The average of these rates at November 1960 was £543 a year.

'B.   To this factor we add a percentage designed to take account of the fact that it is undesirable that pay should be supplemented directly in the ways now customary in outside employment. This economic supplement is intended to fully compensate the constable for his liability to work in shifts, at nights and week-ends and on Bank Holidays without extra payment. It also takes account of the fact that the constable is not permitted to undertake remunerative employment outside the police service. We intend the supplement to provide adequate compensation, too, for the unforseeable and occasional overtime, in excess of a working week of 44 hours, which is inseparable from police life. Indeed it is implicit in our whole conception of the police service that casual overtime of this sort should cease to be expressly remunerated: and we do not doubt that most policemen would prefer that their sense of service to the community should be recognised in a fair and comprehensive rate of pay, rather than that they should have one eye on the criminal and the other on the clock ... ... in present conditions we assess this supplement at 45 per cent of factor A.

'C. The total of A and B takes no account of the constable's value to the community by reason of his duties and responsibilities, or of the drawbacks of police life (exposure to danger, subjection to discipline and a degree of social segregation): ... ... we therefore introduce a third factor into our formula which necessarily relies on a qualitative judgment based upon a broad evaluation of the constable's duties and responsibilities, his way of life, his knowledge and professional skill, and his physical and personal attributes. We put this further supplement at 25 per cent of factors A and B.

'D. The sum derived in this way represents, in our opinion, the appropriate overall remuneration of the constable at the end of the incremental scale. But the constable receives some part of his remuneration in the form of subsidiary emoluments. Of these we attach significance only to his rent allowance or the accommodation provided for him by the police authority: and the overall remuneration must accordingly be reduced, in order to arrive at the correct level of pay ... ... Bearing in mind the wide variety in the standards of accommodation, the insecurity and liability to transfer, and the fact that a police authority has a decisive voice as to where a constable shall live, an appropriate deduction would be £70-£80.

The formula produced the following result;

A. Average minimum or standard time rates 543
B. Plus 45 per cent of factor A 244
C. Plus 25 per cent of the sum of factors A and B 197
                                                                    Total   984
D. Deduct value of housing provision (£70-£80) say 74
Total (pay of the constable at the end of the   £910
         9 year incremental scale)

Two long service increments brought the constable to £970
after 17 years.

The Report was greeted with jubilation throughout the
service, and the Federation, James Callaghan in particular,
were the heroes of the moment. Writing in the *Newsletter*,
Callaghan exulted;

> 'This sort of thing happens only once in a lifetime and
> I am glad I was here to take part in it. I cannot
> remember anything quite like it. We have been making
> history. Even the great Desborough Report, which
> raised pay for a whole generation, was not as good
> as Sir Henry Willink's proposals for lifting the top pay
> of the constable by as much as 40 per cent.'

The local authorities, understandably, took an opposing
view. They were outraged that the Commission had exceeded
its terms of reference by recommending a specific scale,
rather than outlining broad principles and leaving the
calculation of what they meant to the Police Council.
However, the press and the public gave the Report a resounding chorus of approval and in the face of this, they had no
alternative but to accept the *fait accompli*, especially when
it was made known to them that Mr Butler wanted the
Report's recommendations accepted immediately. When the
Council met to consider the report, all that Alderman Hoy
and R E Griffiths could do, was to criticise the Report and
reject its recommendation that the scales of pay should be
reviewed at three yearly intervals, according to movements
in the wage rates of the occupations which formed Factor
A of the formula.

In January 1961 the Council settled the rates of pay of the ranks above constable. The top pay of a sergeant went up from £745 to £1,030, an inspector went from £865 to £1,210, and a chief inspector from £1,060 to £1,445. The increases were in line with the percentage awarded to the constable.

The implementation of the Royal Commission's pay recommendations transformed the police manpower situation. In the first two years, there was a net gain of 7,000 men. The drain of experienced officers was halted and chief officers reported that morale was higher than at any time since the war.

The Federation's other activities at this time had been overshadowed by the Royal Commission. As if to herald a new era of prosperity for the police, the 1960 annual Conference was held in Blackpool in May, thanks to a special Act of Parliament which had removed the stipulation that it must take place in November. Delegates enjoyed the contrast with years of meeting in the austere surroundings of the Methodist Central Hall.

The Federation was pleased that the Royal Commission decided that the London Allowance of £20 should stay as it was for the time being. The Commission agreed with the national Federation that there would be no case for a London rate if the pay was high enough to attract recruits everywhere. They added that the allowance was now well established, so that they would not recommend its abolition 'at the present time'.

Subsequent events were to illustrate how fortuitous it was that Callaghan and Butler had been able to persuade Sir Henry Willink to deal with pay first. A few weeks after the Interim Report appeared, the Government reacted to an increasingly grave economic situation by issuing a White Paper on Prices and Incomes, which imposed strict limitations on pay increases in the public sector. Had the police case gone before the Prices and Incomes Board set up under the Government proposals, the result would have been very different. When other public sector unions sought to use the police pay increases as a basis for their own claims, they ran into the new restrictions, although they were to catch up with the police in far less time than it had taken them after Desborough.

The solidarity among delegates on the floor of the 1960 Conference did not give the JCC an easy ride. To the consternation of the committee, the Conference overturned the decision to buy a freehold property in central London, as the new headquarters. It had been thought that the JCC sponsored motion, asking the Conference to note the purchase, for £20,000, of 30 Newman Street W1, would go through automatically. They considered that they had secured a bargain. The building was a Georgian terrace house large enough to accommodate the needs of the Federation for the forseeable future. The committee had informed the country that a further £10,000 would be spent on repairs and improvements. However, a London delegate had obtained a copy of the surveyors' report, which alarmed the delegates. The report revealed that nothing could be done about the facade of the building, as it was a house mentioned by Charles Dickens and subject to planning restrictions. An emergency motion, instructing the committee to sell the building forthwith, was carried. The committee was obliged to sell the building at a loss. The irony was that it was bought by a property speculator who promptly demolished it, paid a £50 fine for contravening the planning regulations, and built a modern office block in its stead. The Federation found offices to rent in Rathbone Place, the street next to Newman Street, and moved from Camden Town in the autumn of 1961. In the next eight years, they were to pay in rent something like eight times what the cost of buying and refurbishing the Newman Street house would have been. Evans was angered by the loss of Newman Street, and his resentment was heightened by the manner of the 'coup', which had been the work of a London delegate, who could only have obtained the surveyor's report from a committee source. He suspected that the whole thing had been a plot to embarrass him, although the Metropolitan members on the JCC were just as angry about the incident.

An improvement in service conditions secured in 1960 was the facility for members to take up to three days sick leave at a time, without having to produce a doctor's certificate.

It was stipulated that this 'privilege' would be withdrawn from any officer who was considered to be taking undue advantage of it.

Also in 1960, the Federation was alarmed by the contents of the Road Traffic and Road Improvements Bill. This introduced fixed penalties for parking offences, and empowered police officers and traffic wardens to issue fixed penalty notices. Evans wrote to the Home Office to complain that 'the practice of police officers issuing notices in respect of specified offences will not bring about any substantial saving in the use of police manpower and may further exacerbate relations with the public'. He pointed out that under the existing system of dealing with parking offences, a senior officer could take account of any mitigating circumstances before issuing a summons, and it was common to issue many more cautions for such offences than it was to prosecute.

What the Federation was really concerned about was the great expansion of the traffic warden service envisaged by the Bill. Evans put the Federation view in blunt terms;

> '... ... the Police Federation feels that the answer to the problem of vehicles parked in thoroughfares lies in the provision of adequate parking space and the manning-up of police forces to adequate establishments. The appointment of another uniformed body to assist law enforcement in a limited field is not only an unnecessary duplication of responsibility and function, but also uneconomic.'

The Government was unmoved by these objections, and it is doubtful if beat officers, having struggled for years with street parking problems, were as unhappy about losing such soul destroying duties to the new traffic wardens as the Federation suggested.

In the summer of 1960 the report of an 'informal' committee on higher training was issued by the Home Office. Its origin lay in concern about the quality of police leadership, arising from the 'scandals' of the late Fifties. The committee was chaired by Sir Charles Cunningham, the Permanent Under Secretary, and included the Federation and other service associations and the police authorities. The committee started from two basic principles, about which there was no dispute;

1. All entrants should have equal opportunity of promotion.
2. All senior positions must be filled internally.

The Committee examined two suggested methods of selecting and training men for accelerated promotion. One scheme, put forward by the Federation and the Superintendents Association, was to allow a percentage of vacancies on the junior course at the Police College to be open to constables and sergeants by way of a competitive examination and selection. On successful completion of the course, a constable would be promoted to sergeant.

The other scheme was suggested by Sir William Johnson, the Chief Inspector of Constabulary. He proposed a special course of a year's duration (compared with the six months of the junior course). It would be open only to constables, and students would be selected by a board from those who had obtained the highest marks in the national promotion examinations. The course content would be mainly professional and aimed at giving students a full knowledge of every department of policing. There would also be a three weeks' course at a university to study 'some topic outside the ordinary course of police duty' to provide 'a rapid stimulus to acquiring a broad and liberal outlook'. An officer who completed the course, which would contain periodic examinations, would receive automatic promotion to sergeant.

The Higher Training Committee found itself divided between the two proposals. That of the Federations and Superintendents was regarded as far too conservative, while the Federation objected to the Johnson scheme because it clearly identified an elite group of young constables destined for accelerated promotion, and in any case excluded sergeants. It was seen as a devaluation of the junior course at the College, because sergeants on the latter course had no promise of future advancement.

In August 1961 the Government published a White Paper:

Police training in England and Wales. This endorsed the Johnson proposal for a special course at the Police College for young constables. The scheme proposed that each year some fifty to sixty constables who secured high marks in the promotion examination would be selected for a special course designed to give them the kind of training thought to be essential for officers who would one day fill the highest ranks in the service. About half of these would qualify for the Course by virtue of having come top of the examination results list. They would need only the endorsement of their chief constables. The remainder would be selected by extended interview. The selectors would be looking for various qualities, including; an open and inquiring mind; a willingness to learn; the capability of expressing themselves clearly; to form detached judgments and;

> 'keep a balance between principle and expediency; be interested in people; have a sense of humour, and be able to assess character; show an ability to handle a subordinate properly; have drive and vitality; be conscientious and zealous; have the ability to make decisions; be able to disagree without showing antagonism, and; have a stable personality.'

Such paragons, it was hoped, would be found from among those who had done exceptionally well in the examinations. Constables would be given three chances to qualify for selection. Women were not eligible for the course, although this decision 'might be reviewed at a later date'.

An advisory committee from the Police College was charged with drawing up the syllabus for the new course. It had some interesting things to say about its objectives;

> 'They (the students) must anticipate that in years to come they will be expected to live as equals with leaders in the professions, in business, in local government. They must therefore acquire good manners and habits of dress and deportment, and be capable of intelligent discussion on a variety of subjects. In this way they may be able to mix with people in all works of life.'

If this conjures up a picture of fifty or so PC Doolittles arriving at the Police College as raw material to be groomed in the social graces and turned into swans by various Inspector Higginses, it reflects the philosophy which, unfortunately, prevailed at the college in its early days. Now it had moved from the Nissen huts of Ryton to a Jacobean mansion, Bramshill House, standing in acres of Hampshire parkland, the College was seen as a potential rival to the nearby Royal Military College at Sandhurst, so it is not surprising that the same report went on to talk about the values of a 'full mess life, social intercourse provided by team games, formal guest nights and the like'.

The first special course commenced at Bramshill in September 1962. Of the thirty or so constables on the pioneer course, fourteen had got there via their examination placings, and the rest through the selection system. There were three Metropolitan officers on the Course. At first, Sir Joseph Simpson, the Metropolitan Police Commissioner, had not been keen that his force should participate, as he wanted to run a similar scheme in London. He objected to the imposition of a limit on the number of officers that the Metropolitan could nominate, but the Federation and other service associations thought this was necessary. They argued that cadet and probationer training in the Metropolitan were far advanced on the provincial pattern, and if there was to be no quota, the force would have an unfair advantage.

The first special course was hardly an unqualified success. It was soon found that the ability to pass an examination was no guarantee that a student would respond to the academic and intellectual stimuli of a course designed to equip him for future command, and over the years the entry qualifications and selection procedures for the accelerated promotion course have been broadened. In general, the selectors were looking for young officers who appeared to have the potential to reach the rank of chief inspector at an early stage of their careers. Women were admitted to the course in the early years, and some twenty years later, the service had special course graduates in command of most police forces. By the same token, it should be recorded that public and official concern about the calibre of present and future police leaders is, if anything, greater in the Nineties than it was in the Sixties.

The Federation did not maintain its original opposition to the Johnson scheme for long. They knew that criticism in other quarters of the calibre of police leadership, and doubts about the ability of the service to find the next generation of police commanders from its own ranks, made outside intervention more than likely. The Royal Commission, in its final report, was to comment upon the remarkable fact that there was no recent case of a graduate joining the police service, and the report made it clear that they would have made proposals about higher training and promotion were it not for the moves already taking place inside the service. It did propose that the minimum service before a constable could be promoted to sergeant should be reduced from five years to three, a reform aimed at attracting career minded well educated young men. This met with some opposition from the Federation. It was the Federation, in its determination not to have any repetition of the direct entry ideas of Trenchard imposed on the service, which had insisted on the first course being chosen on the basis of the examinations. Faced with the evidence that this was an unsatisfactory method of selection, they agreed to the changes.

A topic which gave rise to a lot of concern from the Federation was the growth of private security services. As the amount of cash in circulation grew, so did the number of attacks, sometimes by armed gangs, on persons conveying money to the banks. The answer was a commercial cash in transit service, which soon became a new target for the gangs. The JCC was worried about the possibility of the uniformed guards becoming a private police force. An incident late in 1959 brought matters to a head. A bank guard, armed with a shotgun, fired five shots at members of a gang who had attempted to hold up an armoured vehicle. It transpired that an unarmed police constable was also in the vehicle. The JCC issued an angry statement;

'It is beyond our comprehension how anybody could authorise the employment of one of our members with a party of civilians, one of whom was carrying a fire-

arm and apparently with instructions to use it if the
vehicle was attacked. We will be surprised if steps
have not already been taken to prevent a recurrence
of this deplorable practice.'

The Committee decided to send a deputation to the Home
Secretary to protest about the issue of firearms to security
guards. They were also concerned about the uniforms worn
by such guards, which were so close to those of the police
as to confuse the public. A director of one of the firms,
Securicor, was a former Assistant Commissioner of the
Metropolitan Police, Sir Philip Margetson. When he was
asked about the uniforms worn by his staff, he replied; 'Of
course they look like policemen. That's the whole idea.'

The Government was embarrassed by the issue and it took
several months before the Home Secretary saw the Federation leaders, by which time the major security firms had
altered their staffs' uniforms to meet the Federation's
complaints. The Home Secretary was able to assure the
deputation that in future no guard would be allowed to carry
a firearm in public. Butler was pleased that the Federation
had raised the question of the large amount of bank notes
in circulation, and that it supported the payment of wages
by cheque or bank credit (most police forces had moved away
from cash payment).

With the pay issue out of the way, the Willink Commission
turned to the reasons for which it had been established. The
outstanding issues were; who should control the police and
how could the citizen be assured that the police would not
abuse their powers?

The Federation's evidence on the other terms of reference
contained some interesting ideas. On the constitution and
functions of local police authorities, the evidence represented
a compromise between opposing views on the committee.
Some members favoured the creation of large regional police
forces as a means of breaking away from the petty approach
of the local watch committees and county councillors. Those
representing the borough forces argued that this would
worsen conditions of service for their members. The Federation told the Commission;

'We value the identity of local forces and would like them to be preserved, but some forces are too small to carry out their functions properly. We propose, therefore, the establishment of regional units of administration, consisting of a regional Commissioner of Police with executive and operational functions, and a regional police authority with functions similar to a standing joint committee. The proposal would also apply to the London forces.'

The Federation said it had no wish to weaken the democratic control of police forces, but the present system sometimes hampered efficiency. Some forces were too small to function properly. It proposed that central government should pay more of the cost of the service. There should be an independent means of establishing what was the correct establishment of a force. Watch committees should lose their powers of promotion and discipline.

On accountability, the Federation said the existing disciplinary system was effective, but a complainant should always be informed of the result of his complaint, and if dissatisfied, should have the right to appeal to the proposed regional police authority. The police authorities should assure a constable who had acted reasonably, that in the event of civil proceedings being brought against him, he would be supported by the police authority.

The local authorities were generally satisfied with the existing arrangements for controlling the police, and expressed fears about the consequences of greater Government control, warning against a 'Minister of the Interior' as in other countries. The chief constables emphasised the autonomy and operational independence of chief officers, relying heavily on a 1931 court ruling *Fisher v Oldham Corporation* to stress that they were not the employees of local authorities. The AMC in particular dissented from this view, saying that while local watch committees could not seek to influence the prosecution process, chief officers were otherwise in just the same position as the director of education or the borough treasurer.

Much of the evidence to the Commission questioned

whether the police should continue to be a locally organised service. Eric St Johnson, the chief constable of Lancashire and a future Chief Inspector of Constabulary, broke ranks with fellow chief officers to call for a national police force, and found support for this in the evidence of the Law Society and, significantly, the Inns of Court Conservative Society. The latter argued that changes in society and the need to have the best leadership of the police, made the case for central control. One of the academic advisers to the Commission, C E S Wade, Cambridge Professor of Constitutional Law, declared that nothing but local prestige stood in the way of a national police force.

On complaints, the service was anxious to preserve the *status quo*. Against this, the lawyers and others argued for an independent system of investigating complaints. Ignoring their own position, they said it was intolerable that the police should be judge and jury in their own cause. Various proposals were made, including a police Ombudsman on continental lines, or independent tribunals.

Some bodies, such as the National Council for Civil Liberties, were very critical of the police, and alleged that the service was losing public confidence. The police insisted, that while their relations with motorists might have got worse, in general the public was very much on their side. The Commission asked the Central Office of Information to conduct a survey, from which the police emerged with much credit. The Commission described the findings as 'an overwhelming vote of confidence in the police, and a striking indication of the good sense and discrimination of the bulk of the population in their assessment of the tasks that policemen have to carry out'. 83 per cent of those interviewed said they had great respect for the police and only 1 per cent said they had little or no respect for them. Although a surprisingly high proportion believed that the police took bribes on occasion, those who thought this admitted that they had no personal knowledge of it. The police scored less well when it came to public satisfaction with the complaints procedure, and relations with young people and motorists.

The Royal Commission did not mention relations between the police and coloured immigrants, who had begun arriving in numbers ten years earlier. There had been race riots in Notting Hill in London in 1958, and race had featured in the previous General Election with the candidature of the former fascist leader, Oswald Mosley, in Kensington. Yet the COI survey did not report separately on the issue, and it was hardly mentioned in oral evidence to the Commission. The sole exception was the National Council for Civil Liberties, which had drawn attention to evidence of tension between the police and West Indian immigrants. The Council noted that the murder of a West Indian by a gang of white men in Notting Hill in 1959 had not been detected and said there would have been widespread condemnation of the police if the colours of the victim and his assailants had been reversed.

The police service at this time was exclusively white, and the Federation had expressed the view that the time was not ripe for the recruitment of 'coloured' officers, as had been suggested to the Royal Commission by the NCCL;

'... ... the recruitment of police from amongst coloured people is a recommendation to be studied carefully. The matter has been discussed in responsible police circles and we understand that there is a large minority view that recruitment should in fact start in the usual way. In particular, efforts should be made to employ coloured people in police stations in the areas where there is a substantial coloured population. Often there are difficulties of comprehension between the station officer and a coloured person who has routine problems at the station. Similarly, a coloured person would feel more confident that his problems would be sincerely understood if dealing with someone of his own background. Finally, one of the best methods of education is integration and the presence of coloured police working side by side with white colleagues would help to dispel the prejudice which undoubtedly exists at the moment.'

Arthur Evans had said in a television interview that a black officer might be well received in a 'liberal' area such as

Hampstead Garden Suburb, but it would be a different story if he had to deal with drunken Irishmen outside a Camden Town pub on a Saturday night, and this was the general police view.

The final report of the Royal Commission was published in May 1962. It rejected the idea of nationalisation, although a few members were in favour, and Dr A L Goodhart, Master of University College and Oxford Professor Emeritus of Jurisprudence, felt strongly enough to argue cogently for one force. He thought it ridiculous that a small borough force should be commanded by a man with the same powers as the head of the Metropolitan Police; 'You don't put an admiral in charge of a minesweeper' was one of his memorable phrases. The Commission acknowledged that there was a very powerful case for nationalisation. It said that a lot of the arguments about local control belonged to the past, and had no practical significance, although there was now a new kind of association with local government. The Commission warned that this must not stand in the way if it was found to hamper police efficiency. Nor did the Commission accept that a national force was a danger to democracy;

'British liberty does not depend, and never has depended, on the dispersal of police power. It has never depended upon any particular form of police organisation. It depends on the supremacy of Parliament and the rule of law ... ... To place the police under the control of a well-disposed government would be neither constitutionally objectionable nor politically dangerous; and if an ill-disposed government were to come into office it would without doubt seize control of the police however they might be organised.'

This said, the Commission still came down in favour of local police forces because, it said, the partnership between local and central government was of immense value. The present system of controlling the police had not failed. The improvements in efficiency that would flow from nationalisation could also be achieved by the present system without much alteration. The strongest impression from the somewhat convoluted arguments and conclusions of the Commission was that the members had no strong feelings either way, but had concluded that the political furore that would follow a proposal for a national force was not worth it, and that the government would probably not act upon it, anyway. Oddly, the Commission said that it thought the optimum size of a police force was about 500 men. It recommended the abolition of police forces of less than 200 officers, and forces below 350 should be retained only in special circumstances. It said there was a case for policing each conurbation with a single force.

The Commission recommended that chief constables should be subject to more effective supervision. Police authorities should have four main responsibilities; to provide and equip an adequate police force; to act as an advisory body to the chief constable; to hire and fire chief officers; and to foster good public relationships. The legal responsibility for the efficient policing of an area should be transferred from police authorities to the Secretaries of State, but they should have the power to call for reports from chief constables on policing matters. Watch committees should lose their powers of promotion and discipline over members of borough forces. Police authorities should be made liable for the wrongful acts of constables and chief constables should have a vicarious liability for them. The Home Secretary should continue to be the police authority for London, but the Receiver of the Metropolitan Police should consult the London local authorities each year before the Metropolitan Police estimates were presented to Parliament.

The Commission recommended that the Home Secretary should become statutorily responsible for police efficiency. He should ensure that police authorities carry out their duties satisfactorily; that each separate police force was efficient; that there was mutual co-operation between forces, and; that satisfactory ancillary services were provided. There should be a central unit for planning and research, under the direction of the Chief Inspector of Constabulary. The Home Secretary should have the power to call for a report from the chief officer on any policing matter.

On relations between the police and the public the Commission said chief constables should ensure that there was a sufficient number of men on the beat, to keep in touch with the public. The Commission agreed with the Police Federation, that officers should be housed in residential areas, and not in colonies of police house and flats. Chiefs should review the practice of transferring officers and take account of the advantage of a policeman's local knowledge. The Special Constabulary should be encouraged and strengthened.

The Commission made proposals for improving the complaints system. It said that the number of complaints was very small and it had no reason to doubt that they were properly examined by the police. The problem was how to devise arrangements which were acceptable and fair to the citizen and the policeman. The decision as to whether a police officer was to be charged with a criminal offence should be taken by the Director of Public Prosecutions rather than the police. Every complaint should be recorded and police authorities must satisfy themselves that complaints were handled correctly. The senior officer investigating a complaint should be from a different division than the officer concerned. The Home Secretary should be more ready to set up inquiries into allegations against police forces. The Commission, by a majority, was opposed to an independent system of investigating complaints, but three members issued a minority report in favour of a Commissioner of Rights who would examine complaints.

The Federation reaction to the Final Report was favourable. In a statement, the JCC said;

> 'Although a single police force for the country might be the ultimate pattern, we feel that to introduce it now would be too abrupt a change. The Royal Commission's proposals will help towards the greater unity of the service. We think it was right to reject suggestions for a separate traffic corps and a national CID. We support the proposals for a stronger inspectorate and for the Secretary of State to have a statutory responsibility for police efficiency.'

The Committee said that members of forces who found themselves subject to amalgamation must have better safeguards in respect of transfers, promotion and housing than had been the case in the last round of mergers in 1946. Mergers should not be based on a minimum strength, but on the needs of each district. Efficient forces should not be abolished just because they were small.

Most of the recommendations of the Royal Commission were included in the Police Act 1964, one of the last measures taken by the Conservative government, which was coming to the end of thirteen years' rule. The Act also included the statutory authority for the Police Council, and permitted the Police Federation, subject to the approval of the Home Secretary, to associate with other bodies. The Federation had reservations about the absence of a specific reference to arbitration in the Bill. This was remedied by the Government in the Committee Stage. The Federation also objected to the setting up of the Police Advisory Board to allow the Home Secretary to consult the police associations and local authorities on non-negotiable subjects, such as training, promotion and discipline. When this was discussed, Henry Brooke pointed out that it was better to discuss such matters in the Advisory Board, over which he presided, than in the Negotiating Board, where he was not present.

The one controversial question concerning the Bill concerned the issue which had led to the appointment of the Royal Commission. The National Council for Civil Liberties, some lawyers groups, and the Labour party, wanted some form of independent investigation of complaints against the police. The Federation saw this as a threat to the members. Evans produced a document explaining why the existing system should be retained,along with the changes in the Bill, and he may well have coined the phrase *The thin blue line*, the title he gave to the document. It received a favourable reaction from the media. The conservative *Daily Express* and the Labour *Daily Mirror* were in agreement that the Federation was right on this issue. The *Express* said;

'Frequently, criminals are supported by hysterical individuals who see the police as 'enemies of liberty'.'

The *Mirror* was even stronger in support of Evans;

'No wonder the police sometimes feel unjustly treated.
They are doing a tough and often thankless job for
a very modest wage packet, and they have to face
piffling complaints about their behaviour. They have
to endure a rigid discipline system which lays down
that once there is a black mark against an officer it
can be held against him for the rest of his career.'

The issue had been revived by the remarkable affair of
Sergeant Challenor, a CID officer at West End Central Police
Station. Challenor was an extraordinary personality. He had
been an SAS soldier during the war and fought behind
German lines with partisans in Yugoslavia. Twice he had been
captured and tortured by the SS and the Gestapo. After the
war, he had joined the Metropolitan Police and quickly
entered the CID, where he became a law to himself in his
dealings with crime. In the West End, he had conducted
virtually a one man campaign against petty criminals and
racketeers in Soho, and had a string of commendations after
securing many convictions. There were frequent allegations
that he planted evidence and perjured himself, and the NCCL
kept a thick dossier of these cases. Challenor enjoyed the
complete confidence of senior officers at West End Central,
who, for too long, saw nothing unusual in a sergeant who
worked well over 100 hours every week and was known to
walk home at night, from Saville Row to Bexleyheath, after
long tours of duty. He called very senior officers 'Me old
darling' and boasted that he would clean up Soho single
handed.

Challenor's downfall came when he found himself drafted
to deal with a demonstration outside Claridges Hotel, where
Queen Frederika of Greece, a woman with past links to Nazi
Germany, was staying on a private visit. Civil liberties groups
wanted her out of the country, and a large police presence
was needed to protect her. Challenor, with three young
uniformed officers who were on temporary attachment as
'aids' to the CID, arrested three men and charged them with
offensive behaviour and possession of offensive weapons.
Challenor claimed to have found a half brick in the pockets

of two of the men. They were unknown to each other, and had been arrested in different places, yet the defence could show that the two half bricks came from the same whole. The case was dismissed and the Home Secretary was questioned in Parliament.

The investigation threw new light on Challenor's other cases, and the Court of Appeal quashed the convictions and lengthy prison sentences which had been passed on several men. Mr A E James, QC, was appointed to consider the circumstances in which Challenor had been allowed to remain on duty when he must have been showing signs of abnormality. After the Claridges case, he became a voluntary patient in a mental home. He and the young PCs were charged with perjury and conspiracy in the 'brick' incident. Challenor was found to be unfit to plead, but sentences of four years and three years imprisonment were passed on the constables, all of whom were acting on his orders. The James inquiry found, to the general astonishment of the public, that no senior officer could be blamed for failing to notice what was common knowledge at West End Central: that Challenor was mad.

Subsequent efforts by Evans to get the savage sentences against the young PCs reduced came to nothing. The Home Office hinted that if no public fuss about the obvious injustice was made, the Home Secretary would be able to release them when the fuss about the case had died down. Evans agreed, but the Home Office did not keep its side of a bargain which, in any case, it would never acknowledge existed. Evans did use the case as a powerful example of what could happen when detectives were overworked on a regular basis, and this helped the Federation secure a better deal for detectives on overtime.

The case also resulted in the ending of the pernicious system of 'aides' to CID. The Metropolitan branch boards had been trying to get it stopped for years. It consisted of posting young men with CID ambitions to the department for short periods. Those with the most arrests for crime stood the best chance of being appointed detectives, and liberal use was made of the provisions of the nineteenth century Vagrancy Act, and the Metropolitan Police Act, which made it an absolute offence for someone to 'loiter with intent to commit a felony'. The only real consequence was to create a wholly artificial picture of detected crime in Central London, and in the process much injustice was done. That it should have continued for so long suggested that senior Metropolitan officers of the time either went around with their eyes closed, or were happy to see the arrest rates maintained in this manner.

Apart from the question of complaints, the Bill's passage through Parliament was unchallenged. These were still the days when a consensus existed between the parties and the police were considered, like the armed forces, to be above the party battle.

SIXTEEN

Evans drops a bombshell

In July 1963 the Federation experienced a 'little local
difficulty', to coin a popular phrase first used, a year earlier
by the Prime Minister of the time, Harold Macmillan. In
the Federation's case, it was apt. Charles White, the JCC
chairman, suddenly resigned from the Committee following
the publication of a leading article in the *Newsletter* which
attacked the reincarnation of a small borough police force
in Luton. The original force had been amalgamated with
Bedfordshire when the non-county borough forces were
abolished in 1946. When Luton gained county borough status
in 1963, it insisted on its right to run its own force. Evans
thought this was a ludicrous decision, because it was obvious
that all the small forces were soon to go, following the
recommendations of the Royal Commission.

White had a personal interest. He was a Bedfordshire
inspector, but had joined as a constable in the old Luton force
and still lived there. The decision to revert to a borough force
was popular with those of its former members who were still
serving. White had been shown the article prior to
publication, but its appearance caused a storm in the area
and he alleged that Evans had 'stabbed him in the back'.

Evans was not upset about the loss of White because he
considered that the chairman lacked the qualities needed to
lead the modern Federation. White's first priority was always
his operational duties in Luton and he rarely made the short
rail journey to London to discuss issues with the secretary.
White was a good committee chairman and had shouldered
his share of the work during the Royal Commission period,
but he had no taste for public speaking and lacked the
outgoing personality required of a post which was coming

more and more into the public eye. Evans was annoyed, however, that White should have resigned just a month after being restored to the JCC and the chairmanship, having left it on promotion from sergeant. In the brief interregnum, the chairman had been Inspector Derek Needham of Hertfordshire, whom Evans regarded as just the kind of young and able official the Federation needed. Needham had left the JCC after the Conference, to make room for White, and taken promotion. He was to become an Assistant Chief Constable in Suffolk some years later. White went on to become a superintendent in the new force, which lasted just two years before being absorbed once again into Bedfordshire.

The new chairman could not have been more unlike Charles White. Reg Webb was a Metropolitan constable who had been the JCC treasurer. A cheerful extrovert, he was a tall and striking figure who always wore a colourful bow tie. He was well known to many people outside the police as the regular Master of Ceremonies when amateur boxing was televised, and he had a profitable sideline as a toastmaster. There was some concern inside the Federation as to how Webb and Evans would work together, because they had clashed so often over the London Allowance, but these fears were groundless. They formed a partnership: Evans was the man of ideas, Webb knew how to put these across on the platform.

The year had begun well for the Federation. The official side had been persuaded to agree, after all, to a formula for ensuring that the pay standards set by Willink should be upheld. They had rejected the Willink proposals for uprating, but agreed to a system of biennial reviews. These would be conducted by examining the movement in the Index of Wage Rates and giving the police the percentage by which they had moved over the previous two years, subject to any discount necessary for movements in rent allowances and 'general economic factors which affect the police to the same extent as the rest of the community'. In December 1962 the Police Council used this formula to agree upon an increase of six per cent for all federated ranks.

James Callaghan warned the members that the agreement was not;

'a gold backed guarantee that the police shall preserve their standards at a time when the rest of the nation are suffering a fall in theirs. On the other hand the agreement does guarantee that we shall enjoy our fair share in the increases in national wealth to which this country can look forward under a properly managed economy.'

With the Willink standard thus apparently safeguarded, the Federation concentrated on other conditions of service matters. Callaghan thought the first target should be weekly hours. He wrote in the *Newsletter*;

'... ... we are listening to an argument from the official side that is entirely circular. It goes like this: the official side says 'we can't reduce the hours until we recruit the men' to which we say; 'but you won't recruit the men until you reduce the hours'. Some way has to be found to break out of this circle. We are faced with heavy retirement from the police service towards the end of 1963 because that is three years' after the Royal Commission pay settlement. We shall therefore need an even larger number of recruits than usual. But there is one aspect of our service that has never had sufficient attention paid to it by the official side. That is, a detailed assessment of why men leave the service once they have joined. If we could slow down the pace of resignation, we would have gone a long way towards the position where we could reduce hours.'

Although the service had made such a large net gain in the post-Willink era, the rate of premature wastage remained high. In 1962, 1,750 men in provincial forces resigned without a pension, a loss of some 5 per cent. They had been asked to give reasons for leaving, and only 47 had mentioned inadequate pay. Almost 800 said they were leaving for a more congenial job, 500 quoted domestic reasons and 150 disliked shift working. At this time, the London forces and Birmingham and Liverpool, making up a third of the service, were still operating a 48 hour week. 15 other forces were unable to fully implement the 44 hour week agreed seven years earlier. A Police Council committee, warned about the expected outflow from September 1963, when retiring officers would have 'averaged' on the Willink scale. The report called for a date to be set for the introduction of the reduced week in all forces. The Federation doubted whether some of the forces which were still paying men and women to work regular overtime needed to do so. It realised that progress towards a further reduction in hours towards the ultimate goal of 40 would not be made until all forces had begun to work the current standard week.

The Federation was disappointed by the performance of the Police Council since Willink. Its hope that the Royal Commission would lead to a new era had not been realised. Its one achievement had been the agreement for regular pay reviews, but on other fronts little progress had been made. The *Newsletter* said;

> 'The theme song of the official side goes like this; 'The police got as much as they are going to get when they won the Willink award. That major uplift has to take care of everything else'. If the police submit a claim for reduced hours, they must be told that Willink is based on a 44 hour week. If they point to shift and week-end work, tell them that Willink took care of that. If they make certain proposals regarding ill health and widows' pensions, they must be told of the great increase in pensions costs since Willink. If they point to the apparently insoluble problems in the CID, they must be told that Willink contains a substantial supplement to compensate for overtime and it is therefore just to expect detectives to work many overtime hours a week above the notional three hours covered by their allowance. At this rate, the feeding of the five thousand will pale into insignificance compared with the multitude of contingencies provided for by Willink!'

Uniformed constables and sergeants had for some time enjoyed the right to choose between time off and payment as compensation for overtime. This did not apply to detectives as it was argued by the chief officers and the official side that whereas overtime in the uniform branch was invariably authorised by a superior, in the CID it was performed at the discretion of the officer concerned. There was no dispute that many detectives were working excessive hours on a regular basis, and that there was little prospect of reducing such overtime because the priority was to have as many uniformed beat officers as possible.

After further prolonged haggling, agreement was reached on a scheme designed to improve compensation for the long hours of detectives. It was a complicated system which required the number of hours worked by detectives in a division to be averaged each quarter. If detectives of the same rank averaged more than eight hours overtime weekly, they would receive a supplementary payment equal to 'approximately 83 per cent' of their detective duty allowance. A further supplementary payment would be made if the average hours worked by the rank in any quarter exceeded twelve weekly. The complexities of the scheme and the anomalies it threw up made it unpopular with CID officers and paved the way for them to be compensated for overtime in the same way as uniformed colleagues. Once this happened, CID supervisors were obliged to ensure that overtime was strictly necessary, and so the problem of excessive hours was partly alleviated.

The Federation's goal of a forty hour, five day week came a step closer when in October 1963, the Police Council agreed to reduce weekly hours from 44 to 42, with effect from July 1964. The staff side had submitted a claim for a 40 hour week a year earlier. This was in line with the standard week in industry, but the official side sought to attach strings to any reduction for the police. The talks had broken up in disagreement and the staff side had referred the claim to arbitration when the official side made a new offer. They had wanted implementation to be postponed until September 1964, the date of the next pay review. The staff side saw this as an attempt to link hours with pay and reduce a pay increase. Secondly, the official side said that for the first year following the change, in forces where the manpower situation did not allow the granting on an extra 13 days off a year (the means by which the 42 hour week could be worked), officers would be expected to continue on a 44 hour week without compensation for the additional overtime, and if this continued into a second year, compensation would be at plain time. Both demands were dropped, allowing agreement to be reached.

One result of the cabinet reshuffle in 1962 was that R A Butler went to the Treasury after a five year stint at the Home Office. He was succeeded by Henry Brooke, a much less significant political figure who turned out to be remarkably accident prone. One of his first encounters with the Federation soon turned into an angry confrontation and got him into deep trouble in the House of Commons. The issue concerned the pension paid to the widow of an officer who had been murdered on duty, or killed accidentally while taking a special risk peculiar to policing, such as making an arrest. The Federation had made a claim for a lump sum payment of around £4000 to be paid in such cases. The official side was sympathetic, but anxious to restrict the payment to cases of the kind that could not give rise to similar claims in other public services, such as the ambulance and the fire brigade. They offered to pay a sum equal to twice the salary of a murdered officer, if the Federation would agree to drop the other part of the claim until they had decided what to do for other services. The Federation was not willing to do this, because it believed that once the pressure was off, the official side would do nothing about the 'accidental' death.

Negotiations went on for months, with neither side prepared to make concessions. Eventually, on the advice of Home Office officials, Brooke decided to break the deadlock by laying a new pension regulation before the House of Commons, giving effect to the official side's proposal to make a payment to the widow of the murdered officer, but not in the other 'special' cases.

James Callaghan reacted by seeking and obtaining cross party support to challenge the regulation. It was normal practice for statutory instruments to go through every day, in batches and 'on the nod'. Callaghan and his allies insisted that the regulation should be debated. On the 8th July 1963, when the debate took place, branch board members from all over Britain converged on Westminster to lobby their local MPs. Dozens of telegrams were sent to MPs from police constituents. Every Member had been sent a detailed explanation of the case. When Brooke rose at a late hour to move that the regulation be approved, the benches on both sides were unusually full. The Home Secretary made a dreadfully maladroit speech, against a background of noisy interruptions from the opposition and dismay among his own side. Callaghan, making a rare speech on a police subject, gave the House chapter and verse on the haggling which had occurred. When speaker after speaker on the Tory side rose to plead with the Home Secretary to think again, Brooke was forced to yield. He did so with bad grace, but the Federation had secured a notable victory and given further proof of its ability to influence events.

One Government decision which did please the Federation was the institution in 1964 of a scheme for compensating the victims of crime. It was intended to provide a lump sum to persons who suffered physical injuries directly attributable to a criminal offence or to the arrest or attempted arrest of an offender. The dependants of persons killed by criminal acts were covered by the scheme, which was administered by a board. A claim had to be deserving of at least £50 compensation. In assessing compensation the board was to apply the principles of common law damages in the civil courts, but lump sums would be reduced by the amount of any payments from public funds, e.g. police pension awards. Members of the Federation were able to call on the funds to provide legal assistance with their claims and from the outset, police officers have figured prominently among the claimants. Through appeals to the Board or in court cases concerning the scheme, its provisions were widened to cover cases in which police were killed or injured while taking 'special' risks when dealing with crime. One example was an officer who fell through a roof when chasing a burglar. In one case, when a young constable was killed in a road accident while answering an emergency call, the Federation took the case to the House of Lords to establish that police would be covered in such circumstances, even though they had not been attacked.

The lump sum payment to widows was the last major cause which Callaghan was to undertake on behalf of the Federation. The Labour Party under Harold Wilson gained a wafer thin victory at the October 1964 election, returning to power after 13 years. At the beginning of the 1959 Parliament, Callaghan had lost his appetite for politics. Now he was one of the most prominent men in the leadership. After Hugh Gaitskell's death in 1963, he had contested the party leadership against Wilson and George Brown, but his candidature was mainly to stop Brown's bid. Before the election, it was decided by the party leadership, that if Labour won, Callaghan would be the Chancellor of the Exchequer. The question of his contract with the Federation was left open. With such a small working majority, it was obvious that the new Parliament would not last for long and both Callaghan and the Federation wanted to keep their options open.

Soon after the new Parliament began, it became clear that Sidney Silverman, the Labour MP who had devoted most of his political life to fighting capital punishment, would be introducing a Private Member's Bill to abolish hanging. In keeping with Parliamentary tradition, MPs would be allowed a free vote on what was seen as a matter of conscience. Given the political change in the House, it was plain to the Federation that Silverman's Bill was likely to succeed. The Federation drew up a memorandum which was sent to every MP. It urged them to retain capital punishment for persons convicted of the murder of a policeman. Evans argued;

> 'We believe that a professional criminal is strongly deterred by the fear of capital punishment. It is also a fact that policemen feel that the special provisions serve as an effective protection. So do their wives and families. The only sure means to test the efficacy of this protection is to remove it, to see what happens. This is the awful responsibility that now faces the members of both Houses of Parliament.'

By a huge majority, the House passed Silverman's Bill. The great majority of the public still believed, with the police, that the death penalty was a just penalty for murder and a deterrent to others. But confidence had been shaken by the case of Timothy Evans, hanged in 1949 for the murder of his baby daughter while he lodged in a London slum dwelling owned by John Reginald Christie, who four years later was hanged for the murders of a number of women. Evans had been charged with, but not tried for, the murder of his wife. His defence all along was that it was Christie, not he, who had killed her and the baby. Evans was a pathetic figure, an illiterate petty thief and pathological liar. Christie in the witness box was presented to the jury as an ex-World War One soldier who had been gassed in the trenches, and he had served during the Second war as a special constable. His own criminal record was not mentioned, and no one in court knew that his squalid little house even then contained the bodies of some of his victims. It fell to Chuter Ede, the Home Secretary in 1949, to tell the House that he had been obliged for years to live with the knowledge that he had refused to reprieve a man he now believed to have been wrongly convicted.

Besides Timothy Evans, MPs were still disturbed by the refusal of a Tory Home Secretary to reprieve Ruth Ellis, the night club hostess who shot dead her playboy lover in Hamsptead in 1956 and had refused to let her counsel defend her at the trial. Her solicitor, George Rogers MP, made a powerful speech in support of abolition. The other outstanding case which helped to tip the scales against hanging was the execution of 19 years old Derek Bentley for his part in the murder of PC Miles at Croydon in 1952, while the youth who fired the shot, Christopher Craig, was too young to hang. Besides these cases, the compromise reached in 1957, whereby some murders were classed as 'capital' and attracted the death penalty, while others did not, had produced anomalies and was regarded as the worst of both worlds.

Prior to capital punishment, fewer than one policeman a year had been murdered in Britain in the 20th century. The execution of Bentley had been followed by a gap of almost seven years (still the longest period without a police fatality). In just twenty months following the Silverman Bill, six policemen were killed. It looked as if Arthur Evans's gloomy prophecy was being confirmed. The service was angry and felt that MPs had exercised their consciences at the expense of police officers' safety.

The end of 1964 brought the first biennial pay review under the Police Council agreement. It produced a general increase of around 9 per cent. A new feature was the introduction of incentives for older recruits, and an undertaking to examine the problems of the seriously undermanned areas. The manpower situation was once again causing concern, and there were signs that the boost provided by Willink was coming to an end. The recruitment and wastage figures for 1964 showed that 5,512 men had joined the service, but 4,888 had left. The 'averaging' factor had retained older men, but this was only a case of delayed natural wastage, as such men would have left earlier had it not been for the loss of pension involved. The net gain in strength of 600 men contrasted poorly with the 1962 gain of 2,500. Moreover, forces were being granted increases in authorised establishments, so that the service had a deficit of 9,000 men on an establishment of 86,000. The most significant wastage was of men who had completed their probation but resigned before pension, over 1,000. The Metropolitan Police lost 423 men in this way, although 100 went to other forces. The reasons given for resignations were still domestic and working conditions. Pay was not a source of dissatisfaction.

With James Callaghan wrestling with the country's economy (and enjoying far less success than he had achieved with policemen's domestic budgets) the conduct of all negotiations was now in the hands of Arthur Evans. He felt strongly, that after the shock of intervention from the Royal Commission, the official side had reverted to type and would do nothing to stop the service from losing the advantages over other occupations which it had just gained. Once again, the problem seemed to be that the official side was wholly local authority minded, and either jealous of the Federation's achievements, or afraid to improve conditions further because of probable repercussions from council staffs. Evans spent several weeks up to January 1965 closeted alone in his office, to the bewilderment of committee members who found that his door was no longer open for a chat. At the next meeting of the JCC, the reasons for this seclusion became clear.

Evans presented the committee with a proposal for a dramatic and unscheduled pay claim. The existing agreement still had 21 months to run, but Evans cited the manpower situation, and prevailing discontent with the attitude of the official side to conditions of service issues, as justification for what could only be seen as a breach of the agreement. Evans held the opposite view, arguing that the Staff Side was merely responding to the undertaking in the 1964 pay agreement respecting undermanned areas.

Evans told the JCC that in his view, the tide of public opinion was running in favour of the police. There was anxiety about a sudden increase in armed crime in London. The manpower problem was one of retention, not recruitment, and ways had to be found of keeping experienced men in the job. His proposals for remedying the problem were;

1. An immediate 'pensionable supplement' of £3 a week for all constables, other ranks to be determined.

2. In forces where undermanning was endemic, such as the Metropolitan, the supplement should £5 a week.

3. The early introduction of a 5 day week.

4. The fixing of realistic establishments.

5. The study and application of man-management techniques.

6. An improved status for the constable.

7. An adequate supply of modern equipment and more assistance from civilians, including traffic wardens.

Evans told the Committee that the pensionable supplements would cost £40 million a year. This had to be set against the estimated cost of crime, traffic congestion and accidents of around £1,000 million a year. He thought the proposals would add 3 pennies a week to the shilling which was the weekly cost of the service to each member of the population.

The secretary outlined a strategy for launching the initiative, and stressed the need for total secrecy. He proposed that the document, once agreed, would be submitted to the Home Secretary, Sir Frank Soskice, and the official side secretary, R E Griffiths, simultaneously, and released to the media immediately afterwards.

In effect, Evans was overturning years of commitment to the national rate of pay, no matter how the proposals were dressed up as 'supplements' rather than pay increases. All the years of argument with London over a pensionable lead for constables and sergeants were ignored. The objection had always been, that if London got more pay, other undermanned forces would follow. Now here was the JCC proposing just such an arrangement. No doubt to his own surprise, Evans did not face any challenge from the provincial members of the committee. Here he showed that he had learned a lot from Callaghan. The committee members had been taken by surprise. Evans wanted to ensure that when they voted on the package, they would stick by the decision later on, rather than claim they had been rushed into a decision. So he insisted that discussion of the plan should be deferred until the next day. When the JCC, having slept on it, came back to the subject the following morning, Evans received unanimous backing and the committee's congratulations were recorded in the minutes. The next step was going to be harder - convincing the Home Office and the official side that more pay was the answer to the manpower situation.

SEVENTEEN

The official side cries: 'Foul!'

It was true that the 1964 pay agreement had contained the undertaking that both sides would examine the problem of the undermanned forces, and in its annual report for that year Evans had stated that the Committee;

'... ... is fully aware of the sensitivity of the implications and will consult all branch board before any decision is taken.'

Before the annual report had reached the boards, the JCC had already decided what it was going to do and there had been no consultation. The explanation offered, was that while the Federation was asking boards for details of their manpower situation, the staff side became aware that 'special confidential discussions' were taking place (presumably involving the official side, the Commissioner and the Home Office) with a view to making manpower proposals about manpower in the London forces. It had therefore been necessary for the Federation to take an initiative on its own.

On the 1st February, Evans and Reg Webb saw R E Griffiths at his office in Belgrave Square, and told him of the claim. He was shocked and angry, all the more so when they told him that the claim would be unveiled at a press conference. The next stop was the Home Office, where an official saw them on behalf of Soskice. On learning what was afoot, the official realised that after all the Federation leaders had better see the Home Secretary.

The document was entitled *The problem*. It opened with a bald statement;

'Owing to serious manpower deficiencies and lack of adequate equipment, the police forces of Great Britain are in grave danger of losing the fight against crime.'

The document claimed that the true shortage of police in Britain was 18,000. It went on to outline the Federation's proposals for remedying the situation. R E Griffiths saw that the Federation had gained a head start in the important jousting for public approval, and promptly issued a press statement of his own. He complained that the Federation had taken an 'unprecedented' step in giving publicity to its memorandum, which 'amounted to a pay claim of very substantial proportions and a breach of an agreement reached as recently as the previous October'. He added that the official side had been considering the problems of undermanning and had been just about to put its own proposals to the Federation.

The response from the Home Office came via a letter signed by Sir Charles Cunningham, the Permanent Under Secretary. It was a dusty answer, pointing out that establishments had been increased by more than 6,000 in the past two years, and that new equipment and technology was being introduced, including personal radios for the men on the beat;

'The Secretary of State welcomes the interest of the Federation in all these matters affecting police efficiency and in the economical use of manpower. He shares their *(sic)* concern about the increase of crime, and their desire to improve recruitment ... ... but he considers that the Federation's memorandum as doing less than justice to the striking developments in the police service which have taken place in recent years.'

As Griffiths had feared, the Federation's new found public relations skills gave them a big start over the official side. *The Daily Mirror*, then the biggest circulation daily paper, backed the Federation:

'WANTED: Twenty thousand new recruits for the police.

ALSO WANTED; The right conditions and incentives to keep them in the force once they have joined.

The police have their own ideas how this can be achieved. Yesterday, their union - the 90,000 strong Police Federation - came out with some suggestions.
'They add up to: Better pay. Better hours. Better man-management. Better status. AND BETTER EQUIPMENT FOR THE JOB.
'Everybody wants better pay. The police are entitled to argue their case. They are certainly one hundred per cent right to demand adequate modern equipment for the fight against crime.'

The *Daily Telegraph* was also supportive:

'A grave and continuing shortage of policemen: this is the excuse on which the Police Federation must rely for giving immediate publicity to their grievances in the matter of pay and conditions of service, notwithstanding the agreement they freely negotiated with the Police Council as recently as Oct. 27. This gave them a seven per cent increase and does not expire until the autumn of 1966.
'The men who hang back from joining the force are not parties to that agreement, however, and those who have left in dudgeon will not be tempted back by citing it. Numerical insufficiency arises from three causes-slow recruitment, early resignation, and wasteful use of police time. The second is the most disturbing. Mr Evans, spokesman of the Federation, says that with an annual intake of 6,000 as many as 2,000 leave voluntarily in a year. This may well be connected with the third factor: much discouragement is caused, for example, by fruitless hours spent in the waiting room of magistrates' courts.'

The *Telegraph* was less impressed with Evans's suggestion that constables should not wear numerals, by which they tended to be addressed by superiors. Evans claimed that no one else was distinguished by numbers, except convicts. But the *Telegraph* poked gentle fun at the idea:

'What about bus conductors, postmen, soldiers, and 007 James Bond? 'There was a king in days of old' who had just this idea, but he found that when he had made everybody somebody, no one was anybody. The 20,000 men Mr Evans estimates are required are likely to think far more of his demand for a rise of £5 a week all round. With more rational use of manpower, less than 20,000 might suffice; yet some increase in pay is surely due anyway.'

The Times also came down on the Federation's side:

'The Home Secretary's letter to the Police Federation this week is an implicit rebuke. It is not a justifiable rebuke, for the Federation's new memorandum on pay and conditions in the police forces of Great Britain gets near to the heart of the matter. There have been, as the Home Secretary says, striking developments in the police service in recent years. These must be presumed to include the long overdue salary increases of four years ago, the Police Act of 1964 and its many changes in the law relating to the police, the establishment of regional crime squads, studies of the use of manpower, a new kind of inspectorate; better trends in recruitment, and the promising experiment of the Bramshill Police College.

All these are sound steps, but they are hardly enough to account for the note of effusive self-congratulation to be discerned in the Home Secretary's initial response to the Police Federation. To agree, as he did, that 'much remains to be done' is hardly a basis for future policy. The difficulties that lie in the way of the development of a modern police force have been discussed this week in three articles written by a Special Correspondent of *The Times**

---

*THE LONELY BEAT was written by the Home Affairs correspondent of The Times, Norman Fowler, and reproduced by the Federation as a pamphlet. Fowler became a cabinet minister and Chairman of the Conservative Party.

Many lawyers, judges and criminologists will agree that the most effective deterrent to the potential criminal is certainty of apprehension.'

The Police Council met in March to consider the pay and allowances aspects of the Federation's document. In response to the claim for £5 a week pensionable supplements for all ranks, and £7.10s. a week in the undermanned forces, the official side tabled its own proposals for dealing with manpower problems;

The London Allowance should be increased to £50 a week and made pensionable;

London members with less than 3 years' service would receive a temporary and non-pensionable allowance of £30 a year. Members with over 3 years' service would receive a further £35 temporary allowance;

In provincial forces with a 'realistic' establishment of not less than 1500, where the strength deficiency was above 25 per cent, and where there had been no improvement in recent years, 'there might be a case for doing something similar'.

The discussions were heated. The official side professed indignation at the 'clear breach of faith' by the Federation. Alderman Bernard Langton of Manchester was loudest in denunciation: 'I never thought I would see the day when the representatives of law and order would be advocating anarchy.' This was the same Alderman Langton who, at a meeting at the Home Office the day before, had praised the Federation for calling for improved equipment, more civilians, and new technology: 'The Federation memorandum contains sound proposals which are worthy of serious consideration' he had said then.

But the row at the Police Council was nothing compared with the storm that broke when the Federation held its Annual Conference in Llandudno in May 1965. Evans had performed a small miracle in keeping the JCC in line with the completely new policy, but the provincial majority on the conference floor was having none of it. After an angry debate on the proposals, they threw out the claim for higher pensionable supplements to London and undermanned forces.

In subsequent years, the JCC was to insist on its status as the sole policy making body, with supremacy over Conference decisions, but Evans and his colleagues regarded the Conference's rejection of pay differentiation as a fatal blow to the whole claim. It took some fast talking by Evans and Webb to persuade the Conference that having rejected the JCC document on the first day, it should debate the subject again on the last day of Conference. In a passionate and brilliantly argued speech, Evans warned the delegates that all they were now left with was the official side's proposals for London, and a nebulous proposal that something might be done for other undermanned forces. He demanded that the negotiators should be given room to maneouvre, and in spite of bitter opposition from opponents of the claim, his plea was accepted.

When the JCC met after Conference to consider the implications of what had taken place, it was felt that the heat could be taken out of the controversy if the pensionable element of the £7.50 weekly claimed for London and the undermanned forces was abandoned. This amendment was endorsed by a special delegate Conference held in August. Meanwhile, further discussions at the Police Council failed to make any progress and the claim was referred to the Police Arbitration Tribunal.

One of the issues raised by Reg Webb in his Conference address to Sir Frank Soskice was the possible recruitment of 'coloured' police officers. Increasing tensions in inner city areas where the proportion of immigrants in the population was increasing had led more politicians and commentators to suggest that the police should no longer be an exclusively white force. Webb said;

'It must be a primary function of the police service, in its dealings with the coloured population, to ensure that equality under the law is not just an abstract principle, but a fact. The Police Federation would never be a party to any policy which meant that coloured citizens were ever less likely to be given justice than others.

'We have read with great interest the articles which have appeared in the press on the subject of the recruitment of coloured policemen. We are told that it is only a matter of time before the first step is taken in this direction, or that you have plans to announce this is the near future. We are not altogether satisfied about the implications of such speculation.

'Whilst I am sure that the more liberal elements which predominate in this country would welcome and encourage a coloured policeman, it is not the liberal and enlightened elements that provide the police with their worst headaches. The time will come, surely, when the process of assimilation has softened many of the tensions which now exist, but I do believe that I am speaking on behalf of the vast majority of service opinion when I tell you that the police service should not become, in this respect, the plaything of the radical reformer. We particularly ask this; *That, if any specific policy with regard to coloured recruitment is contemplated, by which I mean that men are to be recruited because they are coloured, then the police service will be fully consulted before any decision is made.*'

In his response, Soskice agreed that there could be no question of appointing coloured policemen as a social experiment. He suggested that coloured youths who had been brought up in Britain, and who had the necessary qualifications, might start their police careers in the cadet schemes. In 1967, Constable Norwell Roberts from the West Indies joined the Metropolitan Police, and Coventry, Birmingham and Liverpool each appointed a black officer.

The Police Arbitration Tribunal met in November 1965, to consider the staff side's claim for supplementary allowances, and the official side's counter offer. Evans knew that it was always going to be hard to convince the Tribunal that the whole service was under strength, as distinct from the forces which were patently undermanned, but the timing of the hearing could not have been worse. The Government was beset with mounting economic pressures, and staking its future on the 'National Plan', which laid down strict limitations on wage increases. Sir Ronald Morison QC, the chairman of the Tribunal, said that whatever view might be taken of the police dispute, the Tribunal members would feel bound to have regard to the economic crisis, and the Government's policy on incomes.

For the official side, R E Griffiths made a powerful attack on the Federation. It had, he said, fired the first shots in a campaign designed to bring all possible pressure on the official side and stampede the employers into tearing up an agreement and conceding huge pay increases. This action struck at the roots of collective bargaining and was: 'such a shock as to be regarded by the official side as irresponsible ... ...' He insisted that the current national rate of pay was adequate, except for London and one or two larger forces. The solution was to increase the London Allowance from £20 to £50 a year and make it pensionable, and in addition, to pay small temporary allowances as long as manpower remained a problem in London. The case of other under-manned forces could be considered later.

Evans pointed out that the service was now 20,000 below authorised strength, compared with the 12,000 deficiency at the time of the Royal Commission in 1960. He was soon clashing with Sir Ronald Morison, who asked if the staff side claim was not in reality a general pay claim, and as such outside the terms of the 1964 pay settlement which committed both sides to examining undermanned forces. Evans said that every force now needed a special inducement to recruit and retain officers.

Griffiths, in reply, revealed the alliance that had grown up between the official side and Sir Edward Dodd, the Chief Inspector of Constabulary, who had recently been the chief constable of Birmingham. Dodd agreed with Griffiths that no more than half a dozen forces could be regarded as chronically undermanned. Evans had emphasised that staff shortages meant frequent changes of shift and leave days for beat officers, but Dodd said that such changes were made by 'mutual agreement', a view that would not be shared by those obliged to change shifts and days off at a moment's notice. Griffiths was scornful of complaints about the disruption of officers' social lives. He said the Federation seemed to believe that the police service should exist for the benefit of the policeman and not to fight crime.

The Tribunal announced its award just three days before Christmas 1965. It amounted to a total endorsement of the official side's proposals. London Allowance became pensionable and was increased to £50. In addition, constables and sergeants would be paid an allowance of £30 a year in their first three years' service, and £65 afterwards, with 'suitable adjustments' to the existing London rate for the inspector ranks. For provincial forces, the Tribunal said that a committee should be set up by the Police Council to establish conditions for the payment of similar allowances in other undermanned areas.

The JCC view was that the Tribunal had considered it could do nothing else in the face of Government policy, although Evans acknowledged that 1965 had, after all, turned out to be a good recruiting year, with a net gain of more than 3,000 men.

The official side, for the first time since the Police Council had been reformed in 1953, had achieved a total victory over the Federation. Even now, it could not enjoy its moment of triumph, because the press was almost unanimous in condemning the arbitration award. The *Daily Mail* had a cartoon showing a London Bobby being struck across the face with a fish labelled: *Paltry pay rise.* An editorial called the award: 'sheer stupidity'. The *Daily Express* said:

> 'Incredible! That is the only word to describe the rejection of the police pay claim ... ... At a moment when the country is suffering the worst crime wave in history, when the force is 20,000 men under strength, it is unbelievable that the authorities should act in this way.'

The Sun said that the award was 'folly' and urged Jenkins to take emergency action. *The Times* said that disappointment with the award might cause more resignations, a prophecy which turned out to be accurate. The papers were not concerned with the niceties of collective bargaining, or whether the Federation claim had breached an existing agreement. They saw the issue in simple terms. The police were desperately short of men and more money was the only way to get them. This press reaction was music to Arthur Evans, and fully justified his skilful use of the media when announcing the claim, something that the Federation had never done before.

It was also opportune for the Federation that at this time there was a change of Home Secretary. Sir Frank Soskice was not a success in the post, and his successor was Roy Jenkins, who had emerged as one of the most promising members of the first Wilson administration. He saw at once that the arbitration award would be badly received in the service, and moved quickly to calm things down. Early in January 1966, he met the JCC officers at the Home Office. They asked Jenkins to do what Soskice had twice refused to do - set up an independent inquiry to examine police conditions. Jenkins agreed that there was a need for an inquiry, but said it should be conducted by the Police Advisory Board, which included representatives of all the interested parties. He suggested it should cover manpower, equipment and efficiency. He agreed with the Federation that the matter was urgent, and the Board would be expected to report quickly. Taking the hint, the Advisory Board appointed working parties to deal with the topics covered by the inquiry - manpower, equipment and efficiency.

Jenkins was also surprisingly sympathetic to the Federation's pay aspirations. He told Evans and his colleagues that sufficient time had passed since the Royal Commission to justify 'further consideration of the principles which should govern police pay'. The Federation took this as a clear hint that the 1966 pay talks need not be confined simply to the movement in the Wages Index.

A week after the meeting with Jenkins, over 2,500 members of the Federation travelled through a blizzard to an open meeting in Guildford. They were angry about the arbitration award, and especially with the fact that only the London forces had got any money out of it, but Evans was able to assure them that the outlook under Roy Jenkins was not quite so bleak.

This optimistic feeling did not last for very long. The economic crisis was deepening at an alarming pace, and when Jenkins attended the Federation Conference in May, Webb was in a combative mood. He gave Jenkins a blunt warning about the feelings in the service:

> 'If any attempt is made to fob off the police, at this time of crisis, with a diluted pay award in which we are sacrificial lambs on the altar of an incomes policy, no one on this national executive of the Police Federation will be prepared to take responsibility for what will happen to the police of this country.'

It was probably just as well that these were still the days of Federation conferences which excluded the press, as the remarks could have been interpreted as a threat that the police might strike. Webb meant no more than that the reaction of most officers to a second successive pay rebuff would be a huge increase in resignations.

During the General Election, Evans learned that the *Sunday Express* was planning to publish an article about James Callaghan and the fact that his option to return to the Federation if he left the Government was still open. Callaghan was informed, and he and Evans agreed that the contract should be terminated. When the announcement was made, the Tory MP for Bury St Edmunds, Eldon Griffiths, wrote to apply to succeed Callaghan, pointing out that he was the son of a retired Lancashire police officer who had served for a short period as a member of the JCC. After the election, Griffiths was appointed. He had no trade union background and knew nothing about negotiations. Evans and Webb felt that the new adviser would be useful as a spokesman in Parliament.

On the 20th July 1966, the Labour Government, which had been returned to power with a greatly increased majority, introduced a statutory system of regulating pay increases throughout the private and public sectors. Harold Wilson announced that there would soon be a six-months standstill on wages, followed by a further six-months of 'severe restraint', during which groups seeking an increase would have to justify the case for any rise at all, and then the 'norm' would be only 1 per cent. The Government added, that at the same time, prices would be brought under statutory control and frozen.

The Federation was already engaged in negotiations with the official side over the pay increase that was due to take effect on the 1st September. The Government said that where groups had already concluded pay negotiations, implementation must be deferred by six months. New commitments must not be implemented in the rest of 1966, and in the following six months they could only be paid 'if the grounds for exceptional treatment are particularly compelling' Wilson made it plain to Parliament that there would be no exceptions. In effect, this meant that the police would not be able to negotiate a pay increase which reflected the rise in the Wages Index over the previous two years, and whatever was conceded, would not be paid until the beginning of July 1967.

This was a total reversal of the optimistic view expressed by Roy Jenkins just six months earlier. The Federation issued a press statement which outlined the strong feelings of the police;

> '... ... Before the wages freeze was announced discussions with the authorities had already commenced on the question of a salary increase to date from lst September this year. There can be no question therefore but that a review of police pay was already in the pipeline. The Federation would like to make it clear that the cuts in police expenditure and in particular the freeze on a salary increase will seriously damage the morale of the service and also further weaken our resources for combatting serious crime, reducing road casualties and protecting the public. If there are any special cases which will qualify for exemption from the wages freeze the police is surely one and the Federation has made these views known to the Home Secretary.'

The Home Office, in response to a request from both sides of the Police Council for clarification of the police position, said that the 1962 Pay Agreement made it clear that account had to be taken of general economic factors which affected the police to the same extent as the rest of the community. Therefore, the Police Council was bound by the terms of Government incomes policy.

When this reply was received, a deputation of both sides of the Police Council saw Jenkins at the Home Office, and expressed deep concern about the affect of the ruling on police morale. Only a few months before, relations between the official side and the staff side had reached their nadir with the row over undermanning payments, now they were united in trying to preserve the 1962 pay agreement and the Willink pay standards. Jenkins was sympathetic but unable to hold out any hope that the police would be exempted from the general freeze. He said the Government feared, that if this was done, other public sector groups, some with the power to strike, would demand similar treatment.

When the White Paper appeared in November, it made no mention of the position of the police, but on the day that Michael Stewart, the Secretary of State for Economic Affairs, was due to open the debate on it in the House of Commons, Jenkins sent for Webb and Evans to tell them that he had, after all, been able to persuade the Cabinet that the police, and only the police, would be treated as a special case. When Michael Stewart spoke, he told the House:

> 'The Government consider that the police, whose next pay increase was originally due to take effect from September 1966 are in a special position because of their importance in combatting crime. My Right Honourable friends, the Home and Scottish Secretaries, are therefore prepared to discuss in the Police Council an increase payable in July 1967, retrospective to March 1967.'

Most Members of Parliament who heard the statement thought that Stewart was making a small concession to the police, by reducing the delay in their pay increase from nine months to six, but the Government decision was more significant than that. It gave the Police Council the right to go ahead and negotiate under the 1962 Agreement, which was based on the movements in the Wages Index. The Federation was very satisfied. It had achieved something which the entire trade union movement, dealing directly with a Labour Government, had failed to do, notwithstanding strikes by the railwaymen, seamen and the dockers.

Besides being busy with pay, the JCC and the branch boards had been presented with another major task; coping with a programme of amalgamations of police forces. When Jenkins arrived at the Home Office, he was surprised that little notice had been taken of the Royal Commission's view that there were too many small police forces. Civil servants in the police department told him that every one of the 122 existing forces in England and Wales considered itself to be efficient and wanted to remain unaltered. Further, if the Home Office followed the Royal Commission's suggestions, it would still take another twenty years to get the number of forces reduced by a half. The leisurely procedure for amalgamating forces depended on the area reports of the Local Government Boundaries Commission rather than a police efficiency initiative.

Immediately after the 1966 General Election, the Labour Government scrapped the Commission and replaced it with another, with wider terms of reference. This gave the police reformers in the Home Office their opportunity. Jenkins instructed the Inspectors of Constabulary and the civil servants to come up with ideas for a drastic reduction in the number of forces, to be achieved straight away. In the Queen's Speech in April 1966, the Government promised it would;

'press ahead with a vigorous programme of amalgamations to provide the police with the form of organisation best suited to the battle against crime.'

In May 1966, just a few days before he was due to address the Federation Conference, Jenkins took the service and the public by surprise by announcing his intention to cut the number of forces to 49. The plan created a huge new force in Lancashire of over 7,000, which still left two other large forces in the county; Manchester and Salford, and Liverpool and Bootle. All the small forces were to go.

Evans had not received prior notice of Jenkins's intentions, but he gave the plan his immediate and total backing. Addressing the Conference, he urged the branch boards not to allow themselves to get involved in the inevitable local politicking that would go on, as local authorities fought to keep control of 'their' police forces. Instead, he said, they should concentrate on co-operating with the other boards concerned in their particular amalgamations, while the JCC would work to secure guarantees for the members. There was much to be gained for the members, Evans said, from a modernised and reconstructed service. He was able to reassure the Conference that members of borough forces would not be compelled to move their homes following the mergers. Taking Evans's advice, the branch boards formed 'guardian boards' which were soon able to negotiate with the chief constables-designate of the new forces.

Most of the amalgamations went through smoothly. Some police authorities fought to retain their forces, but a succession of local inquiries upheld the proposals. Two forces, Hull and Bradford were reprieved by the Home Secretary but by 1969 the programme of mergers was completed. It was, by all previous standards, a remarkable achievement to have overcome the entrenched opposition of local government and persuade the police service that such drastic upheaval was essential. However, the Jenkins plan suffered from many defects. The law permitted only entire police areas to be amalgamated, so the new forces in heavily populated areas did not reflect the growth of conurbations, and the pattern of boundaries threw up some of the same problems that the scheme had sought to resolve. It would not be long before the service found itself going through another reorganisation.

EIGHTEEN

The Shepherd's Bush murders

T he Federation was grateful to Roy Jenkins for fighting the police corner in the Cabinet discussions on the pay freeze, but the Home Secretary was deeply unpopular with the rank and file, especially in London. One reason was the murder of three unarmed policemen, shot down in a London street in broad daylight in August 1966. Detective Sergeant Head and Constables Wombwell and Fox were patrolling the Shepherds Bush district in an unmarked police car when they became interested in the three occupants of an old car parked close to Wormwood Scrubs prison. Two of the officers got out of their car and began speaking to the men, one of whom produced a gun and killed them instantly. Another of the gang then ran across the road to the police car and shot the driver dead.

The cold blooded killings shocked the nation. Sir William 'Billy' Butlin, the millionaire who pioneered holiday camps, immediately gave Lord Stonham, the Minister of State at the Home Office, a cheque for £100,000 to launch a fund for the dependants of all murdered and injured police officers. The donation was made anonymously, but Sir William's generosity was made known after his death. The fund was named the Police Dependants' Trust, and every Metropolitan officer donated a day's pay to it in memory of their three murdered colleagues. It is today a substantial charity which is of great benefit to injured officers and their families.

The sorrow of the police was mixed with intense anger, most of it directed against the MPs who, eighteen months earlier, had ended capital punishment. Ironically, the murders occurred in the constituency of the only Labour MP, Frank Tomney, who had voted in favour of hanging. Jenkins had inflamed police opinion by appearing, in a television interview immediately after the killings, to dismiss police calls for the return of capital punishment in a condescending manner. He said that a decision on this issue could not be undertaken on a wave of emotion caused by one incident, 'however horrible'. When the Home Secretary addressed a crowded and tense meeting of the Metropolitan Federation in October, he was constantly heckled and half the audience walked out.

Crime had been on the increase, with a rise in the number of armed robberies in London. Jenkins was portrayed by the Tory press as 'soft on crime', (the *Sunday Express* claimed that this was because forty years earlier, his father, a miners' union official, had been jailed for six months following a riot in South Wales during the General Strike). In the face of the hecklers at the Metropolitan Federation meeting, the Home Secretary spelt out a programme for combatting crime, including the introduction of majority verdicts and changes in the laws of evidence affecting alibis. He told the members that he accepted that the maximum penalties for gun crimes were too low and they would be increased. He said he was in favour of modifying the right of silence, as recommended by the Criminal Law Revision Committee (a change not introduced until 1994) and he made it clear that he disagreed with his predecessor, Soskice, who had suggested that nine years in gaol was long enough as a life sentence. Jenkins said that the 'worst' murderers should not be let out until they had served for a term that was 'very much longer' than nine or ten years.

The Federation leadership was worried that the popular resentment felt by the service against 'liberal' penal policies, expressed in terms of personal abuse of Jenkins, was going to be counter productive at a time when the police needed public opinion on their side. The *Newsletter* contained a strong rebuke for the loud mouths who had wrecked the Metropolitan meeting:

'The whole system of dealing with crime and the administration of justice in this country is falling into contempt and policemen are right to give vent to their frustrations. But let us be more careful and accurate in selecting our targets. The onslaught on Jenkins was probably a protest against the state of crime and resentment against those who have pursued their abolitionist and libertarian beliefs beyond the point of reason. It appeared to the public to be an unwarranted attack on a man who had only been in the office for a few months.

What was depressing about so much of the noise at Central Hall was the sheer lack of reason behind it. The police case is very strong. Why then do we find policemen shouting down anything that seems opposite to their views? This Federation has never found difficulties in putting our case. The benefits we have gained in the last ten years were not achieved by booing and slow-handclapping Home Secretaries. They were secured in the cold, unemotional; atmosphere of negotiating chambers and Royal Commission hearings. The loudest mouths braying their fury at Mr Jenkins belonged to the emptiest heads - men who had probably never been to a Federation meeting in their lives before. If they achieved anything, it was to emphasise the dangers of letting the Service run down to the point where such as they belong to it.'

This uncompromising attitude of the JCC did not go down well with all the membership. One board secretary wrote to Evans to say that the 'policies of the present Home Secretary have been received far too complacently by the JCC'. Evans replied in the *Newsletter*:

'We are not surprised at this reaction. We expected it and understand it. In one sense we are grateful to the boards which have written to censure us. They are certainly speaking for a very large section of the membership. In the past, when we have warned the Government and the official side of the likely effect of some of their policies on the morale of the service, we have detected unbelieving smiles. Now Mr Jenkins has seen for himself that there are dangerous undercurrents flowing through the Metropollitan Police and

we pray that he and his advisers have the good sense
to look for the cause of the bad feeling, rather than
worry about the bad manners of the malcontents.'

There were those in the Federation and elsewhere who felt
that the Central Hall hecklers might have helped to influence
the decision on police pay, arguing that the Government
would have nothing to gain by squashing a pay rise for a
service that was clearly in an angry and disillusioned frame
of mind. Evans might have retorted that it was probably more
helpful that the Chancellor the Exchequer, who would have
had a great influence on the Cabinet's decision, was the
former consultant to the JCC. It was also true that Harold
Wilson was deeply concerned about attempts being made
by the left wing union leaders and other elements to turn
the workers' resentment of the pay freeze into a general
strike. If the situation began to deteriorate, the police would
be needed to preserve law and order.

The police pay settlement, when it was announced in the
spring of 1967, annoyed the rest of the public sector
negotiators. It produced a general increase of 9 per cent, way
ahead of the government 'norm' for postponed increases.
While the membership was very pleased with the outcome,
the branch boards were unhappy about the introduction of
a complicated system of age-pointing, brought in to stimulate
the recruitment of more mature officers.

The three reports of the working parties of the Police
Advisory Board were published in January 1967. The manpower report recommended that forces should not insist on
unreasonable height limits, and said that the maximum age
for recruitment could be 40 years for ex-servicemen. Some
members of the working party wanted changes to the
minimum period of service before promotion in the case of
officers who joined with higher educational qualifications.
There was unanimous opposition to the idea of direct recruitment to specialist departments, such as CID and traffic, and
to direct entry to higher rank.

The report said that the causes of high wastage were pay,
hours of duty, and poor man management. The Federation
said that the wastage problem might be reduced by intro-

ducing a forty hour, five day week, and ensuring that all officers got one weekend off in every four. There was unanimity, also, on the need to ensure that police officers were not misemployed on administrative and other tasks that did not require the use of police powers or police experience. More civilians should be recruited for such tasks, said the working party. It called for organisation and methods teams, consisting of police and civilians, to be set up in all forces to examine the use of manpower, paperwork, and other systems.

The report called for the greater use of traffic wardens, the original opposition of the Federation having been tempered by the satisfaction felt by its members at being relieved of tedious duties. The Federation even supported an extension of the powers of wardens, and a greater use of fixed penalties for stationary traffic offences. The Federation had always objected to the use of special constables on a regular basis. Now the working party said that while they must not be used as a permanent substitute for professional policemen, an increase in the numbers of 'active' special constables was desirable.

The report on equipment was enthusiastic about new technology that was coming into use, such as personal radios for beat officers. It supported the greater use of small cars to enable more flexible beat systems to be operated, saying that the service required about 3,000 such vehicles. The working party called for dictating equipment in all stations, to cut down the amount of time spent by officers on report writing and typing. It said savings could be made by greater standardisation of equipment and central purchasing in bulk. It suggested that all forces should have booklets for reporting accidents, thus reducing the paper burden on beat officers. The report welcomed the feasibility study that had been launched to consider the possibilities of having a national police computer to store and retrieve criminal intelligence and records.

Perhaps the most important report dealt with organisation and management. The working party said it had formed three aims; to improve service to the public; increase the interest and responsibility of the policeman; and use manpower more economically. The working party considered that the traditional beat system was no longer effective and called for more flexible systems. One of these, called unit beat policing, was being pioneered at Kirby newtown in Lancashire. It operated on the basis of officers being assigned permanently to one residential beat, as with village constables. Two adjoining such beats would work together, with both officers sharing a small car - the ubiquitous 'Panda' of the sixties - and the team would be completed by a detective constable dealing with enquiries. The team members could exercise their own discretion as to their hours of duty, provided each completed eight hours daily. The idea was that each officer would be responsible for everything that occurred on his 'patch' and so his interest, enthusiasm and job satisfaction would be enhanced. He would become the 'eyes and ears' of the force and in each divisional station an officer would be appointed as a 'collator' to record and disseminate all the criminal information that came in from the beat officers and the public. The report said that adoption of the system would enhance efficiency and cultivate a better understanding with the public.

In subsequent years, attempts to establish unit beat policing as the main system in use in Britain foundered on the manpower shortage which was to get progressively worse. In practice, there were rarely enough constables available to work the system properly, and the unit beat officers were frequently taken away from such duties to fill gaps elsewhere, or to police demonstrations and football matches. Another reason for the system's failure was that supervising officers could not adjust to the idea of constables deciding for themselves which hours of duty they would work. The constables were criticised for spending too much time in the Panda car, when the idea was that they should use the car to drive to parts of the beat, and then patrol on foot. The public began to dislike seeing police officers 'riding around in cars' instead of walking the beat. Yet, before the Panda came into use, some of the critics had rarely seen a policeman in their neighbourhoods in recent years.

The working party concluded that grave man-management problems were a main cause of premature wastage, and low morale. The report called for courses in management skills for supervisors. Evans had called, in *The Problem*, for the abolition of saluting, drill, and collar numbers on uniforms. He argued that everything that was done to enhance the status of officers with rank denigrated the worth of the constable. The working party, while not fully agreeing, went a long way to meeting his points. It said that the time honoured duty parade, with men standing at attention for inspection, should be replaced with 'briefing sessions' where the constables sat at desks. Some forces still held regular drill sessions, which the report said served no useful purpose and were inconsistent with the idea of the constable as a self-manager. It agreed with the abolition of collar numbers.

The publication of the reports attracted more attention inside the service than outside it, but initial response was favourable, especially as money was made available to enable forces to implement a good part of the recommendations. In the end, economic crises and manpower problems meant that the reports did not achieve all that was hoped for. Twenty years later, poor management styles would be identified as a primary cause of adverse stress among police officers. Even so, Evans could look upon the three reports as vindication of the initiative he had launched two years before. A fair proportion of the reports came to be implemented, and their publication challenged some of the practices and beliefs that had been holding back progress in the service.

Roy Jenkins and his Minister of State, Dick Taverne MP, felt that the reports had not done enough to stimulate the recruitment of well educated people. A new working party was established, under Taverne, to examine the question. Its report proposed a Graduate Entry Scheme. This would offer twenty places a year to graduates, who would be selected on the basis that they had the potential to rise above the rank of inspector at an early stage of their careers. After two years' probation they would go on the Special Course at Bramshill, along with the constables selected through the extended interviews. This would give them automatic promotion to inspector within four years, after which further promotion was up to them. The report also proposed that the service should offer twenty university scholarships every year to school leavers with the necessary A levels. They would join the service at 19 and complete their probation before going to university. This part of the working party's report was not adopted, but the graduate entry scheme was instituted in 1967 and continues to the present day.

The publication of the Police Advisory Board reports came just as it was announced that Arthur Evans had been created a Commander of the Order of the British Empire (CBE) in the New Year's Honours List for 1967. This was an unprecedented award for a constable, or any policeman below the rank of chief constable. Some chief constables were heard to criticise the Honour on just those grounds, and suggest that it had come from the personal patronage of the Chancellor, James Callaghan. These critics overlooked one simple fact, no chief constable in the history of the police service achieved as much for the police as Constable Arthur Evans had done in the space of nine years as JCC and staff side secretary.

And then, just a few weeks after the award was announced, Evans was gone. The reason for his sudden departure bordered on the farcical. Some months earlier, he had undertaken the organisation of a visit by Federation members and their families to Canada, to attend the country's centenary celebrations and an international police event organised by the Niagara Falls police. The response was so good that Evans chartered three jet aircraft, signing contracts that could not be cancelled. Only at a late stage did he realise that Government restrictions on taking sterling out of Britain meant that the hotel bills of the party were not covered. He was reluctant to approach his colleagues to discuss a way out of the problem, as members of the Committee were beginning to criticise the amount of time he was spending on the arrangements. An approach was made to James Callaghan, who as Chancellor of the Exchequer authorised a higher sterling allowance for each member of the party, on the grounds that the visit had a business element. This did not wholly resolve the problem. Eventually, a member of the Niagara Falls police came over to London, intending to take the hotel money back to Canada with him. When an attempt was made to withdraw the sum from the bank in cash, the police were notified, in accordance with the rules about transactions in sterling. In the ensuing row, Evans found himself without a friend on the Committee, and would have been shocked to find that some of those he considered his friends were loudest in their condemnation of his actions. He resigned, and in this way the Federation lost the services of its outstanding secretary.

The new secretary was Dick Pamplin, a Metropolitan sergeant who had been the assistant JCC and staff side secretary, and worked closely with Evans. He was to prove to be another able and skilled negotiator, which meant that the sudden loss of his predecessor did not turn out to be the serious blow it had appeared at the time.

The economic pressures on Britain grew worse in 1967 and in November James Callaghan resigned as Chancellor of the Exchequer, following the devaluation of the pound. His place was taken by Roy Jenkins, and Callaghan became Home Secretary. The appointment soon became a classic example of the poacher turned gamekeeper. The Federation had warned the membership that Callaghan could not be regarded as 'our man in the Home Office', but the JCC was still caught unprepared when he announced a series of economy measures at the beginning of 1968. These included a ceiling on manpower growth. In 1967, the service had expanded by 4,000 men. Callaghan set a limit of 1,200 on future expansion. When the Federation protested that this was wrong when the service was still short of 17,000 men, their former consultant replied that this was only a paper shortage, and in his view current establishments were too high. In another move which upset the Federation, Callaghan vetoed the proposal to dispense with numerals on police uniforms, something that had been suggested by the PAB working parties and was intended to get away from the idea of constables as numbers rather than individuals. The Federation was irked because, in vetoing the proposal, Callaghan appeared to be responding to protests from the National Council for Civil Liberties and left wing groups.

More shocks were to come. After two years of negotiations, it had been agreed that Liverpool and Birmingham police qualified for the undermanning allowances. Callaghan refused to ratify the agreement, saying there was no point in paying such an allowance when he was limiting increases in manpower. He annoyed the Federation still further by suggesting that the establishments had become swollen beyond the true needs of the service. Those who remembered how recently he had argued for extra manpower, and accused the Conservatives of keeping establishments artificially low, could not believe their ears.

But the service was particularly incensed by Callaghan's decision to amend the Police Discipline Code to make racial discrimination a specific offence. The Race Relations Bill was passing through Parliament and did not cover the police service. The Federation said that it was insulting to single out the police in such a manner, and that any action taken by a policeman which would justify a complaint of racial discrimination would already be covered by a specific offence. The *Newsletter* said:

> 'This Federation represents 92,000 members in England and Wales. We are certainly not taking sides in the important and sensitive debate which is now taking place on race relations. The Government's job is to legislate, and the police service must, as always, do its best to enforce the law.
>
> 'Before Mr Callaghan advises Parliament to take an irrevocable step, let him pause and consider just what he is doing. No other Member of the House of Commons knows the police as well as he does. We take a real pride in our service and the way in which we have built up a bond of friendship between ourselves and the many millions of fellow citizens who make up the public. We have done this by devotion to duty and ensuring justice under the law for everyone, without asking where they came from, or what was their standing in the community.'

In 1968, the ethnic minorities were still seen as immigrants. The second generation was still at school and the inner city riots of the Eighties lay in the distant future. Complaints against the police by coloured people were regarded as untypical of the prevailing relationships between the police and the newcomers. The police service had recruited only a handful of black and Asian constables.

With the Home Secretary and the Federation at odds over several issues, it was not surprising, that when Callaghan attended the Federation Conference for the first time as Home Secretary, at Torquay in 1968, he ran into opposition. The occasion was anything but the happy reunion between the delegates and their erstwhile hero. In his address, Webb, making his last speech before retiring, angered Callaghan with a strong attack on his veto of the undermanning allowances for Liverpool and Birmingham;

> 'I remember a speaker at this Conference who once referred to the action of Mr Henry Brooke when he was insisting on trying to push an unjust regulation on widows' pensions through Parliament. The speaker said; 'If a Home Secretary gets away with an arbitrary regulation affecting three widows' pensions, he could do it next year on a matter affecting the pay of 80,000 men.' You were that speaker.'

Callaghan's reply was robust and revealed how the realities of office had brought a radical change in his views:

> 'There is only a certain amount of money to be spent on the police. I do not want it to be spent on recruiting large numbers of people unless it can be guaranteed that they are going to be efficiently employed and that the equipment will be available for them.'

He added, that spending on the police had risen by fifty per cent since the Labour Government took office. It was now £250 millions a year and the strength of the service had grown by a 'phenomenal' 10,000 officers in three years; 'there has never been a period like it.'

On race relations, Callaghan was conciliatory, saying that there was 'no hurry' to change the Discipline Code and the matter would be fully discussed in the Police Advisory Board. When these discussions took place, the Board was unanimous in advising Callaghan that it was not necessary to add a discrimination clause to the Discipline Code, and he was happy to drop the idea.

The 1968 Pay Review was conducted under the terms of the Prices and Incomes Act, which imposed a limit of 3.5 per cent on pay increases. The movement of the Wages Index in the period was 10 per cent, so clearly the police were in danger of falling well behind the Willink standard. It was possible, however, to breach the statutory limit if it could be shown that productivity had increased. Besides the 3.5 per cent, the official side offered an additional 3 per cent to take account of the productivity gains arising from the PAB working party reports, but this would not be paid until the following September. It was also ready to concede a 40 hour week as from September 1970, provided that the cost came off the productivity award. The staff side said that the productivity gains were worth 4.5 per cent, and should be paid at once. It rejected the link between weekly hours and productivity, because the whole of industry had now got down to a 40 hour week. The staff side realised that the employers had offered the most that they could under the Prices and Incomes Act, and saw no point in going to arbitration because the Tribunal would also consider itself bound by the Act. It therefore accepted the offer.

The JCC said that the agreement was a retreat from Willink, and felt that the 'loss' was greater than the difference between the 1968 pay rise and the Wages Index change, because the latter took no account of earnings, including overtime, bonuses, and productivity payments which were common in industry. The one police 'perk', rent allowance, was discounted in pay rises, and reductions in hours also came out of the global sum for increases. They were beginning to realise that if Willink was not to be lost altogether, the link with police pay needed to be made with the Earnings Index.

NINETEEN

A show of blue

R eg Gale, a Hampshire inspector, succeeded Reg Webb as chairman of the Joint Central Committee in 1968. He was the first chairman to grasp the public relations possibilities of the position and took every opportunity of appearing on television and radio, commenting on all aspects of policing and giving the 'Federation view'. This helped to keep the Federation's name before the public, but did not please some members of the Association of Chief Police Officers, who considered that the police should, like the Royal Navy, be the silent service. Few forces of that period had press departments, the Association of Chief Police Officers did not seek to speak on behalf of its members or the service, and chief constables did not make speeches or appear on the media. There was annoyance among some chief officers when Gale was the guest chosen by Robin Day to appear on the pioneering BBC radio 'phone-in' programme, *It's your line.* Within a short time, the Federation chairman was appearing regularly on television and becoming well known to the public, while chief officers, except for Sir Robert Mark, the Metropolitan Commissioner in the seventies, remained largely anonymous figures.

An initiative for which Gale was largely responsible was a series of weekend Seminars on important current topics, to which prominent persons were invited. Eldon Griffiths, the Consultant, was an experienced international journalist and publicist, and advised Gale and the Committee that the Federation could increase its influence by making itself known to the opinion makers who exercised considerable influence on public policy. The Seminars, which attracted sponsorship from the International Publishing Corporation, covered such subjects as; the police and the public; drugs, and race relations. Gale also made a point of accepting invitations to speak at conferences on police related subjects, and it was not long before he was attracting attention, on one occasion suggesting that cannabis should be a legal drug, a proposal which shocked many Federation members as well as chief constables.

The Federation was strengthening its organisation all through the Sixties. The search for a permanent headquarters was again frustrated when plans to build an office block in New Malden, Surrey (in the same road as the police station where Goodsall had his office for many years) were thwarted by a ban on new office development in Greater London. In 1969, premises were purchased outright, for about £180,000, in Surbiton. The price represented about ten years rent and rates of the offices in Soho The building was large enough to accommodate all the JCC's requirements for the foreseeable future, and for some years part of it was leased to a tenant. Eventually, the building came to house the offices of the separate central committees as well as the JCC.

In September 1968, the first edition of *POLICE* Magazine appeared, replacing the *Newsletter*. The new journal quickly established itself as an authoritative organ of police opinion.

In its second issue, *POLICE* was concerned about the enormous demonstration against American involvement in the Vietnam civil war. It was scheduled to take place in London at the end of October. 1968. The year had seen similar demonstrations throughout the western world, with pitched battles on the streets of Chicago, Berlin and Paris as protestors clashed with armed police. Thanks to a massive build-up in the British press, with dire predictions of blood on the streets and enormous damage, tension was high as the day came near. There were real fears of a repetition of the deaths which had occurred during mass protests in America, France and Germany. The British police had none of the weaponry or riot equipment available to the police in other countries, and although the Metropolitan was the most experienced force in the country in the policing of demonstrations and disorder, the extent of the violence and civil disobedience used by anarchist and militant groups during the anti-Vietnam War campaign reached heights of ferocity not seen in London since the clashes in the Thirties between the Left and fascists. The press and many Conservative MPs were calling on the Home Secretary, James Callaghan, to ban the event. Sir Joseph Simpson, the Metropolitan Commissioner, assured him that the police could cope, and with some misgivings, Callaghan accepted his advice.

The Federation felt that a ban would have been seen as a police climbdown in face of threats. Reg Gale issued a statement, emphasising that the police would not give way to provocation, and drawing attention to the well publicised intentions of Left wing groups to storm the embassy and discredit the police.

The event turned out to be a public relations triumph for the Metropolitan. The lessons had been learned from July, when the police had been overwhelmed and a dangerous crush of demonstrators in the narrow streets beside the embassy had almost resulted in a disaster. This time, the police response was a massive 'show of blue'. Thousands of uniformed Bobbies, with not a gun, riot helmet or water cannon in sight, walked alongside the huge procession from the Embankment to Trafalgar Square. The demonstrators were allowed to march in line abreast for the full width of the roads, and the feared confrontation became a Sunday afternoon stroll in the autumn sunshine. The vast crowd was estimated at between 50,000 and 100,000 and after the speeches, the great majority followed a planned route down Whitehall to the dispersal point. A few thousand from far Left groups broke away from the march to try to storm the embassy, and a pitched battle ensued with the police in Grosvenor Square. A picture of a demonstrator kicking a policeman in the head went round the world, and the foreign press marvelled at the way in which the British police had handled the march. For at least a short period after this brilliant operation, the Metropolitan Police and the service in general were able to bask in public approval.

In 1969, the Federation celebrated its Golden Jubilee. There was quite a lot to celebrate. The organisation had mastered the art of collective bargaining and functioned as an effective pressure group, able to take on the Government when occasion demanded. The fiftieth birthday was marked by a glittering reception given by the Corporation of the City of London at Guildhall, attended by the Prime Minister, Harold Wilson, and the Home Secretary, James Callaghan, as well as branch board members and former Federation leaders. The Annual Conference at Blackpool was extended by a day to mark the occasion, and delegates heard moving speeches from two of the earliest leaders, Jack Branthwaite and Jack Bates, who had once been a Police Union organiser in London.

In his Conference address to Callaghan, Reg Gale complained that the police had been short changed in the 1968 pay settlement. In spite of the Government's restrictions, he said, the Wage Index had risen by 10 per cent in the past year. It was clear that the pay policy was not working. Callaghan was firm in his response, telling the Conference that an incomes policy would continue for as far ahead as he and they could see. He said the service would need 15,000 recruits over the next two years to increase the overall strength by 2,000 men.

Pay and manpower were once again causes for concern in 1969. Callaghan's edict that the force must not grow by more than 1,200 in 1968 had turned out be a hollow ruling. The net gain was only 207. The flood of recruits which Callaghan had feared, and said the service and the country could not afford, had dried to a trickle. The Federation challenged his announcement that the force could grow by 2,000 before 1970, calling for a national recruiting campaign on a par with the advertising for the armed forces. The main grumble about pay was that the age pointing system was throwing up anomalies and causing discontent among men who found that others with less service were getting more money simply because of their ages.

There was one positive negotiating achievement in 1969 which had a major impact on the number of home owners in the service. This was the agreement on rent allowances. The 1957 agreement had given owner occupiers a better deal than before, but in practice it had major defects. One was that the maximum allowance in a force was supposed to be based on the rents and rates being paid by members who were renting unfurnished accommodation. Very few members rented privately owned property, of which there was a great shortage throughout the country. Most police in rented homes were local authority tenants, and their rents were kept well below economic levels by subsidies. This meant that the force rent allowance had to be fixed at a depressed level, and the vast majority of police owner occupiers were in houses which the district valuers had assessed as having rental values which were well above the maximum rent allowance. The 1969 agreement allowed the council housing subsidy to be taken into account when fixing new limits, but the most important change was that, where the members in rented property was deemed to be insufficient to fix a fair allowance, the district valuer could be asked to assess the open market rent that would be paid on a typical modern police house, and this became the new maximum limit for the force.

The change soon led to a steep rise in the amounts being paid to members in their own homes, and encouraged what became a mass migration out of police accommodation as police officers joined the property owning class. This trend gained further impetus from the amalgamation of forces. The former borough officers were protected against compulsory transfers which would require them to move their homes, and it was not long before equity required that the same opportunity to become house owners was given to all officers in the new forces. Older members of branch boards, recalling the years of housing shortages that followed the war, were able to appreciate how much the situation had changed for the better.

The 1969 Conference carried a resolution dealing with the Federation's relations with outside bodies. The 1964 Police Act had carried forward the prohibition on the Federation being associated with bodies outside the service, but the JCC was anxious to forge links with police associations in Europe. The Conference motion wanted this clause of the Act amended to allow such links. Some delegates feared that this was a back door way of allowing the JCC at some stage to affiliate to the TUC, which was not the intention. The Act was amended, and subsequently the Federation affiliated to the European Union of Police Associations (UISP). This body, which was the largest grouping of its kind, was chosen by the JCC because it was the only one which was non-political and non-sectarian, and exclusive to police officers. Unfortunately, although personal relations with the leaders of the police unions in membership of UISP were cordial enough, the years of membership were not successful. The Federation became increasingly exasperated with UISP because it insisted on being a 'talking shop', passing long winded and pious resolutions about democracy and human rights, but ignoring the need to improve conditions of service and benefits of all police in Europe, and to act as a link with the European Commission and Parliament. After years of seeking reforms and being frustrated by the larger French and German unions in UISP, the Federation left the organisation in 1992.

The mood of unrest which spread through so many countries in 1968 did not have the dire consequences for Britain which many had feared, but in Northern Ireland, a civil rights movement emerged which, for the first time in two generations, galvanised nationalist and unionist factions in Ulster, and reminded the rest of the United Kingdom of problems that had simmered for over fifty years. The Police Federation found itself closely involved as rank and file officers of the Royal Ulster Constabulary sought the help of mainland colleagues.

Until 1968, contact between the Federation and the RUC Representative Body was limited to occasional letters and telephone calls. It was the practice for the pay and conditions of service agreements negotiated in the Police Council to be applied automatically to the RUC, but the force was not represented on the Police Council. In common with the rest of the United Kingdom, the British police service had shown little or no interest in the province. Hostility between protestant and catholic factions had long ceased to be a public order problem in England.

Almost from the outset of 'the troubles' in 1969, the RUC was unable to control events. Militant Unionists, egged on by an agitator then little known outside Ulster, Ian Paisley, broke up civil rights demonstrations, but matters deteriorated sharply when Catholics began to be forced out of their homes in 'mixed' areas of Belfast, and the first killings began. James Callaghan assumed responsibility for Ulster at Westminster. The army was drafted into the worst trouble spots to keep the peace, and Sir Arthur Young, the Commissioner of the City of London Police, was seconded to replace the chief officer of the Royal Ulster Constabulary, who had failed to control the rioting. Sir Anthony Peacocke and his immediate predecessor had presided over a force which was starved of resources and operated as an extension of the sectarian rule of the entrenched Unionist party. Its organisation, rank structure, and management style reflected the barracks mentality of an era that had long departed from the rest of the United Kingdom's police service.

The RUC before 1969 practised the sectarian discrimination which permeated the public life of the province, especially in local government, employment and housing, and of which most Britons had lived in ignorance. The attitude of most RUC senior officers to the civil rights marches, lead by students and Catholic clergy and community leaders, was that IRA gunmen were behind the unrest, using bogus grievances to overthrow the Union. Apart from a brief spasm of violence in the early Fifties, the IRA had been dormant for many years. The RUC was required to be 90 per cent Protestant, although the quota for Catholics was rarely achieved. In spite of this, the RUC was as effective as any in detecting crime and it contained many officers who were the equals at least of their mainland counterparts and knew that the RUC was ripe for reform. With one or two exceptions, such men were not in the force hierarchy.

Sir Arthur Young was close to Dick Pamplin, the JCC secretary, and Reg Gale, and asked them to help the Representative Body become more like the Federation. The Government appointed Sir Edward Hunt, the Everest conqueror, to head an inquiry into the future of the RUC. It included Robert Mark, the Deputy Commissioner of the Metropolitan Police. Pamplin and his assistant, Tony Judge, went to Belfast and drafted the Representative Body's memorandum of evidence to the Hunt Committee. Among other suggestions, this proposed that the RUC should become an unarmed police force as soon as possible, and lose its paramilitary role as the guardian of the border with Eire. In this way lay the RUC's only opportunity of being able to police like a conventional force, seeking the consent of all sections of the community.

The Hunt Committee followed this course when it recommended that the RUC should be reformed along traditional lines. Its most controversial proposals were that the force should disarm, and that the 'B' Special Constables, a wholly Protestant force which was regarded with loathing by the minority Catholic population should be disbanded. The Report said that the force should be integrated with the rest of the United Kingdom as regards its conditions and disciplinary and promotion procedures. It should also become part of the negotiating machinery. There should be a police authority for Northern Ireland, and it was also suggested that there should be interchange facilities between the British police and Northern Ireland.

POLICE gave the Federation's reaction to the Hunt report:

> 'The Police Federation will want to look closely at the idea that current mutual aid schemes between forces might be extended to cover Northern Ireland. There can be no question of any 'reinforcements' from Britain being sent to Ulster in the present emergency.
>
> 'It was inevitable that most of the publicity given to the Report should concentrate upon the disarming of the force and the phasing out of the 'B' Specials, yet it is the internal reforms proposed by Hunt that will have the greater long term effect. Henceforth, the Royal Ulster Constabulary will owe its traditions to Sir Robert Peel rather than Sir Edward Carson.
>
> 'No one should get the impression that the changes are being forced on the RUC. The memorandum submitted by the Central Representative Body suggested many of the changes which have been embodied in the Report. The men of the RUC want nothing more than to be given the opportunity to be police officers in the accepted sense of the word.'

The Federation might have been more concerned about the possibility of its members being asked to serve in Ulster had it known at the time of Callaghan's ideas in this direction. In June 1970, Callaghan told Harold Wilson that he wanted to draft 1500 British police into the province in time for the annual Orange marches on the 12th July, when considerable trouble was expected. This was possible under the Police Act 1970. The request had been made by the Northern Ireland Home Affairs Minister, who was prepared to agree that if they came to Ulster, the British officers would be kept away from the marches and demonstrations and would not be required to operate the provinces' Special Powers Act, regarded by the catholics as the instrument of sectarian rule. Sir John Waldron, the Metropolitan Commissioner, told Callaghan that he would send officers if required to do so, but was adamant that they would be under the command of their own senior officers, not the RUC. It was also decided to draw police from Lancashire and Yorkshire, and Callaghan instructed the Home Office to consult the Police Federation. Before this could be done, the General Election result returned the Tories to power, and nothing more was heard of the plan.

Most of the Hunt Committee's proposals were implemented, although the period of a disarmed force was very short, and the interchange arrangements did not materialise. Some Metropolitan detectives did work briefly in Northern Ireland, but the introduction of Diplock Courts, sitting without juries, and the retention of special powers, made it all but impossible for non-Ulster officers to operate there. More than 200 RUC officers were murdered in the following twenty years and hundreds more were maimed in gun and bombing incidents. In that period, a tight bond formed between the RUC and the rest of the service, epitomised by the ceaseless fund raising of officers on the mainland for charities which cared for the disabled RUC officers and the families of those who have been murdered by terrorists. Every year, under the auspices of the City of London Police Federation, parties of widows and the children of murdered RUC officers have been brought over to Britain to enjoy holidays.

In May 1970 James Callaghan made his third and last appearance as Home Secretary at the Police Federation's Conference. While he was speaking to the delegates at

Llandudno, Harold Wilson was announcing the date of the election. The platform exchanges between Reg Gale and Callaghan were less acerbic than they had been the year before and Callaghan was surprisingly conciliatory on the prospect of securing a substantial pay increase before the end of the year.

The Home Secretary would not have been pleased to discover that as his train bore him back to London and the hustings, the Conference was endorsing a motion of no confidence in the way he had discharged his responsibilities for law and order. Delegates were upset about capital punishment, and the liberal emphasis of the Labour Government's Criminal Justice Act. The service also felt strongly about the Children and Young Persons Act of 1969, which stressed treatment rather than punishment for young offenders. In 1969, the House of Commons had voted to make the abolition of capital punishment permanent. In March 1970, Eldon Griffiths, MP, the Federation's Parliamentary adviser, had failed by only seven votes to obtain leave to introduce a private Bill which would have required that a murderer serving a life sentence for killing a police officer could not be released before the expiry of thirty years from the date of the sentence, except by order of the Home Secretary. The Bill attracted support from some Labour and Liberal MPs, and 173 members supported Griffiths. The 'no confidence' Conference motion was submitted by the Leeds branch board and it was carried against the strong opposition of the JCC. Naturally, it made embarrassing reading for the Government, and handed the Conservative party a weapon to use during the election campaign.

The 1970 Conference was the first at which delegates elected the central committees on a regional basis. There were eight regions, with London electing two members in each rank and the others one. Together with the three women members, this brought the membership of the JCC up to thirty.

Reginald Maudling was the Home Secretary in the new Conservative government. He was to prove a singularly ineffectual occupant of the post, showing little interest in the problems facing the service. There was general relief among the police in 1972 when Maudling resigned in the wake of the Poulson scandal of corruption in local and central government, following revelations of his business dealings with Poulson. One further consequence of the change of Government in 1970 was that Eldon Griffiths ceased to be the Federation's Parliamentary Adviser on taking up a junior ministerial post and the adviser's appointment went to a Labour MP, Alf Morris.

The closing months of the Sixties had seen the police manpower situation beginning to deteriorate rapidly. The 1968 pay agreement had not managed to keep police pay abreast with pay movements in general, and once again experienced officers were leaving the service for higher paid jobs in industry. The situation was bad enough to persuade the official side's negotiators, in January 1970, that there had to be an interim increase in pay before the 1970 review was due to take effect in September. This gave the police an eight and a half per cent increase, but even so, wastage continued to rise at an alarming rate. The actual strength was not falling, because 1970 was the beginning of the thirtieth anniversary of the wartime moratorium on recruiting, which began in 1940, and therefore very few officers would become eligible to retire on full pension until 1976.

The new Conservative Government faced growing law and order problems. Police strengths had grown by 11,000 during the six years of Labour Government, but the service was dealing with a huge increase in reported crime. Whereas the overall figures had increased by under 50 per cent in the Fifties, they doubled in the Sixties. Police wrote;

'The picture is frightening. The rate of increase in the Sixties was twice that of the Fifties. Are we facing the prospect of three million offences by 1980?'

The Federation saw the explosion of reported crime as a clear pointer to the need for further expansion of police numbers, but other influential police voices argued for more civilians rather than extra constables. Sir John Waldron, the Metropolitan Commissioner, who faced a 5,000 deficiency, said in his annual report for 1969;

'In looking to the future I hope to see a highly trained police force, perhaps of not much greater strength than at present, fully backed by a civilian support staff which will carry out all the tasks necessary to keep the trained policeman in the field ... ... I doubt if in an expanding industrial economy the police are entitled to expect more than their fair share of the labour market.'

The Chief Inspector of Constabulary, Sir Eric St Johnston, in his Annual Report for the year, was more optimistic about securing more officers;

'The way is now clear to make every effort to bring the police service up to full strength.'

Many chief constables did not share the Chief HMI's sanguine view. Walter Stansfield, the chief constable of Derbyshire, wrote to *POLICE* in 1970 to explain why he had supported an initiative by local tradesmen to employ private security firms to protect their premises. He pointed out that the county had seen crime rise from 8,000 offences in 1960 to 22,000 in 1969, and that the force was 337 shortage of its strength of 1500;

'... ... while the problem persists we simply could not give the service the public expects without the mobility provided by the Panda car.

'I am as anxious as anyone to see foot patrols operating with their many advantages, not least that of the public image of the policeman on the beat, but until the deficiencies in manpower have been overcome it would be irresponsible of me not to make the best use of our limited resources by ensuring that the men that are available are as mobile as possible.

'An officer in a Panda car does not have to spend all his duty time in the car. My officers are encouraged to park the car and patrol on foot as often as possible. That they are not able to do so as often as I would wish is indicative, I am advised, of the very many calls made upon them. How could it lead to greater efficiency to reduce the number of men in cars and put them on foot?

'My officers are already working overtime to try to bridge the gap between the number of officers needed and the number available. Until there is a really worthwhile gain in manpower extra tasks can only be undertaken by working still longer hours, which could impair health.

'There can be no question that I have delegated my responsibilities to private security organisations but it would be wholly wrong of me to deny the local Chamber of Trade the right to protect themselves whilst at the same time telling them I cannot deploy the officers required to provide the service that they and I would wish.'

The endemic police manpower problems during three decades of almost full employment had brought an end to the years of expecting foot patrol officers to ensure the security of all shops and factories on their beats at night. The private security industry was ready to provide this service to businesses willing to pay for it. Police chiefs were not all that unhappy about losing a manpower consuming chore which had hitherto been regarded as part of the service provided to the public.

TWENTY

Still more upheaval

The Federation saw a further increase in manpower as a first priority for the new Government. *POLICE* wrote:

'As the 1970 pay review approaches ... ... this may well be the last opportunity to tackle the manpower problem. The urgency of the situation is obvious.'

Concern at the rate of premature wastage had prompted the Home Office to survey the reasons why men and women were leaving the service. The survey was conducted by the Police Research and Development Branch, which asked several hundred former police officers to give their reasons for leaving the service. The survey found that a fifth of resignations was attributable to personal reasons, and that such officers would have left the service in any circumstances. Dissatisfaction with pay was the main reason advanced by another fifth, and a similar proportion said that they had left to take higher paid jobs elsewhere. One eighth of the men who resigned said it was because their wives disliked the disruption caused to family life. Others cited discontent about promotion prospects or dislike of shift work. The average age of resigning officers was 25 years, and most had about four years' service.

As the Federation and chief officers were digesting this information about the reasons for wastage, they received the results of another survey which had been commissioned by the Police Advisory Board. This was carried out by the Government Social Survey Department, and more than 3000 officers were interviewed. The survey was intended to assist the PAB working party which was drawing up a syllabus for man-management courses for supervisory officers.

The survey provided a unique profile of the police service at the end of the Sixties. Most serving officers had left school at 15, although about two thirds said they had gone on to some form of higher education and attained some educational or technical qualifications, and many had served a full industrial apprenticeship before joining the police. The great majority of police officers had lived in the force area for at least fifteen years. Three quarters of the respondents had served in the armed forces. Most of those interviewed were married, and said that their wives liked their husband's job, mainly because of the security of police employment.

About a quarter of those interviewed said that their children had been bullied at school because of their father's occupation. There was strong dislike of the requirement on county officers to move their homes frequently, because of the affect on family lives. Most officers disliked living in police houses and there was a strong desire for home ownership among all officers.

The survey found much dissatisfaction with the condition of police stations and offices, and a frequent complaint was of excessive paperwork and bureaucracy. Officers said that they relied on the unofficial grapevine for information about changes in the force, even where these affected them personally.

Four out of five officers told the interviewers they were hoping to be promoted above their current ranks, but only a third of the constables had passed the promotion examination. The promotion system was strongly criticised, with many alleging favouritism and discrimination against them. While two out of five said that they had found life in the police service better than they had expected it would be, half those interviewed said that they had seriously considered resigning at some point, although the vast majority expected to retire from the service with a pension.

The survey showed that morale was surprisingly high, considering the manpower and crime problems that the service was facing. There was not a great amount of criticism of supervisory officers and management, and most officers thought they were supported by their commanders. In future years when such surveys were conducted, it would be found that rank and file dissatisfaction with management style was a constant factor. Perhaps the contrast with this survey is explained by two factors; the high proportion of men with military service backgrounds, and the fact that this was still a time when accelerated promotion and the emphasis on training for higher ranks had not begun to produce senior officers with limited experience of the problems faced by operational constables. Whatever the shortcomings of the promotion and selection system which the Staff College has replaced, it does not appear that the senior officers of this period recorded the low approval ratings of some of their highly trained and well educated successors.

At the start of the 1970 Pay Review, Dick Pamplin, the staff side negotiator, set out his objectives. One was to reduce the period before a constable reached the top of the pay scale from nine years to six. He said in a letter to the official side that the constables arrived at a maximum efficiency level 'much earlier than has been previously thought'. The staff side, he said, would also be asking for three 'long service' increments instead of the current two, to recognise that fact that many constables could not be promoted. Pamplin also called for the abolition of age pointing in the constables scale, which he said had failed to achieve its purpose of attracting mature recruits, was resented by other constables, and was full of complex anomalies. The additional increment he called for would bring the optimum pay of a constable with 18 years' service to the minimum of the sergeants' scale. For other ranks, Pamplin said that the pay system had failed to recognise the value of the long service sergeants and inspectors who were unlikely to advance further up the ladder. They also should have long service increments.

In money terms, the claim submitted by the staff side was for a general increase of thirty five per cent. It called for the constable to start at £1,384, rising to £1,809 after six years, with long service increments. This compared with a current scale of £940 to £1,340 after nine years. The official side immediately said it was 'surprised and shocked' by the size of the claim. It said that wage rates had moved since the last pay review in 1968 by sixteen and a half per cent, of which the police had been given eight and a half per cent in the interim settlement.

The staff side argued that an increase of twenty five per cent was justified to take account of the extent to which police pay had fallen behind other occupations since the Royal Commission report in 1960. The further ten per cent, Pamplin said, took account of the 'vast increase' in police duties and responsibilities since 1960. The claim also embodied the staff side's wish to improve career structures and enhance differentials between the ranks.

The official side's counter proposal was to increase pay from September 1970 by ten and a half per cent. This was improved at a later meeting to twelve per cent. It agreed to reduce the incremental scale to six years, and conceded the additional long service increments for all three ranks, but the package was rejected by the staff side as totally in adequate.

After several months of wrangling, agreement was reached in February 1971. The official side conceded an average increase of sixteen per cent, with special boosts for constables after six, nine and thirteen years' service, and long service increments for the other ranks. The package included the offer of a detailed review of the problems of excessive overtime in the uniform branch and the CID.

The 1970 pay review was the largest increase to have been negotiated by the Police Council to date. It took the starting pay of a recruit from £900 to £1,023, rising to £1,458 after six years service, an increase of 22 per cent. The Federation welcomed the outcome, saying that all the federated ranks now had an improved career structure. It was also pleased to have secured such a sizeable increase at a time when the Conservative government was resisting 'excessive' wage claims in the public sector. A few weeks earlier, it had declared a State of Emergency after power workers went on strike over their pay demands. *POLICE* magazine said;

'The acid test of the agreement will be its affect on police manpower ... ... by weighting the award at precisely the points where the drain has been heaviest, it is hoped that experienced constables will feel it worth their while to remain in the service.'

Meanwhile, the Police Advisory Board was continuing to demonstrate its effectiveness as the progenitor of change in the service. 1970 saw the publication of the report of a working party on staff appraisal. The report began with an acknowledgment that, now that forces were larger, senior officers no longer had the intimate knowledge of all members of the force that was common before, which made a formal system of appraisal essential. It said that the object of staff appraisal was to provide the chief officer with information to help him to:

assess whether each officer was carrying out his duties efficiently or whether he was falling below acceptable levels of performance;

be aware of the capabilities of individual officers;

employ officers on the duties for which they were best suited;

identify officers suitable for promotion, including young officers worthy of early advancement;

identify the training needs of individuals.

The report said that each officer should be given the opportunity to have a regular discussion about his progress with a senior officer of at least divisional command level, and he should thus know at least what his immediate superiors thought of him, and also so that he could state his wishes concerning his future career.

The Federation was in favour of open and fair staff appraisal, although many members had their doubts and feared that it would lead to still more 'secret' files on officers. It was a major cause of complaint in the service that officers were not given access to their personal files, which contained information about their careers, reports from senior officers, and sometimes even anonymous letters about them. Officers were allowed to see only their personal records, which contained nothing more than such details as the date of joining, where they had served, and whether they had passed the promotion examination. In the working party, the Federation had argued for the new appraisal system to be open, with all officers being allowed to see their own appraisal reports. This view was opposed by the chief officers, who felt that if the report was going to be seen by the officer being appraised, the assessment would be less frank. The compromise reached was that the decision as to whether an officer could see the report should be left to each chief officer.

The report acknowledged that officers making assessments would require to be trained in staff appraisal procedures. As with so many ideas on management techniques that the police service was destined to experiment with throughout the Seventies and Eighties, staff appraisal originated in the United States. The PAB report accepted that appraisal was not without its dangers. Experience in the United States had shown that antagonism could occur between those who made the reports and those they reported on. It concluded;

'Staff appraisal should be designed to ensure job satisfaction and full use of the talents of the individual; increased efficiency should then result.'

In the outcome, the laudable objectives of this first staff appraisal scheme foundered on half hearted implementation and inadequate training for the appraisers. In later years, the system came to be regarded with widespread indifference and even contempt among most officers, especially those denied promotion or opportunities to work in specialist departments.

In 1974 another important report from the Police Advisory Board came out which dealt with rank structure and job evaluation. There had been some speculation that the working party would propose a reduction in the number of ranks in forces, and that the chief inspector rank would be abolished. The Report revealed a divergence of views. The technical working group recommended a five rank structure, but the uniform group favoured the retention of the six rank structure. It felt the chief inspector had to be retained to act as the deputy to superintendents in command of sub-divisions, and said that in sub-divisions below 150 in strength, chief inspectors should be in charge. This was the view accepted by the PAB when the report was considered.

The defeat of the Labour Government in 1970 had meant that for the time being the apparent threat to the police pensions scheme, posed by Labour's national superannuation plans, was removed. There was good news on the pensions front in 1971, when Parliament passed the Pensions (Increase) Act. It had long been a complaint of police pensioners that the purchasing power of their pensions was soon eroded after retirement, because of inflation. A succession of increases over the years had failed to keep pace with rising costs. The 1971 Act gave existing pensioners a substantial rise by bringing all public pensions up to 1969 levels, plus a further increase to account for inflation since then. It guaranteed that the purchasing power of public service pensions would be maintained by biennial increases. A further bonus was that pensions increases would henceforth apply from the age of 55 years, instead of sixty. The Act placed public service pensioners at a very distinct advantage over other occupational pensioners. No doubt Members of Parliament realised that they would be substantial beneficiaries through their own pensions. It was not until 1988 that Parliament required all private schemes to be inflation proofed, and even then there was no restrospective element.

Further improvements to the police pensions scheme followed in 1972, when agreement was reached in the Police Council on a new widows' pension. The impetus for change was the requirement that, in order to be exempted from the new state superannuation arrangements brought in by the Conservative government, occupational schemes must at least match its provisions The widow of an officer who died following the inception of the new scheme and had opted to 'buy in' previous service in order that his widow would benefit, would get one half of his pension, instead of one third. Police authorities paid one half of the cost of 'buying-in'. The changes improved childrens and dependants allowances, and there were substantial uplifts in injury provisions. The minimum qualifying period for the payment of a pension was cut from 10 years to five.

The changes also ended one major grievance among police officers. The hated three years averaging requirement, introduced by the Oaksey Committee in 1950, was abolished.

Instead, police pensions would be assessed according to pensionable pay in the last year of service, or whichever of the final three years gave the best result. Pamplin estimated that this change alone would mean an increase of 10 per cent in an officers' pension. It was also agreed to allow officers who retired on ordinary pensions before 30 years' service to commute if they wished to.

The cost of the improvements was considerable, and it was accepted that the contribution of male officers should go up from five and a quarter per cent to seven per cent, while women, who did not benefit from widows' pensions, would pay seven per cent.

Relations between the police and the growing coloured community in Britain was becoming a major social topic. In November 1971 a working party of the newly formed Police Training Council, which under the auspices of the Police Advisory Board oversaw all national training matters, reported on the training of police in race relations. The working party included two JCC members as well as senior officers, civil servants, and civilians with 'special knowledge of race relations in Britain'. The report recommended;

> police training should provide the recruit with factual information and an understanding of the nature of prejudice;

> forces with coloured communities should provide in-force training, including direct contacts with 'coloured people';

> police supervisors should understand the complexities of race relations and the police problems involved;

> courses for senior officers at the Police College should include race relations issues;

> instructors in race relations should be carefully selected and be experienced in policing multi-racial communities and should be trained in their role;

> police cadet training should include community relations;

there should be study tour opportunities to undertake study tours in the 'countries of origin of our immigrant groups' and police forces should consider whether use could be made of visiting police officers from those countries to train their officers, and for 'immigrant' liaison purposes;

conventional training methods should be supplemented where possible by direct contact between the police and immigrants, and role playing exercises.

Twenty years after the first settlement in Britain of people from the Caribbean and the Indian sub-continent, the police service was still thinking in terms of 'coloured immigration'. In 1958 the first 'race riot' had occurred in Notting Hill, London. In 1970, Notting Hill was the scene of a clash between police and marchers protesting against alleged police brutality towards black people. Several police officers were injured, and spokesmen for immigrant groups alleged that the police had used excessive force against the demonstrators. The event received extensive publicity in the media. Police commented;

'In any other place, the incident would have been a 24 hour wonder, but the Fleet Street feature writers and the television pundits saw the words: 'Notting Hill' in the headlines and reacted in all too predictable fashion. 'The picture which has been presented, as a result, is of an oppressed coloured community living in fear of the police jackboot, of blacks being beaten up in police stations, pushed around on the streets and being framed on phoney drugs charges.'

In 1971 the JCC submitted evidence to a Parliamentary Select Committee on Race Relations. It pointed out that the Federation had already sponsored two seminars on the subject, and had held discussions with all the bodies active in the race relations area. The memorandum stated;

'While the race relations problem is part of a far wider social problem relating to housing, employment and living standards, we are conscious that where these social problems apply to immigrants, particularly coloured immigrants, the blame may be attributed, often quite wrongly, to the colour of a man's skin. This is often exploited by alleged spokesmen for the immigrants, either through a mistaken interpretation of the situation, or wilfully.'

On the question of coloured police officers, the JCC told the MPs:

'We do not believe that there is any obstacle put in the way of coloured applicants. The shortage of manpower in many areas and the poor recruiting figures (despite high unemployment) make recruits, whatever the colour of their skin, most welcome, provided they are of the required physical and educational standards. We most strongly support chief officers who refuse to lower their recruiting standards.'

The Federation suggested that among the reasons for the failure to attract coloured recruits could be a reluctance by coloured people to apply, either because they feared being labelled 'Uncle Toms' by their own communities, or because they preferred better paid or 'less exacting' occupations. It added that the service should not seek to deploy black and Asian officers only in their 'own' areas, and urged that where such officers were unsatisfactory, they should be weeded out in the same way that white probationers would be, in spite of the risk of forces being accused of discrimination.

The memorandum urged better training for all probationers in sociology, including the cultural values of immigrants. It rejected the notion that there were more complaints against the police in immigrant areas than in others, and criticised the attitudes of many immigrant leaders. The Federation insisted:

'The Police Service has been second to none in its efforts to help the immigrant, to understand him, and to communicate with him.'

Finally, the Federation warned that 'so-called Black Power' was attracting young supporters;

> 'The fact is that we now have a large number of young coloured people who are to all practical purposes natives of this country. In the main, these young people have not been able to benefit from higher or further education, and are unlikely to get work after school in non-manual occupations. They are bound to attribute this to colour prejudice. It is urgently necessary that the Government pays extra attention to the problems of underprivileged (and therefore 'immigrant') areas, and special efforts are required to minimise discrimination in the employment field for young people. If this is not done, then it will no longer be possible to criticise the vociferous militants as being unrepresentative. On the contrary, they will be the leaders of the black and coloured peoples in Britain.'

In its Report, published in 1972, the Select Committee expressed concern about relations between the police and coloured communities, and recommended the introduction of an independent element into the procedure for investigating complaints. It suggested that independent tribunal might consider appeals from complainants or police officers who were dissatisfied with the outcome of a complaint. A Labour MP, Philip Whitehead, sought to do this through a Private Member's Bill, which he withdrew when the new Home Secretary, Robert Carr, told Parliament that the Government would consult the service and police authorities on arrangements for introducing an independent element into the procedure.

The PAB working party found itself sharply divided on what kind of an independent element, if any, should be added to the system. The Federation was totally opposed to any change. In February 1973, Carr told Parliament that the Government intended to bring in legislation to change the procedure so that there could be an independent ex *post facto* review where a complainant was dissatisfied. This proposal had been advanced by Robert Mark. It was opposed by the

Federation on the grounds that it could put an officer who had been the subject of an inquiry in 'double jeopardy'. Although the Home Secretary stressed that a charge against an officer would not be reopened, such an officer would still have his conduct examined a second time and might be required to answer questions again. If the independent inquiry found that the disciplinary decision had been wrong, the damage to an officer's career could be serious.

However, the JCC realised that the Government was serious about changing the system, and decided to submit its own proposals to the Home Secretary. It suggested the appointment for each force of a 'Police discipline adviser', an independent lawyer who would examine all complaints against the police of a non-criminal nature and advise the chief officer whether to bring a disciplinary charge. The adviser would be authorised to reject frivolous complaints. If a charge resulted, less serious offences could be dealt with by the chief officer, but for graver matters, in cases where the officer denied the charge, a tribunal would be appointed to hear the case and decide on guilt, with the punishment being imposed by the chief officer. An officer would have the right to appeal to the Crown Court against a tribunal's decision.

The JCC told the Home Secretary that its proposals would be simple to operate and need not be more expensive than the existing procedures. They protected the rights of police officers while meeting the requirement of an independent element. The proposals went much further towards satisfying the critics of internal investigations than the Government's proposals.

In April 1973 Robert Carr set up another working group to examine the complaints procedure. When it reported in March 1974 the Conservatives were out of office and Roy Jenkins was Home Secretary again. The report was unanimous in asserting that the investigation of complaints should remain in police hands and said that there was no practical alternative. There should be no interference with the Director of Public Prosecutions' role in deciding whether or not a police officer should be charged with a crime, arising from a complaint from the public. The chief constable's responsibility for the discipline of his force should not be under-mined. No police officer should be placed in jeopardy twice in respect of the same complaint. The role of the police authority in supervising the handling of complaints should not be diminished.

There was a sharp divergence of views among the service members of the working group over the Police Federation's proposals. ACPO and Sir Robert Mark flatly rejected the idea of a Police Discipline Adviser and hearings by tribunals.

In July 1974, Jenkins announced the new Government's proposals for dealing with complaints. They rejected the *ex post facto* ideas of Robert Mark and Robert Carr, and proposed a new independent body to oversee police investigations of complaints from the public. Jenkins told Parliament;

> 'An independent, effective element, commanding public confidence, must be brought into operation while a complaint is being dealt with, both before the decision is taken whether to bring disciplinary action and, in sufficiently serious cases, in the hearing of any disciplinary charge; it would not be sufficient merely to have some kind of inquest after the event, with no power, even retrospectively, to alter the outcome of the case. It is equally important to avoid bringing to bear a disproportionate weight of skilled resources on matters of a minor nature; the new arrangements should provide for the early identification and the expeditious handling by the police of intrinsically minor complaints.'

The plan proposed an independent statutory commission. It would be drawn from a national or regional panel. The initial investigation of a complaint would continue to be in police hands, and the D of PP would continue to decide on criminal matters. The report of the police investigating officer into a non-criminal complaint would be sent to the commission, which would decide whether disciplinary charges should be brought, or to let the deputy chief constable of the force dispose of less serious matters. If the complainant or the deputy chief constable disagreed with the commission's decision, the case would be re-examined by the commission. Serious disciplinary cases could be heard by a tribunal consisting of the chief constable and two members of the commission, or in lesser cases, by the chief constable sitting alone. Where an officer was found guilty of an offence, the punishment would be imposed by the chief officer.

The Government's decision angered Robert Mark, and he cited it as one of the two factors which prompted him, in 1976 to retire from the service (the other, he said frankly, was to safeguard his financial position). He claimed that the independent body would actually hinder him in his determination to root out wrongdoers. Mark, throughout his difficult but historic term in office, had fought a ceaseless battle to rid the force of its deeply corrupt element, which was concentrated in the CID, and to a large extent shielded by the complacency and incompetence of the hierarchy which Mark inherited from his predecessor. The criminality of the CID went to the highest reaches of the department, which had become a 'force within a force'. The extent of corruption had first been exposed by revelations in *The Times*, of all newspapers, of how some junior detectives blackmailed petty criminals and informants, but the real shock came with the arrests of senior officers, including two commanders. They had been controlling the hugely profitable pornography rackets in Soho. All received heavy prison sentences, although one commander had his conviction quashed on appeal. Other officers went to gaol in unrelated cases, but Mark and his deputy, Sir James Starritt, conducted a ruthless purge which saw about 200 CID officers of all ranks either dismissed following disciplinary hearings, or allowed to resign in a hurry.

The Commissioner made no bones about the fact that there had been more than an element of rough justice in the purge. He and Starritt gambled on the suspects' own guilty knowledge of what they had been doing. Such men dared not risk further investigation, especially of their bank balances and life styles, which were invariably well above their modest police salaries and allowances. Mark opposed the Jenkins plan because, he said, unscrupulous corrupt officers, aided by their bent lawyers (another of his targets), would easily pull the wool over the eyes of outsiders and lawyers on tribunals, who would insist on 'due process'.

Although the Federation and Mark disagreed about the complaints system, the Commissioner received total support from the Metropolitan branch boards in his drive against corruption. When approached by detectives who complained about the Commissioner's introduction of compulsory interchange between the CID and the uniform branch, Peter Joiner, the board secretary, told them bluntly that uniform officers were sick of seeing their branch used as a 'dustbin' for failed or suspect detectives.

The JCC saw that the Jenkins plan for complaints went along similar lines to its own proposals. In the consultation period before the changes were eventually embodied in the Police Act of 1976, the proposals were refined. The commission became the Police Complaints Board, and its first chairman was a distinguished academic, Sir Cyril Philips. In recognition of the co-operation he had received from the Federation, Jenkins acceded to a request that previous Home Secretaries had refused. He agreed that police officers should be entitled to copies of letters of complaint about them, and he permitted the Federation to change its fund rules to allow it to give financial support to officers suing for defamation arising from their duties.

Race relations and complaints were just two of the topics occupying much of the Federation's agenda in the Seventies. The 1972 report of a Police Training Council working party on probationer training proposed that the syllabus for recruits followed in the district training centres, that had evolved after the war and seen little change in subsequent years, should be revised completely. The working party found that current training did not reflect the changes in police methods and equipment that had taken place in recent years, and paid too little attention to the role of the police in society. It recommended that the thirteen weeks' initial training course should be cut to ten. The objects of the new course should be to equip the recruit with at least the minimum skills and knowledge he needed for beat duties; to build up his self confidence and ability to deal with the public; to impart a sound understanding of the role of the police in society; and to provide a basis for further training. Particular attention should be paid to the adequacy of first aid, communications and the preparation of files of evidence, and there should be no more than one drill period each week.

The Equal Pay Act 1970 was a short statute. One of its five clauses providing that police regulations should not discriminate between men and women officers in matters of pay and hours. It was only a few years earlier that the Federation had come round to accepting that women should receive equal pay instead of ninety per cent of the men's scales. Even so, the Bill when it appeared took both the JCC and the Parliamentary adviser, Eldon Griffiths, completely by surprise. What should have been a significant achievement for the Federation turned out in the end to be a benefit gained without the involvement of the body that represented the women officers. The reason why the policewomen were specifically provided for in the Bill, was that the police by this time was the only public service which had not adopted equal pay. The Police Council agreed that equal pay would be implemented as from the 1974 pay review.

Meanwhile, the 1972 pay review began inauspiciously for police hopes. When the sides met in September, R E Griffiths said that the Government had suggested to employers, that in the interests of curbing the high inflation that was prevailing at the time, all pay settlements should be subject to a ceiling of £2 a week. He said that the employers therefore felt that they could not offer the staff side the equivalent of the movement in the wage rates index over the previous two years, in accordance with the 1962 agreement. He added that the Government's action could be construed as conforming to that part of the agreement which said that discounts could be made from any police pay rise because of 'general economic factors which affected the police to the same extent as the rest of the community'.

Pamplin launched a strong attack on the official side. He pointed out that no one in the community had yet been affected by the government's 'suggested' £2 limit, because no negotiations had taken place for any other group since the suggestion was made. Police pay reviews took a restrospective view of what had happened in the previous two

years, and the figures demonstrated that all groups had
received substantial increases. Mindful of the way the Federation had used the media in the past, the official side had taken
the unusual step of issuing a press statement before this
meeting. In it, the employers gave a rosy picture of police
pay and manpower;

> 'The copper on the beat, the average British police
> constable, is now earning £40 a week, and in London
> a Detective Chief Inspector is on the £90 mark. These
> are just two of the latest figures released in a survey
> of average earnings amongst 100,000 police officers
> made on behalf of the Official Side of the Police
> Council ... ... these total earnings take account of free
> accommodation for the man and his family, or else a
> tax-free rent allowance, which averages £6 per week
> and £8.50 in London.
>
> 'Present trends in recruitment and wastage are
> satisfactory and give no cause for concern, except in
> one or two difficult areas.'

The figures arrived at by the official side survey not only
took account of rent allowance, they included overtime and
rest day working. The 'average' London constable was working 47.7 hours a week against the national average week of
40 hours in all occupations.

The immediate reaction of Pamplin and Gale was to
demand a meeting with the Home Secretary. They found
Robert Carr sympathetic, if guarded. Pamplin strongly suspected that the coincidence of the police negotiations
coinciding with the Government's attempt to impose a
voluntary limit on pay rises was being exploited by Labour
councillors on the official side, in order to embarrass ministers
who professed strong support for the police, and that R E
Griffiths was not averse to causing a little annoyance to a
group which he considered to have been favourably treated
over the years.

When the talks resumed at the end of October, it was clear
that the Home Office representatives on the official side had
been given fresh orders by the Home Secretary. Agreement
was reached quickly on an increase of 15 per cent. The new

starting rate for a constable was £1,251 a year, rising to £2,061 after 17 years' service. Substantial as it was, the award feel well short of the 30 per cent movement in the wages index over the previous two years, even when account was taken of the six per cent interim increase which had been paid in 1971. Just a week after the pay settlement was reached, the Government announced that it was imposing an immediate freeze on all pay negotiations and pending awards.

Although only a few years had elapsed since the major reorganisation of forces had been completed early in the Seventies the service was faced with another round of re-organisation following the report of the Redcliffe-Maud Committee which proposed major changes in the pattern of local government. The Conservative Government announced that six new metropolitan county councils would be created, to provide area wide services in the major conurbations. This entailed consequential reorganisation of many other county councils and the local government map of England and Wales was virtually redrawn. Although the Redcliffe Maud Committee had spent little time on considering the impact of its proposals on the police service, its proposals, and the Government's decision, meant that police forces would have to conform to the new pattern of local government. The decision meant the end of the remaining city police forces, except for the City of London.

The Federation published its own response to the Redcliffe Maud proposals just before the Government made its decision. It called for a system of regional police administration, but with existing forces retaining their separate identities. The proposals mirrored the ideas which the Federation had put to the Royal Commission in 1962. They called for regional police commanders, and said that there should be no local authority control of forces, except at the regional level. On finance, the Federation wanted the current equal split of policing costs to be revised to 75 per cent exchequer contri-bution, and 25 per cent from local rates. This would reduce local political control of the police.

The 1971 Conference was strongly opposed to the Redcliffe Maud proposals and endorsed the JCC plan for a regional structure, but the Federation was alone in making the proposal. It came as no surprise when in October 1971, the Home Secretary, Reginald Maudling, rejected the idea of a regional structure. In a letter to Dick Pamplin, Maudling said;

> 'I entirely accept the need to keep disturbance to a minimum and have given careful consideration to the Federation's proposals, under which existing force areas would largely be preserved, and grouped in a regional structure. I have, however, reached the conclusion that the boundaries of police areas should continue to coincide with the boundaries of local authority areas. In coming to this conclusion I have been influenced primarily by the desirability of retaining the close link between the police service and local government. This link is not as strong nowadays as would in some ways be desirable and in my view it would be weakened to an unacceptable degree if the Federation's proposals were adopted.'

The Federation kept up its opposition, and Dick Pamplin wrote to every member of the House of Commons Committee which examined the Local Government Bill. He had already managed to persuade two Conservative and one Labour member to table an amendment in the Committee stage which would have allowed parts of police areas to be merged, rather than only entire forces. This, in the Federation's view, would have produced a more rational pattern than simply following the new local government boundaries. The branch boards weighed in with letters and deputations to local MPs and when the amendment came before the Committee the vote resulted in a dead heat, with the chairman following tradition and giving the casting vote against it. It was the closest the Federation was to get to scuppering the Government plan.

This second restructuring of police forces in a decade resulted in 1974 in 43 forces in England and Wales, including the six new metropolitan forces. The latter were to prove more durable than the unpopular metropolitan county councils, which were abolished in 1986.

In 1971 the Metropolitan branch board approached the JCC yet again on the question of a higher rate of pay for London members. This came about largely because Dick Pamplin was wearing several hats. Not only was he the secretary of the Joint Central Committee and staff side secretary, he was the chairman of the Metropolitan branch board. In the latter capacity, he had addressed Reginald Maudling at the previous annual meeting of the board and said, that to improve its manpower situation, there was a need for an 'immediate injection of pay into the Metropolitan Police'. Pamplin had then asked Maudling to do what he knew the JCC could not be expected to do, to place the question of London pay on the Police Council agenda. When Pamplin's speech was published in Police Review, several branch boards sent letters of protest to the JCC.

At its meeting in November 1971 the JCC considered the letter from the Metropolitan board (it was written by the board secretary, Peter Joiner, who was also the treasurer of the Joint Central Committee). It soon became clear that the subject had lost none of its capacity to create discord in the Federation. Pamplin and Gale were anxious to prevent a repetition of past bitterness, and the chairman supported Pamplin's plea that the committee should at least let the issue go to the JCC's pay review sub-committee, which had the task of recommending what should form the basis of pay claims. He hoped, within this much smaller forum, that he could persuade the members to forward the question to the staff side. Where his predecessor, Arthur Evans, had faced opposition head on, Pamplin was a natural conciliator who saw that the only chance of securing a resolution of the London argument lay in persuasion and taking the heat out of the debate if at all possible. He was fully aware of the conflict of interests implicit in his holding the two posts, but he was in a position whereby he could decide when to apply pressure, as the London chairman, and when to cool matters down. The 'old guard' provincial members of the JCC who had gone through the rows of the Fifties were only too willing to get embroiled in the old conflict. Pamplin and Gale were equally determined that the Federation was not going to tear itself apart once more.

The committee rejected the move to refer the issue to the pay review sub-committee, and carried a motion saying that if the Metropolitan wanted to resurrect the London pay issue, the board should table a motion for annual conference. Significantly, when the vote was taken, only the London members opposed the motion, although a third of the JCC abstained.

The controversy did not end there, however, as several members of the Committee, notably Graham Elliott of Liverpool, the deputy secretary, considered that Pamplin was placing himself in an impossible position by retaining the Metropolitan chairmanship when the board was pursuing the London rate of pay claim. At the January 1972 meeting Elliott proposed a motion which 'regretted' the statements made by Pamplin at the Metropolitan annual meeting. Gale made it clear that this could only be interpreted as a vote of censure on Pamplin and if it was carried, he would have to resign as secretary. Several provincial members came to Pamplin's defence, saying the JCC could not dictate to the officers of branch boards. Elliott was obliged to withdraw the motion, but he persuaded the Committee to submit a motion to conference which repeated the policy of opposing pay differentiation and said that the Federation's staff side members must reject any proposals for higher pensionable pay for London 'which had not been presented by the staff side as part of a pay claim'. This was carried.

When the JCC motion was debated at the 1972 conference in Eastbourne,, the delegates voted by two to one to amend it to delete the proviso about an increase for London being part of a staff side claim. This left the Federation with a policy of outright opposition to the London rate of pay. Pamplin argued strongly, but without success, that this was wrong, because the Federation had already accepted the pensionable status of the existing London lead. Therefore, it was obliged to allow it to be negotiated as with any other part of the pay and allowances structure.

The 1972 Conference spent a lot of its time occupied with the constitution of the Federation. Dick Pamplin had prepared a blueprint for a restructured organisation which would embody much more professionalism than in the past. His proposals had been adopted by the JCC, but ran into strong opposition from the delegates to Conference. They rejected proposals that central committees should be elected for three years instead of annually, and to reduce the numbers of delegates to conference.

Pamplin's paper considered and rejected the idea of the Federation becoming a 'free association' which would have given it more freedom of action and association, but would have to become self financing. He called for the removal of the restrictions which prohibited the Federation from involving itself in matters of promotion and discipline affecting individuals, but the Conference rejected the change so far as promotion was concerned.

The closest vote was influenced by the controversy surrounding Pamplin's divided loyalties. Conference agreed, by a majority of 31 votes, that officers of the Joint Central Committee must not hold office on a branch board.

TWENTY-ONE

Pickets and pay codes

During the four years at the beginning of the Seventies when Edward Heath was Prime Minister, the police frequently found themselves in the middle of the conflict between the Government, intent on reforming the industrial relations laws, and the trades unions. Mass picketing was employed in a series of major strikes, including miners, dockers and steelworkers. A large number of police were hurt in clashes with striking dockers at Scunthorpe in Lincolnshire. It was at a Birmingham coke depot, in 1972 that the police first encountered Mr Arthur Scargill, the leader of the Yorkshire miners. He orchestrated the actions of thousands of miners who descended on the depot, which was supplying vital fuel to heavy industry in the West Midlands. By sheer force of numbers, the pickets secured a significant victory by forcing Sir Derek Capper, the local chief constable, to order the operators of the Saltley coke depot to close the gates. Scargill declared that this was 'the greatest victory ever achieved by the working class'. The resultant damage to industrial production brought about a quick settlement of a miners' pay claim the Government had been determined to resist.

The Attorney General, Sir Peter Rawlinson, also saw the Saltley incident as a very significant event. He was furious, and in a major speech uttered a public rebuke to Sir Derek, reminding him and the rest of the chief constables that it was their duty to uphold the rule of law. While Capper retorted that he had acted in pursuance of his first duty, the protection of life, because he feared that a major tragedy could have occurred because of the crowd pressure being exerted by the pickets. Rawlinson, who was also angry because no police action had been taken in other disputes, where 'flying pickets' had caused thousands of pounds worth of damage to vehicles and property at other sites. said that in future he would expect that the ringleaders of any such attempt to prevent lawful business being conducted, would be charged with conspiracy.

Although the Federation was not permitted to be a part of the wider trade union movement, it had always enjoyed good relations with union leaders, something that James Callaghan had encouraged during his years with the JCC. Gale and Pamplin had private talks with Vic Feather, the TUC general secretary, and his deputy, Len Murray, to see if further pitched battles between police and pickets could be avoided. The TUC leaders were just as appalled as the police at the level of violence and damage which had occurred, but they had no locus in the conduct of strikes or the actions taken by TUC unions. Feather had made forthright condemnation of the conduct of the pickets, saying violence had no place in the practice of trades unionism. In a press article, he wrote;

> 'Peaceful picketing has been a lawful practice for 70 years, but assaulting policemen or anyone else is neither lawful nor justifiable. The police are people who are doing their job, and in the main they are trades unionists too. People who cannot control their emotions or their behaviour shouldn't go near a picket line.'

POLICE commented;

> 'It is time that every trade unionist realised that the police protect everyone's rights. If the rule of law starts to count for nothing in this country, the first victims of anarchy or dictatorship might well be the very people involved in industrial disputes. The 'right to work' means nothing in such a society. Does Jack Jones* remember that not so long ago his union was so worried about violence that it sent a deputation to the Home Office to demand greater police protection

---

*Leader of the Transport and General Workers Union, to which the dockers belonged.

for his members? Not strikers, but 'bus crews sick of being beaten up by mindless morons on late night buses'. To the victim of violence, it is immaterial whether his assailant was a man on strike or a youth on the beer.'

Alarmed by the public's reaction to scenes of battered policemen being led away from the picket lines to hospital, the TUC drew up a code of guidance on picketing, which recommended that the maximum number of pickets at any one place should not exceed six at one time. It was a well meant but pious exercise, because the code was virtually ignored in the major disputes that followed over the years.

Violence associated with strikes, together with football hooligans and clashes between racists and 'anti-fascists', public disorder was becoming a major problem for the police service.

In 1973, the use of the Special Constabulary was raised once more by the Federation. It told the Police Advisory Board that in some forces specials were working more hours than the average of four a week recommended in the 1967 report of the PAB working party on manpower. The Home Office agreed to send a reminder to chief constables that specials should be restricted to four hours duty a week, except during emergencies. They should also wear a distinctive shoulder flash indicating that they were specials, and they should not be allowed to wear the diced hatband on their uniform caps. At the same time, the Home Secretary reminded police authorities that he wanted to see more 'active' special constables, and there should be more coloured people among their ranks.

In January 1973, the JCC took a major step towards meeting the wishes of the Metropolitan branch board on the London rate of pay. The initiative came from the inspectors committee. which proposed that the Metropolitan members of the JCC should be given an opportunity to put their case to the committee. Peter Joiner said that the force had not been able to make any headway with its manpower problems, and was still working a 44 hour week. On average, constables and sergeants were working over fifty hours every week. In the board's view, the force would never get down to a five day week unless there was a substantial pay boost to attract recruits and stem wastage. He suggested that this should be at least £500 a year.

Although most of the provincial members, notably Graham Elliott, the deputy secretary, remained vehemently opposed to higher pay for London, the JCC was by now well aware that the Home Office and the official side regarded the Metropolitan Police as a special case. All other forces were making manpower gains. Gale and Pamplin knew that if the London members were given extra money in the teeth of opposition from their own Federation, it would probably lead to a permanent separation, and if that happened the long term losers would be the provincial forces.

The JCC agreed to meet the Metropolitan branch board to discuss the issue, and this meeting took place in April 1973. It resulted in a compromise in which the JCC agreed to sponsor a motion at the following month's annual conference, supporting a 'substantial' allowance for the Metropolitan, and the branch board agreed not to press its claim for the allowance to be pensionable. When the motion was debated at Blackpool in May, not only was the JCC backing an increase for London, support for the motion came from forces throughout the country. It was carried by an overwhelming majority, although the JCC knew that this level of provincial support had been obtained because of its pledge to Conference that it would oppose any attempt to make the London allowance pensionable.

The Government's pay policy was overshadowing all negotiations in 1973, giving rise to more strikes and demonstrations. The police found themselves on both sides of the divide, policing picket lines and marches while the Federation was faced with almost identical obstacles to securing pay improvements. When the Police Council agreed on an 'interim' increase for the police in September, it had to conform to the 'norm' laid down in the policy, of £1 a week plus a maximum of 4 per cent, in order to secure the endorsement of the Pay Board, a body set up by the Government to oversee negotiations. Although the interim increase had been secured without any difficulty from the official side, it caused a row in the staff side, with the constables urging that the global sum produced by the Government 'norm' should be redistributed among the federated ranks, to give a larger increase to lower paid constables. While the sergeants and inspectors would not agree to this during the 1973 negotiations, they did accept that the principle of redistribution should apply when the full pay review came due in 1974.

Earlier in 1973, the chairman of the Pay Board, Sir Frank Figgures invited trades unions and employers to submit evidence on pay relationships, both as between groups of employees and within occupations. The staff side saw this as an opportunity to seek a comprehensive review of police pay, the first since the Willink Royal Commission thirteen years earlier. Dick Pamplin submitted a lengthy memorandum to the Pay Board which was based on research undertaken by Professor Bill McCarthy of the Trade Union Pay Research Unit at Ruskin College, Oxford. The Home Office had been asked, in accordance with the restrictions placed on the Federation by the Police Act, to agree that the Federation could affiliate to the unit. To the Committee's surprise and annoyance, the Home Office replied that in view of the unit's links to the trade unions, it would not be appropriate for the Federation to affiliate.

The submission to the Pay Board claimed that police pay bargaining had failed to reflect the huge increase in duties and responsibilities of the police, although it had just about kept pace with the pay standards set by Willink. It pointed out that the Police Advisory Board had carried out a complete review of the rank structure in 1969, which had resulted in a reduction from nine ranks to seven. The PAB had also arrived at job descriptions for the revised ranks which, the staff side maintained, formed a basis for a substantial upward revision of pay. The official side had expressed sympathy, but nothing had been done, largely because the Government had intervened in pay negotiations to the extent that it had. Pamplin claimed that the imminent threat of a pay freeze had been detrimental to the 1972 pay negotiations, and had resulted in the police getting much less than their full entitlement.

Dealing with relativities between the police and other groups of workers, the memorandum acknowledged the difficulties of making accurate comparisons, but argued that unless some genuine attempt was made to assess what the pay of the police should be, in the light of changes in duties and outside pay, then the service would forever be plagued with manpower problems.

In a second and simultaneous submission to the Pay Board, Pamplin outlined a claim for a £500 a year non-pensionable allowance for the Metropolitan Police, to be paid in addition to existing pay and allowances. The pay legislation required that all such 'special case' claims needed to be approved by the Pay Board. Pamplin had hoped for an early resolution of the issue, arguing that the Metropolitan manpower situation had reached crisis proportions, and was disappointed when it became clear that the Pay Board would look at the police position as part of its general examination of pay in London, which was not due to be published until June 1974.

The official side also gave evidence to the Pay Board in support of additional payments for London. It agreed that there was a 'serious and deteriorating' manpower situation in the capital which was counter to the national trend. It attributed this to significant differences in the scope and pressures of police work in London and the provinces. The official side favoured a substantial increase in the existing London Allowance, while acknowledging that this might not be justified simply on the question of greater costs in London. It therefore hoped that the Pay Board would conclude, that besides compensating for additional costs, London allowances should take account of significant differences in job content between London and outside, and seek to deal with under-manning in a particular job.

Meanwhile, the London police gained some help when the public service London Weighting payments were extended to include them. The amount was abated to take account of rent allowance, but here also there was good news for the force. The board negotiated an agreement whereby the need for individual revaluations of owner occupied homes was replaced by a system of proportional assessment. The district valuer's assessment of the rental value of the 'typical' Metropolitan police house was calculated as a multiple of its rateable value. The same exercise could then be performed by the force, in respect of all owner occupied dwellings. The change brought about major increases in the individual rent allowances being paid, and was quickly taken up by almost every other force. It obviated the need for thousands of separate assessments performed, at great cost to police forces, by the valuers.

A long standing issue was settled in 1973, when the Police Council agreed that constables and sergeants should be able to opt between payment and time off as compensation for overtime. The agreement arose out of a Police Council examination of overtime which reported in 1971. The report recorded disagreement between the staff and official sides on the appropriate way to compensate the inspector ranks. The official side objected to paying chief inspectors for overtime because their rate of pay was above the level at which, in the rest of the public service, overtime was not paid. Their argument for not paying inspectors was that this rank was not under strength and therefore it was more sensible to give them time off than pay them. It agreed that some inspectors were in posts that required long hours, and suggested that they should be paid a commuted allowance. The same arguments were used when the 1973 negotiations on overtime took place. The staff side took the inspectors' case to the Police Arbitration Tribunal, which found in its favour.

In spite of the Government's firm clamp on wage bargaining and attempts to control prices, inflation remained a major problem. The situation led in 1973 to a system of 'threshold' increases by which police pay would rise by 40p weekly for each percentage point by which the Index of Retail Prices rose, above seven per cent. The threshold was first triggered in November 1973 and further payments were made as the Index continued to rise in 1974. The system, introduced by the Pay Board, was intended to protect wages against the effects of inflation, but were of course inflationary in themselves, and the government insisted that the 'threshold' payments could not be counted when basic rates of pay were negotiated.

As 1973 drew to a close, Britain was in the grip of the worst outbreak of industrial strife since the 1926 General Strike. Power workers and miners were on strike. The frequent interruption of energy supplies led to black-outs. The Conservative government was forced to introduce emergency legislation and require industry and commerce to operate a three day week in order to conserve energy. Mass picketing was causing disorder. Early in 1974, convinced that the national miners' strike was politically motivated, Edward Heath called a snap General Election on the issue of 'Who runs the country?' In February, the electorate gave him a dusty, if inconclusive answer, and Harold Wilson returned to Downing Street at the head of a party which did not command a majority in the House of Commons.

At the same time, the Federation lost its own leader. Reg Gale retired because of ill health. He had become the first full time chairman and on occasions had been controversial, such as when he suggested that the use of soft drugs should be decriminalised. When a Sunday newspaper splashed details of his private life across its front page (the story amounted to nothing more than an argument in a pub near his home) the force decided to take disciplinary proceedings, alleging that he had brought it into disrepute. Among his colleagues, there was a feeling that Gale was paying the price for having thrust the Federation to the forefront of the service, and adopting a high profile himself. In the end, he was able to retire in the normal way, but his treatment by the force and his chief constable was a sad finalé for a man who had been an outstanding leader of the Federation and a capable spokesman for the service. The new chairman was Sergeant Leslie Male of the West Midlands.

The Federation also needed to change its Parliamentary adviser. Alf Morris was appointed Minister for the Disabled in the new Government. He had been a quietly effective adviser and very popular with Federation members. The Federation did not rush to fill the post, in view of the new Government's uncertain future. When Labour secured a working majority in the October 1974 election, Eldon Griffiths was reappointed.

The Labour Government had been elected on the slogan of 'getting Britain back to work' and the miners' strike was quickly settled. Other groups, rejoicing in being freed from the straitjacket imposed by the Tory government, quickly followed the miners in securing big increases, and while industrial harmony now prevailed, inflation was beginning to rip once more. In June 1974, Pamplin spelt out the staff side's aims to Brian Rusbridge, who had replaced RE Griffiths as the official side negotiator. Pamplin said that the Government had already shown its willingness to treat some groups as special cases and argued that the police were in this category. He cited a vastly increased work load and the greater risks of violence now faced by the police, as two principal factors to justify a comprehensive look at police pay. The service had gained no reward from productivity and the restructuring of ranks, and could expect to face added problems in the future.

Rusbridge's reply showed that he was more of a conciliator than his predecessor, Griffiths. He told Pamplin that he hoped it would be possible to undertake the wide review the staff side wanted, and the official side intended to undertake a survey of current police earnings, and would consult him about the form it should take. He added that the official side would be ready to take full advantage of the provisions of the pay code, which permitted special increases for special cases.

A combination of a change of government and a new man leading the official side negotiators contributed to a swift settlement of the 1974 pay review in July. The agreement increased pay at each point of the scale by 7.7 per cent, the maximum permitted by the pay code, but the rise was boosted by 'unsocial hours' payments, also permitted by the code, of 9.1 per cent for constables, with other ranks getting lesser increases. In total, a constable's starting pay became £1,632, rising to £2,562 after 17 years. Some money had been found to allow higher increases for junior constables.

There was some criticism among the membership that the unsocial hours increases had been averaged out for each rank, when many members in administrative jobs were not working any unsocial hours themselves. The JCC justified this by saying that while paying the bonuses only to shift workers might seem fairer, it would have discriminated against a large section of the membership.

The agreement also provided that the two sides of the Police Council would conduct a comprehensive review of the whole structure of police pay, although it was agreed that implementation of such a review would depend on whatever statutory arrangements were then in place.

Once back at the Home Office, Roy Jenkins quickly demonstrated that he intended, as before, to press ahead with changing the police service. Addressing ACPO in July 1974, he called for the minimum starting age for constables to be cut from 19 years to eighteen, saying that some young people who left school at this age might not wish to go to university, but could join the police if allowed to do so at once. *POLICE* was not impressed, saying that not more than a handful of new recruits would fit such a description, and if this was the best argument Jenkins could find for lowering the age, he should concentrate on more important matters. The editorial added;

> 'It is not a question of whether a young man or woman can be considered mature enough to serve as a Constable at 19 but not at 18. Recruits are expected to assume responsibilities and powers that can only be discharged by people of maturity, whatever their ages. The overwhelming majority of constables, those doing the great bulk of the operational work of the service, and the group closest to the public, are young people. A difference of a few months in age may be insignificant, but has Mr Jenkins considered in full detail the affect on the cadet schemes? To lower the starting age for constables would mean that forces would no longer be able to run three year courses in which the maximum educational and other opportunities in current training programmes would be available.'

In the same ACPO address Jenkins signalled to the chief constables and the service that the new Government was serious about equal opportunities for women. He said that the service would have to adopt a policy of 'equal opportunities for men and women based on their individual personalities and regardless of their sex'. *POLICE* commented;

> 'If the police service is to follow the Home Secretary's advice it can do so only by abolishing all forms of distinction, including separate career structures and conditions of service. This would not necessarily be to the advantage of the small minority of women who join the service and remain until pensionable age. They have enjoyed favourable career opportunities until now. Some of them feel that their conditions of service will be worsened simply to provide the illusion of full sexual equality, in spite of the fact that common sense dictates that the great majority of policewomen have not joined the service for a career. Integration may prove in the long term to be in the best interests of the service, but policewomen have no history of militant feminism.'

But whether they wanted it or not, the policewomen were about to be emancipated.

TWENTY-TWO

A U-turn on London

In 1974, the Federation proposed to a working party of the Police Advisory Board that the existing code, which set out seventeen major and fifty subsidiary sins of commission or omission which a police officer could be accused of, should be scrapped. In its place, the Federation suggested that there should be a single offence of 'unprofessional' conduct. The idea was attacked by the chief constables, who said that if no specific offence was charged it would be easier for defaulters to escape the just consequences of their actions. There was no support for the Federation from any of the components of the PAB, and the idea was dropped. Years later, the discipline code came under fire for being too specific and legalistic, and chief officers alleged that its precision made it difficult to bring offenders to book.

The problem of overtime in the CID came before the Police Council once again in 1974. Ten years earlier, the Federation had proposed that the only way to deal fairly with the issue was to compensate detectives for extra duty in the same manner as uniform staff, but the official side, advised by chief constables, argued that most overtime in the CID was at the behest of the member who performed it, whereas all uniform overtime was authorised by a superior and subject to supervision. As the problem grew, the Council tried to ameliorate it by introducing supplementary detective duty allowances, based on the average hours of overtime performed by each CID rank in a quarter. This did not work, largely because of the anomalies it created between detectives in the same force, and also because the qualifying amounts of overtime came to be regarded as targets for detectives wishing to increase their income. In the 1974 negotiations, the official side conceded that the allowances should be swept away and detectives should be compensated in the same way as other officers.

The 1974 Conference was held in October instead of May, because of the force reorganisations of that year. Welcoming Roy Jenkins back to Federation affairs, Leslie Male in his chairman's address was concerned about the rapid deterioration in public order which was taking place at the time.

The Federation was concerned about suggestions that the Labour Government was thinking of changing the law on picketing, to allow pickets to stop and talk to drivers of vehicles seeking to enter premises where a strike was taking place. Earlier in 1975 the JCC officers had invited TUC leaders to a private dinner, where the Federation's worries about picket line violence were discussed. The union leaders had said that they wanted to do anything possible to ensure that picketing was peaceful, but complained that police did nothing to stop lorries from going through the lines, sometimes at high speed. This created frustration among the strikers, and led to a loss of control by union stewards. Of the proposition that pickets should have 'stop and cajole' powers, Male told Jenkins that it bordered on lunacy and would lead to more violence, not less. The Home Secretary did not mention the matter in his Conference address, but made it clear to cabinet colleagues who favoured the change, including Tony Benn, that he was against it. The law on picketing was not amended.

The country at this time was facing a much greater threat to law and order than the activities of pickets. 1974 was the year when the IRA stepped up its campaign of indiscriminate bomb attacks on the British mainland. The mass murders in Guildford and Birmingham shocked the nation and led immediately to the introduction of the Prevention of Terrorism Act. The alleged perpetrators of these atrocities were arrested and convicted, but the trials were followed by years of campaigning on their behalf, leading eventually to the quashing of all the convictions.

Jenkins devoted part of his speech to the 1974 Federation conference to sex equality. He acknowledged that the Federation and the other service associations were opposed to the full integration of women's conditions and duties, but refused to make concessions;

> 'The legislation we shall shortly introduce will apply to the police service as to other occupations. A Home Office Bill which excluded the major Home Office service would rightly be regarded as a piece of hypocrisy. But we do of course acknowledge that there are special problems for the police ... ... But let me express the firm hope that the police service will set an example to the rest of the community in adapting to a policy of equality of opportunity for men and women based on their individual capacities, personalities, and merit and regardless of their sex.'

The Federation's claim for a non-pensionable allowance of £500 a year for London members was considered by the Police Council in October 1974. The claim was in addition to the £74 pensionable London Weighting which the London members were now receiving. The Pay Board's Report on pay in London had been published earlier in the year, and the official side felt it had to follow suit with other occupations. Its final offer was £201, which represented London Weighting less the notional value of police housing or rent allowance. The official side said that they were willing to make the award a part of pensionable pay, but they accepted that this was not the current wish of the staff side. At the 1974 Conference, the Metropolitan board tried again to persuade the provincial forces that the award should be pensionable, and again the delegates rejected the idea by a big majority.

There was a surprising reversal of policy on the London issue when the JCC met in November 1974 .Pamplin pointed out that for the first time they were faced with an offer from the official side to make the allowance pensionable. All other public sector groups in London had a pensionable supplement. The committee was no longer debating whether it should submit a claim for the allowance to be pensionable, it was now refusing an official side offer to one section of the membership, and there would be no adverse affect on any other section. He was strongly supported by Leslie Male, who proposed that a delegate conference should be called for January 1975, at which the JCC would recommend that the allowance be made pensionable. There was little opposition to this view.

POLICE tried to explain the reasons behind the sudden change of policy;

> 'If rank and file members feel a little bewildered at the swiftness with which the JCC appears to have changed its long established policy on a pensionable lead for London this is understandable. Yet in deciding to recommend to the special delegate conference that the official side's offer to make the £201 London Weighting award pensionable should be accepted, the JCC is doing no more than bow to the inevitable. Any other decision would have left the police service isolated among all other public service groups working in London.'

The special conference debated the Committee's proposal at great length. There was little of the bitterness and divisiveness which had characterised all previous discussions of London pay, and it was noticeable that some of the forces which had led the opposition in the past, were now in favour of the change of policy. Despite this, when the vote was taken, the JCC motion was defeated by a large majority and the policy of opposing a pensionable lead for London was reaffirmed.

Immediately after the conference rose, the JCC met to consider the implications of its defeat. Pamplin argued that the vote made no difference to the committee's policy, but other members felt bound by it. Male proposed that the pensionable offer should be accepted, and an amendment was moved that the matter should 'lie on the table until after the annual conference in May'. This was carried.

Within two months of the Special Conference, the London allowance was made pensionable, with the Staff Side's concurrence. The Police Council met at the end of January, and the staff side, meeting before the full Council convened, was faced with a proposal from the Scottish Federation that the official side's offer to make the London allowance pensionable should be accepted. It was odd that the Scottish Federation should intervene thus in a matter concerning London, especially when the issue was so sensitive. The only explanation was that Pamplin and Male, having failed to persuade their own committee to ignore the decision of the special conference, needed the Scots to raise the question in the Police Council. If the matter had to wait until after the 1975 Conference, and even in the unlikely event of the decision going in favour of making the allowance pensionable, the London members would lose the operative date on offer, April 1974, and members retiring in the year would not have the allowance reflected in their pensions. The Scottish move tipped the balance, and by a majority the staff side accepted the offer Northern Ireland members, along with the London contingent and Les Male, voted with the majority.

The reaction of the provincial JCC members to the decision was predictable. At the JCC meeting in March 1975, the issue occupied one and a half days. A motion of censure on the staff side members was carried, but no resignations were called for. After all, it was JCC policy to make the allowance pensionable, and in seeking to defer the matter until it had been considered again by Conference, the JCC had been in danger of conceding something that it had always opposed - the power of Conference to make policy. In the end, London members had got their pensionable lead because there was no good reason why they should not have it, and the issue was dead and decently buried. The knavish Scots, it seemed, had got the English off an inconvenient hook.

It only remained for the matter to be discussed for one final time at Conference, and after a low key debate, the decision to accept the pensionable pay offer was carried by a narrow majority.

Another group of police officers who had been waiting a long time for a claim to be conceded, had their wish granted at the same time as the London allowance saga ended. The official side conceded that officers who, before joining the police, had served in the armed forces between 1939 and 1950, would be allowed to count half of their period in uniform towards their police pension. They were required to pay pensions contributions in respect of the period. However, solving this problem only led to another. The cut-off date of 1950 rankled with other officers whose military service fell outside the qualifying period. The date coincided with the concession granted to local government employees in 1950.

Also at this time, the employers conceded a claim to allow members retiring after 25 years' service to commute part of their pensions. However, when the staff side proposed that the pension contribution rate should be cut from 7 to 6 per cent, because police were being required to pay higher national insurance levies, for which they would not receive additional state benefits, the official side said that they would have to wait until the Government Actuary had reported on the scheme.

In April 1975, the staff side presented the employers with a claim for a massive increase in pay. This followed the report of the joint working party on pay. Putting its own interpretation on the working party's findings, the claim contained the biggest single uplift in pay ever demanded by the Federations. It called for the starting rate to be raised from £1,632 to £2,784, and for a top rate of £4,029 after 15 years, as against the current £2,562 after 17 years. Similar increases were claimed for the other ranks. If the size of the claim was not a big enough shock for the official side, there was more to come. The Federations wanted it to be treated as part of the 1974 pay review, because the joint examination had been agreed as part of those negotiations.

The working party's report found both sides in agreement that policing had undergone many changes since the Royal Commission of 1960-62. Workloads had risen, as had productivity. It accepted that the manpower deficiency was probably greater than that revealed by force establishments.

The official side's initial response to the claim was given at a meeting of the Police Council in May. As expected, it was not encouraging. An offer of 14 per cent was made but it came nowhere near to meeting the claim. It was based only on the movement of the wages index since the last review, with discounts, and did not address the outcome of the working party report. After an acrimonious discussion, in which it emerged that the official side would adhere to the letter of the Government's pay restraints, it was agreed that a further meeting would be held at the beginning of June.

Later in May, when Leslie Male delivered his Conference address at Blackpool, he told Roy Jenkins that the police were angry and frustrated over their pay position. He said that if a union had been treated as the police had been by their employers, a damaging strike would have followed.

In June, the Police Council reached a quick and unexpected settlement of the pay claim. The staff side was anxious to reach a deal before the anticipated Government announcement on further incomes restrictions, and there was a real fear that if this came before police pay was settled, the Federations would have to accept whatever limit the Government imposed on pay increases. The negotiators had to consider whether to go to arbitration, or accept an offer that came nowhere near their claim. The official side played it hard, saying that under the rules both sides had to agree to go to arbitration, and it was not prepared to do so until the review period expired in September. This would have delayed any arbitration hearing until Novemnber, and made it virtually certain that the police would be caught up in the new pay restraint rules.

The agreement gave all ranks increases that averaged around 25 per cent, but the negotiators came in for more criticism than praise. Large awards of this kind had become commonplace in all negotiations. The official side accepted that the cost of living had risen by 22 per cent since the 1974 pay review, but said that after deductions to take account of the interim award in 1973, recent improvements in overtime pay, and threshold payments, the police were only entitled to a 14 per cent increase.

In the circumstances, the staff side had done reasonably well in securing a higher award. The agreement meant that a Constable would start at £2,400 and his top pay would be £3,402, far below the £4,000 target set out in the claim. Pamplin's extravagant promises to the Conference were recalled, and the JCC was inundated with angry complaints from branch boards. The main criticism was that the Committee had given wide publicity to its claim and had built up expectations which had now been dashed.

The Federation did not have to endure the angry denunciations of disappointed members for very long. In July, with the national referendum on Europe safely out of the way, the Government issued the long awaited White Paper; *The attack on inflation*. This announced a new pay rise ceiling of £6 a week to apply immediately to every employee over the ensuing year. Those earning above £8,500 a year were to get no increase. Where groups had already settled on a higher award, it could be paid provided it was implemented by the 1st September. Had the staff side gone to arbitration, it would have lost the negotiated rise and police pay would have risen by a flat rate £312. From being the people who had sold the service down the river, the negotiators were now the wise men who had been so clever in settling when they did.

Dick Pamplin's successor as JCC and staff side secretary was Joe Martucci, also of the Metropolitan. He had no experience of national negotiations, but was about to be plunged into the middle of the biggest crisis in the short history of the Police Council. Martucci was not in any way similar to Pamplin. Where the latter had been a conciliator, Martucci prided himself on being a no-nonsense Yorkshireman. Personally a quiet and affable man, he lacked Pamplin's capacity for absorbing and understanding the minutiae of pay bargaining, with all its confusing statistics and relativities. Martucci felt that the Federation should employ professional experts to do this work, while he concentrated on presentation in the Council itself. To this end, he made full use of the research unit at Ruskin College, and also worked closely with Professor Ted Nevin of Swansea University, who had acted as an adviser to the constables' committee.

Martucci lacked Pamplin's patience and wanted quick results. He had no time for the niceties of the negotiating game. He put his case plainly, and looked for plain answers. He had attended only one Police Council meeting before taking over the negotiator's task, but it was enough to persuade him that neither the official side elected members, nor its permanent officials, could be trusted to put the interests of the police before the politics of the situation.

As soon as he assumed office, Martucci went with Les Male to see Jenkins in the Home Office. They were worried that the pay deal might be caught by the impending incomes policy, and warned the Home Secretary that he would have real trouble on his hands if this happened. This was backed up in a speech in Parliament by the Federation's adviser, Eldon Griffiths. The proviso in the White Paper which allowed groups with increases already agreed but not implemented to go ahead, may well have been written with the police in mind, as they were the only significant group that had not completed the current pay round. If so, it was the second time in ten years that Roy Jenkins had wrung such a concession out of his Cabinet colleagues.

The terms of the White Paper, however, caused Martucci and his advisers a lot of concern. The first phase of the new policy, with its £6 weekly limit, was to last for a year. The second phase was expected to be more restrictive, and the fear was that in 1976 the police would not be allowed an increase under the first phase of the pay policy. This apprehension was to prove to be well founded.

TWENTY-THREE

A call to the public

With pay settled for the time being following the 1975 agreement, the JCC turned its attention to the problems of law and order which were mounting at a significant rate. In particular, the committee was concerned about the number of assaults on police officers. Hooliganism had become a regular feature of the football season. For many years, the police role at matches had been concerned with crowd safety and traffic control. From the sixties onwards, outbreaks of mob violence at games, and among supporters on the way to and from grounds, became a major problem. From sending just a token force of officers to matches, senior officers found that finding hundreds of officers to deal with every league match on Saturdays and in mid-week was obligatory. The Federation called repeatedly for firmer action, criticising magistrates for failing to impose stiff penalties on offenders, and the clubs for inadequate preventive measures. More than once, the Federation said that chief officers should refuse to police some matches if they felt unable to ensure that there would be no violence, and called for the closing of grounds where disturbances were regular occurrences.

The Federation was out of sympathy with the penal policies of the Labour Government, although there was little comfort to be had from the Conservative opposition, which was supporting two major measures which were anathema to the Federation; the Bail Act, which required magistrates to exercise a presumption in favour of giving prisoners bail and; enlarging the scope of prison parole. Jenkins said that more than half the prison population consisted of remand prisoners who would not receive a custodial sentence when their cases were disposed of. He told the Magistrates Association that some prisoners, hearing the police object to bail, thought that this meant they could not get it. The Act's requirements would end this situation, and he intended to require magistrates to give reasons for refusing bail.

In an 'open letter' to the membership in November 1975, Les Male and Joe Martucci explained why the JCC had embarked on the campaign to focus public attention on crime. They said that the broad objectives of the campaign were to concentrate public concern on the volume of crime and the burdens thrown upon the police. Next it was intended to highlight violent crime, including attacks on the police. It asked about the effectiveness of the criminal justice system and the weak response of the courts. It called for changes in the rules of evidence, including alibis and the right to silence. It challenged the ambivalent attitudes of some politicians towards violence, especially where it was politically motivated, and it called on the 'silent majority' to be more assertive in support of the police and the rule of law.

The JCC appealed to branch boards to play an active role in the campaign by making approaches to local politicians and the press, and to local organisations such as chambers of trade, Rotary and youth clubs. Martucci told boards that the JCC was preparing briefings and publicity material to assist boards to make such approaches. The secretary went on:

'Members of Parliament who find themselves under pressure from their constituents to say where they stand on law and order will just have to take notice. So will local councillors. Magistrates will have to learn that they cannot dispense justice in a vacuum, impervious to the needs of the local communities ... ... Someone has to give the lead to ordinary people who want to see things change for the better. Who better than their local officers?'

The terms of the 'open letter', especially the references to putting pressure on MPs, upset a number of Labour back benchers. Robert Kilroy Silk, the Member for Ormskirk and a persistent critic of the police, put down a motion in the House of Commons which stated;

'... ... while recognising the difficult and often dangerous job of the police in combatting crime and violence,
and giving full support to them in the proper discharge
of their duties, this House regrets the announced
intention of the Police Federation to campaign against
certain aspects of the law, and believes that the police
force should retain and defend its long established
policy of non-interference in politics.'

The motion attracted strong support from other Labour
MPs. Kilroy Silk said that the Federation's campaign 'could
be a short road to the outrage of a police state'. Martucci
denied that the Federation was being party political and an
editorial in the *Sunday Telegraph* described the MPs
objections as absurd, adding:

'Mr Kilroy Silk and his friends seem anxious to give
law and order a mugging. Whose side are they on?'

Sir Robert Mark was equally concerned about the growth
of crime, and in November 1975 he told the annual meeting
of the Metropolitan Federation that there were only two ways
to make inroads into the 5,000 manpower deficiency in the
force. The first was a large increase in the force's pay lead
over the provinces. The other was to insist that all recruits
to the service spent their first three years in London or in
other hard pressed forces. In 1974, while there had been a
net gain of 1100 in the provinces, the Met had only expanded
by 71. Had it not been for the absorption of the airport police
at Heathrow, the force would have recorded a loss in strength
of 255.

The Federation agreed with Mark that the pensionable
London lead had not made inroads into the force's endemic
manpower problems, but said it was pointless to call for a
massive boost in London police pay when the £6 limit applied.
Mark said in his speech to the Metropolitan Federation that
for far too long the London policeman had been obliged to
bear the burden alone, but other chief constables retorted
that the Metropolitan had preferred to keep its members on
regular and excessive paid overtime rather than take ad-

vantage of the mutual aid arrangements by which forces came to the aid of hard pressed neighbours.

Sir Robert Mark and many other chief constables were pleased when in June 1975 the minimum age for recruits was reduced to eighteen years and nine months. The idea was that recruits of this age could undergo their ten weeks initial training and be ready to go on the streets before their nineteenth birthdays. The Federation stood out on its own against the change, and some years later was to feel vindicated when the Scarman report on the 1981 Brixton riots attributed some of the disorder to the fact that too many very young constables were on the streets.

The 29th December 1975 was a historic date for the police service, when separate establishments for men and women were combined in compliance with the Sex Discrimination Act. In future, men and women would compete on equal terms for entry to the service and for promotion and transfer to specialist departments. The policewomen's departments were dismantled. The service, including a large percentage of women officers, had hoped against hope that the police would be exempted from the Act, along with the armed forces, but the Government was adamant. Although the Act had already passed into law, the 1976 Conference debated a motion calling for the exclusion of the police from its provisions. It was defeated by just 27 votes in a total poll of over eight hundred.

Roy Jenkins made his final visit to a Federation Conference at Eastbourne in May 1976, shortly before he left British politics to become a European Commissioner. He took advantage of the occasion to deliver a lordly rebuke to the Federation for instituting its law and order campaign some months earlier. He agreed with Les Male that the crime situation was 'disquieting', but he said that crime was a continuing challenge, and there was no magical solution. He likened the fight against rising crime to rolling a heavy stone up a hill. Jenkins pointed out that no democratic society had conquered crime permanently. The Federation had de- manded stronger penalties, but Jenkins warned them that he could not argue for spending on the police to be a priority and at the same time call for greatly increased expenditure on prisons. The prison population was 41,000 and rising. This put strains on the prison service which in the long run would be insupportable. He added;

> 'If you want to push the prison population up towards 50,000 and beyond, the plain fact is that in a real world there will be less money to spend on the police, and none of my successors, of either party, will be able to preserve the full priority the police have recently enjoyed.'

He pointed out that Willie Whitelaw, the shadow Home Secretary, had just called for a smaller prison population for 'compassionate and economic reasons', and gave the Federation a blunt warning;

> 'Do not sneer at bail or the Bail Bill, or the parole system. If you do you will be extremely short sighted and damaging yourselves more than you think. We have to take the world as it is, not as we would like it to be. I therefore say to you - by all means emphasise the challenge of crime, and apply sceptical criticism to some approaches to it. But also be prepared first to look at the evidence and to recognise how little the widespread use of prison - no one of course is contesting the need for it for hard and dangerous men - reduces our crime or deals effectively with many of the individuals concerned.
>   'We all believe in the rule of law. But let us be clear what it means. It means the rule of *law*, not that of our own pet prejudices. It means, in a democratic society, the law as passed by an elected Parliament and applied by impartial courts. You cannot have a rule of law while dismissing with disparagement Parliament, the courts and those who practise in them. That is not the rule of law. Your job - and mine - is to uphold the law and not decry it. In your professional capacity you do this remarkably well. You command great public esteem. You are much needed. You have achieved great triumphs in the past year. If after five years as Home

Secretary I had one message for the police it would
be this: *Be more self confident and less self pitying.'*

It was a remarkable speech to such an audience. No Home
Secretary had ever come to the Federation Conference and
challenged head-on the most deeply held prejudices of the
service. It was also a rebuttal of Jenkins's critics in
Parliament and the media, and of the views of Eldon Griffiths
which were holding great sway with the JCC officers of the
time. Jenkins had paid the Federation the compliment of
analysing its law and order manifesto and presenting his
dissenting view. The speech was not designed to win a
standing ovation, but it caused many delegates to think and
it took the steam out of a campaign which, truth be told, had
laboured from the outset and attracted little support among
the wider membership of the Federation.

In any case, soon after Roy Jenkins had shaken the dust
of Whitehall from his shoes and handed the keys of the Home
Office to Merlyn Rees, the Government and the Federation
were at loggerheads in a totally different confrontation. This
time, the word 'crisis' could be applied without exaggeration
to a situation that was fraught with risk.

TWENTY-FOUR

Police pay is a crime!

In July 1976, the representatives of the Police Federations of England and Wales and Northern Ireland walked out of the first meeting of the Police Council called to discuss the 1976 Pay Review.

The immediate cause of the rift with the official side was its insistence that the negotiations must be conducted under the second phase of the Government's incomes policy, which would come into force on the same operative date as the police pay review, the 1st September. The Federations argued that the police had not been given the flat rate £6 weekly increase payable under the first phase, and that they were now entitled to it. The second phase imposed a limit of four and a half per cent for employees earning between £50 and £80 a week, and those above this level were restricted to £4 weekly. A recruit being paid £2,400 would 'lose' £182 a year and a top rate inspector on £4,395 would be £95 a year worse off.

The crux of the Federations' case was that the increase of around 25 per cent negotiated the previous year, was properly a part of the 1974 pay review, because it was partly based on the joint review of pay which was set up as part of the 1974 settlement. Police pay reviews, the Federations pointed out, were retrospective examinations of what had happened to pay rates during the previous two years. Therefore, the police were entitled to the £6 weekly, which other groups had received in the review period.

At the Police Council meeting, Martucci advanced this argument and challenged his opposite number, Brian Rusbridge, to say whether or not the official side thought that the police had received the first part of the pay policy limit, the £6. Rusbridge replied;

'The police, by special arrangement, last year received an amount of money which was not consistent with the £6. It was very considerably in excess. If you say, have you received in the current year the £6 in addition to that, the answer is 'No'. If you say, in the next settlement, will you receive the £6, the answer is 'No'.'

The staff side had met the previous day to discuss its tactics. Its pay sub-committee had reported that the official side was certain to reject the £6 claim and adhere to the incomes policy. The England and Wales and Northern Ireland members agreed that should this be the case, the official side should be given an ultimatum, saying that unless it agreed to take part in a direct approach to the Home Secretary, then the staff side would fail to recognise the Police Council as a negotiating body and seek direct negotiations with the Government. Martucci argued that if the Government was calling all the shots, and the official side was prepared to accept the 'voluntary' pay policy without question, there was no longer any point in talking to it.

The Scottish delegates were in a difficult position. They fully agreed with the claim for the £6, but Scotland was in the middle of the devolution debate, and the Scottish Federation was alarmed at the prospect of having to negotiate on its own, with the Scottish local authorities and St Andrew's House. Police in Scotland were well ahead of other occupations in the pay league, and it would be difficult to sustain that position if the case had to be made solely on Scottish terms. Only a month before the staff side meeting on pay, the Scottish Federation Conference had instructed its leadership that Scotland must remain in the Police Council. This was an understandable position for the Scottish Federation to take at the outset of what was to become a long campaign, but by remaining within the Police Council, the Scottish Federation enabled the Government and the official side to claim that the negotiating machinery was still functioning. As the Scottish Federation stayed on in the Police Council, so the patience of their colleagues in England and Wales and Northern Ireland wore thinner. The issue was not the distant and rapidly receding threat of Scottish independence, the issue was the solidarity of the three bodies representing the rank and file of the United Kingdom police service. Martucci, the staff side secretary, refused point blank to acknowledge the existence of Committee 'C' of the Council, which dealt with the federated ranks.

Immediately following the walk out, Martucci saw Roy Jenkins, who was still at the Home Office until his successor was appointed. He and his officials were taken by surprise, but AS 'Butch' Baker, the head of the Police Department, assured the Home Secretary that the rift was not serious. He (and the Inspectors of Constabulary) told Jenkins that Martucci, as a new staff side secretary, was flexing his muscles, and this would never have happened had Dick Pamplin still been in post. A similarly condescending and misconceived assessment of Martucci had been formed by the official side secretariat. The official side was convinced that the Federations of England and Wales and Northern Ireland would soon be back in the Police Council, if only because they had nowhere else to go.

The official side issued a press statement, regretting and deploring the 'ultimatum' which the two Federations had presented, and insisting that it would not accept it. The action taken, it said, 'is entirely inconsistent with the responsible attitudes shown by the federated ranks over the years and a great deal of damage has been done to the good relationship which has so patiently been built up over the long history of the Police Council'.

The Federation hit back at once through *POLICE:*

> 'If the official side cannot understand why the staff side has refused to play charades with them, that very lack of understanding is a good reason for walking out of the Council. The staff side has told them that no negotiation at all is better than the trappings of negotiation with nothing to negotiate. If they see their role as to nothing more than the messenger boys of Government, then it is to the Government that we must turn.'

POLICE said that the dispute went far beyond the immediate question of the £6 increase. The major issue now was the constitution of truly effective machinery;

> ... ... the philosophy underlying the Council was spelt
> out by the Oaksey Committee in 1949 and is now
> completely outdated. It is based on the belief that the
> police service, because it is unique, must have
> machinery which is restricted in a way that applies
> to no other group ... ... This may have been acceptable
> in 1953 but the whole area of industrial democracy
> has been transformed since then. The most significant
> change has been in the relationship between the
> Government and the TUC. The police are prohibited
> by law from association with the TUC or any outside
> bodies, yet decisions made by the Government and
> the TUC are imposed on the Police Federation.'

In September 1976 James Callaghan, who became Leader
of the Labour Party and Prime Minister after Harold Wilson's
unexpected resignation, chose Merlyn Rees to take over from
Roy Jenkins as Home Secretary, dashing expectations that
the post might go to Shirley Williams, a close colleague of
Jenkins. Rees had little in common with Roy Jenkins other
than his South Wales origins. Formerly a history teacher, he
had risen quietly in the Government ranks and had been
Secretary of State for Northern Ireland, where he was well
regarded by the security forces and detested by Ian Paisley
and the hard line Unionists. His links with the Federation
went back some years, and he had been a junior Home Office
minister. Politicians did not come nicer than Merlyn Rees,
but he knew that in appointing him to the Home Office at
such a time, Callaghan had handed him a bed of nails.

There was an unexpected change in the Federation's
leadership at this pivotal point in its history. Les Male decided
to retire two years earlier than expected, and his place was
filled by the vice-chairman, Jim Jardine of the Metropolitan.
Male had been a good chairman. Although lacking the
flamboyance and innovativeness of his predecessor, Reg Gale,
he had held the JCC together skilfully during the arguments
over London pay and worked in close harmony with Pamplin.

Jim Jardine was an unknown quantity to most of the
Federation membership. A Scot from the borders and an ex-

Military Policeman, he had extensive branch board experience but was not a public speaker and certainly not an extrovert. Nor would his best friends describe him as a profound thinker. At first he seemed a most unlikely choice for a role which was about to be thrust into the national spotlight for the first time. Martucci, his Metropolitan colleague, certainly had his doubts and would have preferred the more articulate and outgoing, but mercurial Inspector Basil Griffiths of South Wales, who had just succeeded Jardine as vice-chairman, to be the Federation's spokesman at this key stage. No sooner had Jardine taken over, than he fell ill and was advised by the force medical officer to take an extended rest. Martucci's immediate reaction was to tell Jardine bluntly that he needed a fit and active chairman to be in the office every day, and he suggested that Jardine should stand down. Shocked, Jardine told his colleagues on the Metropolitan constables' board what Martucci had said. The board's reaction was instant. The members told Martucci that they were the people who had appointed both Jardine and he to the national committee, and Jardine was staying.

The Federation campaign began in September 1976 with a mass meeting at Central Hall, Westminster, scene of the Federation's first Conference fifty seven years earlier. Every seat was taken, and hundreds had to stand in the aisles. Outside the hall, almost as many police officers listened to relays of the speeches. Basil Griffiths, a fiery Welsh orator, whipped up the audience with a speech that promised a fighting campaign to take the police service 'into the 1980s'.

Martucci, making his first ever speech before a large audience, had to follow Griffiths's flights of oratory with a blunt warning to the membership, not to get carried away with heady talk of strikes or working to rule. The audience became restive as he reminded them that no one in the Federation had mentioned the word 'strike', in spite of widespread press speculation about a police service in revolt.

Martucci said that Merlyn Rees should intervene personally, and recalled that the Royal Commission had said that the Home Secretary must play a more direct role in negotiations. But he had no good news for his huge audience. The man in charge of their pay negotiations was telling them that they had nothing to rely upon except the goodwill of Government It was a depressing message and the meeting became something of a shambles as speakers from the floor called for affiliation to the TUC and the right to strike. Eldon Griffiths, MP, was the final speaker. He made a strong attack on the Government and the pay policy, but ran into trouble with the audience when he condemned the talk of striking.

The Joint Central Committee members were themselves surprised to see the depths of anger which the members felt about their pay. One reason for this was the manner in which the Government had capitulated in the face of a national strike by the seamen. In July their union had submitted a pay claim and had been told by the TUC that they were caught by the rule in the Government/TUC agreement that twelve months had to elapse between one pay rise and the next. At Central Hall, Martucci was scathing in comparing what had happened with the seamen and the Government's attitude to the police claim;

> 'I could mention hypocrisy, because that is what we are really talking about. What was the essential difference between the treatment of the seamen and the treatment of the police? We are back to that all important word - strike.'

Martucci wrote to Merlyn Rees in October setting out the Federation's case in full. He pointed out that in the recent review of police pay by the Police Council, the staff side had suggested that pay should be enhanced to compensate police for, among other things, travel to and from work on rest days, enhanced public holiday working payments; 'stand-by' duties, and compensation for changes in rest days. To these, he added, additional leave and reduced pensions contributions.

Martucci told Rees that the Federation had no confidence in the Police Council and had no intention of returning to it. It had been unresponsive to the staff side and refused to consider the police in isolation from other local government and public employment. Party politics had entered into its work and the presence of Home Office officials pre-empted discussions when they impinged on pay policies. Therefore, said Martucci, Rees should replace the Police Council with new machinery operating on the following broad principles;

> police pay should be financed entirely by central government, thus removing local government from the negotiations;

> negotiations should be based on advice from the civil service pay research system;

> the necessary analogues would be a matter for agreement, but the Federation was impressed with the work of the Wynn Parry Commission in the prison service, in setting out pay criteria;

> the Home Office representatives must have power to negotiate.

In November, Rees asked Jim Jardine to see him and Lord Harris, the Minister of State at the Home Office. They talked in general terms about the situation. Jardine told him that the Federation leadership was determined to hold out for direct negotiations with him, and Rees insisted that he could not do so because the Police Council was the only legal negotiating forum. He gave Jardine an envelope containing his considered reply to Martucci's demand for new negotiating machinery.

Rees rejected the idea that the official side had been unresponsive to the police. It had done no more than comply with Government policy. However, he was prepared to have an inquiry into the negotiating machinery. Well aware that Martucci and the Federation were really after another Willink exercise into pay, he stressed that the inquiry, in whatever form it took, would not be allowed to extend its work beyond the question of negotiating machinery.

Rees insisted that the police were entitled only to a Phase Two pay increase and urged Martucci to negotiate in the Police Council for such a rise. he rejected all the suggestions for 'fringe benefits' which Martucci had made, save a minor point about overtime.

Martucci's response was prompt and angry. He wrote to Rees;

> 'We were dismayed by the treatment of our represen-
> tatives who were summoned before you and Lord
> Harris at extremely short notice and presented with
> a complicated letter which they were expected to read
> and discuss without any previous indication of its
> contents. We find it hard to believe that a Minister
> of the Crown would deal with any other body of
> organised workers in this cursory fashion, and I am
> instructed to advise you that we not only resent this
> discourtesy, but regard it as further evidence in
> support of the complaint we made in our letter to you,
> namely that the Federation is still being treated in the
> manner of the 1920s.
> 'We are bitterly disappointed at the unsympathetic
> tone of your letter. This bears more resemblance to
> a civil servant's draft than a communication from a
> Secretary of State who bears a very special and
> personal responsibility to the men and women we
> represent.'

The letter went on to warn Rees that police morale was being undermined and militancy was rising. Martucci con-cluded;

> 'The Joint Central Committee will continue to do its
> best to resist calls for industrial action among
> policemen, but I am bound to tell you that our ability
> to do so depends on your being willing to cut through
> the unresponsiveness of your department and to show
> greater understanding.'

Martucci's warning on militancy in the service was not empty rhetoric. Thames Valley branch board held the first of what turned out to be many force referenda, asking officers if they wanted the right to strike. The result was a two to one majority in favour. Even the citadel of police conserva-tism, the City of London police, voted three to one in favour of the proposition. None of the ballots went on to ask officers if they would actually take such action, but press publicity for the ballots began to worry the authorities. Martucci and Jardine were seen by David McNee, Jim Callaghan's surprise choice to succeed Mark as Commissioner. He urged them to get the Federation back into the Police Council, and said that as London officers they both should realise that the Metropolitan stood to gain a lot from such a move. Sir John Nightingale, the chief constable of Essex and that year's President of ACPO, also thought it necessary to deliver a friendly warning to the Federation leaders that they were sailing close to the wind, so far as the penal provisions of the Police Act were concerned.

In December 1976 branch board members attended a House of Commons lobby in large numbers. They got a good response from Conservative members who were not at all averse to using the police dispute to embarrass the Labour Government, while warning the officers in the lobby that on no account must they go on strike. There was also some support from Labour MPs who opposed the Government's incomes policy.

In January and February 1977, Merlyn Rees and Robert Armstrong, the Permanent Secretary, held long meetings with Martucci and Jardine at the Home Office. Neither side was prepared to move from its original position, the Federation insisting on direct negotiations under Phase 1 with Rees and the Home Secretary reiterating the Government's insistence that only the Police Council could deal with pay. The pressure from the membership was increasing, and Eldon Griffiths informed the JCC at a special meeting in February that the Opposition was planning to table a motion calling on the Government to settle the dispute on terms 'not less generous' than those conceded to the seamen.

The meetings with Rees were unsatisfactory and frustrating encounters. More than once, Rees gave the impression that he did have power to negotiate, and thus encouraged Martucci had pursued the possibilities of a 'seamen' type settlement. Each time the meetings resumed, it was to find that the Home Secretary had shifted back to his original stance.

An extraordinary incident occurred at another such meeting on the 1st March, when Martucci and Jardine found that Rees was accompanied by the Scottish Secretary of State, Bruce Millan. They were informed that the chairman and secretary of the Scottish Police Federation were waiting in another room, and asked if there was any objection to their joining the discussion. Martucci retorted angrily that the Scottish Federation was not a party to the course of action being followed by his organisation and the Northern Ireland Police Federation (whose officers were not present). After the Scottish Secretary had departed, Martucci told Rees that the situation had deteriorated to a dangerous extent. The Federation leadership was doing its best to restrain an angry membership which felt that the service was being treated with contempt. Robert Armstrong urged the Federation leaders to be very careful, he even said that 'the Western world' would be astounded if the British police went on strike, and it would do enormous damage to Britain's reputation abroad. Rees offered to meet the entire JCC if Martucci and Jardine thought this might help. Finally, he asked for 48 hours to take advice from his Cabinet colleagues, after which he would be in a position to make some kind of offer.

The next day, the JCC heard a report on the latest Home Office meeting and resolved to send a final ultimatum to Rees. This told him that everything depended on what he would say to Martucci the next day. The JCC would not recommend any offer to the membership that did not 'materially improve' pay and conditions. Any such offer must be implemented immediately, and contain provision for further advances under the next stage of the policy. If no satisfactory offer was forthcoming, the JCC would on the following day;

'reach a final decision on the current pay dispute and on such further action as may become necessary'

The JCC was careful to avoid any reference to strike action. In fact, all the Committee had decided to do was to plan a national advertising campaign, using a London firm of public relations advisers. The Committee had been concerned to be told by Martucci that the advice of leading counsel was that Section 53 of the Police Act, which prescribed a penalty of two years' in gaol for any action 'calculated to cause disaffection' could apply to any act which resulted in a strike or other form of industrial action, whether or not such a consequence had been intended.

When Martucci and Jardine went to the Home Office on the 3rd March, they fully expected to get an offer from Rees which they could take back to the Committee, at least as a basis for negotiations. As soon as they entered the Home Secretary's room he informed them that he had just finished meeting a deputation from the local authorities, led by Brian Rusbridge, at which they had insisted that he was acting illegally in attempting to negotiate with the Federation outside the Police Council. However, the Prime Minister, James Callaghan, had agreed to meet them as representatives of the staff side in Downing Street on the following Monday, the 7th March. Martucci said this was a blatant attempt to force the Federation back into the Police Council, and if the Prime Minister would only meet them in that capacity, then there would be no meeting. Following a hasty call to Downing Street, the message came back that Callaghan would see them as the officers of the Police Federation.

Immediately after reporting back to the JCC, who agreed that Martucci and other members of the executive would attend the meeting on the Monday, the JCC issued a press statement which condemned Rees for yielding to the pressures of the local authorities and saying he had turned a complete somersault. In view of this, the Committee said, it had decided;

> 'to seek the repeal of all prohibitions placed by the Police Act 1964 on the Federation's freedom of action, and the enactment of legislation to grant to the Federation similar status and protection as that afforded to trade unions under the Trade Unions and Labour Relations Act 1974; and;

> 'to decline all further co-operation in the implementation of the Police Act 1976 in relation to complaints;

and all further co-operation in the various committees affecting the police service.'

The statement went on to call on members of the Federation to fulfil their duties with loyalty, and concluded;

'We have been treated with contempt by an authority well aware of the repugnance felt by all our members against any idea of taking industrial action; an authority which refuses to pay heed to our case because of the impossible position in which the police find themselves in disputes affecting their pay and conditions.'

Had some members of the committee, around half a dozen altogether, had their way, the statement would have made a direct reference to the right of a police officer to take strike action, but the great majority of the committee felt that the statement as drafted, was as far as they dared go. Even so, there were some members of the committee who were privately appalled at the views being expressed by the minority, and when these misgivings became known outside the Committee, they fuelled press speculation about the possibility of a police revolt and rumours of 'reds' in the Police Federation. Ironically, with a couple of exceptions, those wanting to follow a militant line were staunch Tories. One, Basil Griffiths, became a Tory constituency agent when he retired some years later. Jardine, when he retired, stood for election as a Tory councillor.

When the leaders of the Federations of England and Wales and Northern Ireland arrived at 10 Downing Street on following Monday morning, they found that the chairman and secretary of the Scottish Police Federation had also been invited to the meeting. The Scottish Federation was still adamant about staying in the Police Council, and had just rejected further pleas from their brother associations to show solidarity.

As they faced each other across the table in the Cabinet Room, the Federation leaders and the Prime Minister must have reflected on an earlier fateful gathering in that room in 1918, when Lloyd George had capitulated to the Police

Union. The essential difference between then and now, of course, was that in 1918 nearly every constable and sergeant in the Metropolitan Police was on strike.

It was thirteen years since Callaghan had led the Federation's fight for better conditions, now he was confronting the police leaders and telling them he had nothing to offer. The Prime Minister delivered a short lecture, in which his message was simply; 'Get back into the Police Council, you have nowhere else to go.' This was, after all, the man who had so unerringly pinpointed the weaknesses of the same Council, and its constitutional incapability of acting as an independent negotiating chamber for the police service; the man who had described the local authority councillors as the worst employers in the country. He was also the man who had connived with Rab Butler to secure an independent inquiry into police pay. Now he stressed that the upcoming inquiry into the negotiating machinery would not be allowed to look at pay and conditions, so the Federation could forget that line of approach. The tone was bullying and infinitely depressing for the police representatives.

In response, Martucci insisted that everything the JCC had done had been strictly in accordance with legality. Callaghan had declared that there could be no exceptions to the incomes policy. How did that square with the seamen?

Disappointed and disgusted, the Federation leaders went with Eldon Griffiths on the same day to see the new Tory leader, Margaret Thatcher, and the shadow Home Secretary, Willie Whitelaw. Thatcher professed astonishment when told of Callaghan's statements. She suggested that one way out of the impasse was to pay an additional award to the police because of the unique dangers they faced.

Joe Martucci was in an especially angry mood when he faced the JCC members that day. He felt that Home Office officials, notably 'Butch' Baker, and some chief officers, had now decided that the only way to force the Federation to abandon its stance and return to the constitutional path was to get rid of Martucci himself. It was being reported back to him that chief constables were talking to their own branch board officials and suggesting that Martucci was becoming a dangerous liability. He and Jardine were coming under pressure from their own constables' branch board, whose officials had been told by McNee that the two were standing in the way of a possible solution which would be very favourable to the undermanned Metropolitan. Already, a handful of branch boards had written to Martucci to urge him to settle on the official side's terms. Durham joint branch board had passed a motion of no confidence in the chairman and secretary and called for their resignations. Martucci was incensed that the weekly *Police Review* had turned itself into a mouthpiece for the Home Office and the official side. Its editor was a former *Sunday Times* reporter with little knowledge of the police service or understanding of the issues. It called for the Federation to return to negotiations, and said that there were offers on the table that the Federation, because of the 'Marxists' on its national executive, chose not to reveal to the membership.

There were cracks in the united front that the Federation sought to present to the Government and the public, but there was no disputing the fact that the membership as a whole was backing Martucci's refusal to settle for a Phase Two increase. Both sides were beginning to think in terms of the approaching Annual Conference in Scarborough. Rees had accepted the usual invitation to attend and address the conference, but had requested that no TV cameras should be in the hall during his visit. The JCC was worried about angry scenes and demonstrations against the Home Secretary.

On the 25th April, the Home Office forwarded to the Federation what was termed the official side's 'final offer'. This consisted of a general increase of 5 per cent, topped up with 5 per cent of average overtime plus allowances. This worked out at £2.30 a week for a recruit, rising to £3.26 after 15 years. The 'topping-up' gave constables 53p a week and sergeants 39p. The offer included 'forward commitments' to increase the annual leave of constables and sergeants by two days at some future date, and in the light of pay policy prevailing at the time.

The JCC promptly issued a total rejection of the package. In a press statement, it said;

'During Phase I and Phase 2 millions of workers have received total increases of between £8.50 and £10. The police are being offered, for the same period, a maximum of £4 and a minimum of £2.83.

'Acceptance of an award of this kind would merely take the steam out of the situation while not achieving anything for the lower paid constable.'

On the 29th April, the protagonists convened once more at the Home Office, with all present realising that this would be the last attempt to negotiate a settlement. Rees made it clear that the Government would not move any further. He said that the offer on the table had been resisted by the Employment Minister, Albert Booth and the TUC on the grounds that it breached Phase 2. The irony of a police pay offer being submitted by Government for the approval of the TUC, to which the Federation could not belong, was lost on Rees, but not on Martucci.

The JCC found itself divided when it met a week later to consider its position. Martucci said that it was inevitable that Rees would now lay a regulation before Parliament giving effect to the offer. The sergeants central committee thought that the Federation had done everything it could have done, and had at least secured the inquiry into the negotiating machinery. There was now a real risk that having been deprived of an increase under Phase I because of the timing, the police would also lose Phase 2 which was due to expire at the end of July. The sergeants expressed disappointment with the publicity campaign and said no more money should be spent in this way.

The constables central committee took a diametrically opposite view to that expressed by the sergeants. It demanded that the JCC should continue to reject the offer and call upon the membership to work strictly in accordance with police regulations. It said members should be urged not to volunteer for overtime on special occasions and football matches. The constables also suggested that there should be a 'mass march' on London, and a mass lobby of Parliament. Jack Kent of Greater Manchester, the constables' chairman, had emerged as the leading firebrand and was considered by Eldon

Griffiths to be potentially dangerous. Martucci and Jardine, both members of the constables committee, shared this view but realised that Kent was speaking for a large section of his membership. Kent, unlike the majority of his fellow constables on the JCC, was more interested in securing full trade union rights for the police than a pay increase.

The inspectors committee stood by the policy of continuing to reject the offer. The constables' proposal that members should be asked to work strictly according to regulations, and ban voluntary overtime was defeated by 18 votes to 12, but the JCC agreed that a further mass lobby of Parliament should be arranged. Somewhat surprisingly, the proposal for a mass march was carried by a wider margin, 23 votes to 7, although in the end no such event was held. The Federation was advised by the lawyers that the idea sailed too close to the prohibitions of the Police Act.

Early in May the Federation spent £3,600 of the £20,000 set aside for the publicity campaign on an advertisement in the *Daily Mail*. Using the campaign slogans *Police pay is a crime!* and *Up police pay - down crime*, it stated that many policemen were taking home less than £38 a week. Police morale was at a dangerous low ebb while the service was coping with two million reported crimes a year and sustaining more than 12,000 assaults annually. The advertisement asked readers to write to their MPs in support of the police case, and invited them to write to the Federation for car stickers. Within 3 days, more than 4,000 *Daily Mail* readers had applied for stickers. There was widespread coverage on TV and in the press for a rally in Trafalgar Square organised by the unofficial *Police wives support groups*, ironically the fore-runners of the women's support groups which played such a major role in the miners' strike six years later.

On the 17th May 1977, one week before the Federation Conference, Merlyn Rees informed Parliament that he had decided to impose a pay increase of 5 per cent. He said that discussions with the Federation had reached an impasse, but he offered an olive branch;

'... ... acceptance of the offer made on the 25th April (the 5 per cent award) would leave outstanding many

of the problems to which the Federation's representatives have drawn attention in recent discussions.
They argue that police pay has fallen significantly
behind the relationship to outside pay levels recommended by the Royal Commission in 1960; and they
consider that we should be taking account of the way
in which the pressures on the police have increased
since that time: for example, as a result of the increase
in crime and especially in crimes of violence. I cannot
commit myself at this stage to what it will or will not
be possible to do for the police in the next round of
pay policy, but my hope is that there will be scope for
greater flexibility, and I am anxious that we should
not be prevented from considering what may be
possible in future by an indefinite continuation of the
present impasse.'

Martucci, while privately relieved that he and the JCC
would not have to face Conference with the fate of the police
Phase 2 increase undecided, knew that this was not the time
to show any signs of weakening resolve. The Federation's
press statement was as uncompromising as ever;

'We are appalled by the Government's decision to stuff
down the throats of a freely elected body a pittance
which the entire service has already clearly indicated
is inadequate. The sum imposed still leaves large
numbers of constables in provincial forces struggling
to survive on less than £45 a week ... ... The question
now is, will this intensify the desire of the membership
for the right to strike and affiliate with the TUC?
'The Government is acting as a bully against a
responsible body of men and women because it knows
that at the moment they cannot by law take strike
action.'

In the meantime, the JCC members packed their bags
for Scarborough, and what promised to be the most fateful
Conference in the Federation's history.

TWENTY-FIVE

Scarborough flare-up

On the eve of the Scarborough conference, the Joint Central Committee held an emergency meeting. Martucci explained that Rees had acted within his legal powers in imposing the Phase 2 increase, and could not be challenged in the courts. The committee members were sharply divided on what they should do. There were motions on the Conference agenda which called for the right to withdraw labour, and to turn the Federation into a 'free association' affiliated to the TUC. The JCC had decided that it would ask for all such motions to be remitted for it to decide what to do, in the light of developments. Now a majority of the JCC, led by Basil Griffiths and Jack Kent, demanded that the JCC should change its policy and give support to the motions. Jardine had come very reluctantly to the same conclusion. For months he and Martucci had resisted such a course, but both felt a sense of personal betrayal and could see no way out. There appeared now to be not the slightest chance that police pay would be dealt with by the independent inquiry, and with Phase 3 of the incomes policy due to begin in weeks, the Federation was facing a humiliating return to the Police Council, or see Rees imposing the 1977 pay increase without regard for its views.

Eldon Griffiths, MP, made a powerful plea to the Committee to think of the consequences of backing the 'militants'. He accepted that Conference would certainly carry all the motions overwhelmingly, but the JCC, not Conference, was the statutory body that would have to answer for its actions. Its duty was to continue to fight for fair pay for the police. He said that Callaghan and Rees were calling the Federation's bluff, and promised that the Tory opposition would fight the

Home Secretary's order when it came before the House. Griffiths said that he doubted whether, in the end, the police would have the moral courage to withdraw their labour. It would lead to anarchy. 'Would you refuse to guard the Queen?' he asked.

After two hours of heated argument, Jardine put the issue to the vote, and the Committee decided to change its policy and support all the motions on the agenda. The rest of the meeting was devoted to discussing what the Committee could do to control the tempers of the delegates and observers at Conference. Rees had sent a message to say that he would still be coming and would address the Conference. The Committee had decided that it would not be practicable to ban the TV cameras from the hall, and in any case most members wanted them there. Jardine said that he would ask the stewards to eject anyone who misbehaved, but the JCC members had uncomfortable visions of uniformed officers from the local force being brought in to restore order.

Rees was due to address the Conference before lunch on the second day. The usual conference hall at Scarborough was being refurbished and the Federation was meeting in a converted cinema which seated over two thousand people, but was too small to house the number of police officers who wanted to witness the confrontation between Jardine and the Home Secretary. When the proceedings began, every seat was taken and hundreds were milling outside the entrance. No arrangements had been made for an overflow meeting, or to relay the speeches to the crowd in the street.

Jardine had to cope with 'points of order' from delegates who were concerned about what would happen when Rees spoke. A motion to go into closed session to enable the Conference to agree on a course of action, was carried. A large section of the delegates favoured a mass walk-out, others argued that an open show of discourtesy to a Cabinet minister and a guest of the Federation would forfeit public sympathy. An Essex delegate, Inspector Ted Davidson, proposed that as soon as Jardine sat down at the end of his speech, he should be given a 'tumultuous standing ovation'. The Home Secretary should be received in total silence. His speech would be neither interrupted nor applauded. By main-

taining a show of dignified silence, Davidson said, the
delegates would present the right image on television, and
the desired impact on public opinion would be achieved. This
course of action was agreed, but nobody thought to inform
the members from all over the country who were thronging
the entrances, unable to know what was going on inside the
hall.

When the small convoy of police cars carrying the Home
Secretary and his officials arrived, he was hurried inside by
anxious detectives and Special Branch officers, amid a chorus
of booing. This was a foretaste of what was to follow an hour
or so later. Rees looked tense and unhappy, like a man who
had realised at the last moment that he should have heeded
the advice of his officials and stayed in London. He was met
inside the hall by Jardine, who took him directly on to the
platform without telling him of what the Conference had
decided to do.

Jardine's speech recounted the ten months saga of the
dispute. He accused Rees of having failed the police service
by obeying the local authorities' veto on direct negotiations.
He demanded that Rees should confirm whether or not the
police were 'special', and said;

> 'We are special when it comes to doing something to
> support our pay demands. We cannot by law take
> industrial action. We are the police, a disciplined
> service, to whom special considerations apply. But we
> are not special when it comes to ensuring fair treat-
> ment on pay. Then we are tied hand and foot to what
> others decided when we were kept outside the door.'

But Jardine was ready to hold out the prospect of further
negotiations on pay, provided that the Government was
prepared to listen. He spelt out what the Federation was
seeking to achieve in the future;

> 'We have taken a stand on principle and we are not
> to be bought off with peanuts. Under Phase 3 we aim
> for nothing less than the achievement of pay standards
> which will, at long last, give us the proper reward for
> the job that we do.

'We want the full purchasing power of Willink to be restored. We want a proper career structure and decent differentials. We want our pay scales to recognise the unique personal dangers now faced by the police. We want our pay to reflect the police officer's constant commitment to the office of constable. We want our pay to acknowledge the contribution we have made to greater efficiency. We have always co-operated with new technology and it is time for that co-operation to be reflected in our pay.'

Jardine accepted that these aims would be difficult to achieve, but negotiations would have to be conducted by people with the real interests of the police service at heart, and that did not mean the official side of the Police Council. This was why it was imperative that new machinery was set up as quickly as possible. Jardine ended;

'You are not dealing with wreckers. You are dealing with a service made up of men and women who are still, in spite of all, devoted to and proud of being the police of Britain. Literally, their future is in your hands. For God's sake, do not fail again.'

After the audience had accorded Jardine his predetermined standing ovation, Rees rose to reply. His voice and manner betrayed the tension he was feeling, and to make things worse his civil servants had provided him with a woeful speech which hardly began to address the deep seated anger felt in the service. He began by giving the Government version of the dispute, pointing out that special arrangements had been made to allow the police pay increase to go through in September 1975 and insisting that because of this there could be no question of the police being entitled to the £6 weekly increase permissible under Phase 1. He claimed that under the White Paper the 1975 pay award had to be regarded as replacing the £6 that would otherwise have been paid. This was the first time that this had been said in public, and answered the point which Martucci had asked to be cleared up before the 1976 pay review had begun. What was clear was that no one had told the staff side at the time that the pay increase, based as it was on the Police Council's joint examination of pay in 1974, was instead of Phase 1.

Rees agreed that the police were 'special', but said that the Federation's pay ambitions could not be achieved all at once. He had offered a review of the negotiating machinery. Pointing out that the local authorities contributed 30 per cent of police costs, he said they would have to continue to be part of the machinery. The Federation had said that the Government should fund the entire cost of police pay, but that could lead to a national police force.

By this stage, it became obvious to Rees that the delegates were making a silent protest. His attempts to establish a rapport between himself and the audience produced no response. One or two people were openly reading newspapers as he spoke. He looked out across the stage to a sea of stony faces.

The Home Secretary turned to the resolution which the Conference had adopted, to seek the right to strike. To the surprise of some observers, and in spite of the JCC's last minute support, the motion calling for affiliation to the TUC had been defeated. Rees recalled that his father, a South Wales miner, had been out on strike for nine months in 1926, 'and they lost'. He said;

> 'You may feel that in the last few years, because you do not have the right to strike it has affected your position. I do not believe it. The right to strike has not been a significant factor in that time.'

Rees ended with a plea for reconciliation;

> 'A trade union exists to negotiate. Since September 1976 we have not negotiated properly. What matters to me is the next round. I repeat the Prime Minister's words that a police constable has to be put into the position that he once held. I accept that. It has all gone wrong. I want to play my part in getting us out of that situation but I cannot do it alone. I cannot do it unless I can work with you.'

Rees sat down amid the same complete silence. Jardine, looking as discomfited as his guest, muttered some perfunctory thanks and escorted the Home Secretary from the platform. Outside the hall, the crowd of policemen who had been unable to gain admittance had swelled, and too many had spent the previous couple of hours in the local pubs. They knew nothing of the silent demonstration that had just occurred, now they proceeded to ruin whatever good effect it might have had. As Rees emerged, a huge outburst of booing and verbal abuse greeted him. He and his officials had to force their way through the throng to the waiting cars. Special branch officers bundled Rees into the car and as it drove off, at least one man banged on the roof, yelling incoherently at the shaken Secretary of State. The scene lasted a few seconds, and all of it was captured on television for transmission in that evening's bulletins. As the Conference delegates inside were congratulating themselves on an impressive show of disciplined feeling, they had no way of knowing that their colleagues outside had become an unruly rabble, jostling the Secretary of State for the benefit of the media.

A few minutes later, Rees sat down to lunch with Jardine and the JCC officers in a private room in their hotel. Both men carefully avoided any reference to the tense and unprecedented scenes of the morning, and considering all the circumstances, the lunch passed off well. It did enough to convince the Home Secretary that the Federation leadership was not about to lead a mass march of striking police on Whitehall.

After Rees had left for London, the Federation leaders remained in the lunch room, taking stock. The mood was sombre. They knew that the treatment of Rees outside the hall had damaged their cause, but the long term worry was that there was no signpost showing the way to get out of the impasse. And there was no doubt that the level of anger in the service now posed a danger to police stability.

The JCC's post-Conference strategy was outlined in the next issue of *POLICE*;

'After Scarborough 1977 the Police Federation and

the police service will never be the same again.

'The past is past. What matters now is the future and at Conference our members glimpsed the future and will make it work.

'The first step forward can be taken with the inquiry into police negotiating machinery. Mr Rees can delay no longer in establishing the inquiry. The Police Federation will be putting forward its own views on why the Police Council has failed and should be buried. We will be proposing a new body in which the police can deal with the real decision makers, free of the Town Hall mandarins forever fearful of repercussions amongst the firemen, dustmen, and office cleaners for whom they also negotiate. We will be advocating an entirely new approach to the assessment of police pay standards and means of ensuring that standards, once set, are not eroded as Willink was wiped out.

'The second priority will be the longer term examination of the role and functions of the Police Federation. All our history has demonstrated that authority knew what it was doing all those years ago when it killed off free trades unionism in the police and replaced it with a pale imitation of genuine representation. It is astonishing how long the Federation survived, impervious to all the howling winds of industrial democracy blowing everywhere but in police stations. We have a constitution, imposed by Government, which skilfully exploits all the possibilities for division among the membership and withholds all the benefits of unity by a straitjacket of regulations.

'Here we are, a modern police service bursting with technology and efficiency, still saddled with a representative body which lacks even the mildest means of pursuing its cases, graciously permitted to make representations but never to negotiate on a basis of equality.

'Here we are, still singled out for specific exclusion from most, if not all, the benefits bestowed upon every group of workers in Acts of Parliament, designed to improve the employee's job security, working conditions and access to redress in cases of abuse.

'Here we are, still 'special' when it comes to withholding rights because we have 'special' responsibilities. Still not 'special' when it comes to enforcing pay restrictions.

'Here we are. But not for much longer. Scarborough has ensured that changes there will have to be, whether Government, local authorities, chief constables, like it or not. The police officer of today is no less loyal, not a jot less dedicated, than he has always been. But he is no longer going to be patronised and exploited at one and the same time. He wants his place in the sun, and he is going to get it.

'Come what may.'

Or, as 'Jedd', the magazine's incomparable resident cartoonist, put it;

'The Police Federation is like the recipient of a vasectomy - equipped with all the negotiating machinery but lacking the power to strike.'

TWENTY-SIX

Send for the judge

James Callaghan was furious at the Conference's treatment of Merlyn Rees. He felt that the Home Secretary had been the victim of a deliberate ploy to cause Rees and the Government maximum public humiliation. The Federation's former adviser had never liked being criticised on Conference platforms while he was Home Secretary, but he felt that the discourtesy shown to Rees was intolerable. Some months later, Jardine sent the Prime Minister an invitation to address the 1978 Federation Conference on the subject of 'law and order'. Callaghan replied formally to say that he had other engagements, but in an accompanying private note to Jardine, he expressed his resentment in plain terms. He told Jardine that while he was Prime Minister no Home Secretary would ever again attend the Conference. Some months later, Rees declined the usual invitation to address the 1978 Conference, giving the excuse that it would be held too near the expected publication of the Edmund-Davies report.

With Phase 3 of the incomes policy due to commence in September 1977, the official side was anxious that the Federations of England and Wales and Northern Ireland should take part in its discussions on the 1977 pay review. In July the Police Council met for its annual meeting, a hollow event when the representatives of ninety per cent of the service were missing. The Council decided to make a direct appeal to the absent Federations. It issued an invitation to them, either to participate as members of the Police Council, or on 'neutral ground' with an independent chairman. In its most conciliatory mood, the official side conceded that in the previous year the average earnings of the police had increased by only four per cent while the average in the country was eleven per cent. The statement said that both sides were now concentrating upon the identification of 'a proper rate' for the policeman's job in the light of his responsibilities, workload and productivity and the conditions under which he now worked. The statement added that 'particular regard' would be paid to changes in the policeman's job since the Willink Royal Commission of 1960, and expressed concern that, although unemployment was rising, the police were not recruiting enough men, especially mature officers, and wastage was rising.

Martucci was delighted by the Police Council's approach, because it showed the membership that Scarborough had not closed the door on further progress on the pay front, but now he and the Federations were gambling everything on persuading Callaghan and Rees to hand the pay issue over to the Edmund-Davies inquiry. If the Federation were to meet the Police Council, with or without an independent chairman, the chance of that would be gone. He sent back a curt note to Rusbridge and Joe Black of Scotland who was acting as the staff side secretary;

> 'I have to inform you of my Committee's resolve not to enter into any form of negotiations or discussions with the Police Council.'

The JCC members were annoyed that the Scottish Police Federation continued to take part in the Police Council. It was decided that the officers of the committee should approach the Scottish Federation directly. This meeting took place in August. Martucci told Joe Black, that his committee had completed the preparation of a major pay initiative, but he was not authorised by the JCC to divulge details to the Scottish Federation, because Scotland was still in the Police Council and he was determined that the official side would not learn the details before they were submitted to Government. Rees would certainly refuse to discuss the matter so long as the rump of the Police Council remained in being. The Scottish leaders, who were already under great pressure from their own members, agreed to come out of the Police Council.

The first action of the now united Federations was to submit a massive pay claim to Merlyn Rees and the Secretaries of State for Scotland and Northern Ireland. It demanded increases of between 78 and 104 per cent. The claim was set out in considerable detail and represented the work of Professor Ted Nevin, the trade union research unit at Ruskin College, Oxford, and Joe Martucci.

There were three elements of the claim. It sought to restore pay to the standards set by Willink seventeen years earlier; it included adjustments to take account of changes in duties and also the higher productivity achieved through technology and changed working methods, and it included an additional 10 per cent to take account of likely changes in outside earnings up to September 1978.

At the beginning of August, Rees announced that Lord Edmund-Davies, a Lord of Appeal, would head the Committee of Inquiry into police negotiating machinery. The Federation was pleased with the choice, as Martucci had recommended him for the task, on the advice of Professor Nevin.

The terms of reference of the Inquiry were;

'To review the machinery for negotiating those matters relating to the pay and conditions of the police service in the United Kingdom now dealt with by the Police Council, having regard to:

(i) the interests and responsibilities of all the recognised representative bodies for the police service;

(ii) the interests and responsibilities of the Secretaries of State and police authorities for the efficiency, good management and financing of the police service;

(iii) the special position of the police service as a disciplined service responsible for the maintenance of law and order.

The other members of the inquiry team were; Robert Leigh-Pemberton, chairman of the National Westminster Bank and a future Governor of the Bank of England; Cyril Plant, retired general secretary of the Inland Revenue Staff Association, and an old colleague of Callaghan's; Professor John Wood, Professor of Law at Sheffield University and an experienced industrial arbiter, and; Dr Ethel M Gray, principal of Craigie College of Education, Ayr.

The JCC realised that it would require assistance in the preparation of its evidence to the Edmund-Davies Committee and enlisted the services of Lord Wedderburn, an acknowledged expert in constitutional law. It had also brought in the Industrial Society to conduct a survey in forces, to seek the views of the service as to the form of representation they wanted in the future. Wedderburn and the Industrial Society would be investigating what changes in the law would be necessary in order to turn the Federation into an independent trade union within the terms of the Trade Union and Labour Relations Acts of 1974 and 1976. They would also consider how the police could benefit from all the other industrial relations and health and safety legislation of recent years.

Rees called Martucci and Jardine to the Home Office on the 12th September. They informed him that the Federation was as determined as ever not to return to the Police Council. Rees said that 'something had to be decided by someone, somewhere,' and he proposed to talk to the Federation again, when the official side would be in another room, and he would act as a broker. Martucci said that Rees could do this if he wished, but the Federations would not meet the local authorities face to face.

In October, the Federation stepped up its press campaign, in readiness for the expected talks with Rees. The row with the Government was, not surprisingly, a big issue at the Tory party conference at the beginning of the month, while Labour's conference ignored the dispute.

The JCC felt that the involvement of professional public relations firms had not been a great success, mainly because the Federation did not have the kind of money that such firms charged their usual clientele to mount a national campaign. It was decided to do the job 'in house', beginning with a series of advertisements in the most sympathetic newspapers; *The Daily Telegraph*; the *Daily Express* and the *Daily Mail*. These were prepared over a weekend in the Federation offices and rushed round to the papers, who made special arrangements to ensure they appeared on the morning of Monday 17th October. At a time when the print unions held sway in Fleet Street, this was some achievement. The advertisements featured dramatic pictures of policemen who had been injured in demonstrations, and used the slogan *One way to earn £40 a week*. They had an immediate impact, and in the following days television and newspapers featured the police pay issue, concentrating on the worsening manpower situation, rising crime, and dangers faced by the police.

The number of women being recruited was causing concern in the service. Some district training centres were reporting that more than half their intakes were women. The Federation argued that it made no sense to recruit so many women when they spent only three years on average as police officers. In an editorial, *POLICE* said;

> 'The climate of equality for all and Women's Liberation makes it difficult to discuss the police problem without being accused of chauvinism. The number of women officers has doubled since anti-discrimination legislation and the abolition of separate establishments for men and women.
>
> 'The rules have changed but the game remains the same. The decision makers in the police service failed to take a stand against absurdities which were manifest from the start. The advocates of female emancipation ran rings round those who doubted the wisdom of what was proposed. The result has been very satisfactory for a handful of career women, whose appointment to a top post provides the media with a nice little news item. In all other respects, it has failed.
>
> 'Women are still interested in getting married, being housewives, having children. Women are still leaving the police after two or three years' service. So it makes no kind of economic sense to go on recruiting more and more women.

'The stark truth is that the starting pay of a police constable appears to be just about adequate to attract young single women with no family responsibilities, but not young married men. The service has been all too ready to cash in on a rich vein of female recruitment, knowing that the male seam has been just about worked out.'

The total number of women police had risen from just under 6,000 in 1975, the last year before the Sex Discrimination Act, to 8,000 in 1977. Although women still represented only about 8 per cent of total strength, they were becoming a significant proportion of the junior constables most used for street duties. The Federation's unspoken concern was that the recruitment of women was obscuring the alarming drop in male recruitment and helping the Government to present a less disturbing picture of the manpower crisis. Their apprehensions about the rapid expansion in the numbers of women police were shared by Sir David McNee, who in his annual report for 1977, pointed out that women now constituted 22 per cent of the total of probationers in the Metropolitan Police, compared with 11 per cent three years earlier. McNee warned;

'If this striking change in the balance of the sexes in the force continues at the same rate in the future, it will affect significantly the ability of the force to meet its physical commitments. Even in these days of equal opportunity between the sexes, it would be out of the question in my opinion deliberately to employ women officers on duties in which they would be exposed to physical violence.'

In his Report for 1976 the Chief Inspector of Constabulary, Sir Colin Woods, was also worried about the imbalance between the sexes;

'The upsurge in recruiting (of women) has resulted in a large percentage of women officers being on probation. Recruitment of male officers, unfortunately, has not followed the same pattern and in some areas the proportion of women among those performing beat duties is much higher than the proportion of women in the force as a whole. A close watch is being kept on recruiting and wastage trends.'

Sir Colin noted that the first consequences of integrating the career structure of women officers with the men had been a reduction in the number of women holding supervisory ranks, especially sergeants and inspectors.

In October, Merlyn Rees found himself facing another huge and hostile Federation audience. The annual meeting of the Metropolitan Branch Boards was held at Central Hall, Westminster, which had seen so many Federation meetings. Its Great Hall was packed. Rees, sitting alongside Commissioner McNee on the platform, must have known that he was in for a rough reception, and while his presence testified to his bravery, it said less for the wisdom of those who had advised him to attend the meeting. The audience, already in a high state of excitement, was unaware that some senior officers were so alarmed about the prospects of violence, that two van loads of Special Patrol Group officers were parked round the corner from Central Hall, ready to break - up any disturbance.

This time, there was no repetition of the physical abuse which occurred at Scarborough, nor of the 'angry silence.' As soon as Rees rose to speak, the shouting began and as he plodded on with a speech which simply reiterated the Government's view of the pay issue, the volume of disagreement rose, forcing the Home Secretary to abandon his speech. The press was not invited to report the speeches, but outside the hall angry Metropolitan police officers were interviewed for the evening's television news bulletins and the next day's papers, all on the theme of a possible police strike.

The Central Hall meeting took place the night before Rees began a marathon session at the Home Office with the leaders of the Federations, and the local authorities, with both sides being kept apart. At the outset, Rees presented the Federations with a prepared statement. This acknowledged that it was important to establish a proper basis for police pay, and because the Federations would not negotiate within the Police Council, it would have to be done through an independent inquiry.

The statement went on to say that Rees had asked Lord Edmund-Davies to add the pay question to the terms of reference of his Inquiry. He had agreed to do so, and would examine the pay issue at the beginning of the task. The Inquiry could issue an interim report on pay. Edmund-Davies would examine police pay in the light of police responsibilities and workloads, the stresses and dangers to which the police were exposed, the need to ensure adequate police strengths, and the restrictions to which the police were subject. The Home Secretary said that the Government was willing to accept the conclusions of the Inquiry, subject to phasing of any award. The police would at once receive the 10 per cent maximum award payable under Phase 3 of the incomes policy. Rees concluded;

> 'To sum up, this is the offer which I put to you this afternoon: an immediate 10 per cent increase in pay, backdated to the 1st September, and an independent inquiry into the proper basis of police pay, with the Government committed to accept its recommendations. Against the background of Government pay policy, I believe this is a proper offer.'

The Home Secretary said that he was going to increase the size of the Inquiry team, and subsequently Lord Plowden was appointed deputy chairman. The other additional members were Sir Alec Cairncross, the economist and Master of St Peter's College, Oxford; Audrey Prime, a retired NALGO official, and David Bleakley, a former Labour member of the disbanded Northern Ireland Government.

Rees and the Government were conceding all that Martucci and the JCC had aimed for when they walked out of the Police Council fifteen months earlier, but the intervening period had been marked with great bitterness and now a few members of the pay negotiating team saw the offer as tantamount to a sell-out. Martucci had his work cut out to convince all of the Committee, that the time had come to trust Rees.

But if the Federations had their sceptics, the official side's reaction to the Government statement was openly hostile. Rees had met Rusbridge and his team of local authority members before the meeting with the Federations, and they had reacted angrily. After an adjournment, they handed Rees a hurriedly prepared statement which they asked him to read out to the Federations, as well as his own. Rees read it, and told Rusbridge that as Secretary of State he would not read out such a document, because it would end any chance of a settlement. After reading his own statement to Martucci and his colleagues, Rees said that the official side wanted the Federations to hear its statement, but as Home Secretary, he felt that the official side's approach was unhelpful. It was then read to them by Robert Armstrong.

The officials side's statement insisted that the Police Council was still the only legal forum for police pay negotiations. If a settlement was to be worked out, it wanted talks around the table. If this was not possible, then the official side would endorse it 'as though it had taken place in a properly constituted meeting of Committee 'C'.' The official side was still anxious to force the Federations into acknowledging the continuing authority of the Police Council, something it knew that they would not do.

As to pay itself, the official side said that there could be nothing beyond the 10 per cent allowed under Phase 3. Anything more would have to be negotiated, but;

> '... ... local and central government have both to be fully convinced that any future movement in police pay is based upon careful examination of the facts. Taxpayers and ratepayers have a right to be assured that their money is being spent wisely and to be given a clear exposition of the facts of police earnings upon which it is based. Despite the extensive press coverage of recent months the official side have yet to be convinced that the public at large have been given a fair and balanced picture of the facts from any of the participants.'

The official side's counter proposal was that the Police Council should meet forthwith, firstly to agree a 10 per cent increase under Phase 3, and secondly to commence an inquiry into police pay and to complete its investigation within one month. The offer was rejected without discussion by the staff side, as the official side must have expected it would be. Once again, Government was about to by-pass the Police Council and put the future of police pay in the hands of an independent body.

There was nothing to detain the official side members at the Home Office any further, but the arguments in the room set aside for the Federations raged into the night. Martucci and Nevin urged the group to give unanimous backing to their acceptance of Rees's offer. Kent and his few supporters wanted to accept the inquiry but reject the 10 per cent, because acceptance closed the chances of getting anything more in the Phase 3 stage. Martucci argued that if they had been sincere in protesting about the low pay of young officers who were relying on state benefits to make ends meet, they could not expect them to wait for months until more money came along.

It was close to midnight when Martucci and Jardine went into Rees's office to tell him that they had a deal. Afterwards, they went to the press room to meet the industrial correspondents. Both men were hollow eyed and weary, more than a little sick at heart because of the angry words which had been flung at them by a few of their own colleagues during the debate on whether to settle. After they had outlined the terms, the reporters, all experienced in 'doorstepping' many such fraught meetings between employers, union leaders and ministers, told them what they wanted to hear, that they had won hands down. The labour correspondent of the BBC, fixing Martucci's lapel microphone for a TV interview, said; 'I don't know how the hell you've done it. You've not only beaten Rees and Callaghan, you've beaten the TUC.'

TWENTY-SEVEN

A new beginning

T he membership's reaction to news of the settlement of the pay dispute was mixed. There was great disappointment that there was to be no 'extra' money during the current pay review period, to meet the Federations' claim that the police were far behind other workers in the pay league. There was also considerable scepticism about the Inquiry itself. Rees's unhappy performance throughout the dispute had engendered deep distrust of the Home Secretary among many police officers. On a personal level, this was unfair, because Rees was not only a thoroughly decent man who strongly supported the tenets of law and order, he had been living ever since his stint in Northern Ireland with police protection officers as ever present members of his household. He knew and understood what the police wanted, but he was the prisoner of the political imperatives of the time. The Government had been determined not to have its social contract with the TUC undermined by treating the police as a special case. Now it had conceded an independent inquiry and committed itself to implementing its findings, which almost certainly would be far higher than the limits imposed by incomes policy.

Cooler heads among the Federation's activists recognised the depth of Martucci's achievement, because this was very much a personal effort. As with Arthur Evans seventeen years before, the Federation had been fortunate to have a strong man in charge of its pay strategy at a crucial stage. Unlike Evans, who had the considerable advantage of having James Callaghan working alongside him, able to hatch a private deal with a sympathetic Home Secretary, Martucci had been virtually on his own in confronting the Government and the official side. Rees's stance had not been neutral. He had been obliged to back the official side's insistence on acting through the Police Council right up to the last round. The Prime Minister had been equally determined not to concede an independent inquiry, knowing it could open floodgates for the public sector. The JCC and its Northern Ireland ally had begun the campaign without support and with no clear idea of where they were going. Now they had forced Callaghan to change policy, and stood a good chance of restoring the fortunes of the police service. Along the way, they had received no support, and often opposition, from the Scottish Federation, the Superintendents Association, and ACPO, although all the other associations' members now stood to gain considerably from Martucci's stubborn stand. The Inspectors of Constabulary had failed to alert the Home Secretary to the very real danger of a total collapse of morale and the growing possibility of industrial action. On the contrary, he had been assured by them that the Federation's breast beating carried no threat, and that sooner or later Martucci and Jardine would either give in, or be supplanted by others prepared to return to the Police Council.

Jardine also deserved his share of the credit. After an unfortunate beginning, he and Martucci had worked well together, often arguing with fainthearts and hotheads on their own side as much as with the authorities. The chairman had been a surprise success on the public relations front. He was anything but a good public speaker, but he came across on television as an honest Scotsman, completely devoid of guile, defending the put - upon policeman against those crafty bureaucrats in Whitehall and the local councils. People identified with Jim Jardine as they still did with Jack Warner, TV's *Dixon of Dock Green*.

It was Jardine's knack of persuading the public that the police were being badly treated that prompted the complaint about 'misinformation' in the official side's statement. The authorities had not begun to counter the latest public relations offensive mounted by the Federation. While the serious newspapers tended to side with the Government, allowing that the police had a grievance, but not one sufficient to justify a breach of the incomes policy, all the tabloids except the Labour supporting *Mirror* group, gave the Federation unequivocal support. With the public becoming more and more worried about mounting crime and violence, the Tory press was keen to exploit the deep rift between the rank and file of the police and a Labour government which was deeply unpopular.

Callaghan's sharp political instincts had told him that the police row could help to bring down the Government, already worried about its minuscule Commons majority and soon to go into a pact with the Liberals. The police, in effect, could be Callaghan's miners. While he knew that restoring the purchasing power of Willink to the police would be inordinately costly, Callaghan calculated that giving the job of examining pay to Edmund-Davies would resolve the immediate problem, and by insisting on phasing any award, the cost could be kept within manageable bounds, at least to start with. Callaghan realised he would have trouble in placating the TUC leaders, who would find the capitulation to the Federation hard to explain to union negotiators, but the time it would take Edmund-Davies to produce a report was important to the Government. This was why, in Cabinet, Callaghan overruled Albert Booth, the Employment Secretary, and allowed Rees to make peace with the police.

To a great extent, the Federation's success in forcing the Government to change its mind on an inquiry had to be shared with the media. Never before had the Federation run such a sustained and effective campaign to keep their dispute in the public eye. Sue Harris, in an unpublished thesis for her MA degree from Brunel University, analysed more than 500 news stories and features which dealt with the Federation's claims, and interviewed all the crime reporters of the national papers who (rather than the labour correspondents) had covered the campaign from start to finish. She concluded that it was the publicity campaign which kept the pay claim alive when otherwise it would have been doomed to fail;

> 'Overall the police dispute received a fair press. It was quite remarkable how few lies there were, how little opinion and how factual the accounts of police events

were. Papers and journalists were quite positive about
the plight of the policeman. *The Sun* in particular
mounted a very vocal campaign on behalf of the police
force. *The Guardian* appeared almost consistently
negative in its attitude.

'Without any doubt the police campaign must be
seen as influential and effective. The regular demonstrations, meetings, and statements to the press made
a consistent impact on the public mind, the fact that
the police were dissatisfied was kept to the forefront
of public attention.

'The campaign made appropriate use of the media
by continually feeding the press with news and views
about the pay situation. To succeed a campaign must
not be allowed to die and the police campaign did not.
It was kept alive for a long time by carefully planned
publicity and I believe had it not been for this
persistent use of the press the police pay claim would
long ago have been a closed subject.'

To which it needs only to be added that the press coverage
owed more to the carefully nurtured relationship between the
Federation and the regular crime reporters over the previous
twenty years, than to the somewhat maladroit efforts of the
professional public relations companies who were briefly
employed during the campaign. The Federation got many
thousands of pounds worth of coverage for nothing. Besides
doing a few favours for the Federation, the crime reporters
were acknowledging their debt to the people on whom they
depended to do their jobs - operational police officers
throughout the country. They may not have understood the
subtleties of negotiations or the politics of the issue, but they
went in to bat for the police when they were needed the most.

Martucci, in a message to the membership in a supplement
to *POLICE*, explained why the Federations' had settled for
10 per cent and an inquiry;

'We have accepted the Home Secretary's offer because
we believe in our case. We do not have to trust the
official side, and certainly not the Government. But

we do have to trust Edmund-Davies. He is the man
we asked for in the first place to inquire into our
negotiating machinery. Now he is going to examine
police pay.'

Martucci stressed that the Government had committed
itself to accepting the findings of the inquiry, subject to
phasing. To those members worried about phasing he
suggested, somewhat implausibly, that it was possible that
some of the Edmund-Davies award could be backdated to
September 1977. He said the Federation would be arguing
for the 78 - 104 per cent claim which had been submitted
to Rees.

Edmund-Davies let it be known that the Committee wished
to begin the examination of police pay by considering the
question of whether the police should have the right to strike.
The Federations submitted their evidence to Edmund-Davies
in December 1977. They claimed that the police had fallen
about 21 per cent behind the earnings of non-manual workers
since Willink.

The document put forward two ways of finding a suitable
mechanism for ensuring that once a proper level of police
pay was decided upon, it would be maintained in the future.
The first was the 'comparability approach'. This took as a
starting point the New Earnings Survey figure for full time
male non-manual workers, which stood at £92.55 for a 40
hour-week. To this should be added amounts to take account
of the special factors in policing which made the job less
favourable than the average conditions elsewhere, with
deductions for factors where police conditions were better
than in other occupations. This was the approach favoured
by Willink in 1960. The Federations listed the 'less favourable' factors as; unsocial hours; restricted career structure;
limitations on private life; personal danger; the continuing
commitment of a police officer to his position, and; the
prohibition on trade union activity. They said there was
'general acceptance' that hours worked between 8pm and
6am on weekdays and Saturday and Sunday working justified
a premium payment of around 25 per cent. Roughly half the
police service worked 'unsocial hours' whereas this was not

common in non-manual occupations. Averaged over the service, this premium worked out at twelve and a half per cent of the £92.55.

The Federations said that the police career structure, with eighty per cent of the personnel in the rank of constable, compared very badly with other non-manual callings. A premium of £10 was suggested, to compensate for this. A further 20 per cent of the £92.55 would take account of the remaining 'less favourable' factors.

The deductions for the advantageous factors were assessed by the Federations as 50 per cent of average rent allowances, and 7 per cent of the £92.55 for the pensions advantage. The calculation worked out at £118.92 weekly. This would have produced, in April 1977 a constables scale of £5,140 rising to £7,260, compared with the actual scale of £2,530 - £3,276.

The second, and less conventional approach, was called the 'constant requirement approach'. This was strongly advocated to the Federations by Professor Ted Nevin but had lead to heated arguments. It owed a lot to the market forces approach put to the Royal Commission by the Treasury. Expressed in simple terms, it asked two questions;

'what level of net recruitment is necessary each year to maintain a police service fully manned to the United Kingdom establishment of 134,000?, and;

'what level of pay is necessary in order to ensure that this level of net recruitment is in fact achieved?'

The answer to these questions was based on a formula which took account of the length of service profile of the service. In order to meet all contingencies, including resignations and retirements, Nevin concluded that police pay had to be high enough to ensure that 6,900 recruits joined the service every year. He rejected the notion that the rate of police recruitment was 'mysterious and unquantifiable', and offered an analysis of recruitment and wastage over 30 years up to 1975 which showed that variations in recruitment and wastage could be explained by the rate of pay; the ratio of unemployment to unfilled vacancies; changes in authorised establishments, and the shortfall of actual strengths to establishments. This made it possible to predict recruitment and wastage figures. Using Nevin's formula, a constable's pay would have started at £4,110 in 1975, rising to £5,820. These figures fell far short of the comparability approach, and brought into question the Federations' wisdom in allowing Nevin's thesis to go to Edmund-Davies as an alternative to comparability. The figures on which Nevin had worked out his formula were two years out of date, but it was hardly a convincing argument to say, as he did, 'it may well be that the up to date statistics would produce scales nearer to those obtained by the 'comparability' approach.' Fortunately, the Inquiry found it all too esoteric and theoretical to merit further consideration.

The Federations urged Edmund-Davies to ensure that his recommendations on pay were accompanied by a continuation mechanism to guard against future erosion, and suggested that the control group against whose earnings the police should be compared, should be full time, adult non-manual male workers.

On the right to strike, the Federation said that in recent years this right had been enshrined for everyone save the police and the armed forces. It pointed out, that when the courts had ruled in a recent action that a strike by postal workers broke the law, the Government had immediately changed the law to make a postal strike a legal event. The Federation went on;

> 'We do not believe that the onus lies on us to argue the case for enjoying the same rights as other workers. On the contrary, it is for those who would oppose our policy to justify their opposition ... ... we cannot believe that any responsible person would nowadays argue that the prohibition on the right of a police officer to withhold his labour should remain, and at the same time that the pay of the police officer need not embody a specific weighting to take account of the limitations which are thus placed on him and his representative body in pursuing legitimate claims for better pay and conditions of service.'

The united front among the Federations was briefly disturbed when the Metropolitan Branch Board, without troubling to tell the national Federation what it was up to, submitted a claim direct to Edmund-Davies, demanding that in addition to any general increase to the police, the Inquiry should award £1,000 in pensionable pay to the Metropolitan. The Board claimed that it had been taken by surprise when Rees decided to refer the pay issue to Edmund-Davies: if so, it must have been the only branch board in the country not to have realised that this was about to happen. Having gone directly to Edmund-Davies, Harry Slipper, the Metropolitan Federation secretary, then wrote to Martucci hoping that, nevertheless, the JCC would support the claim. The JCC could do no such thing. It had conceded the pensionable London weighting element some years earlier, but national Federation policy was to seek a £500 non-pensionable allowance for the Metropolitan, and this was the JCC's submission to Edmund-Davies. It was more by the accident of timing than design that the Metropolitan move did not reopen the old arguments for long, but the opportunistic strategy of the branch board angered and embarrassed Martucci, himself a Metropolitan officer. He knew the board was working in concert with David McNee, who promptly gave the £1,000 claim his full support.

The evidence of the Association of Chief Police Officers to Edmund-Davies spelt out the problems that beset almost every force. Crime had increased by 176 per cent over 1960, while police strengths had grown by 47 per cent. Traffic volume had doubled, as had the number of traffic offences. Public order problems had become much worse, and a new feature was the level of violence and hostility directed at the police. Violence against police officers was a serious problem, and the police use of firearms had increased in line with armed robberies and terrorist incidents.

The chief officers were, naturally, totally against police officers having the right to strike; as were the Superintendents' Associations, but all the service representative bodies were in accord that the absence of the right to strike required adequate reflection in police pay.

The chief officers' pay proposals fell well short of the

Federations' demands. They thought that a 30 per cent uplift was needed to restore police pay to the standards set by Willink, and a similar amount was needed to take account of increased duties and responsibilities, workloads, and the absence of trade union rights.

> '... ... wide publicity has been given to a wish freely expressed in various forces to possess the right to strike, but we are convinced that this springs not from any real; desire to take industrial action, but from deep feelings of frustration over levels of pay and an inability to do anything about them; we are equally convinced that any attempt now to lead the service out on strike would fail.'

ACPO said that giving the police the right to strike would make the oath of office 'meaningless'. Any affiliation to other bodies (such as the TUC) could make difficult, if not impossible, the position of the police in dealing with public order problems arising during industrial disputes. Here ACPO cited the very recent strike called by the Fire Brigades Union, in which the role of the police (working alongside the army) was vital to the safety of life and property. However, it followed that the denial of the right to strike placed a responsibility on authority to ensure that police officers were adequately compensated in cash terms, and given guarantees for the future.

The official side's evidence to Edmund-Davies was the first opportunity the service had been given of seeing what conclusion the local authority leaders had reached. It amounted to a proposal that a 'fully fledged' constable, with at least four years' service, should be paid the same as the average male worker. This would have meant at most an increase of 12 per cent. To offset such unwonted largesse, the official side suggested that overtime at the end of a shift should no longer be paid for, and there should be no additional compensation for working on bank holidays. The official side also proposed that rent allowances should be consolidated into pensionable pay, and that any pay formula should stipulate that rent allowance should not exceed 15 to 20 per cent of pay. It called for the ending of the compensatory grant system, by which officers were reimbursed by police authorities for the income tax paid on rent allowances. For the third time in thirty years, the local authorities had gone in front of an independent inquiry into police pay and suggested that there was no significant problem to worry about.

The 1978 Annual Conference was overshadowed by the deaths of five delegates from West Yorkshire, who were killed when their coach overturned on the journey to Blackpool. This was the first time a Federation Conference had not been addressed by the Home Secretary of a junior minister. The coach tragedy cast a pall over the proceedings, and the atmosphere was further subdued by the uncertainty over Edmund-Davies. Martucci found no difficulty in routing the few critics of the decision to settle for an Inquiry and a Phase 3 award.

The only time the Conference came to life during three days was a debate about women police. Several motions demanded that the Federation should seek amendments to the Sex Discrimination Act. One argument was that women could not cope with the physical dangers of street duty. Ian Westwood of Greater Manchester said:

> 'We want to recognise the abilities of our women colleagues. Women will be police officers first, in their own department. I do not want our women to be so equal that they equally face the dangers of the streets. The service has room for men and women, but get the proportions wrong and the mixture will fail.'

West Midlands' way of restricting the numbers of women recruits was to abolish the separate height requirements for women candidates. A Greater Manchester delegate, Jack Charlton, claimed that women in his force wanted to go back to a specialist department;

> 'What could be better than to bring in a distraught woman or child, the victim of an attack, and to take her along to the policewomen's department and be sure

that the result would be an expert statement covering all points? This no longer occurs. We have young girls walking the streets who are expert in nothing.'

A woman's view came from Inspector Vee Neild of West Midlands, a future JCC general secretary. She said that the issue was training and qualifications, and challenged anyone to say that a policeman dealt with a road accident or a burglary better than a policewoman. Philip chambers of the Metropolitan, who for many years was a dissenting voice to the prevailing views of the Conference, spoke up for the women. He warned the delegates against scapegoating women because of the pay and manpower problems of the service. But Elizabeth Denford, a woman inspector, said that the public was beginning to notice that the police service was wearing skirts. The Sex Discrimination Act, she said, had helped the Government to hide the manpower shortage. Another woman delegate, Margaret Heathcote, called for a limit on the numbers of women, saying that on current trends women would constitute half the strength of her force in four years' time.

Ann Hogben of the Metropolitan was the first woman to hold a national appointment as chairman of the Sergeants' Central Committee. She told the Conference that the clock could not be turned back. Women had joined since 1975 in the expectation of being involved in the full range of police duties with equal opportunities. She said that the JCC supported the call to change the Act, to enable forces to have separate establishments for men and women, but held out no hope that this would be achieved.

As spring 1978 turned to summer, the rumour mills ground at full speed, helped by some imaginative reporting in the press. In July, almost two years to the day after the Federation walked out of the Police Council, Edmund-Davies published his conclusions on pay and negotiating machinery.

The Committee endorsed the views of Desborough and Oaksey on the unique place of the police in society. It said that in a parliamentary democracy, the concepts of law and its impartial enforcement were fundamental. The instruments essential to the continued fulfilment of these concepts were;

an independent judiciary to interpret the law, the police to maintain and enforce it, and the armed forces to protect the nation from external aggression. These three groups were unique in society and essential to its continuation.

Edmund-Davies took as his starting point 1960, the year of the Royal Commission. He said the constable of 1978 was more likely to be in a Panda car than riding a bicycle, and would be in touch with his base through a personal radio, which did not exist in 1960. Yet he was as isolated as his predecessor when faced with the need to take instantaneous action. The qualities required of a policeman were unchanged since Willink, what had changed was the general challenge to authority and increasing recourse to violence.

Edmund-Davies said that the pay structure must have the ability to permit the service to meet the demands made upon it. Despite the technological advances of the recent past, the man on the beat remained the kernel. It was also important to offer an attractive career which offered variety and opportunities. The report said that using civilians, whose numbers in the service had trebled since Willink to 34,000, to do some police jobs had obvious advantages but had to be weighed against the need to provide a varied career. Three quarters of the service were constables and most retired in that basic rank, and the long service constable had an important part to play.

Edmund-Davies was concerned about the number of women officers, which stood at 8,000 out of a total strength in England and Wales of 108,000 (in 1960 there had been 2,000 women). Some forces found that women now made up one third of their intake of recruits. Referring to the Police Federation's view that the Sex Discrimination Act should be amended to allow a limit to be put on female recruitment, Edmund-Davies said it was too soon after the Act to form a view on its affect on the service, and in any case its recommendations on pay should provide an impetus for the recruitment of both men and women.

Edmund-Davies noted that more than half of recruits resigned during their probation, but said the loss of more experienced officers was more disturbing, with about 2,500 officers who had completed their probation resigning in 1977.

The report said that pay was a major factor. The Inquiry therefore proposed to amend the incremental structure, to give annual increases in the first eight years, and then a 'top' rate after 12 years. This would mean that a constable would reach maximum pay three years earlier than at present. As an additional incentive to the constable who was unlikely to be promoted, after 15 years' he would receive the same amount as a sergeant after one year in that rank. To emphasise the reason for this overlapping of the ranks, Edmund-Davies did not extend it to the other grades, something which left the sergeants' with a sense of grievance for many years afterwards.

As with previous inquiries, Edmund-Davies accepted that it was not possible to equate police work with other jobs for pay purposes. The report accepted that there had been a loss of ground since Willink, mainly affecting the long service constables, but the loss was partly offset by the other emoluments, mainly rent allowances. Account had to be taken of increased workloads and responsibilities, and the limitations on private life and trade union involvement.

After taking account of all these factors, the Inquiry recommended that constables' pay should start at £3,600, an increase of 30 per cent, and the top rate, after 15 years', should be increased by 45 per cent to £5,700. The senior PC would thus overlap the newly promoted sergeant, who was to receive £5,450 on promotion (40 per cent more), unless he or she was already at the top of the PCs scale. The Inquiry acknowledged that overlapping was against Federation policy, but said it was common practice elsewhere in the public service.

The report said nothing about differentials between the Federated ranks, but recommended that the six years incremental scale for ranks above constables should be cut to four years.

The superintendents did particularly well out of Edmund-Davies, which somewhat rankled with chief inspectors. The Superintendents' Association said that their relative position had worsened since chief inspectors became entitled to claim payment for overtime in 1974, and proposed that the differential between the superintendent and the chief inspector should be increased from 17 to 30 per cent. Edmund-Davies said it was inappropriate to pay officers of this rank for their overtime. The Committee considered taking chief inspectors out of the overtime ranks also, but because the arbitration award had been so recent, decided not to do so. The chief inspector was to receive £7,900 a year at the maximum, and the Inquiry recommended that the superintendent should start at £9,800, a considerable increase on the previous differential. The award lead to many chief inspectors asking if they would not be better off, either on their own, or in an 'officers' association' with the superintendents.

The chief officers, who had so signally failed to back the Federations' stand, also had good reason to be pleased with Edmund-Davies. The report recommended that the current link with chief officers in local government should be broken. It accepted that there had been a substantial increase in the duties and responsibilities of chief officers, and that as with the lower ranks, it was almost impossible to find a comparable post for salary purposes. The Report recommended that all ACPO ranks should be paid on a 'single salary point' basis, eliminating increments. Under the proposals, the pay of the chief constables of the smallest forces went up from £11,500 to £16,600, and those in command of forces with the largest population band rose from £13,500 to £20,500.

For London, the Inquiry recommended that pensionable London weighting should be £319 year, plus a non-pensionable allowance of £650, which was awarded specifically to help overcome the manpower problems of the capital. The Inquiry recommended that the undermanning allowances in London and undermanned forces should cease to be paid when the new scales were introduced.

The Inquiry urged that the full award should be paid as from the earliest due date - 1st September 1978, but the Government insisted on phasing the award over two years, with one half being paid as the first instalment. As a concession members who retired on and after the 1st September 1979 could have their pensions calculated on the full Edmund-Davies award.

In percentage terms, the Edmund-Davies result was very similar to the boost given to police pay by Willink, and the broad result of the Inquiry had been to restore the police officer to that niche in the pay league. It fell well short of the optimistic proposals of the Federations, but it was all 'new money', additional to the incomes policy awards to which the police were also entitled. To ensure that the new standards were maintained, Edmund-Davies proposed that they should be updated each year according to the movement in the earnings index for all workers.

Edmund-Davies, as expected, declared that the right to strike would be incompatible with the responsibilities of the police service and contrary to the interests of the nation. The report said;

> 'We do not think it is open to doubt that the three Police Federations genuinely consider that up to the present they have been at a substantial disadvantage in negotiating on pay and conditions of service by reason of their lack of 'industrial muscle' due to the absence of any right to strike.
>
> 'In common with all those who submitted evidence for our consideration, this Committee is satisfied that the absence of the right to strike is a serious deprivation for any worker. It is essential that the police should not suffer in pay because they are deprived of the right to strike, and that it should be put beyond doubt that they are being treated fairly.
>
> 'Such an important limitation on the freedom of action of members of the police force renders it even more essential;
>
> (i) that the machinery for determining police pay and other conditions of service commands the confidence of all sections of the service;
>
> (ii) that the absence of the right to strike be borne in mind by both sides when negotiating and should lead to an award that does full justice to the claims of the police, and;
>
> (iii) that there should be speedy arbitration at the request of either party.

The report made it clear that the new pay standards reflected the absence of the right to strike, but the Committee declined to reveal what precise value had been put upon this factor.

Dealing with the negotiating machinery, Edmund-Davies rejected the Federation's plea for direct negotiations with central government. However, they conceded that the Federations were justified in complaining that the local authorities exerted too great an influence on the official side, and were too prone to equate police pay and conditions with those of local government employees. This was largely because the official side secretariat was the same as that which acted for the employers on all local government bargaining The Federation complained that although both joint secretaries were supposed to have equal standing, it was to the official side secretary that chief constables and police authorities turned when disputes arose as to the interpretation of Police Council agreements. The Inquiry recommended that the new body it proposed, to be called the Police Negotiating Board, would have its own independent secretariat, and an independent chairman and deputy chairman. Moreover, the official side should include magistrates in its ranks, as they were important members of police authorities. The latter proposal was strongly resisted by the official side, on the grounds that unelected members were not accountable to electors for the way they spent public money.

POLICE had no doubt that the outcome was a total triumph for the Police Federation;

> 'The reason why the police service has received such a tremendous boost in its pay standards is because the Police Federations (of England and Wales and Northern Ireland) stood up and fought. Of course some will cavil about the size of the award, grumble about phasing, bemoan the fact that the long service constable has overtaken the newly promoted sergeant, or complain about differentials. But all our qualifications should be put in their true perspective; in the same week that the Government nailed its hopes to the mast of 5 per cent pay rises for the rest of the nation, it

accepted that police pay shall rise, by September next year, by the full extent of Edmund-Davies plus *the amount by which other earnings rise in the same period.*

'Our trust in Lord Edmund-Davies has been fully vindicated. Whilst stressing that the police service must never be given the right to strike, he has deliberately included compensation for its absence in the new scales. The Committee has recognised the dangers inherent in a police service wracked with dissatisfaction over its pay. Provided that this and future Governments stand by the pledge to honour Edmund-Davies, the system by which police pay is adjusted in future to take account of average earnings should give to the new standards the permanency which was never achieved after Willink.

'So much for the toothless tiger.'

Not everyone was so pleased. The editor of *The Guardian* was particularly scathing;

'One of the biggest (and most literal) confidence tricks in recent times has been pulled off by the police with the decision to give them a 40 per cent pay rise.'

The Observer was just as miffed;

'With law and order the next most popular election issue to inflation, any Government standing even mildly in the way of the Police Federation's demands was on a hiding to nothing. Mr Whitelaw rushed in with a promise that the police would get their 40 per cent increase at once under the Tories, instead of the two stages offered by Labour. In this atmosphere of Dutch auctioneering, we must be grateful that the Federation did not ask for free holidays on the Costa Brava for all ranks.'

TWENTY-EIGHT

A federation, or a union?

The immediate consequence of the Edmund-Davies pay award was a remarkable turn round in police manpower. As early as October 1978, the service started to gain strength through increased recruitment and a sharp drop in premature wastage. Many officers who could have retired decided to serve for at least one more year in order to get the benefit of the new rates in their pensions. The loss of more than 1000 officers in 1977 was offset by a rise of almost 2,000 in 1978, all of it coming in the last quarter of the year. At the end of 1979, the strength of the service in England and Wales stood at 118,000, a net gain of 5,000 over the end of 1977.

Edmund-Davies still had to report on the structure and role of the staff associations. It did not take the Federation long, after the outcome of the pay inquiry, to abandon most of the objectives it had said it was seeking. The JCC was ready to accept the reformed negotiating machinery proposed by Edmund-Davies, it gave the Federation most of what it had wanted by breaking the umbilical cord between the negotiating body and the local authority negotiating bureau in Belgrave Square. Henceforth, the joint secretaries would have equal status, and it would be the negotiating body's own secretariat, provided by the Office of Manpower Economics, which would interpret the meaning of agreements, not the official side or the Home Office.

A survey for the Federation by the Industrial Society suggested that, despite the results of the local ballots, most police officers remained firmly opposed to the right to strike. The survey did, however, favour a much stronger Federation than before, a free association which could be affiliated to the TUC if the members so wished. It recommended the formation of a confederation of police federations, and said that consideration should be given to including the Superintendents Association and the staff associations of non-Home Office forces, such as the British Transport Police. The Industrial Society said it had found widespread dissatisfaction with the Federation, caused mainly by poor communication with the members. It suggested that the Federation should be reorganised along regional lines. Other proposals were that the annual conference should become a biennial event, and that the JCC secretary and his deputy should be elected by a ballot of branch boards, and serve as such until retirement.

The Industrial Society's report was one of the subjects on the agenda of the special delegate conference which met in London in September 1978 to consider such matters as the Federation becoming a free association, and the right to strike. In its submission to Edmund-Davies on the future of representative organisations, the JCC proposed that all forces should have a joint negotiating and consultative committee, so that all ranks would become involved in policy making and decision taking. It pointed out that the Police Act and the Police Federation Regulations limited the rights of branch boards almost as much as when the Federation began sixty years earlier. Boards were empowered; only to make written or oral representations to chief officers and police authorities; send a copy of such representations, if they wished, to the Home Secretary, and; in matters of importance they could appoint a deputation to speak to chief officers or police authorities. In practice, most chief constables had long since introduced direct discussions with board officials, but the extent of consultation depended entirely on the management style of the chief officer, and consequently, almost everything hinged on whether or not branch board officers were able to establish a good rapport with the chief constable. The Federation told Edmund-Davies;

'The relationship between the police officer as an employee and those concerned in the management of the police service differs in certain crucial respects from management/employee relationships in all other civilian occupations. Because members of police forces serve under a code of discipline, and are obliged at all times to obey any lawful order given by a superior officer, the chief officer and those with delegated management responsibilities are in a unique position in their dealings with the representative body. Without question, this limits the effectiveness of a branch board. It may make representations, but authority makes the final decision.

There is no formal machinery for registering dis-agreement, conciliation or arbitration. A branch board which is dissatisfied with a management decision has very few avenues left open for further action. It may seek to raise the matter again with the chief officer; it may take the matter to the police authority; it may ask a central committee to make representations on its behalf to the Secretary of State; it may ask Her Majesty's Inspector of Constabulary to look into the matter. Experience has indicated that all such ap-proaches are likely to fail, unless it can be established that the chief officer's decision is contrary to the requirements of the relevant police regulations, or is otherwise so perverse that it cannot be upheld. Invari-ably, the answers from the Secretary of State or HMIs are to the effect that the matter in question is one within the discretion of the chief officer and they cannot intervene. The result leaves the branch board feeling dissatisfied and this is heightened by the knowledge that nothing more can be done. The mem-bers of the force, seeing the branch board unable to make progress, conclude that the Police Federation is ineffective.'

There was a marked contrast at this time, between the progress which had been made at a national level by the Police Federation in establishing direct liaison with the Home Secretary, the Home Office and the HMIs, and the situation that prevailed in some forces where chief constables, them-selves reared in the service of the Thirties, kept their branch boards at further than arm's length.

The JCC told Edmund-Davies that some boards, fed up with trying to make headway at local level, had tried challenging chief officer's decisions in the courts, and with varying success. The courts would only intervene if it could be shown that the chief constable was acting contrary to the appropriate police regulations. In any case, the Federation said, the courts should not be regarded as appropriate for resolving management issues in the police service.

The Federation accepted that informal consultation procedures existed in many forces, but said they were inferior to a formalised structure for consultation and negotiation. A problem with informal arrangements was that chief officers would consult on some matters, and not on others. Sometimes consultation was offered only after the event, and branch boards found themselves reacting to decisions of which they had not been told. Informal discussions, without agendas and minutes of decisions, lead to misunderstandings and distortions. Branch board officials were sometimes asked to give a Federation view on matters about which they had been unable to talk to their boards The police service had lagged far behind the major developments in joint consultation, such as workers' councils, in other occupations. All recent legislation on this subject, which had strengthened the rights of trade unions at shop floor level, had excluded the police and the armed forces. The Bullock Report recommended worker directors on the boards of public and private companies, and the Police Federation had adopted a policy of seeking Federation representation on local police authorities, citing the precedent of teachers' representatives on local education authorities.

The Federation painted a graphic picture of the authoritarian nature of police management;

'The strongest influence acting to prevent the establishment of more effective local representation for members of police forces is the nature of management practice in the police service. Chief officers are regarded as commanders of disciplined forces. The hierarchical structure is based on the areas of command of senior officers. In the police service, management decisions are translated to subordinates as orders, with failure to comply being regarded as a disciplinary offence. The chief officer has authority over all matters that deal with the operational conduct of the force. He does not recognize the right of the police authority to intervene in operational matters. He regards day to day management and deployment of the force as his sole prerogative. It follows that the chief officer of a police force is in a unique position as a manager when compared with the remainder of senior management in all fields of employment. He enjoys this unique position because of the nature of the police service. The chief constable as a manager is never faced with a hostile or uncooperative work-force. On the contrary, there has always existed within the service a ready acceptance of the need for discipline and a common understanding between those giving the orders and those receiving them, that the interests of the service are the paramount consider-ation. Strengthening the ability of branch boards to negotiate on matters affecting their membership will not threaten this position. It will possibly, even probably, make management a more difficult task by requiring chief officers to justify decisions, but there is no reason why relationships between them and their branch boards should not be harmonious.'

The Federation drew a clear distinction between negotiable and non-negotiable subjects. They suggested that negotiable matters should be mainly questions of local application and interpretation of negotiating agreements reached by the Police Negotiating Board. There was already a good example of this in practice, as since 1957 branch boards had been responsible for negotiating local rent allowances with police authorities, with the right to go to the national conciliation panel in the event of failure to agree. On consultation, the Federation said;

'Given the special responsibilities of chief officers, we accept that there are certain matters where negotia-tion is inappropriate, and in these we seek the right of formal consultation before chief officers make final decisions. It would not, for example, be realistic to expect that a chief officer would have to reach full agreement with his branch board by negotiations before seeking an increase in the authorised establishment of his force. There appears to be no reason, however, why the establishment of the force should not be discussed through the consultative machine, so that the branch board could advance its ideas on the manpower requirements. We do believe that the subjects which would have to be reserved for consultation rather than negotiation would be relatively few in number. Apart from questions of individual discipline or promotion, there do not appear to be any aspects of police management which should be excluded from either consultation or negotiation. There should be a uniform decision as to which matters are 'negotiable' and which are 'consultative' to avoid this issue becoming a matter of local interpretation by chief officers.'

The Federation proposed that the Joint Negotiating and Consultative Committees (JNCCs) should consist of the chief constable and nominated senior officers as the management side, and representatives of the branch board as the staff side. The JNCC was intended to supplement, not replace the branch board, which would remain the primary form of representation, but it would be for the board to decide what powers should be given to its JNCC members to conclude agreements. It was axiomatic that the JNCC members would be bound by the policies of their boards.

The Federation realised that the constitution of police authorities was outside the Edmund-Davies Inquiry's remit, but it said there was a need for direct liaison between the police authority and the branch board. There were a number of 'non-operational' subjects, such as police housing, buildings and equipment, where the views of the branch board ought to be communicated directly to the police authority.

The Federation proposed that there should be local arbitration where there was a failure to reach agreement with the chief officer on a negotiable subject. The JCC ended its submission thus;

> 'Sixty years ago, the Desborough Committee saw no greater role for the Police Federation than a forum at which members might consider matters affecting their welfare and efficiency and bring their views to the notice of authority. Thirty years later, the Oaksey Committee took matters a stage further by introducing a form of Whitleyism into national negotiations. Oaksey was influenced by developments outside the police service since 1919, and by the obvious sense of responsibility displayed by the Police Federation over the years. Thirty more years have passed and the Police Federation invites the Committee to conclude that police officers, holding one of the most responsible offices open to individual citizens, can be trusted to operate a modern system of local consultation and negotiation in the most responsible manner.'

The Federation's views on local negotiation and consultation upset the chief officers. ACPO told Edmund-Davies that, contrary to the impression given by the JCC paper, chief officers accepted the need for consultation. However, it suggested that some Federation representatives needed to learn to put forward views for the general good rather than their own preferences. Some matters could not be left for consultation because chief constables carried personal responsibility and it was their heads that would roll if anything went wrong. ACPO said that there were occasions when a chief constable as a manager faced a 'hostile and unco-operative' workforce, although not surprisingly no details were given. It claimed that the wide consultation arrangements asked for by the Federation would impose an 'intolerable' constraint on the day-to-day direction of the service.

ACPO took strong exception to the Federation's proposal for liaison committees with police authorities. It would be necessary to give similar rights to Superintendents and ACPO ranks, and this would make the chief constable's position impossible. The police authorities might take decisions against the chief constable's advice.

In further evidence to Edmund-Davies, the JCC called for the lifting of some of the irksome restrictions which the regulations imposed on the private lives of police officers. The Federation had lost an Appeal Court decision in which the right of a chief constable to order a policeman living in his own home to move into a police house, and to deny him rent allowance when he refused to move his family, had been challenged. There had also been several examples of police officers being told that their jobs were in jeopardy because their wives ran small businesses in the force area. The JCC proposed that no restrictions should apply unless it could be shown that they were designed to 'secure the proper exercise of the functions of a constable', such as the ban on political activity. It also wanted an appeal tribunal, because the chief constable was the only judge of these issues.

Two hundred and fifty delegates attended the special delegate conference. Before they got down to discussing the JCC proposals, together with more than two hundred amendments from branch boards, several boards attempted to halt the proceedings. Greater Manchester claimed that it had obtained counsel's opinion that the conference was unlawful, and Mike Bennett, the board chairman, threatened that it would go to court if it did not agree with any decisions that the conference might take. The main complaint was that there had been no separate rank conferences. It was left to a future Sergeants' Committee secretary, Ken Brown of the Metropolitan, to point out that if the conference was aborted, the Committee would be free to give what evidence it liked to Edmund-Davies.

Once the Conference was under way, the JCC was overturned in its attempt to assert that the JCC was the policy making body. Not so, said the delegates, Conference made the policy. Speakers attacked the JCC for back tracking on a free association. Martucci argued that Conference gave the JCC an opportunity to explain its policies; 'You cannot tie our hands,' he insisted, but the vote went against him by a big margin. Inspector Colin Jones of South Wales, said; 'Time after time this Conference has been misled into thinking it is not the policy making body. It is, it was intended to be, and it will go on being if you support it.'

The JCC was defeated again over its wish to retain separate representation for policewomen, but this time the margin was just three votes. The Committee accepted that eventually there should not be separate seats for women on committees and boards, but argued that they should be retained while the Federation was trying to get the Sex Discrimination Act amended.

Another defeat for the platform involved the JCC proposal that elections should be held every three years instead of annually. A big majority agreed with Ken Brown that annual elections kept officials on their toes. The JCC argued that three yearly terms protected a good representative against arbitrary removal, he said, but their remedy was to protect incompetent or unpopular people for three years. Devon and Cornwall proposed that voting in Federation affairs should be by proportional representation. Stuart Cadmore, a future Constables' committee secretary, said that constables should command at least half the votes. An opposing view came from Essex, which wanted the abolition of separate rank representation. Both motions were defeated, and in effect the conference voted for the *status quo* so far as elections and voting were concerned. It also rejected proposals to reduce the size of Conference.

Ian Westwood of Greater Manchester, a newcomer to national affairs and a future vice-chairman of the JCC, lead the opposition to the JCC's proposal for a restructured Federation, rather than a trade union. He said that the decision to back free association and the right to strike had forced the Government to hand the pay issue to Edmund-Davies. Now the attitude of the JCC was that we had got the money, and everything was solved. This was naive. Government incomes policy would not go away. The members needed a Federation with powder and shot, at present they were going up against tanks with muskets.

The conference was swayed by a powerful speech from Colin Jones. He paid tribute to Greater Manchester for fighting for a principle for so long, but said; 'This is about deeply held principles. You are asking people like me to throw away the principles on which we joined the job twenty years ago. It is not now necessary. The position has changed.'

Joe Martucci, who had never seen free association as anything but a bargaining ploy, said it could only mean a trade union with the right to strike and Parliament would never allow it. He added; 'We cannot be unique and at the same time be the same as all other workers. We either go down the road that Edmund-Davies has shown us, or we go for free association. And that puts us with the 'five per cents' of incomes policy, and the dole queues.'

The JCC had comfortable majorities for its rejection of free association and the right to strike, and for its proposed new constitution, taking account of the considerable changes which the special conference had insisted upon. But the special conference ended in disarray, with Jardine losing his temper in spectacular fashion when his attempt to close the proceedings with much of the business still to be done was challenged by the disaffected minority, who thought they had been outmaneouvred by the JCC. Stuart Cadmore of Devon and Cornwall, a future secretary of the Constables' Committee, wrote to *POLICE* to complain about what had happened; 'I keep talking of the JCC when I mean Joe Martucci and Jim Jardine. To save money in the future perhaps we could have tailor's dummies as the JCC sitting behind them.'

The major changes in the Federation which the JCC proposed to Edmund-Davies were for station representatives for constables, as well as divisional branch board members. It said that all branch board secretaries should be full time, and their divisional duties should be undertaken by another member elected for the purpose. There should be six branch board meetings a year instead of four, and the JCC proposed that regional meetings should be held every quarter. They would not usurp the functions of force branch boards, but would deal with regional matters, such as training and regional crime and traffic squads.

The JCC proposed that the chairman, secretary and treasurer of the Committee should be full time appointments, along with the secretaries of the separate central committees.

It asked that all three JCC officers should be paid at the rate of the highest rank represented by the Federation, the London chef inspector, and this rate should be pensionable.

In July 1979, the Edmund-Davies Committee wound up its task with a report on the staff associations and some other aspects of police conditions of service. It said that the long-standing pattern of representation, based on three separate rank levels, was widely accepted and should continue. It was inevitable that there would be strains from time to time, but the Inquiry was satisfied that it worked well. Edmund-Davies said that it was still necessary to have a statutory framework because of the important role of the police, but there should be more flexibility and the Federation should have control of its own affairs as far as possible. Because of the existence of regulations, the Federation had in the past adopted a too rigid approach, seeking binding rules instead of informal agreements. It was 'unfortunate' that the Federation felt the need to go to court to establish uniform enforcement of regulations. The Inquiry proposed that there should be a minimum framework of regulations, governing such matters as constitution of boards, elections, the ban on political use of the funds, and the voluntary status of subscriptions. Other matters should be prescribed by rules made by the Federation itself.

The Inquiry recommended that secretaries of joint branch boards should have full time facilities and be additional members of the boards. It rejected the demand for six meetings a year, saying chief officers could grant additional meetings where necessary. Although the three Federations were unanimous in rejecting single rank and proportional representation, these ideas had been put to Edmund Davies by eleven constables' branch boards, of which two said that without such changes, they would prefer a constables' association. Edmund-Davies agreed with the majority view, saying;

> '... ... the present structure has many advantages. Because of the range of ranks represented, there is a diversity of approach and experience which, when welded together, gives to the Federations a unity and

strength of purpose which serves them well. That a common approach can be achieved in almost all cases is a matter of fact. Were the present balance to be disturbed we think the Federations might well disintegrate into separate rank associations, and this would mean the end of the Federations as we know them. The resultant individual bodies would be weaker in respect of finance, consultation and negotiating power and national influence.'

The Report noted that the Federations had made a complete reappraisal of their previous position and reversed their policy of seeking 'free association' status. They now asked for the repeal of Section 44(2) of the Police Act so that they could make their own decisions as to which bodies they could associate with. Two joint boards had submitted evidence demanding that the Federation should become a free association. The Report, to no one's surprise, came down firmly against free association;

'The police must not have any political bias and our conclusion was that free association could endanger their impartiality. This would be true, even if the police did not exercise any previously conceded right to free association, because if they had that right it *might* be exercised at short notice by resolution of a special conference; and public confidence and trust in the police might be undermined by the knowledge that right existed. The Federations have shown themselves to be mature and responsible, and we do not doubt them when they asserted that they did not want to join the TUC or have political affiliations. But organisations can change their character and aims, and leaders come and go with the years. Indeed the Federations changed their policy on free association between 1977 and 1978. Our view is therefore that it would not be appropriate for the police staff associations to have the right of free association without any limitations, and we recommend accordingly.'

Dealing with the Federations' view that the police should have all the rights bestowed in legislation on other workers, except the right to strike, Edmund-Davies said the problem was the unique constitutional position of police officers, who were not employees but officers of the Crown, and said many complications would arise from giving them employee status. The nature of the policeman's job made it inevitable that some of the benefits, such as aspects of health and safety, could not be given. There was no evidence, the Inquiry said, that the police had suffered from the absence of statutory provision in this field, but it understood the Federation's anxiety and suggested that the Home Office and police authorities should 'make every effort' to ensure that the police received all the relevant benefits of industrial legislation. Once legislation was passed, the benefits should be passed on to the police without delay. This could be done through the Police Advisory Board, or where appropriate, by the new negotiating body.

Edmund-Davies did support the Federations on the right of access to police authorities. The report recommended that staff association representatives should be entitled to attend police authority meetings as observers in duty time, but could be excluded when confidential matters were under discussion. Also, there should be machinery to enable the staff associations to put their views to the authority in an informal setting. On a regular basis, there should be meetings consisting of the representatives, the chief constable, and members of the police authority.

The report rejected the Federation proposal that chief constables should have a statutory duty to consult the staff associations, but said the aim should be to make such an obligation unnecessary. It therefore accepted, almost in its entirety, the Police Federations proposals for joint negotiating and consultative committees in all forces except the Metropolitan - 'where special considerations apply'. The JNCC would consider major matters of force policy and any negotiable matters affecting the whole force. All parties on the JNCC should be able to enter items for discussion on the agenda. The chief constable should ensure that all major matters of force policy were entered for discussion.

On the other matters raised by the Federations, the Inquiry said the existing restrictions on private lives of officers should continue, but should be 'interpreted as liberally as possible both in relation to police officers and members of their families'.

Promotion, said Edmund-Davies, must remain a matter for the chief officer. Each force should review its staff appraisal system and there should be a promotion appeal system, comprising a board of senior officers who were not involved in the officer's last promotion board and not currently his direct supervisors. Each force should examine its promotion system and adopt the best features of schemes in other forces.

The Inquiry rejected proposals from the Federations to change some aspects of disciplinary procedure. It said there was no evidence to justify the appointment of an appeal tribunal with a legal chairman, but the possibility should be kept under review. The Federations had pointed out that nearly all appeals were decided on paper in the Home Office, and no reasons were given for the decision of the Secretary of State. Edmund-Davies said this could be pursued through the PAB.

The Inquiry agreed that all probationers liable to be dismissed as unlikely to become efficient constables should have the right to an interview with a senior officer before a final decision was taken, and to be assisted by a Federation representative.

On the role of women, the Inquiry said that in appropriate cases, departments of men and women officers should be set up to work with juveniles, women, missing persons and sexual offences. Efforts should be made to reappoint women officers who had resigned to have families, and their shifts should be designed to take account of temporary family commitments. Women should retain separate representation in the Federations, but the situation could be reviewed in the light of the workings of the Sex Discrimination Act.

The Edmund-Davies saga occupied three years. Its most dramatic aspect was the new pay structure, but its other work had been fundamental to the role of the Police Federation as an integral part of the police service. With both major parties openly committed to preserving the new pay standards, ordinary policemen owed a lot to the patient work of Lord Edmund-Davies and his colleagues. As with the Willink Royal Commission, the influence of the Inquiry's secretary was crucial to the outcome. Neil Morgan of the Home Office police department had been seconded to this task and he had done a remarkable job in ensuring that the team gained the confidence of the police, and that its members were shown the extent of the problems facing the service. The Federations had been lucky to have been virtually given the right to choose the chairman of the Inquiry, but their other stroke of luck was to have had Neil Morgan acting as its secretary, rather than some other mandarin of the stamp of 'Butch' Baker, the man who had given such disastrous advice about the state of the service to a succession of Home Secretaries.

There was one last postcript to Edmund-Davies. Joe Martucci and Jim Jardine did not forgive and forget all the months of opposition and sniping from the sidelines. Jack Kent, their most persistent and effective critic, was ousted from the chairmanship of the constables' central committee. Kent had been seen as a strong contender to succeed Jardine as the national chairman, a prospect which horrified Eldon Griffiths as well as a number of Home Office officials. Kent was one of those Lord Edmund-Davies had in mind when he pointed out that the 'character' of the Federation might change in the future. The Manchester man had chosen to be a loose cannon and throughout the period had publicly distanced himself, not only from Martucci, but from his own central committee. Kent took his removal badly, but in truth, and for all his great ability, conviction and commitment, he was too mercurial a figure to be trusted with high office, and he spoke only for a small minority of the service which wanted to establish a very different kind of body to represent the rank and file. Martucci's ruthless streak had been used on this occasion to clear the way for a more settled and peaceful future for the Police Federation.

TWENTY-NINE

The inner city's burning down

In April 1979, fed up with the 'Winter of discontent' in which the social contract he had nurtured with the trades unions collapsed amidst the bitterness of the health ancillaries and council workers' strikes, the electors ejected James Callaghan from Downing Street and installed Margaret Thatcher at the head of a Conservative government with a comfortable majority in the House of Commons. No sooner had she stood in Downing Street and quoted St Francis of Assisi in her remarks about healing the nation's divisions, than the new Home Secretary, Willie Whitelaw, implemented his party's pre-election promise to pay the full Edmund-Davies award to the police, back - dated to the lst September 1978.

In the election campaign, Joe Martucci and Jim Jardine took the Police Federation as close as they dared to outright intervention in party politics. As soon as the election date was announced by Callaghan, and acting on strong advice from Eldon Griffiths, they retained the leading firm of public relations advisers and lobbyists, Charles Barker Lyons, to mount a 'law and order' campaign. The ease and speed with which they were able to do this demonstrated the total grip that the chairman and secretary had of their JCC colleagues. A meeting of the executive committee of the JCC was simply told that the campaign had commenced. Further, a manifesto would be produced and circulated to every candidate standing in the general election, demanding to know whether or not they supported the views it expressed. Seeing that the 'manifesto' was principally the work of Eldon Griffiths, and was virtually a verbatim reproduction of the Tory policy statements and campaign promises on law and order, there was no doubt at to which party the Federation was backing on this issue.

Nor was there any doubt that in this election the overwhelming majority of Federation members, always regarded as natural Conservative voters, would be enthusiasts for Thatcher. The party was already committed to implementing the whole of the Edmund-Davies increase, which meant that every serving officer stood to gain hundreds of pounds from a Tory victory. Thatcher was also speaking the strong language they had not heard from the Labour Government; promising to strengthen and support the police, and get tough with criminals. The police agreed with Thatcher that Labour had been 'soft on crime', and were apprehensive about the outcome of the Royal Commission on Criminal Procedure, which Callaghan appointed in 1978 following concern about police interrogation methods which had been expressed by many Labour MPs and others in legal and civil liberty circles.

After the election, *POLICE* told the membership why the Federation had intervened in the election campaign;

> 'In taking the unprecedented step of a public challenge to all candidates and parties to declare themselves, the Police Federation was not seeking to support or attack any party. We sought from those who wanted the people's votes a clear indication of what they were actually going to do, as distinct from what they were saying, about the challenge of crime to our society.'

The editorial called for a new Criminal Justice Act which would 'spell out to the courts the determination of society to meet and defeat crime.' It added that 'the dangerous experimentalism, the trendy and half baked penology, of the past two decades, must be abandoned.'

The 1979 Conference was held in Blackpool just a week after the election. Willie Whitelaw did not attend to receive the grateful thanks of the delegates for the handsome pay present. Instead, a totally unknown Minister of State, Lord Belstead, walked on to the platform to a huge standing ovation. There was a touching moment when Eldon Griffiths, who hoped and expected to play a leading role in the new

Government, told the delegates that he would have to give up being the Federation consultant. He was presented with the Federation Bowl, in recognition of his outstanding services, and joined James Callaghan and Roy Jenkins as recipients of the organisation's highest honour.

A couple of weeks later, the membership was informed that Mr Griffiths would be staying with the Federation. The anticipated Government job was not offered to him, probably because Mrs Thatcher regarded him as a loyal supporter of Edward Heath. Martucci told the JCC that Griffiths was the only man to act for the Federation in Parliament. The Labour MPs who had survived the Tory landslide had no love for the Federation after its open intervention in the election, which included press advertisements and cost £20,000. When Jim Jardine wrote to all newly elected MPs to congratulate them on being elected, several Labour members wrote back to say, in the words of the MP for Wood Green, Reg Race, that the Federation had made its bed and could lie on it. In any case, the policies of the new Government on law and order were fully in line with the wishes of the Federation, and it was difficult to think of a Labour MP who would be prepared to advocate those views on behalf of the Federation, or whose constituency party would agree to his working for it. A tentative approach had been made to Alf Morris, who did not wish to resume the post, saying that he would be too busy as the Opposition spokesman on the disabled. Martucci said it was essential that the Federation's adviser should be able 'in good conscience' to speak and vote in harmony with the Federation, otherwise he would not carry conviction in the House or with the membership.

If the police welcomed the change of Government, the summer of 1979 brought a further boost to morale when the first pay review to be conducted under the Edmund-Davies formula produced an increase of 13.5 per cent. This took the starting rate for a constable to £4,086, and at the 15 year point it became £6,470. Welcome as it was, the increase demonstrated the level of wage inflation in Britain at the time, and the failure of the previous Government's attempts to hold it down.

The period just before the General Election had been marked by increased disorder in London and several cities, consisting mainly of street clashes involving the racists fascists of the National Front and a broad alliance of students, Trotskyists, and similar groups. Usually, the demonstrations degenerated into running battles with the police, in which officers were injured.

The Federation leadership disagreed with the refusal of the Metropolitan Commissioner, Sir David McNee, and provincial chief constables such as Alan Goodson of Leicestershire, to ban National Front marches which were bound to degenerate into riots After a particularly violent confrontation at Southall in London, the Federation demanded that better protective clothing and equipment be issued to officers expected to deal with riots. The death of an anti-racist demonstrator, Blair Peach, during this demonstration became a *cause célèbre*, with an allegation that Mr Peach had been killed by a blow from the baton of an unidentified officer from the Special Patrol Group.

Just a week before the election, Martucci and Jardine met Merlyn Rees as Home Secretary for the last time, to express concern about public order. They told him that there should be a review of the Public Order Act immediately after the election, to ensure that the police were given the power to prohibit marches which carried a threat to public safety. The Federation also said that electoral law should be altered to allow a local authority to refuse to allow its premises to be used for election meetings where a similar threat was present. They thanked Rees for resisting demands for a public inquiry into the complaints made against the police at these events. The Home Secretary said that the allegations must be dealt with through the new complaints procedure. Some years earlier, in his report into a similar riot in Red Lion Square, London, Lord Justice Scarman said that no useful purpose was served by appointing special tribunals whenever a public disturbance occurred. Within a couple of years, Lord Scarman would find himself again presiding at just such an inquiry, following the Brixton riots. After the election, the new Government introduced a review of the law of public order and public meetings.

One of the first actions taken by Margaret Thatcher was to ensure that Parliament had a further opportunity to consider the restoration of capital punishment. Jim Jardine wrote to Willie Whitelaw to set out the Federation's case. He said that terrorism had added a new dimension to the debate, citing bomb outrages in Britain and the deaths up to then of 130 police officers in Ulster. He argued that terrorists acted in the full knowledge that if convicted their own lives would not be taken.

Jardine pointed to the sharp rise in homicides since 1965, and criticised the 'diminished responsibility' rule which allowed killers to plead guilty to manslaughter rather than murder. He said that there had been a significant increase in the criminal use of firearms since abolition. The Federation encouraged branch boards to lobby MPs on the issue, and the opponents of hanging also mobilised their forces for the debate. The vote, when it came in July 1979, resulted in the rejection of a motion to restore capital punishment, by an overwhelming majority, setting a pattern in which, irrespective of the political make - up of Parliament, there is always a substantial majority opposed to capital punishment. Soon after the vote, Jardine addressed a Conservative meeting in London, and said that the Federation had to accept the result, but the law should be changed to ensure that in the case of some murders, including those of police officers, a life sentence should mean what it said. He referred to calls which had been made in some quarters for the arming of the police;

> 'We are opposed to any general arming of the police. Nothing would do more to damage the close relationship of trust and confidence between the police and the public than the conspicuous wearing and using of guns by the police. Then there is the danger of escalation. Criminal gangs, confronting police armed with Smith and Wesson's, would take to sub-machine guns.'

He added that the police would now require 'easy access' to modern weapons, whenever they were needed, and more officers must be trained in the proper use of firearms. They should also have effective body armour. Finally, he called for strict controls over all firearms, with shotguns being treated in the same way as other firearms, a call that annoyed the shooting interests.

Towards the end of 1979, the JCC submitted detailed evidence to the Royal Commission on Criminal Procedure. It pointed out that reported crime had reached two and a half millions a year, and that only forty per cent were 'cleared - up'. The JCC said that the chances of arresting, still less convicting, the more dangerous, cunning or resourceful criminals were diminishing. Accepting that there had to be limits to police powers in a free society, the Federation said that the other side of the civil liberties argument was that proposals to strengthen the rights of suspects should be balanced against the interests of society. Making specific proposals, the memorandum said there should be a statutory code of practice governing police procedures in investigating crime, and arresting and detaining suspects. There should be a police power to arrest when an officer had reasonable grounds for suspecting that an indictable offence had been or was about to be committed, and also when a suspect failed to give his name and address in the case of summary offences. The police should be able to detain a suspect for up to 72 hours before being required to bring a charge or release him, with magistrates being able to authorise continued detention in appropriate serious cases. The police should have a general power to search an arrested suspect.

Dealing with the suspect at the police station, the JCC said the Federation, with some reservations, supported an experiment in the tape recording of interviews with suspects in police stations, but evidence of other statements made by an accused should continue to be admissible in court. The Federation criticised the right to silence, and suggested that the police caution which had to be administered to a defendant when being charged, telling him that he was not obliged to say anything, should be amended to say that if he exercised the right, adverse comment about his silence might be made at the trial The prosecution as well as the judge should have the right to comment on the defendant's silence. The JCC said that a defendant should either give sworn evidence in court, or remain silent, he should not be allowed to make an unsworn statement on which he could not be cross-examined.

The Federation expressed concern at the rate of acquittals in contested cases, and asked for a power to take fingerprints from all arrested persons over the age of 14. It was often vital to medically examine a suspect for evidential purposes, but this could not be done without his consent, therefore a power to conduct an examination was required. The JCC added that in spite of recent criticisms, it believed the law on identification procedures was satisfactory.

One of the major issues before the Royal Commission was whether the police should continue to take the decision to prosecute in cases other than the serious offences where the decision was taken by the Director of Public Prosecutions. The JCC said the current practice was excellent and it was opposed to a national prosecuting system. The solicitors departments of police forces, or local lawyers who gave advice on whether to prosecute, did an excellent job, the Federation said.

The Royal Commission, one of whose members was the former JCC secretary Dick Pamplin, did not publish its report until January 1981. Although it said the right to silence must remain unchanged, many of its proposals came close to the Federation's views, and succeeded in angering the civil liberties' groups who had hoped for sweeping additional safeguards for suspects. The chief anger was directed against a proposal that all police officers should have the power to stop and search a suspect on reasonable suspicion of possession of an article which it was an offence to possess in a public place. POLICE pointed out that this did no more than to extend to the rest of the service a power that the Metropolitan police and some large provincial forces had possessed all along.

The Federation could not foresee that a Conservative government under Margaret Thatcher, far from implementing the proposal to give all police additional search powers, would shortly take the power away from the Metropolitan and other forces, in the interests of improved race relations.

In 1980, the House of Commons Home Affairs Select Committee issued a report on race relations which called for the scrapping of the 'suspected person loitering' offence, contained in the nineteenth century Vagrancy Act. A strong campaign against 'Sus' had been mounted by a coalition of pressure groups, with strong support from the Opposition parties. The report referred to widespread belief among members of the black community in inner cities that the police used the 'Sus' law to discriminate against them.

The Metropolitan Police submitted evidence which denied that this was so, and said that the sustained campaign for the repeal of 'Sus' had 'increased the difficulties faced by police officers in their attempts to establish good relations with black youth.' If this was the case, the Committee retorted, then the sooner it was repealed, the better, although the MPs agreed that this would make comparatively little difference to relations between the police and young black men.

The Report said that there was evidence that the police used 'Sus' as a useful back-up when they had not got enough evidence to convict for actual or attempted theft, but knew that somebody was 'up to no good.' The Federation's view was that if the clause was to be repealed, the law on attempts to commit crimes would have to be strengthened to ensure that the police had power to arrest.

In 1980, the 'Sus' offence was abolished by the Criminal Attempts Act, which introduced changes to the law on attempts to commit crime. It made it an offence to interfere with a motor vehicle, and removed the loophole that a person could not be convicted of an attempt to steal if there was nothing to be stolen, such as trying to 'pick' an empty pocket.

An immediate consequence of the abolition of 'Sus' was that police in inner London areas found that many young black people believed that the police had lost the power to stop and search people on reasonable suspicion that they had committed, or were about to commit crime. The generic term 'Sus' had been applied to this practice, and it was the abolition of the power to stop and search on suspicion that the pressure groups had been demanding.

The Royal Commission on Criminal Procedure proposed that there should be a limit of six hours in the time that a suspect could be detained before being charged, or 24 hours on the authority of a senior police officer. Magistrates could authorise further detention for periods of 24 hours.

The Commission suggested that once a suspect had been charged by the police, a locally appointed Crown prosecutor should take charge of the case, with the power to vary the charge or to drop the case. It also proposed that local police authorities should take charge of the force prosecutions departments, while saying that the power to prosecute must remain the prerogative of the chief constable. *POLICE* commented;

> 'There is so much of value in this report that it must not be allowed to be quietly dropped after the usual consultations and Parliamentary debate. It provides the police with a much clearer statement of their powers than has ever been available in the past, and it helps towards a greater understanding of the rights of the suspect. A Government committed to reducing the problems of crime has a clear duty to act during the lifetime of the current administration.'

At Easter 1980 race relations burst into the headlines in the most dramatic and frightening manner. One afternoon the chief constable of Avon and Somerset was meeting local Federation officials at the divisional headquarters in Bristol, when the officers drew his attention to the scene beyond the windows, where a huge pall of smoke was rising above the city. The police had made an afternoon raid on the somewhat incongruously named Black and White Cafe in the predominantly black St Pauls area. The cafe was notorious for illegal drinking and supplying liquor and drugs to youngsters of school age, many of whom milled around the premises during the raid, and as police removed crates of beer, they began throwing stones. Within moments a large and hostile crowd had arrived to outnumber the thirty police officers engaged in the raid. For two hours, they did what they could to quell the violence, reinforced by a few more officers, but they were hopelessly outnumbered and after a third of the officers engaged in the street battle had been injured and were forced to withdraw. As soon as they did so, the mob began to loot shops and set fire to buildings, destroying a bank and burning parked cars. When the riot began,. many motorists were trapped and put in fear by the roving gangs of mainly black youths who smashed their car windscreens and robbed them. After the withdrawal was ordered, the police put a cordon around the St Pauls area. During the riot, six police cars were destroyed and fifteen more damaged by stone throwers. Fire service personnel and vehicles were stoned, and over a hundred rioters were arrested.

The chief constable, Brian Weigh, took the controversial decision to keep the police out until reinforcements arrived from surrounding forces. This left the law abiding people caught up in the mayhem unprotected for more than four hours, for which the police were criticised heavily. Rank and file opinion in the force was that the chief and senior officers had mishandled the situation. Many off duty officers, hearing of the violence, had reported for duty and been told that they were not required. It became obvious that the force, in common with almost all others outside London, had no effective contingency plans to deal with mass disorder on such a scale. Only a month earlier, a senior Home Office official, Brian Cubbon, had been to Bristol to confer with the police and local community leaders, and had been informed that race relations in the city were very good.

The St Pauls riot was the worst to have occurred in Britain for sixty years. It mirrored the scenes which had been seen in Northern Ireland since 1969, but this time TV viewers witnessed live scenes of huge fires and rioters throwing stones at the English police. Even as the fire service was dampening the embers in St Pauls, politicians and editors were speculating on where the next riot would occur, with most pointing to the racially tense inner city districts in London, particularly Brixton. Willie Whitelaw was alarmed at the demonstration of virtual impotence of police commanders and instructed ACPO to prepare an immediate report on what was needed to prevent any recurrence.

Jardine wrote at once to Whitelaw to demand that the Police Federation be consulted about any proposals for changes in the way police dealt with public disorder, citing the Edmund-Davies report on the importance of consultation.

It was, after all, the Federation's members who had to bear the brunt of the violence. The Federation was far from impressed with the handling of the Bristol riot, and concerned about the lack of equipment and training of the police. Whitelaw replied that this was an operational matter and was being dealt with by the chief constables. The Federation and the Superintendents would be shown the draft recommendations of ACPO, and in the meantime could 'feed in' any views it might have to the Home Office. This, said Whitelaw, complied with the spirit of Edmund-Davies. Jardine replied to call this answer 'disappointing' and said it was far short of the intentions of Edmund-Davies. Whitelaw took the point, and invited the Federation and the Superintendents Association to put their views personally to him at the Home Office. *POLICE* commented on the lessons of St Pauls;

'What disturbs some members of the force and outside observers is the apparent absence of any contingency plan to cope with serious public disorder in the area. If an airliner had fallen on the centre of Bristol, a plan was ready to deal with it. If there had been a train disaster, or a major explosion, the plans were there. But a mob of young blacks suddenly going on the rampage? the totally unexpected emergency appears to have caught the planners on the hop. Is this true of other areas where serious disorder has always been a possibility, and after Bristol becomes more likely?'

Brian Weigh took exception to the *POLICE* report of the riot, whilst making no attempt to answer the questions it had raised. He wrote that the problem was manpower;

'All of us are only too aware of how thin the blue line is when confronted by sudden emergencies, and now especially so when the antagonism is entirely against the police and fire is part of it. Only the largest forces will have sufficient manpower quickly - fast response by fully equipped task forces may help, but the risks are enormous, especially where there is firing of police vehicles - and in the ultimate, manpower in consider-

able strength, properly protected and well organised,
is the only answer.'

In June 1980, Joe Martucci retired, and Constable Leslie
Knowles of South Wales became the secretary. Martucci had
always intended to go when he had completed twenty five
years' service. although the JCC would have wished him to
remain in charge during the formative period of the new
negotiating machinery. Leslie Knowles did not occupy the
secretary's chair for long. He had been elected unopposed
after Sergeant Gordon Meredith, whom most members would
have supported for the post, stood down because he was close
to completing thirty years' service and there was an unwritten
rule, that in conformity with its policy of seeking compulsory
retirement after thirty years', Federation officials should not
serve beyond this point. Meredith would have been a popular
choice among the membership. He was awarded the George
Medal after being seriously wounded in an incident in
Coventry in which a young constable, Peter Guthrie, was shot
dead. When he was elected unopposed, Knowles told the
Committee that he could serve for three more years, but he
had not taken account of his service in another force before
joining South Wales. This came to the notice of the JCC
officers a few months later, and they told Knowles, that
although this was 'broken service', it counted towards the
'30 year rule'. Knowles in any case was in poor health at this
time, and he decided to retire. His successor was the deputy
secretary, Inspector Peter Tanner of the Metropolitan.

The outcome of the review of policing arrangements for
handling disorder was submitted to Willie Whitelaw in
August 1980. Its main conclusions were that each force must
ensure that it had enough trained officers to deal with sudden
disorder. Effective mutual aid between forces, by which units
of trained officers could be sent to assist forces with problems,
were essential. All officers must receive common training
in the public order aspects of their duties.

The Federation representatives involved in the review had
pressed the chief officers and the Home Office for the
immediate introduction of protective clothing and equipment
of the kind in use among continental police forces and the

RUC. The chief officers and Home Office officials baulked at this. The report said;

> 'Police forces have responded to the rising incidence of violence in recent years by introducing a limited amount of personal protective equipment for police officers, chiefly shields and a reinforced helmet. This is a step the police have taken with the greatest reluctance. However, chief officers, and the community as a whole, have a duty to ensure that police officers are adequately protected during disorderly incidents.'

Within a very short time, the police were to have need of the new mutual aid requirements when rioting broke out on a scale which easily surpassed the level reached at St Pauls.

On the domestic front, the Federation suffered a significant reverse in the Court of Appeal in the case of *Starbuck v Goodson*. This was a test case which concerned the entitlement of an officer whose rest day was cancelled at short notice to be paid compensation. The chief constable of Leicestershire, Alan Goodson, decided to cancel all rest days in the force in order to police a National Front demonstration in Leicester. He took this action 14 days before the event. The ruling ruined PC Starbuck's planned family holiday, for which he had already paid. The force told him that all he was entitled to was another day off to be taken at some later date. This had been a sore point with the Federation for years, and the Federation backed PC Starbuck in a High Court action where the judge upheld the chief constable's interpretation of the relevant police regulation.

At the appeal hearing, Lord Denning, the Master of the Rolls, sided with PC Starbuck. He said that the contention by the police authority that it could change an officer's rostered rest day at will, so long as at least 8 days' notice was given, and not compensate him for the inconvenience to him and his family, was wrong. It meant that the chief constable had full discretion, and no such discretion should be vested except in plain words in the regulation. Unfortunately for Starbuck and the Federation, the two other judges disagreed with Lord Denning. The Master of the Rolls was scathing about the terms of the regulation, which he thought was almost impossible to understand. He asked the counsel for the police authority if it could be amended to put things right, and when counsel said he was sure the Federation and the Home Office would now 'put their heads together' Lord Denning retorted; 'They have put their heads together at fairly regular intervals, and that is what has caused the trouble. If they put their heads together and produced regulations which made sense, that would be a different matter.' The ruling lead to protracted negotiations with the official side, and to the introduction of annual duty rosters, which years later were to be condemned as inhibiting chief officers from effectively deploying their manpower resources.

There was good news for the police in the outcome of the 1980 pay review, although once again it reflected spiralling wage inflation throughout the working population. The increase was 21.4 per cent, which meant that a constable's starting pay rose from £4,086 to £4,956, and a top rate PC with 15 years service, on £6,470, went up to £7,848. In two years, therefore, the police had received salary increases which were greater in total than the uplift provided in the Edmund-Davies report.

THIRTY

The judgement of Scarman

In July 1980 the House of Commons Home Affairs Committee published its report on a special investigation it had conducted into the deaths of persons in police custody. The inquiry was the culmination of a long campaign which had been spearheaded by a Labour MP, Michael Meacher, whose allegations became wilder as the campaign went on. Before the Select Committee decided to examine the evidence, Mr Meacher had even questioned whether some persons who had died in police hands from heart failure, or from choking on their own vomit (a common occurrence with drunken prisoners) might not have died from these causes at all, but as a result of ill-treatment by the police. The case that had excited Mr Meacher's closest attention was that of a man named Kelly who had died in Liverpool. He made allegations about Kelly's injuries that were repudiated by Professor Alan Usher, the Home Office pathologist who had conducted the post mortem. Meacher was unabashed at being shown to be wrong. Another member of the Home Affairs Committee and a former junior minister in the Home Office, Alec Lyon, proposed unsuccessfully that police officers in cases of deaths in police custody should be deprived of their right of silence.

The police deeply resented the tone and content of Michael Meacher's campaign. It was unfortunately typical of the readiness of a small number of Labour MPs, mainly but not wholly on the Left, who were ready to attack the police whenever the opportunity occurred. Most allegations, apart from deaths in custody, involved racialism, brutality or corruption. Persistent criticism by MPs in the House was matched in the country by a clear rift between many Labour party activists and the police service. In 1980 and 1981, Labour gained control of a large number of councils, including the metropolitan authorities.

The new police authorities were predominantly left wing, and many sought to adopt a more interventionist role. This lead to a series of confrontations with chief constables, notably James Anderton in Greater Manchester and Kenneth Oxford in Merseyside, where the new chairman of the police authority was a formidable woman, Margaret Simey, who had been a lone voice in the Seventies in calling for changes in the constitutional position of police authorities and chief constables. The country's largest authority, the Greater London Council, was not a police authority but the ruling Labour group set up a 'Police Committee' with an annual budget of over £2 million. Its purpose was to monitor the activities of the Metropolitan Police, and to campaign for the force to be brought under the control of the GLC. Some Labour controlled London borough councils set up police committees to act as watchdogs in their areas. There were several examples of persons being employed by the GLC or the boroughs in their 'police units' at substantial salaries, who were also Labour councillors and the 'chairs' of police committees in other authorities. A new breed of activists emerged, paid out of the rates to criticise the police, while the GLC 'police committee' doled out grants to disparate 'community' groups and law centres, to keep pressure on the police.

Alec Lyon MP, told the Labour police authorities that the increasing size of police forces, and the creation of public relations departments 'dedicated to putting across the policy of the chief constable' had led to a new breed of assertive chief constables who 'spurned political control only to indulge in politics'. It was, Lyon argued, just as desirable for politicians to control chief constables as it was for them to control the armed forces and the civil service. He advised police authorities to insist that their forces adopted 'community policing' as operated in Devon and Cornwall by chief constable Alderton, saying tartly that it was not enough to put a few officers back on the beat and make them the children's 'Uncle Charlie' for the neighbourhood, if the rest of the force was still maintaining its reactive police tactics to undermine the judgment of the community. Lyon's enthusiasm for community policing was not shared by some other Labour figures, such as Ted Knight, the far-Left leader of Lambeth Council, who described it as 'having a copper's nark on every street corner'.

A newly elected Labour MP, Jack Straw, introduced a Private Member's Bill in the Commons to extend the powers of police authorities. It sought to give police authorities power to give directions to chief constables in such matters as community policing and whether police patrolled on foot or in cars. Police authorities should be able to appoint superintendents as well as chief and assistant chief officers. They should be able to order investigations into specific complaints, and be entitled to see the HMI's report of his annual inspection of the force.

Straw recognised that the frustration felt by Labour members of police authorities (which was shared by some Conservatives who resented the independence exercised by local chief officers) was caused by the abolition in 1964 of the old watch committees in the city and borough forces. As he wrote in *POLICE*;

> '... ... although the watch committees had no more formal powers over the policing of their areas than the county joint committees, their power of appointment and promotion of *all* officers inevitably gave them considerably more influence in practice over policing policies, and made the officers of the forces more sensitive to the wishes of the elected members.'

Which, after all, was what convinced the Royal Commission in 1962 that watch committees should lose their powers of promotion. Straw's Bill suffered the usual fate of controversial Private Member's Bills, and Willie Whitelaw assured ACPO that the Government had no intention of introducing a democratic police authority for the Metropolitan Police.

This period of sustained criticism of the police from the labour and trades union movement marked the breakdown of the broad concensus on policing which had grown up over the previous forty years. After the hostility between the police and strikers in the early part of the century, and the street battles caused by fascists and their opponents in the Thirties, when the Left accused the police of supporting the fascists, there had been a long period of relative tranquillity on the labour and political fronts. The Attlee post-war Government had been strong on law and order, reassuring rank and file police officers and chief constables that Labour in office could be as supportive of the police as the Tories had always been.

The two principal factors which contributed in the late Seventies to the rift between the police and Labour were the tensions between the police and young black people in multi-racial areas (exacerbated by the increasing politicisation of social issues), and the frequent resort to mass picketing by trades unions in industrial disputes. Here too, the same Trostkyist and far-Left groups which agitated against the police in the inner cities, were active on the fringes of every significant industrial dispute. in this period. The police, especially after Thatcher came to power, were seen by many Labour supporters and others, not as neutral enforcers of impartial law, but as agents of the anti-trades union Government - 'Maggie's boot boys'. It was argued in these circles that the Tories had bribed the police by paying the whole of the Edmund-Davies award as soon as they took office, and giving top priority to spending on law and order. Therefore, the police were expected to 'do the Government's dirty work' in breaking strikes and suppressing protest.

In the spring and summer of 1981, urban rioting in England reached a scale that had never been witnessed before. The worst outbreak was in Brixton, fulfilling forecasts that an eruption would occur in this South London hotbed of tension. During three days of rioting and looting, over four hundred officers were injured and shops and other commercial buildings were burned down. In addition to being attacked with hand held weapons and bricks and stones, the police were the targets of crudely made petrol bombs, which the rioters had prepared and stored long before the 'spontaneous' rioting occurred.

The riots in Brixton, and simultaneous disturbances involving the police and gangs of young people at fairgrounds and seaside resorts, showed that existing protective equipment, and public order training and command strategies were inadequate. Many officers had been injured because they lacked riot helmets and shields. Some had improvised during the riots, using plastic dustbin lids and milk bottle crates to ward off the bricks and petrol bombs.

Immediately following the Brixton riots, Jim Jardine and the new JCC secretary, Peter Tanner, met the chairman and secretary of ACPO to discuss the situation. Tanner, before becoming a JCC member, had been an experienced operational inspector in Tottenham with a reputation for leading from the front. He was incensed by the scale of injuries suffered by the police and the lack of protection they had been given. He had seen the sophisticated weaponry and personal protection equipment used by the German police to deal with street riots, and demanded that, at the least, officers should be supplied with the riot helmets worn by continental officers. The best the British police could do up to then was a conventional police helmet made of stronger material with wide retaining straps. In practice, it offered little or no protection.

Jardine and Tanner found that ACPO was still resistant to the adoption of 'riot gear' - NATO helmets, flame proof overalls, steel capped boots, and short shields (to allow officers to move forward rather than crouch behind static ones) - for fear of damaging the historic pacific image of the British Bobby. It was a view with which the Federation leaders had lost patience and they told ACPO, that if the chiefs would not support them in their demands for proper protection, they would go directly to the Home Secretary. They knew that Whitelaw, with his experience of Northern Ireland, was privately appalled by the number of injured officers. He favoured the adoption of water cannons, as used on the continent and in the past in Ulster, but the Commissioner and ACPO were against them. The ACPO leaders agreed that a joint approach was needed, and at the end of April, the three associations met Whitelaw to discuss public order.

The JCC issued a long statement, which emphasised the Federation's demand for better protection of its members;

'Too many police officers are being asked to face mobs whilst wearing ordinary police uniform and have virtually no defence against missiles and petrol bombs. We now call upon the Home Secretary, as a first priority, to ensure that all police officers when ordered to deal with riots are wearing headgear which is capable of withstanding a blow from a missile and which protects the face, and have sufficient protection to avoid the risk of serious injury to other parts of the body.'

The statement also called for police vehicles to be reinforced to afford protection for their occupants against missiles and fire. As to the 'image', the Federation said;

'We are under no illusions about the path which the police service is being forced to follow. A decade ago, the idea of the police requiring riot shields, helmets and visors and body protection on the streets of England and Wales would have been regarded as unnecessarily alarmist. Yet all these things have come to pass and it is now necessary to provide special training in the containment of riots in every police force. As the violence shown to the police has become increasingly vicious, so the police response has had to become progressively more organised and disciplined. Society cannot be far away from making the choice between withdrawing the police from the streets, thus allowing the mob to vent its fury on property and people, or equipping the police to enable them to go on the offensive in the manner of continental police forces. We believe there is still time and opportunity for the Government, Parliament and all people in authority to take steps which will obviate the need for such a choice.'

Following his meeting with the staff associations at the Home Office, Whitelaw set in train an immediate review of protective equipment. He had already announced that Lord Justice Scarman would conduct an inquiry into the causes of the Brixton riots, a decision which incensed Sir David McNee, who was not even consulted about it.

At the Federation Conference in May 1981, Jardine spoke up for the young constables who were being blamed in the media for insensitive behaviour in Brixton and other inner-city areas;

> 'I think it is time the public recognised that nowadays the young police officers working in inner city areas soon acquire a vast store of bitter experience and their maturity is remarkable. The public owes these young officers an enormous debt of gratitude, not only for their courage, but for their determination to do the job according to the oath they took on the day they were appointed to the police service ... ... How many people stop to consider the size of the task which faces the young men and women in police uniform, who are put on the streets after a minimum training period, and expected to maintain the rule of law amongst people who, in many cases, have nothing but contempt for the ordinary values of our society?'

In July, more riots took place in Brixton, and there were similar outbreaks in Handsworth, Birmingham, Moss Side in Manchester, and in Toxteth, Liverpool, where the looting and damage was comparable with Brixton. It was widely believed that these disturbances owed much to a desire by local elements to imitate the mayhem in Brixton, which had been portrayed so dramatically on television while it was actually happening. It was also noted in these areas that the Government's reaction to Brixton had been to set up a public inquiry, and give widespread publicity to the social problems of the area, as well as giving voice to grievances against 'heavy handed and oppressive' policing. The mobs had discovered the advantages of anonymity amongst crowds, and of lawbreaking in darkness.

The police response to the 1981 riots was more effective than the chaos which had reigned in Bristol a year before. Following ACPO's public order review, training had been stepped up and police support units were sent to the aid of the forces where the outbreaks occurred. At Toxteth, for example, officers who had spent the morning working in Dorset and Hampshire villages found themselves before midnight patrolling unfamiliar streets in Toxteth. The ferocity of the Toxteth riots was probably greater than anywhere else. It reflected years of animosity between the criminal fraternity in the small Granby enclave of inner Liverpool, mainly young black or mixed - race men, and the police. When the local police station was beseiged on the first night of rioting by a crowd intent on burning it to the ground, one of the few officers defending it fired two canisters of CS gas at the rioters, several of whom sustained injuries because the projectiles were not suitable for riot dispersal. It was the first and only instance of gas being used against rioters in England.

At Moss Side, Manchester, while his officers struggled to keep order and dodged bricks and petrol bombs, chief constable Anderton found himself locked in confrontation with Labour councillors and local 'community leaders'. One of the councillors was Mrs Gay Cox, the deputy chairman of the Greater Manchester police authority. She led a demand that Anderton should dismiss the senior police officer in Moss Side and make a public apology to the local community for the 'provocative' actions of the police. Further, they demanded that the heavy police presence in the area should be withdrawn. Anderton said that he was 'absolutely dismayed' by this 'appalling proposition'. He told Mrs Cox that the suggestion was outrageous and he would not crucify one of his senior officers to placate the disgruntled members of the community. In a report to the Labour controlled police authority, Anderton wrote;

'We hear a lot nowadays about the much heralded concept of 'democratic community policing' and the need for more involvement of local representatives in the management of police affairs. Well, if this was a practical example then all I can say is - God help us!'

Meanwhile, Kenneth Oxford, the chief constable of Merseyside was also under strong attack from his left wing police authority. During the rioting, a young man who had got in the way of a police vehicle was killed, and immediately the cry of 'Murder' was raised, although a jury acquitted the police driver of a manslaughter charge. Many wild allegations were made against the police, and these were given credence in the inflamed atmosphere of the time. Jim Jardine went to Merseyside to address a packed annual meeting of the local Federation. He launched a strong attack on Margaret Simey and the police authority, and made a vigorous defence of Oxford. There was a certain irony in this, because not long before, the JCC had been forced to ask the Home Secretary to intervene in a bitter row between Oxford and the Merseyside branch board, caused largely by Oxford's autocratic managerial style.

Merseyside police authority was faced with a very large bill for riot damages following the Toxteth disorders, but Margaret Simey refused to criticise those who had burned and looted. 'They would have been apathetic fools not to have rioted,' she declared, to the fury of many Liverpool citizens. Seeing that the riots brought Mrs Thatcher's Secretary of State for the Environment, Michael Heseltine, hot foot to Toxteth to see for himself what was wrong, and the city subsequently received massive urban renewal grants from the Government, it could be argued that the mobs had achieved more for inner-city Liverpool in a few nights of rioting than the local authorities and central government had managed over a generation.

Speaking to the annual meeting of the Metropolitan Branch Boards later in 1981, Willie Whitelaw praised the courage with which officers had faced the rioters, but said that insofar as the disorders were a manifestation of the breakdown in trust between the police and some of the communities they served, trust had to be rebuilt and the task would not be easy. It would be a long, slow and often unrewarding process. Not all criticism of the police came from those with a political interest in undermining the relationship between the police and the public. There was genuine concern that police objectives and methods should be adapted to meet current circumstances;

'We must therefore examine what we can do to restore

the standing - credibility even - of the police in those areas where it has been lost or damaged. If we are to break down the barriers of suspicion and mistrust, we must identify and eliminate the causes of tension and we must seek to learn from the lessons - and mistakes - of the past.'

But John Newman, the chairman of the Metropolitan Federation, was in no mood for bridge building when he told Whitelaw, at the same meeting, that his members had been subjected to verbal and physical abuse to a degree that was 'as unacceptable as it was inevitable'. Newman alleged that the force had played the game of 'low profile policing'. As to alleged police racism, he said;

'The police officer sheltering behind a riot shield from a barrage of petrol bombs, cannot be expected to exude love and harmony towards the ethnic minorities, if it is they who are throwing the bombs.'

In its evidence to the Scarman Inquiry into the Brixton riots, the Joint Central Committee accepted that the relationship between the police and the multi-racial inner city communities was a very difficult one;

'Here the police are the representatives of the rule of law. Their duties bring them more frequently into conflict with the population and the public does not offer anything like the consent and cooperation which is generally to be found elsewhere.'

The Federation accepted that some officers had fallen below the high standards expected of the police, but told Scarman that it rejected the picture of a bullying, uncaring police service which had been painted by its critics. While the Brixton riots had been exceptionally ferocious, the Federation pointed out that disturbances had become more frequent at football matches, seaside resorts and industrial disputes. More than 14,000 officers a year were being assaulted.

The memorandum criticised excessive leniency by the courts when dealing with violent offenders and asked Scarman to bear in mind that ordinary law-abiding people in the inner city were most at risk from the rioters. They were the victims of the same 'muggers' that the much criticised police operation in Brixton had been aimed at, and they were entitled to police protection.

Dealing with the criticism, of 'insensitive' young officers, the Federation pointed out that a third of the constables in the Metropolitan Police were under 25 years of age, and the proportion of young officers rose when applied to constables on street duties. Therefore, the lion's share of street duty was being performed by young officers. Training was a key issue;

> 'The British police service spends less time and money on training than its contemporaries in other countries. There is very little structured in-service training and now that the manpower situation is so much healthier, we hope that the money can be found to effect major improvements in the field.'

The Federation rejected 'facile' comparisons of current police officers with the 'halcyon' days of the past when mature officers performed the duties now being undertaken by very young policemen and women. The young officers had borne the brunt of police duty for a long time. In twenty years, crime had trebled. Technology, particularly personal radios and the greater use of vehicles, meant that officers were now dealing with situations as they occurred, rather than arriving after the trouble was over. Personal stress, caused by job pressures, was now recognised as a police problem;

> 'Police work today is not conducted in the atmosphere of respect for authority and acceptance of the police role that used to be the case. Police officers have to establish a position of authority that once was taken for granted. There is a far greater tendency among the public to challenge police authority, and nowhere is this more marked than amongst the younger section of the population.

'In inner city areas these pressures are heightened by encounters between the police and young black people. It seems to be an almost automatic reaction, whenever a police officer stops and checks a young black person, or decides to arrest him for an offence, that the officer will be accused of victimising the young person simply because he is black. This has made a great many younger officers extremely wary in their dealings with young black people.

'The police in inner city areas have made strenuous efforts to improve the relationship between themselves and the black community ... ... all too often the initiative is all on the side of the police ... ... there are too many people around who claim to be community leaders when 'agitators' would be a more appropriate description. When young blacks hear well educated and eloquent political activists telling them that they are the victims of police oppression, and that their attacks on the police are a way of achieving a better way of life, it is small wonder that they are believed. The voices of reason and moderation tend to be swamped.'

Lord Scarman's report on the Brixton riots was published in November 1981. He began by saying that the problems of policing a deprived multi-racial area like Brixton could not be considered without reference to the social environment in which policing occured. The area suffered intense social deprivation. A third of the population of Brixton was black and the proportion was greater among young people. Black people faced more severe problems here than white people. Family, unemployment and discrimination problems existed. Young black people felt frustrated. They spent much of their lives on the streets and were bound to come into contact with criminals and the police.

Scarman said that many young black people in Brixton had been 'spoiling for a row' with the police. They resented 'Operation Swamp' in which large numbers of officers had been on duty in the area to combat widespread street crime. The riots were 'communal disturbances'. with strong racial elements, but they were not race riots. They had been

At Scarborough in 1990, Home Secretary David Waddington stages a solo walk to a cool reception from the Conference delegates, and studiously ignores the media throng.

Conversation piece at Bournemouth in 1991, when Kenneth Baker, seen with Federation chairman Alan Eastwood, rushed back to the House to deal with dangerous dogs.

How *POLICE* cartoonist "Jedd" saw the appointment of BAT Industries chairman Sir Patrick Sheehy to head Kenneth Clarke's Inquiry.

Sheehy could not understand police opposition to the report.

Inquiry member Eric Caines invited Michael Howard to "take on the boys and girls in blue".

Roy Hattersley MP as Shadow Home Secretary mended fences between the Federation and the Labour Party.

Vee Neild, the first woman to be general secretary of the Federation.

Wembley Arena, July 1993.
23,000 members came to
"Say 'No' to Sheehy".

(Right): Tony Blair MP:
"Government and police
should fight crime, not
each other".

(Far right):
Robert Maclennan MP;
surprising star of the
Wembley rally.

(Far left): Dick Coyles:
Warned 1992 Conference
of threat to Edmund
Davies.

(Left): An unmistakeable
message from the rank
and file.

Clarke explains his decision to set up an inquiry at a press conference. Neild and Eastwood look pensive.

Alan Eastwood and the author confer on the Conference platform at Blackpool, 1993.

Lyn Williams secured the post-Sheehy deal by tough negotiating stance.

Metropolitan officers "trial" the new batons, banned by Clarke but permitted by Howard.

Michael Howard with Federation chairman Fred Broughton (Metropolitan) at Surbiton in 1994.

5 POINTS?

50 POINTS?

500 POINTS?

?

Do you believe the Police should compete against crime... or against each other?

Could you assess the value of each of the actions above? Should an act against terrorism earn a police officer more than an act of kindness?

Should a caution pay less than a 'collar'?

Impossible, isn't it? But this is exactly what the Sheehy report proposes.

Under the pretext of improving efficiency this report, headed by the chairman of BAT Industries, wants to treat police officers as if they were employees of, say, a cigarette company, awarding points for personal performance and linking these to financial rewards.

This demonstrates a profound misunderstanding of what makes a police officer tick. Police work is *not* a job like any other, and our main motivation is and has always been a vocation to serve the community and to be recognised for doing so.

Of course we don't oppose change or increased efficiency or answerability, but introducing personal competitiveness into police work can only have a negative effect.

It encourages over zealous 'bookings' to provide evidence of 'performance' and pits one officer against another, destroying the co-operation and teamwork that is vital to an efficient fight against crime.

What's more, by proposing fixed-term contracts the report fails to recognise that citizens join the police because it is the *only* job they want to do, and after 10 or 20 years of service they cannot easily find another.

The Sheehy report would like to transform the bobby on the beat into a career hungry points-scorer, and by doing so will destroy a whole tradition and culture of service.

We don't want this to happen. If you don't either get on to your MP now.

Otherwise chasing bonuses may soon become more important than chasing criminals. **THE POLICE FEDERATION**

ASK YOUR MP TO OPPOSE THE SHEEHY PROPOSALS

Leslie Curtis welcomes HRH Princess Margaret to a Police Federation sponsored charity concert at London's Festival Hall in aid of the NSPCC in October 1984.

spontaneous, but there was evidence of leadership and organisation, and white people had been seen helping to distribute petrol bombs. The riots, said Scarman, 'were essentially an outburst of anger and resentment by young black people against the police'.

The Report referred to a loss of local confidence in the police, caused mainly by; 'hard' policing methods; lack of consultation about police operations; suspicion of the complaints system, and; unlawful and racially prejudiced conduct by some police officers.

Scarman acknowledged that the dilemma facing the police in Brixton was; how to cope with a rising level of crime, and particularly of street robbery (mugging) - while retaining the confidence of all sections of the community, especially ethnic minorities. He said that while both the police and local community leaders had to share some of the responsibility for the riots, once they had broken out, the way the police had handled them was 'to be commended, not criticised'.

Scarman offered a series of ideas for preventing a recurrence of inner-city rioting. Vigorous efforts were needed to recruit more black officers, and there should be special additional training, including education, to assist black candidates for the force. The police should seek means of identifying racial prejudice on the part of applicants for the service. Police recruits should receive a minimum of six months full time training rather than the current ten weeks, and this should include race relations training. Community relations courses should be compulsory for all ranks.

Dealing with criticism that much of the trouble was caused by young and immature officers, Scarman said that they were an invaluable part of the force but should be given the correct guidance and supervision by sergeants and inspectors. Close supervision was essential in stop and search operations.

Scarman called for more 'community based' policing by home - beat constables in inner-city areas. There should be a statutory requirement on the Metropolitan Police to consult community leaders. He agreed that the law on police search powers was 'a mess', and said that the new Criminal Attempts Act should be carefully monitored. Lay visitors should visit police stations to supervise the treatment of prisoners. There should be an independent element in the police complaints system.

Scarman was opposed to a new Riot Act, which the Federation had called for, but recommended that advance notice of a procession should be given to the police. If existing law was inadequate, there should be a new power to ban a 'racist' march.

The Federation gave a general welcome to the Scarman report, especially the call for extended training for recruits and probationers. Jim Jardine described it as a 'historic' report. He said the Federation supported the recruitment of more officers from the ethnic communities, and welcomed Scarman's rejection of quotas or lowered entry standards. He agreed with Scarman that existing operational methods should be reviewed, and said it was right that there should be consultation with the local community, provided that 'consultation' did not become 'control'.

On complaints, Jardine said that the Federation had abandoned its long standing opposition to an independent complaints investigation system;

> 'We are convinced that criticism of the system will not be ended until there is a wholly independent investigative body. We support complete independence in investigation, but would insist on greatly strengthened civil rights for police officers to be introduced at the same time.'

This was a reference to the Federation's demands that police officers should have the right of legal representation at disciplinary hearings, and that there should be independent adjudication of disciplinary charges as well as independent investigations of complaints.

Jardine said that every interested party should look upon Scarman as a 'new beginning'. It would be a tragedy, he said, if some groups, because they were disappointed that the Report did not agree with their own views, rejected the opportunity to work to bring about a permanent improvement in society.

THIRTY-ONE

'Kill the Bill!'

The Joint Central Committee's decision to support a wholly independent complaints system was a complete reversal of policy. It resulted from the 1980 Triennial Report of the Police Complaints Board. This proposed that a special investigation team, made up of police officers, should investigate 'serious' cases, by which it meant those high profile complaints which attracted widespread media and political attention, such as the death of Blair Peach in Southall. The Police Advisory Board set up a working party to examine the introduction of an independent element into the complaints system, but the Federation became increasingly frustrated when its own proposals for changes to the discipline procedure, which it had been urging for some years, were not considered to be a part of the exercise. The working party failed to find much common ground between any of the parties on the PAB, and at the Federation's suggestion, Whitelaw agreed to appoint another group, chaired by Lord Belstead, the Minister of State, which would examine all outstanding complaints items. When this met, however, its Terms of Reference from the Home Office excluded the changes that the Federation wanted to be considered.

The JCC wrote to Whitelaw in November 1981 to express its frustration at the lack of progress on discipline. The House of Commons' Home Affairs Committee was also examining the complaints issue and the JCC reminded MPs that police officers, as well as complainants, were entitled to fair treatment;

> 'The discussion about the police complaints system has concentrated upon the need to ensure satisfaction

for the genuine complainant. The Police Federation does not disagree with this objective, but over the years the position of the police officer has tended to be overlooked. It is a serious matter for a police officer to be subjected to a complaint. Even a relatively minor matter causes him considerable anxiety, and in the most serious cases he has a great deal to lose. The financial consequences of dismissal from the police service run into many thousands of pounds in lost salary. It is also a serious matter for a police officer to be demoted in rank, or find himself barred from promotion because of a disciplinary conviction. Yet he is expected to face all the paraphernalia of the investigation system and the police disciplinary system with a minimum of personal protection ... ... he should at least have the elementary civil rights that would certainly be available to a person facing a criminal charge, or to an employee enjoying the statutory protection of employment legislation.'

The Federation told the MPs it had decided to support a wholly independent system because the arguments about the police being judge and jury in their own cause would not go away so long as investigations remained in police hands, and would certainly not be resolved by tinkering once more with the existing one.

Speaking in the Commons' debate on the Scarman report, Eldon Griffiths, strongly opposed the Scarman proposals for automatic dismissal of police officers found guilty of racial discrimination. The Home Office had submitted an outline of such an offence to the Police Advisory Board. Griffiths told the House;

'There is no room in the police service for racially prejudiced policing. The Police Federation believes that if there are officers who act that way, they should be asked to leave, but the proposals by the Home Office are not acceptable. The existing code, as Lord Scarman knows, covers the whole area of racial discrimination. Nothing would be more discriminatory against the police than to subject them to a new offence of racial prejudice that would apply to no other section of the community.'

Whitelaw eventually accepted the Federation's argument that racial discrimination should not be a specific offence against police discipline. Griffiths went on to speak of the Federation's new policy on complaints;

'I do not always support the views of the Police Federation. In this case, I agree with the Federation. Its proposals reflect the fact that over the years its members have become sick and tired because however the system is tinkered with - it has been tinkered with seven times - it still cannot meet its critics. So the Federation, perhaps emotionally, has said that it wishes to be shot of the whole procedure of complaints against the police. It wants an independent investigation system.

'At no time, however, has the Federation proposed that crimes should be investigated by an outside body. What the Federation has said is that complaints by the public against the police - which in most cases do not involve crime - should be investigated by an outside body. That is entirely right.'

'Entirely right' or not, when the Federation's proposal came before Parliament some time later, as an amendment to the Police and Criminal Evidence Bill, it was Griffiths who invited MPs to reject the whole concept of independent investigations. In the Scarman debate, however, he had identified the practical problem about independent investigations: the great majority of 'serious' complaints started off as allegations of crime, which would have to be investigated by the police. The Federation's 'independent' system would have to wait until a criminal inquiry was over before the disciplinary issues could be investigated.

ACPO objected strongly to the Federation's call for independent adjudication of disciplinary charges. ACPO told the Commons' Select Committee that this would undermine the chief constable's responsibility for the discipline of his force. The Federation replied that its proposal applied only to cases arising from complaints, not internal matters. Others criticised the idea of independent investigations because of the cost and the problem of where the independent investigators would come from. The Federation estimated that the current cost of using senior police officers to investigate complaints cost £10 million a year, and pointed out that other bodies, such as the Post Office, Customs and Excise, and the Department of Health and Social Security, appeared to find little difficulty in finding competent investigators to handle complex inquiries. More surprisingly, opposition to independent investigations came from some of the most vociferous Labour critics of the system. Alec Lyon MP, argued that the Federation favoured outside investigators because it would be easier 'to pull the wool over their eyes'.

The pay review of 1981 was the third to be conducted under the Edmund-Davies rules, resulted in an overall increase of 13.2 per cent. The starting rate of a constable rose from £4,956 to £5,610, and the top rate PC went up from £7,848 to £8,883. During the negotiations, the official side revealed its increasing anxiety that the police pay bill was rising too rapidly. It reminded the staff side that Edmund-Davies had said that either side should be able to propose variations to the formula. It accepted that police pay should continue to be linked to the earnings index, but wanted a joint examination to see whether there was a case for changing the method by which the link was made, or whether the pay structure itself should be changed. The staff side responded that it would take some convincing that there was any case for changing the system, and if anything, the increasing crime rate and other factors which the police had to contend with, suggested that there was a 'strong case' for enhancing, not reducing, Edmund-Davies.

There was at this time little respite for the police from the sustained criticism of Labour politicians and the press. The Metropolitan was in the eye of this storm, with allegations of corruption and the fiasco of an intruder in the Queen's bedroom at Buckingham Palace, a catastrophe which led to Willie Whitelaw sending the Permanent Under Secretary to ask David McNee to resign as Commissioner, a proposition he rejected. Roy Hattersley, Labour's shadow Home Secretary, showed that a right winger could match the invective of the Left when he immediately demanded that the Metropolitan should be broken up into four or six area forces, each controlled by a democratically elected police authority, with its national duties, such as state security and VIP protection, being carried out by a small force answerable to a committee of the House of Commons. *POLICE* commented;

'Mr Hattersley has declared that an incoming Labour government would actually do this, but politicians have a commendable habit of revising their intentions once they are saddled with responsibility and confronted by reality. All the same, the threat of a Met' break-up is one more item on Labour's growing agenda for the police service. This agenda includes such commitments as; a local police authority for London; the abolition of the Special Branch and 'political surveillance'; the disbanding of the Special Patrol Group, and; promotions of senior officers by the new police authorities.'

The issue of capital punishment was raised yet again by the Federation in March 1982, following the murders of three police officers in the space of a few weeks. The Joint Central Committee decided to place advertisements in several national newspapers, calling for the return of the death penalty, and inviting readers to return a coupon, expressing agreement with this view, to the Federation headquarters. The response was remarkable; within three weeks of the advertisement appearing, more than 250,000 people returned the coupons.

Questioned in Parliament, Willie Whitelaw said that he remained personally opposed to capital punishment and Mrs Thatcher, a committed hanger, said that she could not see the matter being debated again during the lifetime of the current Parliament. The Federation came under attack for its campaign from liberal opponents of the death penalty.

John Alderson, the chief constable of Devon and Cornwall, wrote in *The Observer*;

> 'Care needs to be taken that those who accept appointments as parliamentary advisers do not become political advisers and spokesmen. In the past this was avoided by the convention that advisers changed when elected to Government. It was more than just coincidence that the Police Federation spent £30,000 on an unedifying campaign for sentences of death at a time when the far Right was pressurising the Home Secretary for the same thing.'

Parliament did get another opportunity to debate capital punishment. Several Tory MPs put down amendments to the Criminal Justice Bill, but again the Commons reaffirmed abolition by an overwhelming majority. Police feelings on the subject were further inflamed soon after the debate, when three more officers were murdered in England.

Jim Jardine retired in June 1982. He had been the chairman of the Police Federation through six significant and event filled years. becoming better known to the members and the nation than any previous Federationist. The JCC chose as his successor Leslie Curtis, a Surrey constable, who defeated Jack Kent and Pat Johnson of West Yorkshire in the election. Curtis was an experienced JCC member but hardly known outside the committee. He was a dour man, inclined to be stubborn and sometimes arrogant, who lacked Jardine's charisma or a personal following among the membership, which made many Federationists wonder how he could follow Jardine's act. He did not try to emulate his predecessor, but even his critics conceded that he was a hard worker who was committed to the advancement of the Federation. His early weeks in office were notable for a series of public relations gaffes, starting with his first press conference when he annoyed the JCC by saying that he had been the 'right wing' candidate for the chairmanship. Later he told a meeting of the far-Right, anti-immigration Monday Club that the speech he was making would be different if addressed to 'dark skinned' people, and again when he told a television interviewer that calling a black man a nigger was no different from calling a Welshman 'Taffy'. But his touch became surer as he learned what being the chairman entailed, and in six years in office he did a good job in keeping the disparate groupings on the JCC more or less together.

The pay review of 1982 was the first since the Tories came to power to present the staff side of the Police Negotiating Board with a real difficulty. While the staff side had rejected the official side's proposals for a review of Edmund-Davies, it had agreed, at the urging of the independent chairman of the PNB, Lord Plowden, to take part in a joint examination of the police pensions scheme, with neither side committing itself to any course of action. The Government Actuary was asked to produce a report on the costs of the scheme. This report concluded that the contribution of serving police officers should be increased from 7 to 11 per cent of their pay, with women paying 8 per cent. As soon as the report was available, the official side told the staff side that it expected the new contribution rates to be accepted, to apply from 1st September 1982, the date of the pay review. The staff side said that it was awaiting its own actuarial report on the scheme, but agreed that it would negotiate on the contribution rate as soon as the pay review was dealt with.

At the July 1982 meeting of the JCC, Eldon Griffiths spelt out the politics of the police pay issue. The Government was seeking to secure drastic reductions in the annual wages increases of public sector workers, and the police were now at the top of the pay 'league'. It looked as though the Edmund-Davies formula would produce another 10 per cent at least, and this would be a big embarrassment to the Government as it sought to enforce restraint on other employees. He told the Committee that the Government was disappointed that, with police forces up to full strength, crime was rising and the detection rate was falling. He suggested that it might be expedient if the Federation was to offer an increased pension contribution. It was advice that was not welcomed by a large proportion of the JCC, who thought that Griffiths was being patronising and too ready to take the side of his own Government on an issue which affected their members' incomes.

Lord Plant, one of the members of the Edmund-Davies Committee, had become an unofficial adviser to Peter Tanner on pay matters, and he attended the July meeting of the JCC. His message was not very different from that of Eldon Griffiths. The Treasury was pointing out that police pay increases had outstripped civil service settlements and was calling for a halt. The Government had made its pledge to uphold Edmund-Davies, but the outside pressures were now very strong. He suggested that the Federation should accept the need to raise the pension contribution, and offer to phase it in over the next few years.

The JCC was sharply divided on the issue, with the constables pressing for outright opposition to any increase in the contribution. The majority view was that the staff side negotiators should be allowed to get the best deal that they could. The staff side's hopes of securing concessions received no assistance from its own actuaries, who reported that the government actuary's conclusions were accurate, and that the cost of the pension scheme had risen by a fifth since Edmund-Davies.

At the July meeting of the staff side, it was agreed, with the constables' of England and Wales dissenting, that it should offer an immediate pension contribution increase of one and a half per cent, with talks about further increases to follow. But when the full negotiating board met the next day, it was clear that the Government had already decided that the full 4 per cent pension contribution increase would be imposed at once. The formula had produced a 10.3 per cent increase, taking the constable's starting rate to £6,189 and his top rate to £9,798. This was agreed, but when the committee of the PNB which dealt with pensions met, immediately after the pay settlement, it was made clear by the official side that there would be no concessions. The staff side's offer was rejected at once, and the official side said it would report the 'failure to agree' to the Home Secretary straight away.

Whitelaw agreed to see Tanner and Curtis at the Home Office on the day after the PNB meeting, but this was only to tell them that there was no alternative to what was proposed. The same day, the Home Office issued a press statement which announced that police pay would be increased by 10.3 per cent, but as the pension contribution was going up to 11 per cent, 'effectively' the police were only going to get 6.3 per cent. This got the Government off an embarrassing hook with the rest of the public service.

The Home Secretary was able to take this decision because it was not possible to seek arbitration on a pensions issue. But he was still required to lay the enabling regulation before Parliament, and if any MP 'prayed against' a draft regulation, it would have to be examined by the Committee on Statutory Instruments, a rare procedure. Eldon Griffiths was against this course, advising the JCC that it would not make any difference and would focus Parliamentary attention on the fact that police pay rise were outstripping the rest of the public sector (except in the fire service). His attitude incensed some members of the JCC, and the sergeants' wanted to demand that he publicly oppose the contribution increase. Tanner reminded the JCC that it could not tell its adviser how to vote in the House.

It was left to Cyril Smith, the idiosyncratic Liberal MP for Rochdale, to steal a march on Griffiths by tabling a prayer against the regulation. The Committee on Statutory Instruments met to consider it, with Griffiths devoting his speech to attacking Smith's 'opportunism'. Seeing that the object of the exercise was to try to stop the pension contribution being raised, many members thought Griffiths was more concerned with the politics of the matter than with arguing the case for the police. When the Committee submitted its report to Parliament, the tiny band of Liberals in the House voted against the regulation, but was not supported by either of the major parties. The Tories agreed with Whitelaw, and the Labour whips were not going to ask their members to go into the lobby to support the Police Federation.

The way in which the Government had imposed the pension contribution rise rankled with the JCC. Peter Tanner persuaded the official side that if in the future there was disagreement on a pensions matter, the independent chairman should be asked to seek conciliation before the Home Secretary made a final decision.

Tanner had another worry to contend with. Egged on by the Labour councillors who dominated the official side, Belgrave Square was busy with plans to bring about a drastic reduction in the cost of rent allowances, described by the councillors as an unwarranted 'tax free perk'. In July 1982 the official side said it would soon be tabling proposals to change the basis of rent allowance and wanted this to be achieved by the following April. There was some relief when the official side said in October that it was not ready with detailed proposals, and any change could not be implemented before April 1984. The reason for the delay, was that the Home Secretary favoured changes in rent allowance, not total abolition as called for by the local authority interests.

The annual meeting of the Metropolitan branch boards in October 1983 was another of those occasions when anger among the rank and file boiled over. The hall was crowded with more than 2,000 officers present. The causes of the anger were not hard to find. Rank and file officers felt they had been made scapegoats, in the Scarman report and by the Government, for the failures of senior officers in inner city policing The Government's action in abolishing the 'Sus' law was seen as a capitulation to the criminal elements in the inner cities. The months of press and media allegations had also built up resentment, as had the imposition of the higher pensions contribution, and now there was anxiety about the threat to rent allowance. The same Federationists who had cheered Willie Whitelaw in the past, now gave him a rough ride. He was visibly angry about the content of the speech by John Newman, the chairman of the Metropolitan Federation, and the belligerent manner in which Newman delivered it. When the barrackers tried to shout him down, Whitelaw rounded on them; 'Show me one word or action where I have failed to support the police,' he demanded.

The new Commissioner, Sir Kenneth Newman, was treated in the same fashion by the unruly element in the audience when he talked of the need for 'sensitive' policing, but he was applauded for promising that henceforth he would not allow his officers to be the 'Aunt Sallies' of the mobs.

The Central Hall meeting did considerable damage to the reputation of the Federation. The next day, Mrs Thatcher told the House of Commons that the behaviour of the officers who had shouted Whitelaw down was 'disgraceful'. It must have seemed like base ingratitude to a Prime Minister who felt she had put the police at the top of her priorities. The press reaction was strong. The *Daily Telegraph* said;

> 'Those responsible for such rowdyism should think what effect their behaviour has on enemies who rejoice at their every failing and also upon their wider public. If the police themselves cannot keep their patience and manners for the Home Secretary then the public have grounds for apprehension.'

The Guardian, of course, went to town on the Federation ingrates;

> 'What Mr Whitelaw and Sir Kenneth Newman found on Wednesday night was base ingratitude. The serried ranks of Federation members are, apparently, oblivious of the special treatment they have received and oblivious, too, of the stark contrast between their situation and the desperation they see on so many street corners.'

The *Daily Express* acknowledged that the police had many problems which needed to be put right, but 'acting like a bunch of Militant Tendency at a Tory garden fete is not the way to do it.' However, the *Daily Mail* had some sympathy for the hecklers, pointing out that their pay increase had been almost halved by the pensions levy, but it suggested that the real cause of the discontent was different;

> '... ... much more of a cause of resentment seems to have been their impression that the police have been made monkeys of in aid of progressive ideas about policing in coloured areas.'

In December 1982 the Government published the long awaited Police and Criminal Evidence Bill. It was the most comprehensive criminal justice measure since the Act of 1948, and immediately it attracted howls of protest from the

Left, civil liberties and ethnic minorities' interests, and the lawyers. The GLC's 'police committee' alone spent more than £250,000 of London ratepayers' money on a 'Kill the Bill' campaign. The cause of the outcry was the perceived extension of police powers, although the Bill, for the first time, defined the limits of powers when dealing with the investigation of crime and the detention and questioning of suspects. The Bill enacted the majority of the proposals of the Royal Commission on Criminal Procedure (the prosecutions matters were left for a subsequent measure, the Prosecution of Offences Act).

Initially, the Federation welcomed the Bill, as it had the Royal Commission's report. It extended the powers possessed by constables in London and some cities, to stop and search persons and vehicles on reason able suspicion, to the whole of England and Wales, but these powers were strictly circumscribed with police officers being required to record all 'stops'. The Bill defined precisely the circumstances in which police could enter premises to search for stolen property and other evidence. It simplified powers of arrest, giving the police the power to detain for offences which had not previously carried it, but only in order to ascertain the true identity of the offender, or prevent harm or 'public mischief'.

The Bill imposed strict time limits on the detention of suspects before being charged, and gave detained persons a statutory right of access to a solicitor, and the circumstances in which this could be delayed or withheld. Codes of practice were drafted which governed police actions during investigations and interrogations of suspects. Confessions found to have been obtained under duress would be excluded at trials.

The Federation was less happy with the Bill's proposals on complaints. Its call for an independent system was ignored. With the original Bill, Eldon Griffiths had persuaded the Committee on the Bill to accept the principle of legal representation for an officer charged with an offence which could result in a penalty ranging from a fine to dismissal, but this was not included in the revised version. The Bill introduced three main elements regarding complaints: minor complaints would be dealt with through an informal conciliation procedure; more substantial matters would be investigated under the supervision of the Police Complaints Board, with some minor criminal matters no longer being referred to the Director of Public Prosecutions, but being dealt with under the disciplinary procedures, and; the appointment of an independent assessor to supervise 'serious' cases, which would always be investigated by a police officer from another force than the force concerned in the complaint.

The Bill was strenuously opposed in Parliament by the Labour and Liberal parties, assisted by the 'Kill the Bill' alliance in the country. Its passage was halted by the 1983 General Election, at which the Conservatives, riding on the national euphoria after the Falklands triumph, and assisted by the most overtly Left wing programme ever put forward by Labour, won a greatly increased majority. After the election, the Bill was brought back in a much altered form. One of the major changes was that the Home Secretary accepted a statutory obligation to introduce the tape recording of interviews with suspects in police custody, something that the Federation had accepted for some time. Another was that the Police Complaints Board would be replaced by a Police Complaints Authority with greater powers of intervention and control.

The Federation was far more critical of the new Bill. It said that far from creating 'policing by coercion', as alleged by its main critics, the Bill had now shifted the balance of justice in favour of the suspect and would make the work of the police investigator more difficult than ever. The elaborate 'checks and balances' in the Bill would add an enormous new bureaucracy to the police service, without any corresponding increase in police resources. In this respect, the Federation was worried about the new duties and responsibilities of police custody officers. It pointed out that a single arrest would now require no fewer than fifty entries in official records, and the police made some two million arrests every year.

On complaints, the Federation said that the Bill strengthened the rights of complainants, something to which it did not object, but there was nothing in it which improved the vulnerable position of the police officer, and it would press for the right of legal representation to be included. The Federation had secured some important concessions on discipline during discussions with the Home Office. Instead of having appeals to the Home Secretary decided on the written submissions of both parties, a Tribunal would be appointed to hear each appeal against dismissals or loss of rank, and one of the three-member panel would be a retired Federationist. Chief officers would be advised by Home Office circular to follow the criminal rules of evidence at discipline hearings.

The Federation was strongly critical of one of the new proposals, to allow a chief officer to give deputy chiefs the responsibility for hearing 'less serious' disciplinary charges, although it would have accepted this if legal representation was available for charges where an officer stood to lose his job or his rank.

During the Committee Stage of the Bill, a most unlikely alliance was forged between the Federation and the Law Society, with the National Council for Civil Liberties adding its support later on. After discovering the amount of common ground between them, the Federation and the Law Society put forward proposals for a new system of dealing with complaints. This would differentiate between criminal and other matters. If a deputy chief constable considered that a 'non-crime' complaint was serious, he would pass it to a Police Complaints Tribunal for independent investigation and adjudication. The Tribunal would also hear appeals from decisions of chief constables in lesser cases. There would be provision for conciliation between the complainant and an officer.

The Federation/Law Society plan was forwarded to Leon Brittan, who had succeeded Willie Whitelaw as Home Secretary immediately after the 1983 General Election. Brittan rejected it on the day he received it.

During the General Election Margaret Thatcher promised that the new Parliament would be given another opportunity to vote on the death penalty. There was some optimism among the supporters of restoration, because the new House was considered to be the most right wing in history. Thatcher caused confusion by telling Robin Day on television that if the House voted to bring back hanging, the Government would introduce legislation. Subsequently, she said it would have to be done by a Private Member's Bill. Opposition to the death penalty was on this occasion unusually strong. There were press reports that Home Office officials would resign rather than implement a change, and several judges were said to be ready to do the same. The new Home Secretary, Leon Brittan, lost a lot of personal credibility by saying that he would support hanging for terrorists, except those convicted in non-jury trials in Northern Ireland. The vote against restoration was higher than ever before.

The Police Training Council published the report of the working party on probationer training in the summer of 1983. Set up in the wake of the riots and the Scarman Report, it proposed the biggest ever shake-up in recruit training. Recruits, it said, should serve for at least seven months in full time training before being allowed to patrol the streets on their own. When they went out on the beat in this period, they would be accompanied by an experienced 'tutor' constable. Throughout the remainder of his two years' probation, the recruit would be subjected to continuous monitoring and assessment. He would receive three more full time training courses in this period, designed to underpin the formal and on-the-job training he had already received. Finally, he would return to the training centre for a final assessment course. The new curriculum would concentrate on the need for the recruit to understand the society in which the police operated. The report said;

'Policing is a profession requiring a combination of personal qualities, knowledge and social skills. All these should be developed through the training given to the probationer, so that at the end of the probationary period he or she would not only have professional ability, but also that considerable degree of personal confidence which is necessary in facing the public and doing the job well. We have particularly in mind that many recruits join the service at an age when their experience of life and society may be limited.'

The report stressed that recruits must learn that very high ethical standards were demanded of them. They must have a firm commitment to human rights and understand that the use of force must be restricted to circumstances where it was unavoidable. Probation, said the report, should be regarded as a two years' 'apprenticeship' and recruits should not regard themselves as fully integrated police officers until they had completed this period. This view somewhat alarmed the constable Federation representatives on the working party, who suspected it might be used to reduce the levels of recruits' pay. The Federation otherwise gave the report an unreserved welcome.

The 1983 pay review produced an 8.4 increase and once again the size of the award was embarrassing for the Government. The starting pay of the constable went to £6,708 and the top rate to £10,620. During the pay talks, the official side referred to 'widespread concern' about the level of police pay and compared it to the average of around 5.5 per cent being achieved elsewhere in the public service. The official side invited the staff side to take part in a joint examination of levels of pay in the police in relation to outside employment. The staff side declined the invitation but said it would consider any proposals that the official side came up with. The official side declared itself 'disappointed' with this response, and as it happened, so were key members of the staff side. A few weeks later, after Tanner warned that the official side would go ahead with the review anyway, the staff side agreed by a single vote to join in it.

At the end of 1983, the Government announced a clamp - down on police expenditure. It had been realised for some time that the burgeoning cost of the service was becoming a major topic in the Cabinet, and the replacement of Whitelaw with an out and out monetarist, Brittan, presaged what was to come. Home Office circular 114/83 nevertheless came as a rude shock to the service and was to become the definitive document governing police expenditure for the rest of the decade. It pointed out that the cost of the service in 1982-3 was £2.4 billion, compared with £1.4 billion in 1970-1. In this period, the numbers of police had gone up by 24,000 to 121,000. The circular said;

'After this rapid growth a period of consolidation is desirable, not least because the constraints on public expenditure at both central and local government levels make it impossible to continue with the sort of expansion which has occurred in recent years.'

In future, the circular stated, forces would not be allowed extra officers unless the Home Secretary was satisfied it was making the best use of available resources. The HMIs would assess whether forces had the correct manpower priorities and were making the maximum use of civilians, thus freeing police officers for operational tasks. Each additional post would have to be justified, and the police authority must have indicated a readiness to fund it. Increases in police numbers would not be approved if police officers were found to be doing work that could be civilianised.

The circular made it clear that previous Home Office guidance on the numbers of civilians to be employed no longer applied. These had paid too much attention to the views of chief constables and the staff associations. The Federation, while accepting that there was a role for civilians in the police service, had always been concerned about reduced opportunities for 'inside' jobs for officers who were not up to the physical grind of wholly operational tasks. ACPO was unenthusiastic about civilians because they lacked the flexibility of deployment offered by police officers, and in the forces which served only one county, civilians were employees of the county council, not the chief constable. In the mid-seventies, ACPO had expressed concern about the expansion of trade union activity among police civilian staffs, and had suggested that they should be subject to a 'no-strike' agreement, proposals which the local authorities had firmly rejected. Now that police officers were so much more expensive, the attractiveness of civilianisation had become irresistible.

Brittan called on the chief officers and police authorities to set clear objectives and priorities, and deploy their police manpower accordingly. The circular said that forces which had carried out major reviews of their structures, and used their manpower more efficiently by changing shift patterns and working methods, had increased their operational strength without recruiting more police officers.

It soon became clear that Home Office circular 114/83 meant exactly what it said. Some chief officers were outraged by the degree of control that the Home Office and the Inspectorate at once began to exert. Geoffrey Dear, the chief constable of West Midlands, for example, was seeking an increase in the size of the force of 300. He was told that not one would be approved until he had completed a programme of further civilianisation. The message from Government to the police was plain enough; the party was over.

THIRTY-TWO

From Orgreave to Broadwater Farm

1984 opened with the service mourning the three Metropolitan officers who were murdered when terrorists exploded a bomb at Harrods store. PC Jane Arbuthnot became the first woman officer to be murdered in England (she was soon to be followed by PC Yvonne Fletcher, who was shot dead by a member of the staff of the Libyan Embassy as she escorted a protest march past the building). Several other officers were seriously wounded as they tried to guide Christmas shoppers in Knightsbridge to safety. It was a further reminder, were any needed, of the extent to which terrorism had become an ever present threat.

The Joint Central Committee was meeting in Cheshire in March, when Leslie Curtis received a telephone call from David Hall, the chief constable of Humberside and that year's president of ACPO. Hall told him that because of major problems caused by mass picketing of pits in Nottinghamshire, the National Reporting Centre, set-up to co-ordinate requests from forces for mutual aid, had been activated. Several forces had been instructed to send support units to Nottinghamshire. Hall's purpose in calling Curtis was to say that only the most basic accommodation could be arranged for the hundreds of officers who had been drafted in to the coalfield, but efforts would be made to improve the situation.

It was the beginning of the year long battle waged by Arthur Scargill and the National Union of Mineworkers against projected pit closures. Before it was over, well over a thousand police officers would be injured in pitched battles with strikers and their supporters, hundreds of miners would be arrested for public order offences, and several deaths would occur. Relations between the police and the mining communities which supported the strike would sink to their lowest ebb for sixty years.

Policing the coal strike required the greatest concentration of police strength ever deployed over an extended period. The Federation found itself involved, at local and national level, with questions of the welfare and safety of thousands of officers who manned the police lines throughout the coalfields of England and Wales. The Federation accepted that at the outset living conditions would be primitive, but as the strike wore on there was growing anger at the lack of improvement. Officers slept on the floors of disused aircraft hangars at RAF stations. Many of the buildings used to house the police lacked elementary sanitary provisions. There were many complaints about inadequate catering; unreasonable over-crowding; lack of privacy and storage space for personal belongings. Peter Tanner worked hard to secure improvements but his approaches to ACPO produced only limited responses from Hall and his colleagues.

The ACPO leadership, and the chief constables of the host forces, seemed to think that because this was a national emergency, the Federation and the PSU officers would have to put up with the conditions, because it would be prohibitively expensive to improve them. Officers who complained were reminded that they were getting overtime payments for the long hours on the picket lines. Morale among the officers living in this state was not helped when, as in some cases, senior officers were housed in comfortable hotels or guest rooms at police establishments while their men went without hot water and queued for the portable lavatories. Nor were matters assisted by the Nottinghamshire force, which attempted to save money by reneging on an earlier PNB agreement concerning the payments to which members away from home on PSU operations were entitled. These irritations were offset by the substantial overtime earnings of members throughout the strike period, but they showed the organisational capabilities of police management in a very poor light, to say nothing of the absence of contingency planning for a strike which had been expected for a long time. Almost two years later, the dispute over compensation was the subject of an arbitration case which recommended the payment of 'hardship' allowances in cases where the standard of sleeping accommodation offered to PSUs on secondment to other forces fell below basic standards. Later, the Police Negotiating Board concluded an agreement to cover future events, and agreed that this could be applied to claims arising from the miners' strike.

Although so many officers sustained injuries in the dispute, the great majority were not serious, which the Federation attributed to the provision of protective equipment, something it had insisted upon after the urban riots of three years earlier.

A feature of the strike was the ceaseless propaganda war waged between the NUM and the government. Scargill and the majority of the Labour leadership depicted the police as the shock troops of Thatcherism, determined to grind the miners into the ground. Scargill and his closest supporters in the divided union leadership were confident that he could repeat the success of the mass picketing tactics of twelve years' before, when he had forced the police to close the vital Saltley coke depot in the Midlands. The police were equally determined that this time the mass pickets would be repulsed wherever they appeared. Each morning became a guessing game as police intelligence reports to the NRC tried to assess where 'Arthur's Army' was headed. These daily confrontations at pits, docks and power stations throughout Britain, made dramatic TV news pictures and the role of the police became a major issue for debate. While the miners complained that the reporting of the violence was biased against them, some programmes sought to depict the police as the aggressors, and Curtis found himself giving daily television and radio interviews, defending the membership from criticism.

The Federation leadership was disturbed by what it saw as Government inertia in dealing with the strike. Trade union law had been drastically changed by the Tories since coming to office, and secondary picketing was outlawed. Yet neither the TUC nor the Government seemed prepared to make use of the new laws against the NUM. The strategy appeared to be to confront the mass pickets, and rely on the criminal law to deal with the violence which grew worse as the bitterness of the miners and their families increased.

Addressing Leon Brittan at the 1984 Federation conference, two months into the strike, Curtis demanded that the Government should use the civil law to deal with the picketing. He drew no response then, nor on several other occasions during the year when he repeated the call.

The coal strike was a cause of more friction between chief officers and Labour controlled police authorities. Merseyside and Greater Manchester threatened to take legal action because the authorities had not been consulted by the chief constables before officers were despatched to other force areas. South Yorkshire police authority, with several miners on its Labour group, imposed strict financial restrictions on the chief constable, which he was able to overturn in the High Court. After the pitched battle between the massed pickets and the police at the Orgreave coking depot in South Yorkshire, the police authority instructed the chief constable to get rid of the force's police horses and dogs as an 'economy measure'. It argued that the chief constable had landed the ratepayers of South Yorkshire with an enormous bill for the hundreds of police from other forces who had been drafted into the area, where the vast majority of the community were solid supporters of the miners, and therefore cuts had to be made from the ordinary budget. The Home Secretary intervened and the instruction was withdrawn, but relations between the force and the police authority had broken down to an alarming degree. The other Metropolitan authorities complained that they had been no more than frustrated spectators as their chief officers sent mutual aid to other forces at the behest of the National Reporting Centre. The issue was 'operational' and therefore entirely for the chief constable to decide, while the Government and the authorities met the cost.

As the strike wore on, the Federation leaders had their doubts about the policies being pursued by some chief officers. Charles Maclachlan, the chief constable of Nottinghamshire, succeeded David Hall as the year's President of ACPO in 1984 and became responsible for the National Reporting Centre, and for articulating the ACPO viewpoint to the media. The post was allocated on a rotational basis, but the choice could hardly have been more inappropriate for the time, simply because MacLachlan's handling of the strike in his county, where the bitterness between striking and working miners was at its height, was insensitive and bordered on the belligerent. His officers' tactic of stopping convoys of cars containing pickets on motorways had attracted widespread comment and doubts as to whether it was legal. Soon after taking over the NRC and the Presidency of ACPO he figured in a furious row with Gerald Kaufman during an hour long debate on BBC television, in which he lost his temper and declared that the police in Nottinghamshire were concerned with the miners who had refused to strike - the only ones that mattered. There was a feeling in the Federation, shared by a few chief officers who had begun to issue calls for a more conciliatory approach from the Government and the National Coal Board, that ACPO's efficiency in ensuring that some working pits stayed open in the face of mass picketing was being used by the Government to prolong the strike. There were mutterings in political circles about collusion between chief constables and pit managements, and several operations involved using hundreds of officers to allow a handful of miners to go to work in a pit where everyone else was on strike. There was also a strongly held opposing view in the service, that on no account must Scargill's tactic of mass intimidation be allowed to succeed.

The Federation leaders, and probably the great majority of chief officers, would have been shocked had they discovered that there had been secret political collusion between the chairman of the National Coal Board, Ian MacGregor, and Margaret Thatcher. At the outset of the strike, with Scargill's flying pickets rampaging through the Nottinghamshire pit villages, MacGregor met Thatcher, along with Leon Brittan and the energy secretary, Peter Walker. He was furious that the police seemed to be adopting a strictly neutral stance as between the pickets and the working miners. According to his account *(The enemy within, 1986)* MacGregor said the battle was between 'men who want to work and a bunch of thugs, yet the police seem to want to keep out of it.' He said that if this had been America, the National Guard would have been called out, a comparison which might have reminded the Ministers of the massacre of students at Kent State University in 1968.

As a result of this meeting in Thatcher's study, MacGregor claimed, the police National Reporting Centre was brought into action, and the first support units were on their way to Nottinghamshire within a few hours. This flatly contradicted MacLachlan's claim that it was he who got in touch with Sir Laurence Byford to say that the scale of the picketing was too great for his force to handle alone, and that David Hall had then, as ACPO president, activated the NRC. The idea that this was done without the tacit support of ministers was always difficult to accept, but MacGregor makes no bones about it - the NRC was set up as a result of instructions from central government. This is consistent with information given at the time to this writer by two chief constables, but David Hall insists that MacGregor's version is completely wrong. Throughout the strike, MacGregor writes in his book, whenever he heard of local police chiefs seeking to keep the peace between the factions, and dissuading some miners from going to work, he complained in person to the Home Office. MacGregor also revealed that it had been a deliberate policy not to take civil action against the NUM, under trade union law, but to rely instead on the police enforcing the criminal law. The hundreds of ordinary police officers who bore the brunt of the missile barrage hurled at them at Orgreave would have been incensed to know that the chairman of the NCB did not give a damn whether the coking plant stayed open or not. It was, according to him, all a ploy to keep the massed pickets there, and away from Nottinghamshire. For this, police officers were injured, and hundreds of thousands of pounds wasted on a riot trial which failed to convict anyone, to say nothing of the substantial compensation which the South Yorkshire police authority had eventually to pay to those arrested at Orgreave.

In October 1984 there was a major public row between Leslie Curtis and Gerald Kaufman MP, the shadow Home Secretary, over a speech which Curtis made in Humberside while the Labour Conference was taking place in Blackpool. The debate on the miners' strike at the party conference was understandably emotional and bitter, with the police being assailed by almost every speaker from the floor. Louise Christian, a London solicitor who worked for the GLC 'police committee', said that the police were not, as some apologists had suggested, 'the meat in the sandwich': 'The police,' said Ms Christian to huge applause, 'are the salmonella in the sandwich.' A brave speech in defence of the police from Eric Hammond, leader of the Electricians' Union, was howled down. He was a lone voice of sanity in what was otherwise a public lynching of the police.

Curtis felt that the attacks by Labour speakers had to be answered, and he was concerned about the motion, passed without dissension by the Conference, which instructed a future Labour government to adopt the policies on the police advocated by the GLC. Before delivering his Humberside speech, Curtis had broken his journey to Hull at Harrogate, where the Superintendents' Association was meeting. He held a press conference to tell the police correspondents what he was going to say that evening, and to stress that he was not going to say that the police would not work with a Labour Government. In the speech, Curtis said;

> 'The police service deeply, bitterly, and fearfully, resents the Labour Party's verdict on the police. We are fearful, because we wonder how it will be possible to serve the people of this country, in some future crisis of this nature, if the party in power adopts a policy of blaming the police, and forbidding them, incredibly, to intervene to restore law and order, if the lawbreakers happen to be engaged in an industrial dispute.'

The speech ended with a plea from Curtis to the Labour leadership to take stock of the 'dangerous polarisation of political opinion about the police.' He said the Police Federation was willing to take part in genuine discussions about the issues involved. Neil Kinnock, the Labour leader, responded to the speech by saying that the motion carried by the Conference would not be included in the party's manifesto for the next election. He said the call to ban the police from intervening in an industrial dispute was 'a nonsense'.

Gerald Kaufman was in no mood to be conciliatory. He went on television immediately to say that Curtis should be ashamed of himself, and several papers (and the TV news bulletins) reported that the chairman had said the police would not work with a future Labour government. This brought him public censure from the Attorney General, which was withdrawn when Curtis sent him a text of the speech, while Leon Brittan said that Curtis had been right to speak out after the 'disgraceful' debate at Blackpool. At the Superintendents' Conference, the Federation's fraternal delegates, Peter Tanner and the treasurer, Trevor Laws, were asked to leave the hall while the meeting passed a motion which distanced their Association from the speech. The superintendents appeared more annoyed that Curtis had called a press conference at their Harrogate hotel, than with the actual contents of the speech. The clash marked the nadir of relations between the police and the Labour Party, and prompted people on both sides to recognise that some fences needed to be rebuilt.

The Federation's domestic concern at this time was with rent allowance. The official side's proposals for change represented a drastic lowering of the allowance. Eight out of every ten officers in the service was in receipt of rent allowance. The average amount paid was £1,500 a year, and the annual cost was put at £240 million. The official side suggested that instead of relating the force rent allowance to the rental value of a typical house provided by the police authority, it should be based on the average rent of a council house, less 30 per cent. This would have halved the current levels of the allowance. Inevitably, the matter went to arbitration where the staff side had little difficulty in persuading the Tribunal to reject the official side's proposals in their entirety. The arbiters accepted that Edmund-Davies had taken account of rent allowance when fixing pay levels in 1978 and they said that it would be invidious to attempt a revision of rent allowance in isolation from a general review of pay and conditions. The decision marked a considerable victory for the staff side, and in subsequent years, when escalating house prices increased the 'rental values' of police houses, the biennial reviews brought increasing benefits to the owner occupiers in the service.

The official side on this occasion was obliged to lick its wounds, and plan its next attack on the 'tax free perk'. This came almost at once, and from an unexpected quarter. The Home Office sent a circular to police authorities saying that in future he would not approve negotiated increases in rent allowance maximum limits unless he was satisfied that the 'selected house' was within an area where rents were not above the average for the whole police area, and had a rateable value of around the average for police provided accommodation. The implication was that branch boards and police authorities had selected houses which were at the top of the quality range, thus producing artificially high maximum limits. There was some justification for this view, as in some forces only a minority of officers occupied houses which attracted the maximum rent allowance. The circular warned;

> 'The Secretary of State intends to keep the maximum limits of rent allowances under review. In the light of future developments, he may need to consider whether further steps are necessary to limit the additional costs to police funds.'

Tanner was incensed at the Home Office's move, and wrote to Brittan to protest that the Home Secretary was exceeding his powers, because the regulation gave him power only to approve or disapprove of a force maximum limit, not to instigate a review of it. He added that the ruling on the rateable value of the selected house meant that police authorities had to take account of one bedroomed flats when calculating the average rateable value of its properties. He described the Home Secretary's warning on future action as a threat, and an attempt to take over the function of the negotiating body. Referring to the arbitration decision, he added;

> '... ... your circular has been taken by the Police Federation as an indication that you are a poor loser and I am sure that this is not the case.'

Brittan and the Home Office were unmoved by Tanner's warning, and within a short time the Home Secretary had rejected new maximum limits in three forces. The Federation took him to court, and in the High Court some eighteen months later Mr Justice Kennedy ruled that the circular was indeed *ultra vires*, because there had been no consultation with the PNB, a decision which was upheld by the Court of Appeal.

The Police Negotiating Board reached agreement in 1984 on changes in the arrangements for compensating officers for overtime and rest day and public holiday duties. The agreement provided that where less than 8 days' notice was given of a requirement to work on a rostered rest day a member would receive payment at the rate of time and a half for the cancelled rest day, and be given another rest day in lieu. When between 8 and 28 days' notice was given, the member would be paid time and a half for the day, but would not get another rest day. Where more than 28 days notice of the cancellation of rest day was given, the day would simply be re-rostered. This agreement was to come under strong attack in future years, with chief officers' maintaining that it limited their flexibility when wishing to deploy manpower. The Federation regarded it as a considerable achievement, because arbitrary and short-notice changes of rest days had a bad effect on the morale of members.

The other major concern of the staff side in 1984 was pay. The joint review of the Edmund-Davies pay levels had, as expected, produced widely divergent views. The staff side maintained that the method of updating pay since 1978 had produced precisely the objectives set by Edmund-Davies. It argued that the average earnings index understated the true level of increases in incomes, because it excluded fringe benefits. The official side maintained that the formula had been over generous to the police, and should be changed to prevent this happening in the future. They proposed that future pay reviews should take account of a new index - the 'underlying' index - which they thought would produce a lower level of increase.

After the intervention of Professor Hunter, the independent chairman of the PNB, the pay review of 1984 resulted in an

increase of 5.4 per cent, for all federated ranks except probationers and recruits. These were excluded because the pay
of police recruits had, since Edmund-Davies was introduced
six years earlier, outstripped pay in comparable employment.
It had moved ahead of average pay for graduates, for instance,
by over 10 per cent. The Constables Central Committee was
opposed to the 'freeze' of recruits and probationers' pay, but
was outvoted by the remainder of the staff side. The top rate
PC moved from £10,620 a year to £11,193.

The Federation scored a notable Parliamentary success in
1984, when the Government was forced to concede that police
officers should have the right to be legally represented when
facing serious disciplinary charges. The change of heart
followed a strong campaign by the Federation during the
Committee Stage of the Police and Criminal Evidence Bill.
The Federation took full page advertisements in national
papers on the theme that of all the weapons a police officer
faced, the most dangerous could be the pointing finger. It
was a victory secured at high cost, because the lawyer's bills
for advising and representing police officers in disciplinary
trouble have to be met by the Federation, and comfortably
exceed six figures every year.

As part of the campaign to persuade MPs to back its
proposals, the Federation commissioned a MORI poll which
found that 66 per cent of the public backed its call for wholly
independent investigations of complaints, and 82 per cent
agreed that an officer was entitled to be legally represented
in disciplinary matters. However, the House rejected the
Federation inspired amendments to the Police and Criminal
Evidence Bill which would have introduced an independent
system. The outcome was never really in doubt, and whatever
slight chance the Federation stood was effectively torpedoed
when Eldon Griffiths, having tabled the amendment, proceeded to rubbish it in his subsequent speech.

Another setback for the Federation came during the final
stages of the Bill's passage, when the Government accepted
an amendment which implemented Lord Scarman's recommendation that racial discrimination should become a specific
disciplinary offence. The Police Advisory Board had been
unanimous in advising Willie Whitelaw that such a clause

was unnecessary. Lord Scarman had the satisfaction of having used his membership of the House of Lords to secure his objective. He had failed twice when the original Bill was before the House of Lords. This time, by just six votes, he managed to defeat the Government, which decided to let Their Lordships have their way. It particularly irked the Federation that this decision was not taken on the merits of Scarman's amendment, but as part of a deal between the party whips by which two other amendments on different matters would be rejected if the racial discrimination clause was accepted. During the Third Reading debate, Eldon Griffiths made an angry and cogently argued speech attacking a new Home Secretary, Douglas Hurd, for pusillanimity, but when he pushed the matter to a vote, just 30 MPs joined him in the lobby.

The replacement of Leon Brittan as Home Secretary by Douglas Hurd came not long after the Federation's 1985 Conference, at which the prevailing mood of the delegates was anger against a Government seen to be 'letting down the police service'. An emergency motion was carried, which expressed 'grave concern' at the impact of Government policies on the police service and the fight against crime. Leslie Curtis attacked Brittan and the Government for its handling of the coal strike. Brittan's response was both inept and patronising, and drew heckling from the audience.

At this Conference, dissension and personal rivalries among the Joint Central Committee surfaced. The sergeants committee found itself alone on the JCC in adhering to the tradition of retirement of JCC officers after 30 years' service. It had adopted a policy of not supporting any candidate for office who had completed full service for pension, and at Conference the sergeants' committee members and their supporters on the floor wore stickers which drew attention to the fact that Peter Tanner was seeking a further three years in office although he had more than thirty years' service. At the post-Conference meeting, he fought off a challenge from the deputy secretary, Pat Johnson of West Yorkshire, and then an alliance of members of the constables' and inspectors' committees ensured that Alan Eastwood, a sergeant who had played a leading role in the '30 year' campaign, was not re-elected as JCC vice-chairman.

The Federation was concerned at this time about the future of the provincial metropolitan forces after the Government decided to abolish the six provincial metropolitan councils, along with the GLC, in 1986. The alarm bell sounded because the Local Government Bill contained a provision which would allow one of the new Metropolitan district councils, if it so wished, to become a police authority and set up its own force. The Federation knew that some of the new councils would, all things being equal (especially finance), be willing to break away from the existing metropolitan forces. The Federation believed that these forces had proved their worth in policing the large conurbations, and it would be follow to go back to the old city and borough system. Griffiths sought an assurance from the Environment Secretary, Patrick Jenkin, that he would refuse to embark on the break-up of the metropolitan forces. Jenkin declined to do so, but added that no change would be permitted unless a case could be made showing that it would be effective and efficient. This simply added to the uncertainty felt by the provincial forces, and the Federation leaders saw Hurd to express their concern. He made it clear that he would not entertain any proposal for change, but the Federation wrote to him to say that he could not bind a successor, and it was important to resolve the future of the forces concerned. Hurd replied that while it was true that a future Home Secretary might take a different view, he was convinced that every Minister would be bound to consider applications for changes in the light of his total responsibility for the service.

In the autumn of 1984, the IRA achieved its most spectacular propaganda coup with the bombing of the Grand Hotel at Brighton whilst it was being used by Mrs Thatcher and the cabinet during the Tory conference. The Premier herself was the target and narrowly escaped death. Several politicians and guests were killed, and others injured. The incident highlighted the lax security at major political conferences, a consequence of the party's own refusal to adopt stricter standards. From then on, the annual party conferences have become a major commitment for the host forces, each costing several million pounds to police.

For the Federation there was an ironic footnote to the Brighton tragedy. Earlier in the year, it had tried to persuade Leon Brittan or a junior minister to attend and address a major conference on Terrorism which had been organised in Germany by UISP, the European Union of Police Associations. Most of the interior ministers of other European states attended and spoke, as did the police heads of anti-terrorist forces. The answer from the Home Office had been that the event clashed with the forthcoming Tory conference, and in any case, terrorism in Britain was no longer considered to be a major threat. The British delegation to the conference flew black from Germany on the night that the Grand Hotel was blown up.

The service was finding the effects of Government restrictions on expenditure increasingly onerous. During the twelve months of the miners' strike, when over 6,000 officers from other forces were engaged in the coalfields, restrictions on recruiting and the fact that many forces could not afford to fill existing vacancies meant that the number of police officers in England and Wales fell by more than a thousand.

1985 was one of the most traumatic and tragic years in British police history. Within weeks of the coal strike coming to an end when the miners were forced to accept the inevitable, inner city rioting came back with a vengeance, with eruptions in Brixton, Toxteth and Handsworth, Birmingham in the summer, and then in the autumn came the riot on the Broadwater Farm estate in Tottenham, when PC Keith Blakelock was murdered in appalling fashion.

The chief HMI, Sir Lawrence Byford, reported that this time there were new and 'sinister' aspects of the rioting, which was being prompted and co-ordinated by criminal elements. He said that the petrol bomb was now the weapon of first resort for rioters, who displayed a contempt for human life. Two people were killed by rioters at Handsworth. Byford added that the riot highlighted the need for the service to have ready access to adequate reserves of trained personnel and equipment to enable them to mount a swift and effective response. He warned, however, that the root feeling of alienation which lay behind inner city disorder was beyond the ability of the police to solve, and they could do no more than mitigate the most violent consequences. The service must continue to recognise that CS gas and 'baton rounds' may be necessary.

Neither CS gas nor baton rounds were used in any of the riots of 1985, although these exceeded the 1981 events in ferocity. Officers equipped with baton round launchers were deployed at the height of the Broadwater Farm riot, but were not given orders to open fire. The handling of this riot came in for almost universal condemnation by the rank and file of the Metropolitan Police, who felt that the conduct of senior management on the night contributed to the casualties suffered by the PSUs, and left the rioters exulting after giving the police what local MP Bernie Grant described gloatingly as 'a bloody good hiding'. Sir Kenneth Newman ordered an internal inquiry and immediately promised that nothing would be swept under the carpet, but the inquiry dragged on for months and its report was never made public. Police anger over the death of Keith Blakelock and the horrific injuries suffered by several other officers was heightened when *POLICE* published evidence to show that local senior officers had ignored or played down many warnings, from officers working full time on the tension ridden estate, that an 'uprising' was being planned and could happen at any moment.

When the annual meeting of the Metropolitan Branch Boards took place soon after the Tottenham riot, Douglas Hurd decided not to face the massed anger of the rank and file who packed the Central Hall. He preferred instead to deliver a lecture to a prisoners' aid group. *POLICE* said;

'Had Mr Hurd, who is the police authority for the Metropolitan Police, chosen to attend the meeting, he would have been left in no doubt as to the depths of anger felt by ordinary officers against what they see as the mishandling of the Tottenham riot, and the policing policies which have been followed in the inner city since 1981.'

The magazine said the service had been 'Scarmanised';

> 'There are thousands of officers who believe that Lord
> Scarman's 1981 report has had a devastating effect
> on the quality of leadership and decision taking in the
> police service. Senior officers appear to have been
> 'Scarmanised'.'

POLICE pointed out that in the four years since Scarman
police organisation had been changed to comply with his
conclusions. Training had been improved and more attention
was being paid to social conditions. The 'Sus' laws had been
repealed and the Police and Criminal Evidence Act enshrined
the rights of suspects under interrogation and detention.
Racial discrimination had been made a specific offence
against police discipline. Yet the police were still under attack,
verbally and physically. At Handsworth, Toxteth, and Tottenham, said *POLICE*, senior officers had followed a policy of
avoiding confrontation at all costs, in the vain hope that peace,
no matter how uneasy, could be maintained. This had been
an illusory peace, as the victims of the petty and serious
crime which had been allowed to flourish in these areas in
the absence of a stronger police presence, had found out to
their cost. It said that prior to the riot the Broadwater Farm
estate was being paraded by the Department of the Environment and Haringey Council as 'a beehive of flourishing
rehabilitation and positive community involvement' which
cloaked the ugly reality of criminal gangs ruling the estate,
robbing and terrorising the inhabitants, and making daily war
on any police officers who dared to venture near.

In later years, the horror of that night in 1985 would return
to haunt the consciousness of the Metropolitan Police. There
was great satisfaction when three young men were convicted
at the Old Bailey of Keith Blakelock's murder, but following
a lengthy campaign and the Home Secretary's reference back
of the case to the Court of Appeal, the convictions were set
aside as 'unsafe', mainly on the ground that the senior
detectives in charge of the investigation had tampered with
the notes of interviews with a suspect. Counsel for the Crown
referred to the 'dishonesty' of the officers having destroyed

the credibility of the prosecution case. In 1994, another jury would decide that the officers had not tampered with the notes, nor had they committed perjury. A detailed second police investigation into Blakelock's murder was said to have found insufficient evidence to prosecute any other person.

The riots had demonstrated yet again that police resources were thin on the ground when they were needed the most. The manpower restrictions continued to bite hard, and when Mrs Thatcher, addressing the Tory conference in 1985, singled out 'strengthening the police' as a major priority for the Government, Leslie Curtis was quick to take up the challenge. Speaking in the aftermath of the riots, Thatcher assured her adoring audience that, 'the Government will continue steadfastly to back the police. If they need more men, more equipment, different equipment, they shall have them. We do not economise on protecting life and property'.

In a long letter to Douglas Hurd, Curtis hoped that this 'unequivocal' statement would be translated into positive action. He said it indicated that the police service had established its case for additional resources, and spelt out how the restrictions on the previous two years had hampered the fight against crime and disorder. He cited Sir Kenneth Newman's analysis of how the increase of almost 4,000 officers since 1979 in the Metropolitan had been more than offset by the loss of regular working on rest days and cuts in police overtime; cash limits; establishing the 700 strong Royalty and Diplomatic Protection Group, and putting another 750 officers in district support units as an instant emergency reserve. In all, the force had thus 'lost' almost 5,000 officers in the five years that it had recruited an additional 4,000. Curtis said that provincial forces had similar problems. The forces in the large conurbations had all lost strength in 1985. Hurd responded with an offer to discuss manpower and resources with Curtis. He reminded him that expenditure on the police had risen since 1979 from £1.1 billion to £2.8 billion, an increase of a third 'in real terms'. As the Federation suspected, the Premier's law and order rhetoric on the Conference platform did not signal any loosening of the strings of the policing purse.

THIRTY-THREE

The widow's mite

Politics rather than economics dominated the talks on pay in the summer of 1985. The staff side found that what should have been simply the formal ratification of an increase of 7.5 per cent had turned into a wrangle between the Labour dominated local authority representatives, and the Tory government, which was preaching hair shirt restraint in public sector pay. The official side informed the staff side that it agreed that 7.5 per cent was the correct amount, but would not agree to it until the police authorities had received a guarantee from central government that it would be funded for a full year.

The staff side was annoyed because the negotiators could see the artificiality of the issue. Having made its point, the official side agreed at the next meeting to conclude the agreement. The starting pay of a recruit became £7,212, rising to £12,033 after 15 years.

The Federation was more genuinely upset about the Government's policy of encouraging people to take out private pensions schemes, as a means of reducing reliance on the state earnings related scheme. Employees in public service pensions schemes were also being encouraged to opt for private pensions. The legislation allowed such employees to opt out, although the Federation tried and failed to exclude police officers from the right to do so. There were financial incentives from the Government to encourage opting out. The Federation was angered to discover that any officer who opted out would still be covered by the special accident, injury and death in service benefits of the police scheme. It recognised that many younger officers, and especially married women who saw themselves as unlikely to stay in the police for the full thirty years to qualify for a maximum pension, would be tempted to opt out.

The Federation had two major concerns about opting out. If a significant number of younger officers did so, it would not be long before the reduced contribution base put a strain on the ability of the scheme to fund current pensions. More importantly from a Federation viewpoint, it was undeniable that no private sector scheme could match the benefits available under the police scheme, particularly early retirement and dependents' payments. The Federation ensured that every member received a pamphlet setting out the available options, and warning officers that opting out was a decision they could come to regret. In fact, comparatively few officers opted out, and some years later a number of those who did discovered that they had been misled by smooth talking pensions salesmen into joining a much inferior scheme.

The long running problem of football hooligans came to a head in 1985, with the deaths of many Italian fans in a riot in Brussels, when Liverpool supporters ran amok before the start of the European Cup final. A serious riot by Leeds United fans at Birmingham City's ground resulted in one death, and on the same day over fifty people died when a stand caught fire at the Bradford City ground. Hooliganism was not a factor at Bradford, but the other catastrophes came as no surprise to the service. The Federation had warned for years that disorder and the poor state of some grounds would lead inevitably to tragedy, and in the twenty years since the hooligan problem had first surfaced, several murders of football followers had occurred. Calls from the Federation for chief officers to have the power to ban matches at which public safety could not be guaranteed had always been rejected, as had suggestions for all-seater stadia.

The Joint Central Committee gave evidence to the Inquiry into the Safety of Sports Grounds, presided over by Mr Justice Popplewell. Many of his recommendations coincided with the proposals put forward by the Federation. They included; an extension of police powers to search fans for offensive weapons; an additional power of arrest of persons causing disorder at matches; and making new criminal offences of the throwing of missiles and chanting racist slogans at matches. The Federation was critical of the Act which was rushed through Parliament, immediately after the Popplewell Report, to control the possession and consumption of alcohol at grounds and on coaches going to and from matches. It criticised the decision to ban the sale of alcohol at most parts of the ground, but to permit it in 'executive boxes'. It also complained of the limited power to search for alcohol, granted by the Act, as falling far short of Popplewell's proposal. Within a couple of years, the appalling tragedy at Hillsborough would galvanise Government and football clubs into more decisive action.

1985 also saw the advent of the Crown Prosecutions Service, established under the Prosecution of Offences Act as an independent prosecution service for England and Wales. This followed the main proposals of the Royal Commission on Criminal Procedure and brought to an end a long tradition by which all prosecutions, save those major offences reserved for the Director of Public Prosecutions, were instigated by the police. The Federation had told the Royal Commission that the police should retain the right to prosecute, but privately it was not an issue on which it felt strongly. It soon became clear, however, that the new service had got off to a bad start, and many of the problems could not be dismissed merely as teething troubles. The root cause seemed to be that the CPS was from the outset seriously underfunded and understaffed, and the quality of many of the prosecutors dismayed the police. The 'independence' of the prosecutors contrasted with the relationships which forces had enjoyed in the past with their own prosecuting solicitors, and there was dismay about the number of cases in which the CPS refused to go to court, or substituted charges of lesser gravity than the police considered to be justified by the evidence. Other complaints were of unjustified 'plea bargaining' between prosecution and defence lawyers, in which the police were not consulted, and of a failure to explain, either to police case officers or to the victims of crime, why decisions had been taken.

The service had to get used to the idea that these prosecutors saw themselves, not as facilitators of the police case against defendants, but as neutral officials, attaching equal weight to the interests of justice and suspects, as the Royal Commission had intended. The effect on police morale was serious, and greatly under appreciated by the Government and the CPS. The JCC raised these concerns with the Home Secretary and the Lord Chancellor's Department, without securing any concessions.

In 1986, the Federation thought that at long last it had righted an old injustice, which affected elderly widows of police officers whose husbands had served before the widows' pension scheme was improved in 1956. These widows received only a fixed rate pension, which in 1986 stood at £13.89 a week. Of the 6,000 widows affected, many did not qualify for a state widows' pension because of their age. The Federation had been trying to secure an improvement for many years, and had at last reached an agreement by which the widows would in future receive a pension of one third of their late husbands' pensions. For a constable's widow, this meant a rise of £1.41 a week. The annual cost of the agreement was estimated at £500,000 a year, a drop in the ocean of police pensions costs, and more than offset by the increased contributions of the police. To the astonishment of everyone, and the disgust of the Federation, Douglas Hurd vetoed the agreement. He said he did so because of the possible repercussions on other public sector schemes, yet the Government had established the precedent in 1980 when similar concessions were made to the widows of servicemen who died in the 1939-45 war. It was the first occasion since collective bargaining was introduced in the police service more than thirty years earlier, that a Home Secretary had refused to ratify a freely negotiated settlement in the PNB.

More than 100 MPs of all parties, including former Home Secretaries Leon Brittan and Willie Whitelaw, had signed a motion urging justice for the 'preserved rate' widows. But Hurd remained unmoved. The Home Office was quite content to let the problem of the impecunious elderly police widows be solved by the course of nature.

Even before this row had died away, Hurd found himself in trouble with the police once more over a proposal that police officers should no longer be eligible to claim compensation from the Criminal Injuries Compensation Board in respect of injuries sustained as a result of an assault or while trying to effect an arrest. This arose from an earlier report of an inter-departmental committee, composed entirely of civil servants, which recommended that the scheme should exclude anyone who held any office or emplopyment which required them to arrest offenders or prevent the commission of crime. The committee said that the Edmund-Davies pay scales took account of the police officer's special exposure to physical danger.

Once again, Hurd displayed an arrogant and obdurate disregard for consultation. The inter-departmental committee's report was published in November 1986 and on the same day Hurd announced that the proposal to exclude the police from compensation would be incorporated in the new Criminal Justice Bill. He found himself assailed in the Commons by Gerald Kaufman, enjoying the opportunity to champion the police for once, and by a deeply embarrassed Eldon Griffiths. After some sharp exchanges and lame explanations, Hurd reluctantly agreed to talk to the Federation. Following a meeting with Curtis and Tanner, Hurd was happy to change his mind.

One report of particular importance to the police that was published in 1986 concerned the use of firearms. The subject had been given media prominence during the Eighties after a succession of cases in which something had gone wrong during a firearms operation. In 1982, police hunting a man who had shot and wounded a Metropolitan police constable, stopped a car being driven by the man's girl friend, which they mistakenly believed to contain the suspect. The man in the car, Stephen Waldorf, was shot several times by the armed police officers, and subsequently two officers were tried at the Old Bailey for attempted murder and acquitted. In the West Midlands, an officer shot and killed a five year old boy during a raid on the home of the boy's father, an armed robber. The officer was charged with manslaughter and acquitted. The 1985 Brixton riot was sparked off after an armed police raid at the home of a wanted suspect resulted in an officer shooting and wounding the man's mother. He was charged with unlawful wounding and acquitted.

The prosecutions of the officers in these cases emphasised

that every police officer who carried a firearm on duty bore a personal responsibility for the decision to fire the weapon. The Federation felt strongly that the existing guidelines provided insufficient guidance to officers faced with life or death decisions that must be taken instantly in highly stressful and dangerous situations. The report of a Home Office working party, on which Leslie Curtis represented the Federation, concluded that there was little wrong with the existing procedures, although Curtis himself had earlier criticised the training courses given to officers as wholly inadequate. The report recommended that armed response vehicles should provide 24-hour cover. Some police officers and outside observers thought that the report amounted to nothing more than a total endorsement of existing practices and policies, and offered nothing in the way of ensuring, as far as possible, that similar tragedies did not recur.

Sir Cecil Clothier, the first chairman of the Police Complaints Authority, had declared his determination that the new body would adopt a high profile, in sharp contrast with the restrained stance of its predecessor, the Police Complaints Board. He was true to his word in the Authority's 1986 annual report, calling for the dismissal of 'sub-standard' officers. He said that in the course of investigations, the authority came across a few police officers who were 'clearly unsuitable to hold the office of constable', although there was insufficient evidence to proceed against them for disciplinary offences. Clothier pointed out that the police did not have the civil service or armed forces procedures for getting rid of people who consistently failed to come up to required standards. The Federation saw this as a means of circumventing the disciplinary procedures, which afforded protection to officers against arbitrary dismissal. It would be a back door method of getting rid of officers whose 'faces did not fit', said *POLICE*;

'The real danger of Sir Cecil Clothier's enthusiasm for hanging black sheep is that unscrupulous management might welcome a convenient and relatively unchallengeable way of getting rid of officers for all kinds of undisclosed reasons. Anyone who doubts that senior police management would behave in such a fashion, doesn't begin to understand the extent to which the balance of power in the police service is firmly in the hands of the hierarchy.'

The 1986 pay review produced an identical increase, 7.5 per cent, to that of the previous year. This was three times the Government's current target for wage increases. Once again, there was a political wrangle between the local authorities and the government, with the former seeking assurances, which were not forthcoming, that police authorities would not be penalised if the cost of the award took them over government cash limits. Brian Rusbridge said that unless satisfactory assurances were obtained on this point, the official side would not be able to approve the award due in September 1987. The constables' pay scale was now £7,752 on appointment, rising to £12,936. Later in the year, the Police Arbitration Tribunal rejected the staff side's claim for an increase in London Allowance, which had been 'frozen' since 1981. The tribunal accepted the official side's argument that there was no acute shortage of manpower in the Metropolitan Police.

An initiative of the policewomen representatives to the Federation Conference in 1986 lead eventually to a substantial change in the law concerning evidence of children in sex cases. Women officers had complained of a ruling that a very young child could not be allowed to give evidence in cases where the defendant was alleged to have sexually abused that child. As so often the only witness was the child, molesters were virtually immune from justice unless there was sufficient circumstantial evidence to convict them. Initial approaches to the Home Office brought an immediate rejection from David Mellor, the Minister of State, but after a lengthy campaign, in which the Federation worked with other interested groups, the law was changed to allow child victims to give unworn evidence over a live video link.

The police came in for considerable criticism after the television screening of an episode in a series *Police* produced by Roger Graef, in which the Thames Valley police was subjected to the 'fly on the wall' technique, with cameras ever present during weeks of routine policing. The episode showed CID officers behaving in a uncaring and callous fashion to a woman of low intelligence who alleged that she had been raped. Their indifference, ineptness, and obvious lack of sympathy for the woman came as a rude shock and lead to immediate demands that there should be major changes in the way that police dealt with women complainants. The officers were in fact simply demonstrating the prevailing male police culture of that time. For generations, officers had been taught to be sceptical about complaints of rape. Trainers would tell recruits that the accusation was the easiest to make and the hardest for an accused man to disprove, and that in any case many complainants had 'asked for it'. Among the public, it was assumed that the conduct of the Thames Valley detectives was typical of what women could expect if they complained of assaults or rapes, and as such it did enormous damage to the reputation of the police. What the programme also exposed was the consequences of the Sex Discrimination Act, following which the policewomen's departments were scrapped, and the unique expertise which they had built up over many years was all but lost to the service.

In October 1986, the Home Office issued a circular which endorsed most of the proposals of an inquiry conducted by the Women's National Commission - *Violence against women*. It recommended the setting up of separate facilities for interviewing and medically examining women and children in sex and abuse cases, with more female police surgeons. Following the controversy surrounding the TV programme, most forces overhauled their procedures and established departments, staffed by men and women, to specialise in these areas The police attitude towards allegations underwent a major change, with the interests of the victim becoming paramount.

Following the 1987 pay review, which resulted in a 7.75 per cent increase, the starting pay of a constable rose to £8,352, and the top rate PC received £13,938. Again, the official side rejected an application for an increase in London Allowance. It said that it wished to undertake a full review of the Edmund-Davies formula. The staff side said it would not co-operate in such an examination unless the official side agreed to discuss London Allowance. The official side said that there was no recruiting problem in the Metropolitan Police, which was up to strength, but accepted that there was of retaining experienced officers. It pointed out that the objective of the allowance, to bring the force to full strength had been achieved. Later in 1987, the Police Arbitration Tribunal again upheld the official side's refusal to increase the London Allowance.

In July, the Police Arbitration Tribunal awarded an increase of 7.5 per cent in London Weighting, the pensionable supplement paid to London employees in the public sector, which was intended to compensate them for the assumed additional costs of life in Greater London and which the London police received in addition to London Allowance. This became £990 a year.

As the service faced ever mounting increases in its workload, with crime escalating year by year, and social factors deteriorating rapidly, the effect on individual officers was becoming more marked. The Federation was aware of the attention being paid to stress problems among American officers and at the beginning of the Eighties the JCC approached ACPO to ascertain the extent of the problem in England and Wales. Anecdotal evidence suggested that there was a direct link between increased sickness absence rates and mental rather than physical illnesses among officers.

A working party drawn from all the staff associations concluded that stress was a problem, and that one of the major causes of adverse stress appeared to be unsatisfactory and sometimes oppressive management styles. Examples of this were cited as; unjust criticism; unrealistic expectations of officers' performances; excessive autocracy and a lack of concern for the individual. The working party contrasted management systems in forces. The good ones were seen to produce competent professional officers, but these were offset by bad systems in other forces, which threw up problems of recruitment, training, career development and discipline. The report called for management support systems to assist officers with their health and welfare problems, to deal with the difficult demands which policing placed upon them and their families. In particular, it called for a much more informed and caring approach to the effects of post traumatic stress among officers.

The working party continued to examine the subject in following years, and in 1987 a major report was placed before the Police Advisory Board. This recommended the establishment of a dedicated occupational health unit in the Home Office, charged with progressing work on the organisational and other problems which the working party had identified as being associated with stress. The proposals were supported by the staff associations and the police authorities, and the unit was established. As usual, however, the problem of the gap between intentions and achievement boiled down to a shortage of resources. In some forces, branch boards provided the funds that enabled members suffering from stress to be counselled by psychologists. At the same time the Home Office, police authorities and chief officers, were complaining about the cost of ill health retirements, many of which could have been attributable to adverse stress.

In what became known as the 'Hungerford Massacre' in 1987, a man ran amok in the area and shot and killed 14 people before committing suicide. He used a Kalashnikov automatic rifle, for which he held a firearms certificate. One of the dead was a policeman, Constable Roger Brereton. The Police Federation saw the tragedy as a consequence of the refusal of the Government to recognise the menace of such high powered and lethal weapons in private hands. On three occasions since the Conservatives took office in 1979, the Federation had approached Home Secretaries to call for tighter restrictions on firearms. The Federation wanted shotguns to be brought under the rules governing 'Part One' firearms, and had called for a ban on all automatic weapons. The Government was more in sympathy with the powerful shooting lobby of farmers and gun enthusiasts, and on each occasion the Federation was told that there was no need to legislate. When ACPO asked the Home Secretary at least to change the law so that shotgun owners should be made legally responsible for the safe custody of weapons and ammunition, and must notify a change of address, the shooters called this a gross interference with the liberty of the subject. Yet thousands of shotguns were being stolen every year, and many ended up in the hands of armed robbers. Meanwhile, deadly automatic weapons were being offered to British enthusiasts by mail order firms. For £500, or £50 a month, anyone with a certificate could obtain a Franchi STAS12, which fired 11 shells before reloading, could empty its magazine in 11 seconds, and was fitted with telescopic sights. The Hungerford incident followed closely on two other cases of multiple murders committed by assailants with 'legal' firearms.

This time, Douglas Hurd, the latest Home Secretary to dismiss Federation anxieties about guns, was compelled to take action and the private possession of automatic and semi-automatic weapons was prohibited under an Act, brought in almost record time, and in spite of the furious condemnation of the shooters.

Guns were not the only danger facing the police on the streets. The Metropolitan Police, strongly supported by the London Federation, was urging the Government to take action to control the menace of knives. Following a series of knife attacks on police the Federation was demanding legal curbs. Again, the Home Office had at first suggested that the existing law on offensive weapons was adequate, but with public and police concern mounting, Hurd told the annual meeting of the Metropolitan Federation that the Government intended to outlaw the carrying of knives, and 'of course, there will be a parallel power to search'. When the relevant amendments to the Criminal Justice Bill were published, however, the police were disappointed with the weakness of the Government response. The new offence did no more than update an existing ban by putting on the defendant the onus of proving that he had a reasonable excuse for carrying the knife. The promised power of arrest allowed an officer, 'on reasonable suspicion' to search for a knife, subject to the existing restrictions of the Police and Criminal Evidence Act. There was no power, as the police had requested, which would allow them to search persons at the scene of a crime, such as a pop concert or disco, after a stabbing had occurred. The Federation said the police would say 'thanks for nothing' to the Home Secretary. It pointed out that in the first nine months of 1987, there had been nearly 2000 street robberies reported to the police in London in which a knife had been used, an increase of 44 per cent.

Curtis wrote to Hurd to protest about his reneging on the promise to give police a new power of arrest to search for knives. He said that Hurd had given the public the impression that he was strengthening police powers when he had done nothing of the kind. Douglas Hogg, a junior Home Office Minister, replied that it was 'difficult to conceive of circumstances in which it would be in the public interest to create additional powers to search for knives, or arrest knife carriers'.

Early in 1988, the official side gave the staff side advance notice of its likely approach to the next pay review. It accepted that the existing system of relating pay to the underlying average earnings index should remain, save for another 'freeze' on the pay of recruits, and for possible discounts to take account of the fact that constables' pay was inflated by the affect of increments. For London, the official side changed its mind again, and wanted to remove the London Allowance from recruits to offer an incentive to experienced London officers to stay in the police It also proposed that London inspectors and chief inspectors should lose their pay lead over the provinces.

The official side next turned its attention to rent allowance. It proposed that recruits who became eligible for rent allowance should lose the compensatory grant by which income tax on the allowance was reimbursed. It wanted the rates element of the allowance to be deleted and said that future increases in the allowance should be based on the retail prices index, not the district valuers' assessments of rental values. It proposed another look at allowances paid to detectives and the end of the system of reimbursing NHS prescription and treatment charges, except where these arose from injuries or illnesses related to police duties. The official side also wanted a woman officer's right to pay during maternity leave to be restricted to those who undertook to return to the police after giving birth. Finally, it proposed changes in entitlements to paid sick leave, and greater flexibility in duty rosters.

The Federation saw that it was likely to be confronted with quite a formidable package of reductions from current conditions of service. It assured its members that it would be approaching the pay review from a totally opposite direction, looking for financial recognition of the additional workload, responsibilities and dangers faced by the police since Edmund-Davies. POLICE said;

> '... ... not only police officers will find it hard to understand why the Government and the local authorities should be seeking to undermine the existing structure of police pay and allowances ... ... The official side is well aware that they are opening negotiations with a group that is, by statute, shorn of all the conventional weapons of industrial action. They need to be reminded that the underlying principle of Edmund-Davies was that this unique advantage to the employers must not be exploited.'

THIRTY-FOUR

Hurd turns the screw

The signs of strain in what the general public had come to see as a cosy relationship between the police and the Tory Government came into the open at the Federation's 1988 Conference in Scarborough. Leslie Curtis made a strong attack on the official side's readiness to attack the pay and conditions package. He told Douglas Hurd that for the first time in ten years, the police felt that their living standards were under threat. He accused the official side's elected members of being jealous of the Edmund-Davies standards enjoyed by the police, but made it clear that he held the Home Secretary responsible for honouring the Government's pledges to uphold those standards. Curtis and Tanner knew that while Ministers maintained they were honouring the pledges given to the police, Hurd's civil servants on the official side were more hawkish than the councillors in attacking rent allowance and other benefits. The Federation view was that, under pressure from the Treasury, Hurd was seeking further cuts in the burgeoning police budget. Hurd appeared rattled by the strength of Curtis's onslaught, which went down well with the angry delegates. He said that it was fair enough for the Federation to put its case and fight its corner, but he added;

> 'do not let anyone deceive you about where your support comes from. It was this Government that fully implemented Edmund-Davies. We have continued to honour it'.

This was an oblique reference to indications of a thaw in the previously frosty relations between the Federation and the Labour Party. Hurd knew that Curtis and Tanner had talked to Roy Hattersley, the shadow Home Secretary, and this was something that appeared to worry Eldon Griffiths, who made his second 'farewell' speech at this Conference. It lasted almost an hour, and contained a rebuke for what Griffiths saw as the Federation's lack of gratitude to his party's Government;

'The worst way to proceed is to attack your friends. There is no evidence that Ministers have inspired the official side's papers (on drastic revision of the Edmund-Davies package) ... ... it is not the case that the Home Secretary is conniving to reduce the policeman's standard of living. This charge simply will not wash. It will be treated by Parliament and the public as one of those exaggerated allegations that devalue only those that make them. Not even your closest allies on the Conservative side of the House will respond to the assertions that the Government is letting down the police with anything but deep resentment. And it's no good looking to the Opposition for practical help. They may relish the prospect of the Government colliding with its 'pals' as they see them (the police); but in present circumstances there is no way that Labour can, or will, convince either trade unionists or its left wing majority; that the police should get more of the Opposition's fire power than the health workers or the teachers or the seamen.'

Eldon Griffiths had been the Federation's Parliamentary Adviser for 18 years in all. He had fulfilled a completely different role from the negotiating one occupied by Callaghan, his predecessor, but in later years he adopted an openly confrontational approach to his work for the Federation in Parliament, which alienated non-Government Members of Parliament, and his annual addresses to Conference had become more and more political in tone and content. Griffiths had also presumed that he had the right to criticise as well as support Federation policies, and there was lingering resentment on the JCC over the independent complaints issue and his action over the pension contributions rise. When considering a successor, the committee officers would be anxious to ensure that a more consiliatory figure was chosen.

Leslie Curtis retired in the summer of 1988 after six years as chairman. His successor was Alan Eastwood, a Metropolitan sergeant. Eastwood had become the vice-chairman for the second time a year earlier, following his removal from that office because of the '30 year' rule controversy. Shortly afterwards, Peter Tanner retired as general secretary. There were four candidates for the succession. Three were constables and the fourth an inspector. In the Committee vote, on a 'first past the post' basis, the constables cancelled each other out and the inspector, Vee Neild of the West Midlands, was elected. For the first time, a woman took charge of the Police Federation, something that the early leaders who fought against the very idea of women in the police service would never have thought possible.

The new parliamentary adviser, appointed in March 1989, was Michael Shersby, a little known Tory MP. The Federation advertised the post in the Parliamentary house journal and it attracted about a dozen replies. Eastwood and Neild had told Roy Hattersley that they would prefer to have an Opposition MP this time. Hattersley decided that one Labour name would be put forward, to be considered with other short listed applicants. The Labour MP who applied was well qualified for the post, having some previous police connections and a close knowledge of current problems, but he destroyed his own chances at the interview when he explained that his constituency party would make difficulties for him if he took up a paid post with the Federation. In any case, Shersby was the unanimous choice of the JCC officers, who were impressed with his grasp of detail and obvious sympathy for the police.

The discussions on rent allowance at the Police Negotiating Board found no common ground between the sides. The official side argued, that as the Government was abolishing the domestic rate and replacing it with a community charge to be levied on every adult, the rate element in the allowance should be discontinued. The staff side said that the community charge was simply a replacement of one form of local taxation with another, and the police authorities should continue to reimburse the cost to the police, while paying the charges of police officers living in police accommodation. When the matter, as was inevitable, came before the arbitration tribunal, it had no hesitation in rejecting the Federation's claim, saying that there was no reason why the police officer and his wife should be exempted from community charge.

The Tribunal proposed that rent allowance should be replaced with a new allowance, called housing allowance. The arbiters said that an allowance based on housing costs should continue to form a part of police pay. They said it should continue to be separate from basic pay because there were special factors which determined where a police officer could live, and they could be required to move their homes from time to time. The allowance should be paid to all officers, with those living in police accommodation paying rent to the police authority. The housing allowance should be calculated in each force by averaging out the global sum paid to members as rent allowance and would be taxable. Thus the allowance would in future have no regard to the value of the house an officer occupied. The position of serving officers would be protected. They would continue to receive rent allowance at the current level of payment, but future uprating would be according to an agreed index based on average housing prices in an area. The compensatory grant for tax paid on rent allowance would be phased out, but a corresponding proportion of the rent or housing allowance would become pensionable.

The Tribunal was anxious to stress that its award was not made in order to reduce costs to police authorities, but to modernise the element of housing assistance in the police pay package, in the light of changes such as the community charge. The award stated, that apart from requiring officers to pay their own charges, no officer should be worse off as a result of the award. The arbiters said;

> 'The allowance has become an integral part of police pay. Our concern has been to put it on a footing which is more in conformity with modern practice, that is to say a taxable component of pay, and less likely to attract criticism as an outdated concept.'

Vee Neild told the membership that it should be reasonably satisfied with the outcome. Although the Federation had lost the claim for reimbursement of community charge, it had never expected to win it, because the new charge was not property related. The main thing, said Neild, was that the rates element of the old rent allowance would be consolidated in the new housing allowance. Much hard bargaining with the official side lay ahead, she warned, but meanwhile the staff side had fought off, by the strength of its arguments, a determined attempt by the official side to inflict major damage on the living standards of members.

The Tribunal instructed the two sides of the PNB to work out the details of the new allowance. It soon became clear that the official side had not expected such an outcome from their efforts to make a substantial cut in the cost of housing aid. In particular, they objected to paying housing allowance to all members of police forces, because by making police officers tenants of police houses paying rents, they would secure the same statutory 'right to buy' which had become so popular with council tenants. To avoid this, the official side said the Government would seek to introduce legislation to deny police officers the right to buy their police houses, which they argued, were required by police forces for strategic purposes. Many police house occupants wanted the right to buy their homes as sitting tenants, with the substantial discounts from market values that were available to council tenants, and the staff side would not negotiate their rights away. The two sides could not reach an agreement on this issue, and on several other points.

The staff side was angered when, in the middle of talks between the sides, Douglas Hurd intervened to say that he intended to veto substantial parts of the arbitration award. It was apparent that he too had been expecting greater savings from the exercise, but yet again Hurd displayed a curious, aloof arrogance towards the negotiating and consultative processes of the police service.

In a letter to Professor Laurie Hunter, the independent chairman of the PNB, Hurd said that after consulting Cabinet colleagues, he had to warn him that the Secretaries of State would not be committed to accept any agreement on rent allowance, simply because it was based on the decision of the arbitration tribunal. He singled out the proposal that the new housing allowance should take account of what the force had paid in domestic rates in the previous year, the proposal to pay housing allowance to police living in provided houses and charge them rents, because of the right to buy legislation, and the suggestion that future upratings could be based on housing cost indices. Hurd feared that this would perpetuate the recent experience of substantial increases in housing aid at every biennial review. Nor, said Hurd, would he be likely to agree to the compensatory grant element being phased into pensionable pay.

As no progress could be made in the talks between the sides, the matter returned to the arbitration tribunal. The staff side case was presented, as at the previous hearing, by James Anderton, its chairman. It was felt that he was more likely to argue the case effectively, and stand up to the official side's spokesman, than the relatively inexperienced Vee Neild, who as staff side secretary might have been expected to present the case. By common consent, Anderton was a first class advocate for the police case.

Sir John Wood, and his colleagues were clearly annoyed by the attitude of the official side and the indication from the Home Secretary that, whatever they recommended, he was likely to impose his own version of housing allowance. In its second judgement, delivered in November 1989, the tribunal stuck to its first principles. It accepted the official side's view that police officers should not be allowed to buy police houses as sitting tenants, and said it expected the federations to agree that this should not happen. The tribunal did not explain how the federations had the power to deny any of its members the legal right to buy that they would acquire as paying tenants. However, this was something of a side issue, and did not affect the tribunal's thinking on its main recommendations. The arbiters stressed that the objective of the first award had been to establish that police pay should in future consist of two elements - pay and a housing allowance, which should be differently indexed, but should be consolidated as far as possible for tax and pensions purposes. In an implicit rebuke to Hurd and the official side, the tribunal added;

> '... ... any inclination to pick and choose between the individual changes that we have suggested is likely to destroy, to the advantage of one side or the other, the fairness of the solution we have proposed, which we believe takes account of the need not to add to the expense of the police service and is based on clear and sensible principles.'

Shortly after the second ruling, Hurd left the Home Office to be replaced by David Waddington, who promptly carried out his predecessor's intention and vetoed the arbitration award. He rejected the proposals so far as they included the rates element in the 'kitty' from which the new force housing allowance would be calculated, and the proposal to pay housing allowance to police house occupants. The uprating process would be through reference to the retail prices index and not the building societies' index of house prices. The compensatory grant figure would not be absorbed into pensionable pay. For good measure, he added other provisions which worsened the position of officers who were married to each other.

Anderton and Neild saw Waddington immediately after his veto and found him adamant that the award could not be accepted. A protest meeting in Central Hall, at which more than 3,000 members were present, and approaches by branch boards to Members of Parliament had no effect. Roy Hattersley, the shadow Home Secretary, secured Opposition support for a motion which condemned Waddington's interference with arbitration, but Government whips used delaying tactics to delay the debate reaching the floor of the House.

The housing allowances, paid to new entrants, averaged about two thirds of the rent allowances which they replaced, resulting in very substantial savings on the police pay bill, in addition to the saving resulting from the abolition of rates, which alone was estimated to be a third of the total rent allowance bill of around £500 million a year.

The 1988 and 1989 pay reviews came and went while the

protracted arguments over rent allowance were going on. In 1988, as it had warned the staff side earlier, the official side insisted on a second freeze on the pay of police recruits, on the grounds that the starting rate was advancing far ahead of commencing pay in comparable employment. The average gross earnings of non-manual males of the same ages as police recruits were £8,780 and the starting salaries of graduates was £8,500. These compared with the PC's starting rate of £10,512.

The official side also complained that average salaries of the federated ranks had increased faster than the level intended by the Edmund-Davies pay formula, due to the impact of annual salary increments. It said that the underlying earnings index took account of increments in other occupations, so in effect the police were getting double compensation. Anticipating that the actual increase in the underlying index would be around 8.5 per cent, the official side therefore proposed, in addition to a freeze on the starting rate, that the pay of constables should be increased by varying amounts of between 5 and 8.5 per cent, to take account of the 'overpayment' of previous years.

The official side also put forward its proposal to scrap the London Allowance for new entrants and introduce a non-pensionable retention allowances of £1,050 a year for officers with five years' service. It also proposed changes to various allowances and sick pay arrangements, and to maternity pay.

The staff side rejected the official side's arguments, and counter claimed that in addition to the 8.5 per cent movement in the underlying index, police pay should be adjusted to take account of the shortfall between the movement of the index and the actual movement of police pay scales since the previous award. Also, it wanted the 'overlapping' principle introduced by Edmund-Davies, by which the top rate of the constable exceeded the starting pay of a sergeant with less than fifteen years' police service, to be extended throughout the federated ranks' pay structure. After the initial pay talks had broken up without any sign of agreement, Tanner sent a document to every MP, outlining the reasons why the Federations felt aggrieved by what was seen as an attack on police living standards. In a covering letter, he said;

'The essence of the Police Federations' case is this:
the British people are threatened with mounting crime
and violence. To beat back lawlessness ... ... to contain
the unending risk of public order breaking down ... ...
to defend our country against drugs and terrorism, the
police force needs more manpower.

'Cutting down police living standards is not the way
to do this. Yet the official side's proposals are damaging police morale. If implemented, they would drive
many younger officers out of the service while demo-
tivating the rest.'

The letter was intended to alert Government backbenchers
to the strength of police feelings on the issue. Their postbags
already contained many letters from constituents who were
concerned about the growth of crime, and quite a few Tory
MPs who received the document, expressed to Hurd their
unease about the dissatisfaction felt by the police. The
exercise may have helped to break the deadlock, as the official
side was in a more conciliatory frame of mind when the talks
resumed. It was finally agreed that police pay should be
increased by 8.5 per cent, and the official side dropped its
proposals for 'tapering' the increases. The staff side was
obliged to agree to the freezing of recruits' pay. The official
side's proposal to end the London inspectors' pay lead was
deferred, pending the outcome of discussions about London
allowance and a retention allowance. In turn, the staff side
dropped its claim for an additional 4 per cent to make up
the 'shortfall' on the underlying index. The outcome of all
this was that starting pay stayed at £8.352 and the top rate
PC rose to £15,123. The 1989 pay review was a much more
straightforward matter, with a general increase of 9.25 per
cent. Starting pay rose to £9,900, and top pay became
£16,521.

The Federation reacted angrily to the revelation that,
immediately after the privatisation of a number of ports in
1989, a 'private police force' had been established at Parkestone Quay. All the new dock owners had terminated the
previous port authority's contracts with the British Transport
Commission Police to provide police services to the dock

areas. Security was being provided by private firms, but at Parkestone the employees of the company providing security had been sworn in as special constables, under a 19th century Act, and had all the powers of constables on the dock and in its immediate vicinity. Federation concern about this move was heightened when it emerged that this had been done with the blessing of Essex Police, which had even vetted the prospective employees of the firm and given those appointed to the new 'police force' a crash course in police law and powers. *POLICE* commented;

> 'Overnight, and apparently with the blessing of the Home Office, Sealink have created the first truly 'private police force' in Britain. The implications of the move are quite enormous.'

Alan Eastwood, the new chairman, lodged an immediate complaint with Hurd, and described the swearing in of the security staff at Parkestone Quay as a 'blatant abuse of the principles of the Special Constabulary.' The Home Office reply was non-committal.

The Federation highlighted its concern about the issue by making the theme of its 1989 Conference - *Policing for people - not profits*. Addressing Hurd, who was attending his last Conference before handing over to David Waddington, Eastwood said that the Federation was suspicious of 'tentative' moves to give the private security industry a bigger say in crime control, such as the proposals that the Police National Computer, the forensic science service, and police telecommunications might be managed by other agencies. The Metropolitan Police had contracted the removal of illegally parked vehicles to a private concern. Eastwood asked how long would it be before the private sector administered stationary traffic in towns altogether. He referred again to the private force set up at Parkestone Quay, and the absence of Home Office concern at what was happening, a policy of 'benign non-intervention'. Private security patrols were dressing up in police-like uniforms, equipping themselves with dogs, and claiming that they could make 'citizen's arrests'. In his reply Hurd accepted that there were grounds for concern about the less reputable security firms. He said that the Government looked to the industry to provide self regulation, thus ruling out legislation.

The Government returned to the issue of football hooligans in 1988 with the publication of its Football Spectators' Bill. This followed the appointment of a working party which contained just one police representative, an ACPO appointee. The Federation had sought and been refused representation on the working party, and it was not impressed with the Bill's answers to a problem which was a constant headache for its members. The main provision was for a national membership scheme at League clubs and restriction orders on convicted hooligans to prevent them from travelling to matches abroad. With English clubs banned from Europe following the 1985 Brussels disaster, it was felt essential to be seen to be taking such action. The Federation said that the Bill did not provide the answer to the major scourge of soccer related violence. It supported the action taken by Luton Town, which had introduced a 'members only' admission policy and banned all away supporters from its ground. The Bill, said the Federation, left the organisation of a membership scheme to the football authorities, the very people whose neglect of the problem had created the need for legislation.

But the debate on football hooligans was soon to be seen in a terrible new perspective. On a sunny April afternoon in 1989, 95 Liverpool supporters were killed, mostly through crushing, while attending an FA cup semi-final at Hillsborough stadium in Sheffield. Lord Justice Taylor was appointed to conduct a public inquiry.

The Police Federation's evidence to the Taylor Inquiry emphasised that, although it was not suggested that hooliganism was the cause of the tragedy, the barriers and locked gates which had so much to do with the deaths of the people in the overcrowded narrow paddock behind the goal at the Leppings Lane end of the ground, had been erected as a deterrent to hooligans. Had there been no history of disorder at grounds, there would have been no barriers.

The Federation told Taylor that a football membership scheme as proposed by the Government was not the answer to crowd problems. The Minister for Sport had claimed that with such a scheme in operation, 'the hooligans will simply not travel to matches'. The reality, said the Federation, was that the vast majority of offenders could not be apprehended. They took advantage of the anonymity of large crowds, and a great deal of hooliganism and crime took place well away from the grounds. The Federation was convinced that it was essential to segregate supporters, and a national membership scheme could not do this. Its support for the Luton scheme was emphasised. The authorities had a duty, said the Federation, to take drastic action to reduce opportunities for crowd misbehaviour. All clubs should restrict admission to members of their membership schemes, although there could be reciprocal arrangements with other clubs, which could be rescinded in the event of trouble. The Federation added;

'Football itself has consistently failed to meet its responsibilities. Its irresponsible attitude is epitomised in the evidence it has given to this inquiry, calling for a return to selling alcohol at grounds on match days. It should be representative of wider interests.'

Lord Justice Taylor's report put the major share of the blame for the tragedy on the South Yorkshire Police, and in particular on the senior officer in charge. The gross overcrowding had been caused by the failure to cut off access to central pens in the paddock. These were already full when a main gate was opened, on police instructions, to release dangerous pressure from the crowd outside the Leppings Lane turnstiles. The victims were crushed by the efforts of late arrivals to force their way into the pens. Taylor accepted that the problems facing the police were aggravated by 'the presence of an unruly minority who had drunk too much', and by Sheffield Wednesday's confused and inadequate signs and ticketing system. His interim report covered most aspects of ground safety, and his final report contained the key recommendation for all spectators at matches to be seated.

The South Yorkshire police were stunned to find themselves saddled with the majority of the blame, and felt that Taylor had deliberately understated the extent to which the behaviour of drunken Liverpool fans outside the ground, trying to force an entrance before the game started, had contributed to the tragedy. Taylor claimed that police strategy in policing football over recent years had paid undue weight to a 'minority of trouble makers.' *POLICE* commented;

> 'In this phrase, he dismisses all the mayhem, the rioting, the injuries, and even the deaths, as a relatively minor consideration, not justifying the alleged subordination of safety considerations to the need to contain the hooligans.'

But Taylor had delivered his verdict. South Yorkshire police officers, many of whom were traumatised after their harrowing experiences of that awful day, had to live with the residue of blame for a tragedy which, in the opinion of many, had been waiting to happen.

THIRTY-FIVE

The service examines itself

One consequence of the Home Office restrictions on police numbers was that chief officers began to pay more attention to ways in which available manpower could be deployed with maximum effectiveness. At the same time, ACPO began to complain that chief officers were inhibited from introducing more efficient working methods because of the 'rigid' shift system, with its insistence that the normal working day should be eight continuous hours, and 'Victorian' regulations which over-compensated officers if they were required at short notice to change their days off or work overtime on a rest day.

Far from being a survival of a bygone age, the regulations were of very recent origin. The annual roster, about which ACPO made loud complaints, was introduced in the mid-Eighties following the Court of Appeal ruling in *Starbuck*. It was true that the requirement to work on a rest or public holiday with very short notice carried a high premium rate of compensation. But this had been done deliberately, by agreement of both sides of the PNB, in order to end bad management practices which had played havoc with the domestic arrangements of officers.

In 1988, ACPO conducted a survey to discover the extent of violent disorder in country areas. It revealed a widespread problem, made worse because the police in country areas and small towns could not give assistance to local officers when disorder occurred, as would be the case in large towns. ACPO and the Home Office set up a working group to examine the response to sudden disorder of this kind. The JCC asked for, and was refused, membership of the group, which made the committee suspect that the object of the

ACPO exercise was to launch a further attack on the police regulations. The suspicion was confirmed when the group published its report in the following year. It contained a strong attack on the regulations, claiming that they prevented police commanders from mobilising extra strength to deal with anticipated disorder. The working group had one possible solution for dealing with disorder in country areas where, because of the distances involved, the call out of off-duty officers, rather than mobilising those on duty elsewhere in the force, was seen to be 'a reasonable alternative' (by management, of course).

However, it soon became apparent that there were circumstances in which rank and file officers were quite prepared to work outside the terms of police regulations, to the mutual benefit of themselves and hard pressed police commanders. In 1989 the Portsmouth division of Hampshire police agreed to go over to the 'Ottawa' system, named after the Canadian force where it was conceived.

The Ottawa system used 5 reliefs and ran over a 5 week pattern. It broke away from the rigid pattern of 4 reliefs working a 28 day rota of night, late and early shifts, which gave no weighting to busy times and provided the same cover over 24 hours, without regard to operational needs. Under Ottawa, officers worked for 10 hours each shift on 'days' and 'lates'. Of 7 nights worked, 6 were eight and a half hours long and one was 9 hours. Over a five weeks period, this added up to 200 hours, giving the required 40 hours duty a week. The advantages for the officers were that they got four 'extra' rest days in every five weeks, and two weekends off in that period. The operational advantages were that almost double the usual number of officers could be on duty at peak periods, the number of overtime claims was reduced, and improved morale lead to reduced sickness rates.

The system was adopted in the Portsmouth area as an experiment, but after six months it was deemed so successful that other divisions opted for it, and soon 'Ottawa' was being adopted in other forces. The JCC came in for considerable criticism for failing to endorse this trend, but the Committee was concerned, that once having given up hard won benefits and the protection of the regulations, members could find themselves being exploited with further demands for working outside the ambit of police regulations. The JCC objections were not sufficient to halt the momentum towards 'Ottawa', but significantly after the system had been tried in a large number of forces, some managements began to doubt that the operational advantages were in fact being achieved and discontinued the system, much to the disappointment of operational officers who strongly supported 'Ottawa'.

The Home Office was quick to spot the difficulties which the popularity of Ottawa created for the JCC. The Inspectorate had argued for some time that much greater flexibility could be achieved if the regulations allowed managements greater discretion without incurring financial penalties. The rank and file enthusiasm for Ottawa provided the opportunity for introducing changes without, it seemed, provoking a hostile reaction among the workforce.

In 1990 the Home Secretary wrote to the bodies which constituted the Police Advisory Board, setting out proposals to change police regulations in order to provide a 'framework which allows the maximum of local flexibility in the arrangement of shift systems and duty rostering'. He proposed to replace the annual duty roster with a requirement to give officers 12 months notice of the days when they could expect to be on annual leave or on rostered rest days. Instead of a requirement to show starting times on each day, there would be four hours flexibility, with seven days notice of the actual starting time. The daily tour of duty could be between eight hours and twelve and the length of the working week could be variable, provided that it averaged 40 hours in 12 weeks. The 'penalty' rate of compensation where a rest day was cancelled with less than 8 days notice should be paid in future only when less than 6 days notice was given, and compensation for working on a rest day should be reduced if the requirement to work arose from the previous day's duty.

The Federation expressed its annoyance that the Home Secretary had acted in this way. For months, the official side had been telling the PNB that it wanted to examine these issues in a joint group. The Federation had been trying, without success, to get specific proposals out of the official side, yet now the Home Office was bringing proposals forward in a forum which had no power to negotiate. The Home Office replied that they were seeking an early resolution of the matter, so that new regulations could be brought in as quickly as possible. The Federation and the Superintendents' Association managed to persuade the rest of the Police Advisory Board to recommend that these matters should be discussed in the PNB.

1990 saw a brief echo of the 'officer class' concept of the Trenchard era, when it emerged that Mrs Thatcher was a supporter of an idea, said to have originated inside her policy unit in Downing Street, that a new accelerated promotion scheme should be introduced. designed to attract able young graduates and other potential high flyers. ACPO officials had expressed concern about a 'top secret' seminar which was held at Bramshill, consisting of senior civil servants and a few invited chief officers, who were not present as ACPO representatives. Various accounts of the proceedings began to circulate in the service. It was said that Government misgivings about the calibre of senior management had been voiced by Ministers and Tory MPs, who were worried about police performance. The feeling was that the Government had not reaped the anticipated benefits of increased spending. A Police Complaints Authority investigation of allegations against the police who had protected the Murdoch press plant at Wapping against mass picketing for several months, which was prepared by Northamptonshire police, was severely critical of senior Metropolitan officers for their tactics and alleged lack of control over some officers who were accused of using unnecessary force (an allegation that led to an angry public refutation from Scotland Yard). It was reported that the Premier had mooted the idea of offering some of the armed forces officers who were being made redundant by defence cuts, the opportunity of joining the police in middle management posts. She had queried why it was considered essential that a chief constable should always be a career police officer. In remarks to an ACPO conference in the summer Waddington appeared to put flesh on the rumours when he suggested that officers pursuing the path to the top ranks need not have served in every level above constable. This prompted Alan Eastwood to write to Thatcher;

'We are greatly concerned about press reports that you and other members of the Government favour the recruitment of armed service officers to senior positions in the police service. These press reports contain unattributed statements alleged to have been made by Ministers and Members of Parliament about 'dead beat' chief constables, poor police performance, rising crime rates and allegations of police corruption. The impression is given that the service requires an influx of army officers to restore morale and improve police probity and performance.'

Eastwood agreed that there were deficiencies in the way in which senior officers were selected and trained. The Federation had attacked 'Butterfly Men', officers who spent their careers in single minded pursuit of the next promotion, and flitted from force to force in the process, and had been strongly criticised by ACPO for its remarks. But Eastwood was adamant that it would be a disaster to depart from the principle of promotion from the rank of constable. He said there should be a thorough examination of the role of Bramshill and the extent to which universities and higher education institutions could improve police management training, and suggested that Thatcher should convene a meeting with the staff associations to discuss the issue. Thatcher's reply was brief and far from reassuring. She told Eastwood;

'It is essential to ensure that police leadership is of the highest calibre. All organisations need to consider how best to recruit talent and subsequently to develop it. All organisations stand to benefit from 'an injection of new blood and new ideas'.

But she added, that as 'no decisions are imminent', a meeting in the near future would not be productive. Within a few weeks, Thatcher was out of Downing Street, as her colleagues concluded that the Conservatives stood to benefit from an injection of new blood and new ideas.

The *Operational Policing Review* was the result of an initiative launched in 1988 by ACPO. Roger Birch, the chief constable of Sussex, was that year's President and unlike most of his immediate predecessors, a vocal critic of the Government's policies towards the police service, especially the financial restrictions. Birch was also a strong believer in involving all the staff associations in speaking and acting for the service, something else which distinguished him from the general run of ACPO officials over the years. His invitation to the Federation to join in a comprehensive review of the current state of policing was accepted at once, and the JCC agreed to put office space, staff, and its computing and printing facilities at the disposal of the review team. The Federation also paid the cost of a major public opinion survey to ascertain the citizens' views of the police, and what they felt to be the priorities of policing.

The feeling in the service was that the public did not understand the gravity of the problems it was facing. The police were seen as the favoured public service, able to get Government money where others, like education and health, could not The Government propaganda machine constantly spoke of its commitment to strengthening the police, and how much money the service was costing, but the reality was that cash limits on police forces meant that many vacancies went unfilled and applications for additional officers were either refused by the Home Office, or drastically reduced. Meanwhile, there was no let-up in the mounting workload of the police.

Birch was resentful of what he deemed to be deliberate 'rubbishing' of the efforts of the police in some Government circles, where it was hinted that the police had been given everything they needed to fight crime, and had failed to get results. Ministers showed open impatience with chief officers who complained about inadequate manpower. It was suggested that the service needed to import more business acumen into its management, to stop the wasteful use of police resources, and that perhaps the police were concentrating on the wrong things. The staff associations hoped that the *Review*, when it appeared, would lead to a better informed debate about policing.

The *Operational Policing Review* was published in March 1990. It was a wide ranging review of the state of the service, and its conclusions reflected police anxiety that traditional policing was under threat, largely because the service was neither large enough, nor sufficiently well financed, to meet its existing commitments and deal with rapidly increasing demands. It acknowledged that in the previous fifteen years the service had been given increased resources, but these had not kept pace with additional demands. Forces had been forced to drastically revise working methods, which had been subjected to greater internal controls. The proportion, around 85 per cent, of total spending which went on personnel costs, left the service with no room for capital investment and expenditure on the equipment required in a modern service. This had inhibited long term planning, and to a serious lack of management information.

The *Review* found that traditional policing had been 'substantially eroded' and police effectiveness had been reduced as a result of systems which had been introduced to compensate for staff and technology shortcomings. Instances of this were; a 'graded' response to reported crimes and incidents, and crime 'screening' by which some offences were not investigated because they were not regarded as serious enough to justify the use of resources, or there was little or no prospect of detecting the offenders; 'inflexible' police regulations (a view which contradicted the Federation's position), and the compulsion placed on the service to cope with an ever increasing level of operational and organisational demands.

The *Review* said that the service could not achieve greater efficiency whilst retaining the job satisfaction of police officers. Although the service had become 'dramatically more efficient', the overall effect on individual officers had been to reduce their sense of 'service' as a necessary component of their task. Police work, in consequence, had been reduced to a series of mundane tasks that were aimed at increasing police efficiency, but not the quality of service. The *Review* concluded that there was a 'desperate need' for the service to be clear as to what should be the critical indicators of success, and to standardise measurement of common activities across forces. The gross lack of adequate information technology was identified as the reason why forces had made hugely expensive and often wrong decisions when installing computer systems, most of which were incompatible with those of other forces.

The *Review* defined 'traditional policing' as being low on numbers and powers, and high on accountability. It was undertaken with public consent, with people being allowed to express their policing needs. The culture was expressed by a single constable, close to his community, policing his beat with the consent of the general public, armed only with his lawful powers and his discretion. Traditional policing, the *Review* stated, was under threat because of the financial pressures exerted by central government. The police were being torn between competing and contradictory demands. Some police tasks were being withdrawn or handed over to the private sector, a development which struck 'at the very heart of core policing'. Private security had already carved out a role in the public order field, ranging from the increasing use of security firms at football matches and major public events, to employing security guards in magistrates courts. Large out-of-town shopping centres were 'policed' by security guards, and there had been a proliferation of private uniformed patrolling of residential estates.

The *Review* said that the bulk of additional resources since 1974 had been used to meet additional demands, not to secure traditional policing. A great deal of money had been wasted in a vain search for 'increased efficiency' and 'value for money' solutions, designed to put more officers on operational duties, but which were found to be impractical. A major argument of the *Review's* authors was that the pressure for greater efficiency in the use of resources had in many cases produced the opposite effect to that intended. The *Review* found that greater civilianisation had created problems, with tensions between police and some civil staffs, who suffered from low pay and poor career structures.

The *Review* published the findings of three simultaneous surveys of opinion among police officers, civilians, and members of police consultative groups, bodies which had been established after 1985 under the Police and Criminal

Evidence Act. The police survey showed that police morale was mainly satisfactory, and where this was not the case, the main cause was management style. Police officers felt that the current 'split' between foot and mobile patrols was about right, but felt that any additional resources should go into foot patrolling. They saw response to emergencies as the main priority of the police and wanted to concentrate their efforts on the arrest and detention of offenders. Crime prevention and community policing were seen to be of less importance. Most police respondents agreed that 'strong, positive policing', resulting in the arrest and prosecution of offenders, produced far better results than the community constable's 'caring' preventive style.

These views contrasted sharply with the opinions of most of the respondents to the public survey, conducted by Harris Research Centre. Approval ratings for the police were high, but not as high as in some other polls of the time, with 77 per cent of respondents agreeing that the police did a 'very' or 'fairly' good job, and 19 per cent saying they were performing badly. Adverse views were held most strongly among young adults, and there was a marked difference of view between urban and suburban and rural areas, with dissatisfaction with the police running at 22 per cent in inner cities.

A third of respondents said they felt unsafe when out alone in their neighbourhood after dark, with half the women interviewed saying this. The survey found that people were worried about things that they associated with policing, but were either not police tasks or received low priority, such as litter in the streets, graffiti, and street parking. Fewer people expressed concern about disorder in the streets, drunkenness, domestic disputes and noisy parties. Nor did people think that hard drugs, street robberies, or attacks on women were frequent local occurrences.

The public was in no doubt that there were too few police on duty where they lived. Seventy per cent complained of inadequate police coverage. Only a third of respondents could recall seeing a policeman on foot in their area in the week before they were interviewed. A quarter claimed never have to seen one. Eighty two per cent said that the police operated in their areas in cars, and the image of the traditional beat

Bobby appeared to have been replaced by the police car. When asked whether the police should perform on foot or in cars, 72 per cent said more officers should be deployed on foot. 'Community' police officers were very popular with the public.

The major difference between the views of the police and the public came with the question of policing styles. The police favoured firmer policing while the public opted for the greater use of police discretion and a more caring approach. The public put crime prevention at the top of the agenda, and the police favoured the arrest and prosecution of offenders.

Looking to the future, the *Review* anticipated that the Government would maintain its pressure for efficiencies and cost savings. It feared that this would oblige the police to concentrate on 'measurable' performance indicators at the cost of the very style of policing that the public favoured. There would probably be more privatisation, especially in the technological areas, and there would be an increase in centralised units, such as the National Criminal Intelligence Centre. The growth in the number of elderly in the community would require the police to extend their caring role, which could bring them into conflict with central priorities. The *Review* said that the gap between the affluent and the poorer sections of the population would most likely widen, bringing more tensions between the police and the 'have nots'.

The *Review* said that the choices open to the police were to retain the present organisational structure, to move to larger regional forces, or become a national force. Greater centralisation would continue, and ACPO would assume a more prominent role in policy making.

The *Operational Policing Review* did not evoke much of a response from the Home Office. ACPO set up working groups to examine some of the major issues it highlighted, such as quality of service. But the word filtered back to the service that senior civil servants were dismissive of the *Review* and regarded it as just another example of special pleading to justify more resources.

Discontent over the rent allowance veto was a primary

reason for the cool reception given to David Waddington when he attended the Federation's 1990 Conference in Scarborough. The Home Secretary had caused annoyance by sending a long letter to all MPs to counter the arguments being put to them by the Federation. Waddington said there had been an 'enormous' increase in spending on the police since 1979, the bulk of which had gone in wages and allowances. The 'generous' rent allowances had escalated to an alarming degree. It had just been increased again, by 57 per cent, in the Metropolitan Police, and this bore no relationship to the actual increase in housing costs. The system of comparisons with open market rents had meant that police were receiving sums far in excess of what would be realistic compensation for not living in a police house, which after all was the basis of the allowance. Waddington told MPs that he was not bound by an arbitration award. This one, he claimed, would have uprated existing rent allowances at a cost of up to £110 million, and additional expenditure could not be justified.

Waddington had made some concessions. The arbiters had awarded a transitional allowance to occupants of police houses to compensate them for having to meet water rates. This amounted to £300 a year for three years. The Home Office had said that this could not be paid but Waddington now accepted that it should be. He had also agreed that forces whose rent allowances had not been uprated since 1988 could have their existing allowance uprated by the movement of the housing factor in the retail prices index, thus ensuring that their 'red-circled' allowances would be calculated on the same basis as other forces.

The small concessions had done nothing to placate police anger by the time of the Conference. An emergency motion calling for a repetition of the 'angry silence' accorded to Merlyn Rees thirteen years earlier, was carried in closed session, against the strong opposition of the platform, which argued that the media would condemn the police for being seen to be greedy and intransigent.

Waddington, unlike Rees, was warned in advance of what the delegates had decided, and chose to put on a little show of his own. He dismissed the Ministerial car and walked the

mile from the hotel to the hall, surrounded by reporters and
television cameras, staring fixedly ahead and ignoring the
microphones thrust under his nose. It was a shrewd depiction
of a Home Secretary at bay, about to confront the revolting
constabulary. In the hall Waddington met his critics full on.
Eastwood attacked him over the rent decision, and assailed
the Government for failing to support the police in the face
of sustained media criticism. Waddington reminded the
delegates once again of what had been spent on the police
since the Tories came back to power and said;

> 'I can go no further and you must now come to terms
> with the new arrangements. No Home Secretary can
> always give you what you want, and I have not been
> able to do so on rent allowance. There will be a debate
> in Parliament before long, and I hope that when it
> takes place, and everyone has had his shout, we'll draw
> a line under the matter and move on to other things.'

The press reaction to the Conference's silent reception of
Waddington was universally hostile to the Federation. The
Daily Mirror, normally opposed to the Tories, said the Federation had behaved with the sort of childishness that would once
have earned a child a clip around the ear from a Bobby. *Grow
up, Copper*, was the advice from the editor of *The Sun* and
the *Daily Express* told 'police moaners' that with crime rising
the taxpayers were wondering if they were getting value for
money; 'more work and fewer wails are in order'. *Today* told
its readers that the Police Federation were 'Britain's finest
whingers and whiners' and said the police had failed to earn
their extra corn. *The Times* delivered a crushing verdict;

> 'For the Police Federation to accuse the Government
> of undervaluing its work is little short of cheek. No
> group in the public sector has been more succoured
> since Mrs Thatcher came to power in 1979. Certainly
> no group has been treated so well with so little obvious
> return.'

The press onslaught was exactly what Eastwood had
warned the Conference would follow any kind of demon-

stration against Waddington. It was a massive public relations blow which left the Home Secretary in total command of what could have been a tricky Parliamentary situation. *POLICE* said;

> 'Luck plays its part in these matters. Mr Waddington's good fortune is that this dispute has come to a head while all the other anxieties about the police are so prominent. It does him no harm at all to be seen to be slapping down uppity Bobbies. If the police are to lose thousands of pounds a year, so what? It is the price to be paid for not reducing crime; for not detecting it; for the Guildford Four and the Serious Crime Squad; and for all the sins, real or imagined, of which the service stands accused today.'

When the Labour motion attacking Waddington's veto on arbitration was debated in the House of Commons in July, the Government won by 293 votes to 191. Just six Tories, including Michael Shersby, defied the party whip to vote with the Opposition. Other Conservatives who had promised branch boards their support, either backed Waddington in the Lobby or were not in the House. Some erstwhile supporters said they could not back the Federation after its churlish treatment of the Home Secretary at Conference.

Besides revealing the bitterness of the dispute with the Government over the arbitration award, the 1990 Conference had provided a further indication of the healing of the rift between the police and the Labour Opposition. Roy Hattersley became the first Shadow Home Secretary to address the delegates, and he was given a rousing welcome. With Labour doing well in the opinion polls and a General Election in the near future beginning to look a possibility, Hattersley was shrewd enough not to make promises on pay, but pointed out that the Labour members of the official side had opposed the Home Secretary's veto of the arbitration award, while omitting to mention that most of them had wanted to abolish all forms of housing aid to the police.

There was better news for the Federation's membership when the 1990 pay review resulted in a 9.75 per cent increase.

This increased the starting rate by almost £1,000 a year to £10,866, and the top rate PC went up to £18,132. There had been some disagreement among the staff side members, because the official side had rejected the claim that the 'overlapping' system, by which top rate PCs received more basic pay than newly promoted sergeants with less service than they had, should be extended to sergeants and the inspector ranks. The official side pointed out that the current system, by which the top of the scales for the ranks above constable 'butt-ended' to correspond with the starting pay of the next rank had been endorsed by Edmund-Davies. Following the rejection of the claim, the staff side decided, by a majority vote, not to seek arbitration on the matter.

Arbitration was required to resolve lengthy negotiations over hours and leave. Early in 1990 the staff side asked for increases in annual leave, to 25 days a year for probationers, up to 35 days after 10 years' service. The official side proposed a joint working party to consider this claim along with the Federations' call for the working week to be reduced from 40 to 38 hours, and improvements in overtime compensation. The staff side rejected this because it felt that the annual leave claim stood on its own and should not be mixed up with the other issues. When the matter came to the arbitration tribunal, the official side said it had costed the annual leave claim at £125 million, or 3.7 per cent of the pay bill, which would rise to 10 per cent if the other claims were conceded. The tribunal said that the items should be considered together, and took the unuusal step of adjourning the case for a year to give the sides a chance to settle by negotiation.

The official side, following the adjournment of arbitration, put a package of proposals to the staff side which amounted to the Home Office's demands for cuts in overtime compensation and flexibile rostering, submitted some months earlier to the Police Advisory Board. The meetings of the working party during 1991 took the issues up to and beyond the 12 months deadline set by the arbitration tribunal. This was extended for three months by the Tribunal, which made it clear that a further delay would not be acceptable. The staff side at this point said it would return to the arbitration tribunal to seek an interim award, because 1991 would have come and gone without any improvement in the annual leave situation. The annual leave claim was eventually settled, early in 1992, with an increase of one day a year across the board. Further negotiations on the outstanding issues were then overtaken by events, of which more later.

THIRTY-SIX

All officers are equal

Towards the end of 1990, the service was confronted with revelations of racial discrimination against Asian and black officers. In Nottinghamshire, an Asian officer took his complaints to an industrial tribunal which found that he was the victim of discrimination from colleagues and superior officers during the time he was an 'aide' to CID (attached to the department with a view to becoming a regular detective) and when it was decided not to appoint him on a permanent basis. The officer was awarded substantial damages and the revelations were a blow to the reputation of the force. The JCC felt that the case also pointed to glaring omissions in the Federation's service to members, because the officer had not been assisted by the Federation although the case had taken almost two years to reach a hearing. The fact was that the Federation had not considered its policy on equal opportunities, and the subject had not been covered in its training programme for branch board officials. When this case was followed in quick succession by several others, all indicating that black or Asian officers had been subjected to inexcusable racist remarks and actions from white officers, the committee decided that action could not be further delayed.

The committee knew that the Metropolitan Police had just conducted a series of residential seminars for the several hundred non-white members of the force, and had been shocked to hear of their experiences. They had complained that they were subjected to careless racism, unfunny jokes, and job customs and practices which put them at a disadvantage.

At the same time, women officers began to bring complaints to industrial tribunals of sexual discrimination and harassment. In its annual report for 1991, the JCC acknowledged that in the 15 years since the Sex Discrimination Act, very little had been done by the service to ensure that women officers enjoyed equality of opportunity and treatment. Equal opportunities considerations had put support for part time working and job sharing at the forefront of Federation activities in the year. As with non-white officers, police women were stating, in a number of surveys, that they were being subjected to high levels of harassment. The Federation and police commanders hoped that the introduction of formal grievance procedures would encourage officers who experienced victimisation or harassment to come forward at an early stage, rather than go to Industrial Tribunals, but it was recognised that just as this unacceptable conduct could not be eradicated overnight, so it would take time for victims of discrimination to gain confidence in the grievance procedure.

Expressing concern about reported discrimination and harassment cases involving women and ethnic minority officers, the Federation declared;

> 'Our duty is to every member and we cannot tolerate a situation in which a growing number of colleagues join us from the ethnic communities and find themselves exposed to various forms of discrimination. We urge all our members to be mindful of the harm that is done by such things. Similarly, officers are entitled to be protected from sexual harassment in the workplace.'

The JCC set up an equal opportunities committee, which organised seminars for branch board representatives. The Federation supported the establishment of grievance procedures for resolving internal problems of this kind. It also published the Federation's Statement of Intent on Equal Opportunities;

> *'The Police Federation commits itself to the eradication within the service of any racist or sexist behaviour and*

any acts or practices which are indirectly discriminatory of grounds of race or sex;

'We will support the principles of equal opportunities and give assistance, where appropriate, to our members;

'We support the training of all police officers to achieve the elimination of all unfair discrimination and a force which affords full equality of opportunity;

'We believe that the implementation of these principles will guarantee fairness and equality in our service to the public.'

The Federation's own electoral arrangements for women officers lead to discussions with the Equal Opportunities Commission. It was accepted that the Federation regulations would be amended to ensure that a 'women's representative' had a seat on every board and committee. The Commission had objected because male officers voted only for male candidates, and women for women. The revised procedure enabled officers of both sexes to vote for all posts.

In another development that would have surprised Federationists of earlier generations, the Equal Opportunities Committee held discussions with the Gay and Lesbian Police Association, and was happy to confirm that its equalities stance included opposition to discrimination against homosexual officers. A decade earlier, the discovery that an officer was homosexual would have been followed by his or her speedy departure from the police.

Part time working and job sharing schemes were subjected to trials in six forces in 1991, involving about 200 officers. Although there was little enthusiasm for job sharing, part time working was an attractive proposition, allowing many women officers (the scheme was open to male officers as well) to return to policing after children had become old enough to be cared for by relatives or nurseries. The service gained because it was able to retain the services of experienced officers. Even so, the fact that the principle of job sharing was accepted so readily within the service, underlined the extent to which the police no longer saw themselves as set apart completely from developments outside the service. Only a few years earlier, the Federation and chief officers would have raised a long list of reasons why part time working was just not possible in a disciplined, 24 hour service like the police.

Concern about high levels of sickness among police officers, coupled with suggestions of malingering, prompted the Home Affairs Select Committee of the House of Commons to investigate the subject. Its report rejected the notion of widespread abuse, but expressed concern at variations in sickness levels between forces. The MPs accepted that management failings influenced sickness levels and recommended more occupational health units. It also proposed that officers over 40 should be subjected to compulsory medical checks.

In another sickness related issue, the Police Complaints Authority's criticisms of the practice of allowing officers who were subject to disciplinary enquiries to take early retirement on grounds of ill health was echoed in another Report from the Select Committee. This prompted the Home Office to remind chief officers that such retirements must be restricted to genuine sickness cases, and not used as a means of avoiding disciplinary action. Proposals were put to the Police Advisory Board, which included Home Office advice, that if chief officers thought that an accused officer's medical condition was being 'misrepresented', the disciplinary procedures should be expedited to prevent the officer retiring before they were completed. Also, in serious charges, the Home Office said it would be inappropriate to allow an officer to retire unless the medical evidence was that his condition was unlikely to improve. In cases of doubt, the hearing of charges should go ahead, with the chief officer forming his own view of the medical evidence. The Federation reacted angrily to what it saw as draconian measures aimed at mollifying the PCA and the MPs. The Police Advisory Board agreed to tell the Home Secretary that the only change needed was to call in an independent doctor where the officer's doctor and the police medical officer disagreed about his condition.

The problems of sergeants who acted as custody officers had concerned the sergeants' committee since the introduction of the Police and Criminal Evidence Act. The Federation view was that it was illegal to require constables, even if they held acting sergeant's rank, to act as custody officers. The JCC took the Dorset force to the High Court to seek rulings that the chief constable was under a duty to appoint sufficient custody officers at each station designated to receive prisoners, and that 'acting' sergeants were not eligible for the role. The judge ruled in favour of the Federation that a custody officer should normally be available at every designated station, and he expressed the opinion that acting sergeants could not perform the role, but the Court of Appeal overturned his decision.

Kenneth Baker's first, and as it turned out, last visit to the Police Federation Conference in 1991 was literally a flying one. His helicopter landed outside the conference centre at Bournemouth a few minutes before he was due to speak, and immediately afterwards he was on his way back to London to introduce his Dangerous Dogs Act in Parliament. This, yet again, was an issue on which previous calls from the Federation had been ignored or rejected. The Federation had drawn attention to the menace to the public and the police of pit bull terriers, some of which were owned by street drugs dealers, and had been told that existing legislation was adequate. Now, following the savaging of a little girl, Baker rushed through an Act to ban the breed and similar types.

Baker found that the Federation was in the mood to do a little biting itself. Alan Eastwood's address complained of a criminal justice system that was clearly failing to convict the guilty, and of the worsening consequences of the economy squeeze on police expenditure. He said that forces were running out of money to maintain normal recruiting levels and now there were cuts in crucial capital programmes. Baker, like his predecessors in the post, responded with a recital of the extra money that had gone into policing, thanks to the priorities which the Tories attached to law and order.

In October 1991, the JCC launched *The Policing Agenda*. There were indications that a general election would take place in the autumn, or the early spring, and the Federation was anxious that law and order would form part of the election debate. At the joint meeting with Northern Ireland and Scotland, all three Federations agreed to support the *Agenda*. It dealt with all the issues confronting the police;

manpower and resources; police powers and duties; and the criminal justice system. It set out nine key areas, dubbed *Nine points for the law*, where the Federations felt that action was called for, in order to reverse the rapid escalation of crime over recent years.

NINE POINTS FOR THE LAW

1. *Law and order must be a first priority of government and a first claim on resources.*
2. *The police must have the means and the power to protect life and property.*
3. *Punishment must fit the crime, not just the criminal.*
4. *Victims must be compensated and helped to recover from their ordeals.*
5. *Priority must be given to cutting crime among the young.*
6. *More emphasis must be placed on crime prevention and partnership between the public and the police.*
7. *Criminal trials must become a search for truth.*
8. *The bail scandal must end.*
9. *There must be a Royal Commission on policing.*

In amplification, the Federations said that there should be common ground between the parties that law and order was not a party political issue. It said the criminal justice policies of all the parties failed to tackle crime and would not allay public anxiety. It had taken twenty years for reported crime figures to rise from one million to two million a year, and only ten years for them to rise to five millions. It was time to re-establish public confidence in the ability of the police to prevent crime, and of the criminal justice system to punish offenders while protecting the public from crime.

The great bulk of offenders were children and young adults. Juveniles were responsible for a large proportion of domestic burglaries and car thefts. Juvenile justice seemed incapable of dealing with persistent young offenders who committed scores of offences, were arrested frequently, but almost always returned to the streets to go on committing offences. Local authorities failed to provide secure accommodation for juveniles deemed by the courts to require it.

By the 'bail scandal', the Federations meant the fact that one third of persons charged with burglary were already on bail when arrested. The Federations saw the Bail Act, and constant exhortations by Government Ministers to magistrates not to remand offenders in custody (and to avoid passing custodial sentences) as the cause of this situation. *The Policing Agenda* challenged the received wisdom that Britain locked up too many offenders.;

> 'The opposite is the case. Over the past 30 years the emphasis of criminal justice has moved towards the abandonment of imprisonment as a punishment for non-violent offenders, and towards 'rehabilitation'. Parliament has lost sight of the victims of crime.'

The trial system was criticised. The Federations believed that miscarriages of justice were caused in part by the adversarial system. It pointed out that wrongful acquittals greatly exceeded wrongful convictions, and said both were miscarriages of justice. The Federations would welcome changes to make the criminal trial more of a search for truth and less of a jousting match between lawyers. On compensation for victims of crime, it suggested that this should be paid from public funds and recovered, where possible, from offenders.

On resources, the Federations said that the police were being expected to perform miracles in the face of draconian cash limits. It was no coincidence that the recent expansion of private security operations in the crime control field coincided with these pressures on police resources.

The document argued that a Royal Commission was needed to examine every aspect of policing; to look at the most effective means of reducing crime; the way in which the police are organised and controlled; and the adequacy or otherwise of existing police powers.

Copies of the agenda were sent to all MPs, and under covering letters to Kenneth Baker and Roy Hattersley. Speaking to the Tory Bow Group at a conference fringe meeting in October, Dick Coyles, the JCC vice-chairman, spelt out the extent of police dissatisfaction with the Government's performance and the state of crime. He said the police were sick and tired of being criticised for their alleged failures to clear up crime when their hands were tied by the system and the lack of resources. He bluntly told his audience;

> 'No government in history was elected on a more explicit or stronger law and order platform than was this one. Do you remember the conference where Willie Whitelaw talked about the 'short sharp shock'? What have we got now? Punishment in the community, community service orders, yet more 'radical alternatives' to custody. Gone are the detention centres and the approved schools. Gone, in fact, is any kind of sanction that will really deter young villains.'

The Federations' had hoped that the *Agenda* would stimulate a proper debate on law and order in the run up to the election. When the campaign began early in 1992, the subject was hardly mentioned, but within a short time it would become the issue which most concerned the general public, and prompt the politicians into promises of action.

In 1991, following public concern about a succession of cases where it was held that convictions were unsafe, the Conservative Government appointed a Royal Commission on Criminal Justice, with Lord Runciman as its chairman. The three staff associations submitted joint evidence. In summary, this suggested an end to the current adversarial system in the courts, to secure greater openness and fairness in both the investigation and the trial. it called for pre-trial reviews to address such issues as the admissibility of evidence. The staff associations said the rules governing the right of silence impeded justice. Previous convictions should be admissible where defendants denied intent. The evidence called for more resources for the Crown Prosecution Service, and said that police investigations would benefit from the introduction of tape and video recording. The associations were critical of the costs of the system. Justice should be speeded up, and the right to elect for trial by jury should be removed. It was also proposed that the prosecution should have a right of appeal where an acquittal was thought to be perverse.

In yet another Cabinet reshuffle, in April 1992, Kenneth Clarke became the sixth Home Secretary since 1979. It was an appointment that caused foreboding in the service. Clarke had emerged from bitter battles with the teachers and the health service. The rumour was, that Mrs Thatcher's Rottweiler was about to be turned loose on the police. The apprehension felt by many was summed up by *POLICE*;

'This month the Police Federation conference delegates will see the new Home Secretary in action. Some pundits suggest that he has been put into the Home Office to 'take us on'. Having vanquished the health workers and the teachers, he is apparently expected to grind the prison officers into the dust and then turn to the Police Federation; 'the last bastion of trade union reaction in Britain', as one critic describes us.'

In the same issue, the political columnist Edward Pearce offered the Federation sound and prophetic advice;

'... ... the man is, if not amenable to reason, worth getting at before he makes irrevocable decisions for your own good. If you want to knock out the idea of 'massive waste in the police', compile the papers now. In handling this gifted, bossy, irksomely assured but quite decent man, do get your retailiation in first.'

Sound advice though this was, it was already too late. Only days after taking over the Home Office, Clarke gave the Federation a taste of his methods. For all the disagreements that had occurred between the Federation leaders and his Conservative predecessors, their personal relationships were cordial, but Clarke revelled in his 'bruiser' reputation. A week before the Federation Conference, he met Alan Eastwood at the Home Office. It had been customary for Federation chairmen to discuss their Conference speeches with Home Secretaries. Eastwood gave Clarke the complete text of his address, and while they talked, Clarke skimmed through its contents. As he read, his initially affable mood changed, because the speech was deeply critical of Government policies and in particular, of the financial restrictions on the service. Tossing the speech on the desk, Clarke told Eastwood that if this was what was going to be said, he might as well stay away from the Conference. He said;

> 'I didn't go to the teachers conference, nor the BMA's. I don't have to go to yours. I've looked up my legal obligations towards the Federation. I am only obliged to consult you. No more, no less. If that's the way you want it, so be it.'

Eastwood was badly shaken by this outburst. but agreed that the speech would be amended, and within minutes Ian Burns, the Head of the Police Department, was on the telephone to Eastwood's speech writer in Surbiton, 'suggesting' a series of amendments to tone it down. The feeling in the Federation was that Clarke had staged the confrontation, having been advised by several pundits that the police had had it too good, and it was time to take them on.

If Eastwood was upset by this opening example of Clarke's bullying style, he and the whole police service were about to be given a major shock. As he travelled up to Scarborough, Clarke sent a message ahead to say that he wished to have a private meeting with Eastwood and Vee Neild before he went on to the platform. The only room that could be found was the stage electrician's space behind the stage. Eastwood met Clarke on arrival, and he and Neild took him to this place.

Clarke was surprised and annoyed to find that, although uninvited, the Chief Inspector of Constabulary, Sir John Woodcock, and the President of ACPO, Brian Johnson of Lancashire, had joined the party. Both had no prior idea of what Clarke was about to say. He told his listeners that he was going to announce that he was setting up an 'independent' inquiry into police pay and conditions.

THIRTY-SEVEN

Say 'No' to Sheehy!

C larke spent most of his Conference speech explaining why he had decided to go for an independent inquiry. He said it would cover roles and responsibilities; careers and performance; management; leadership, and; 'rewards that come with new responsibilities, and new ways of doing the job.'

Clarke told an attentive but clearly shaken audience, that they had his full support. He accepted that the service had already done a great deal to reform itself, with extensive civilianisation and many forces concluding structure reviews which had slimmed down managerial ranks, and said it was time to review the impact of such changes;

> 'What we should be seeking to do is to give individual police officers a clearer idea of the roles they are expected to perform, to let them know how well they are doing it, and to reward them in accordance with their role and performance.
>
> 'I shall want the inquiry to examine whether there can be more flexibility in the determination of police pay to recognise the increasing flexibility of roles and responsibilities ... ... (and) to recommend what, if any, changes would be appropriate in the rank structure and pay arrangements.
>
> 'It will be concerned with asking and answering the questions; 'Have we got the right pay and career structure for the future? Are we rewarding the right people fairly? Is a blanket increase in pay for every rank and every officer, irrespective of type of work or competence really the best way of reimbursing the police for the huge spectrum of work that they do?'

Clarke denied that he was destroying Edmund-Davies. The inquiry was not based on any criticism of pay levels, which were 'fully justified'. But the time had come to move on;

'... ... if you are to be enabled to do your jobs better we need, as Edmund-Davies suggested, to be able to propose variations to meet the changing circumstances.'

What Clarke was proposing was nothing like the fine-tuning which Edmund-Davies had envisaged would be necessary from time to time. It was a root and branch re-building of the entire pay structure, sweeping away the principles of a national rate of pay; uniformity of remuneration between officers of the same rank and length of service in the rank and the incremental scales, which had been the bedrock of the system for seventy years.

Eastwood, in his address to Clarke, ended with a repeat of the Federation's call, in *The Policing Agenda*, for a Royal Commission. He had been careful to add that he was not expecting such a Commission to deal with pay and negotiable matters. Now he knew that Clarke was appointing an 'independent committee' that would deal with virtually nothing else. He had been given no opportunity to consult with his JCC colleagues since the extraordinary last minute briefing at the back of the stage, and spent most of the time that Clarke was speaking, considering what his immediate response would be. He realised that the media would see the inquiry as a 'massive shake-up' for the police, and that any immediate show of dissent would be dismissed as the natural instinct of a powerful trade union whose first instinct to protect its members' interests. When Clarke sat down to polite applause, Eastwood rose to say that the Federation welcomed the inquiry, because 'we have nothing to hide'. He diffused the growing tension in the hall by giving Clarke a surprise present - a toy dog, a reference to his widely reported denial that he was a political Rottweiler, 'more of a cuddly pooch'. As a public relations ploy, it left Clarke lost for words and ruined his big dramatic moment. He had been expecting the Federation to react as the teachers' or the health unions had when confronted with his abrasive tactics.

Eastwood's 'we'll wait and see' reaction was not the response that some delegates and members of the JCC had wanted to hear, and while the chairman was repeating the line in a joint press conference with Clarke outside the hall, Dick Coyles, the vice-chairman was telling the delegates that in his view, Clarke had spelt out the end of Edmund-Davies. This was what most of them thought, and several delegates said so in interviews with reporters.

In July, Clarke announced the composition and the terms of reference of the 'Independent Inquiry into Police Responsibilities and Rewards'. Neither the staff associations nor the service as a whole were encouraged by what they heard and read. Clarke had refused to consult the staff associations about the composition of the Inquiry. This was in contrast to 1977, when Rees had accepted Lord Edmund-Davies, knowing he was the Federation's choice, and the terms of reference had been agreed with the Home Secretary. The Federation had been shown the draft terms of reference and had criticised them as being too narrow, with insufficient emphasis on the size of the police task or the special nature of policing, but its view had not lead to any change when the terms were announced.

The man Clarke chose to head the Inquiry was virtually unknown outside the world of multi- national business. He was Sir Patrick Sheehy, the 62 years old head of the giant conglomerate; British - American Tobacco Industries.

The other members of the five man team were Professor Colin Campbell, vice-chancellor of Nottingham University (Clarke was a Nottinghamshire MP); John Bullock, joint senior partner of the huge accountancy firm, Coopers Lybrand; Sir Paul Fox, former managing director of BBC Television, and Eric Caines, Director of Personnel for the National Health Service. Clarke's announcement said the team brought together experience in management, law and accountancy. None had any direct knowledge of the police service. The Federation immediately pointed out that the team was entirely representative of top management.

The inclusion of Eric Caines told the Federation that the 'independent' tag attached to the inquiry had to be taken with a generous pinch of salt. Caines was a lifelong civil servant whose track record was of clash after clash with the public sector unions. At the Home Office, he had been the architect of *'Fresh start'* a complete restructuring of the pay, conditions and working practices of the prison service, which had been fought all the way, but unsuccessfully, by the Prison Officers' Association, whose industrial action caused police cells to be used to house remand prisoners and imposed a major added burden on the police. Caines had gone on to push through the staffing reforms in the NHS, appearing to relish the confrontations with the BMA and the unions as much as Clarke himself.

The terms of reference of the Sheehy inquiry were;

> *To examine the rank structure, remuneration and conditions of service of the police service in England and Wales, in Scotland and in Northern Ireland, and to recommend what changes, if any, would be sensible to ensure;*
>
> > *rank structures and conditions of service which reflect the current roles of police officers;*
> >
> > *enough flexibility in the distribution of rewards to ensure that responsibilities and performance may be properly recognised in changing circumstances;*
> >
> > *remuneration set and maintained at a level adequate to ensure the recruitment, retention and motivation of officers of the right quality;*
>
> **having full regard to:**
>
> > *the principle recommended by the Edmund-Davies Inquiry that police pay should reflect the special nature of the police officer's role;*
> >
> > *the principles set out in the police service statement of common purposes and values;*
> >
> > *the need to ensure affordability and value for money in public spending.*

The Home Office statement added that the Inquiry would take account of the findings of specially commissioned studies into current police roles and responsibilities; force manpower profiles and the impact on career development of changes in police retirement policy; the recommendations of the Audit Commission which was in the middle of a comprehensive examination of police costs; all work currently being undertaken on manpower and personnel issues, including police performance measures and indicators; developments in pay generally, and; the special position of the Royal Ulster Constabulary.

The Home Office chose the management consultants Ernst and Young to carry out the studies into police roles and responsibilities. The Federation turned to another leading firm in this field, Touche Ross, to conduct parallel surveys on its behalf. Touche Ross had tendered for the Home Office work, but the Federation was encouraged by a survey it had recently conducted for the three police associations, as part of a joint report, *Improving management standards* which rejected performance related pay for the police as a mechanistic and unworkable system. It could have been this report which ruled Touche - Ross out of the running for the Home Office survey.

The Federation quickly added other professional advisers to the team set-up to assist with the preparation of evidence to Sheehy. Touche-Ross conducted an opinion survey among the Federation's membership. Seven thousand officers of all ranks, weighted by length of service and roles, were invited to complete the questionnaire and 75 per cent of them did so. The results showed that the members felt there were many things wrong with the service.

Officers in all departments expressed concern about the low status of the uniformed constables. They were seen as the key to policing, facing increasing hostility, yet lacking the support and understanding of senior officers. Uniform patrol was seen as the dumping ground for poor performers, and the first source of labour for other tasks when demand arose. Junior officers had little time for superiors who, in dedicated pursuit of their own advancements, flitted from force to force and showed no concern for those about or below them. Senior officers were described as remote and out of touch. Some respondents said it would be a good idea if senior officers occasionally donned a PCs uniform and went out on duty on a Friday or Saturday night.

There was widespread agreement that, while a rank structure was essential, it was top heavy and there was too much overlapping of duties and roles. A large majority supported the abolition of the posts of chief inspector and chief superintendents. Most officers were satisfied with their pay. Asked about alternative systems, they were strongly against differentiation between officers of the same rank performing different roles, and performance related pay. Sergeants disliked the overlapping system which meant that top rate PCs got more than some newly promoted sergeants.

There was a total lack of confidence in the staff appraisal systems used in the service, but much of the criticism was of a lack of frankness about poor performers. The respondents said that the current appraisal systems were not suitable for pay related appraisals. There was anxiety about proposals to abolish payment for overtime and rent and housing allowances. Officers wanted the length of service for maximum pension reduced, pointing out that in America the period was often only 20 years. Some respondents supported the idea of short term contracts, but mainly for senior officers.

The results of the survey were among the issues taken into account in the preparation of the JCC's evidence to Sheehy. The Committee knew that some of the ideas being talked of - performance related pay and fixed term contracts - were already in place or about to be introduced in several forces in New Zealand and Australia. Neild and Eastwood, with three other members, were sent to these countries to discuss the experiences of the police associations there. The constables' committee sent members to California on a similar mission.

The JCC was faced with major problems. With the rank structure being so prominent among the terms of reference, each separate committee had to put the interests of its own rank at the forefront of its thinking. The inspectors were encouraged by a surprising readiness of their own members to accept that there was a case for abolishing the chief inspector rank, and the JCC was able to agree that current chief inspectors should be assimilated as superintendents, on the grounds that their workload and responsibilities were more analogous with that rank.

The Federation had adopted the slogan *Only our best will do* to spearhead its response to Sheehy and the demands for change. In the opening paragraphs of its evidence to Sheehy, the JCC said;

> 'The police service is committed to real change. Police forces have adopted quality of service, not as a pious slogan, but as a real motivator. This is nothing less than a new ethos of policing and it deserves to be recognised as such.
>
> 'Were it not for the fact that this country is facing a grave financial crisis, with unemployment close to 3 millions, the Police Federation would be urging the Inquiry to recommend a substantial increase in police pay, in recognition of how much more difficult, complex and dangerous, police work has now become.'

The Federation's asserted that the Edmund-Davies system had served the police and public well. It had not achieved excessive pay levels and had ensured the recruitment and retention of high calibre police officers. The Federation said that pay should reflect the unique nature of policing, while rewarding experience and expertise. It was not appropriate to compare police pay with other occupations or through a pay review body. The system of determining police pay according to the index of earnings should be retained, but the non-manual workers index should be used. Home Secretaries should not be able to veto arbitration awards unless they could demonstrate there was an overriding national interest involved.

The JCC rejected the concept of performance related pay, but told Sheehy that it would not be opposed in principle to the introduction of appraisal related pay, provided that a separate pay appraisal system was introduced and the incremental structure was retained. Increments were defended on the grounds that they offered progressive rewards and compensated officers who could not be promoted to the next rank; rewarded the acquisition of skills learned on the job, and; recognised experience and encouraged the retention of experienced officers. The Committee accepted that there was popular support in the service for greater rewards for operational officers at the 'sharp end', but said a shift allowance would be a crude and ineffectual way of doing this. The incremental scales should be extended with opportunities for additional rewards for such officers.

The Committee proposed an extra incremental scale for each of the federated ranks. It accepted that within the scales, officers could reach the maximum pay of the rank within either the same or fewer increments than they did at present. Beyond current maximum rates, further increments could be available to reward the best performers. These proposals could be embodied in a new pay spine system.

Overtime, said the Federation should continue to be compensated by payment or time-off at the option of an officer. It should not be likened to overtime elsewhere, because it was unpredictable and arose out of incidents on duty, or because of demands on the service. The need for overtime was not evenly spread and fell mainly on the uniformed officer. If compensation for overtime were to be reduced or ended, it would lead to managerial abuse. The Federation reminded Sheehy that for several years it had been trying to get the basic working week reduced to 38 hours. The evidence also argued for the retention of the national standard of pay, and for housing and rent allowances to remain as an essential part of the remuneration package.

The Federation was firmly opposed to fixed term contracts. It asked Sheehy;

> 'Is policing a job like any other, or a vocation which requires total commitment from men and women prepared to devote the greater part of their working lives to the service?
>
> 'That is the issue raised by the idea of short service contracts. It is being put forward as a means of getting rid of the 'job for life' concept which has been at the heart of career policing for generations. Now it is claimed that short term engagements would benefit the service and the public, because if an officer wished

to continue to serve after the term was completed, he or she would have to satisfy high standards of fitness, performance and competence.

'We say that the case against short term contracts is overwhelming. The loss of job security would seriously jeopardise the quality of recruits. It would deter graduates and others with special qualifications, and older applicants.'

The best means of ensuring the fitness and competence of officers, said the Federation, was through an effective appraisal system. What was needed was a 'culture that supports and rewards achievements'. The JCC opposed the introduction of an 'incapability' procedure for getting rid of officers who performed poorly, although the Touche Ross survey showed extensive rank and file support for it. The Federation also asked Sheehy to recommend the retention of current sickness arrangements, because they were appropriate to the risks and injuries which officers had to face. It added that the police pensions scheme was fitted to the distinctive career patterns of the police service and should remain as it was.

The Federation devoted much of its evidence to a detailed critique of police training. It called for the setting-up of a 'police university', able to award degrees and diplomas, with responsibility for all police training.

The role of the constable as a 'beat manager' should be recognised. The role of the sergeant needed to be redefined. Sergeants were the first level of management who spent much of their time attending incidents with constables, checking paperwork and acting as custody officers. They were asked to be administrators, trainers, facilitators, trouble shooters, and law enforcement officers. Sergeants needed more training on promotion, and there should be sufficient sergeants to ensure that they could fulfill their role.

More than half of the inspectors said they had a 24 hour responsibility and the average overtime worked by an inspector was between five and six hours a week, with most saying that they claimed for much less. Many inspectors were put under pressure not to claim for any overtime at all.

The JCC gave oral evidence to Sheehy in January 1993. It was a depressing experience for the five strong deputation which confronted the Inquiry members. At first, Neild had been told that the Inquiry could spare only an hour to hear what the JCC wanted to say. Only after protest was it agreed that there should be no such time limit. Sheehy was courteous and anxious to refute an article which had just appeared in the *Daily Telegraph*. It purported to summarise the 'decisions' which the Inquiry had already arrived at. These included fixed term contracts, performance related pay, and differentials between roles and forces. Sheehy stressed that the team was still taking evidence and had not begun to write its report.

The exchanges between the JCC members and the Inquiry team were perfunctory, only coming to life when Eastwood pointed out that some of the proposed changes had been introduced in the NHS and they had destroyed morale. Caines saw this as a personal attack and exploded. He said that he and his colleagues had been appalled by the low morale of the police, and the lack of confidence in senior officers expressed to them by Federation members.

The Federation's evidence to Sheehy was minutely detailed, and filled two volumes, with copious appendices. There were times during the meeting with Sheehy and his colleagues that the JCC members began to doubt if the team had bothered to read it, a fear confirmed after Jeff Moseley, the secretary of the Sergeants' Central Committee, had explained about research undertaken into the role of sergeants, and Sheehy suggested that he might send them a copy. It was already a part of the evidence.

The evidence of the Association of Chief Police Officers to Sheehy was not received with enthusiasm by the Federation. It recommended overlapping pay scales, with progression depending on satisfactory performance and the highest part reserved for those 'deserving particular recognition'. ACPO said it would prefer to remove all overtime payments but this would not be realistic for sergeants and constables. Unforeseen overtime should not be compensated for an initial period. It wanted changes to compensation for rest days cancelled at short notice, and called for the restoration of the old requirement that officers should parade for duty before their starting times, without compensation. Inspectors should have 24 hour responsibility and their salaries should reflect this. Sick pay should be limited. Police regulations were unduly restrictive and hampered chief officers from deploying their resources. They should be replaced by an advisory code of practice.

The Home Office on this occasion departed from its customarily neutral stance when giving evidence to such inquiries. It said the service needed to adopt good management practice from other occupations. The current rigid system of ranks and pay and conditions of service, it claimed, militated against this. On rank structure, it said that it did not follow that all forces had to have every rank in its structure, nor was it necessary for officers to pass through each rank on their way to the top.

Pay, said the Home Office, should provide flexibility, not inhibit it. Pay points should be determined in other ways than simply length of service. Pay should give the police an assurance that it would reflect their roles and responsibilities, with emphasis on the central importance of beat duties, and be simply and easily understood. Housing and rent allowances should be phased out with compensating pay adjustments. Overtime compensation should be reduced.

The Home Office suggested that once constables had completed their probation, they should be offered short term contracts of ten years' duration. It agreed that short term contracts for senior officers would give greater clarity to their roles, but asked if they would deter officers from seeking promotion.

The official side of the PNB asked Sheehy to abolish the requirement for a rank structure and leave it to the discretion of the police authority of each force. Housing and rent allowances should be phased out, and there should be flexible pay rates which would be fixed locally. The Home Office should no longer control police establishments. It accepted that local flexibility on pay would lead to a labour market and competition between forces, and suggested a system of undermanning allowances would help the 'unpopular' forces. The official side was sceptical about performance related pay but wanted chief officers to have the right both to reward good performers and withhold pay from poor ones. Only the basic rate of pay should be paid for duty on bank holidays. For all other overtime, constables and sergeants should not be paid, but given time off, again at basic rates.

The official side complained that the cost of pensions was rising too fast, with seven pensioners for every ten constables. This ratio would increase because pensioners were living longer and an increasing number of officers were retiring on pensions which were enhanced on ill health grounds, which it said was an abuse of the system. It suggested that officers who were considered unfit for the full range of duties should not be allowed to retire on ill health pensions, but moved instead to civilian posts. It rejected the idea of extending the period of service for maximum pension, but only because it believed that this would lead to more ill health retirements.

In their evidence, the Inspectors of Constabulary pointed out that under current force reorganisation schemes, two out of every five officers above the rank of inspector would soon be redundant. They called for a severance scheme, saying that at present superfluous chief inspectors, superintendents and senior officers, were being offered 'non-jobs' in the hope that they would leave the service on pension. This was unfair to them and to the service.

The HMIs, all former chief officers themselves, were scathing about some of their erstwhile colleagues;

> 'It has to be accepted that some of the present managers of the police service are not as capable of meeting the challenge of change as some of their subordinates; some senior officers are facing a service of a type which they did not join and facing demands for which they have neither the training nor the skills.'

In order to expedite the succession of their more modern and accomplished subordinates, the HMIs suggested that the out of date and unadaptable chief officers should be given the opportunity to retire with dignity, in other words, with a 'golden handshake'. The compulsory retirement ages, which allowed provincial chief constables to stay until they were 65, should be swept away, as should the restriction which did not allow an ACPO officer to go out on pension until he was 55 years of age. No commercial organisation, said the Inspectorate, would attempt to carry out major change without displacing managers who could not be expected to drive it through.

The Inspectorate agreed with the Federation, that the ranks of chief inspector and chief superintendent should be abolished and absorbed with the superintendents, but the latter should be graded according to responsibilities and paid accordingly. The Inspectorate criticised the Edmund-Davies pay system, saying it was clearly intended to make the police a white collar profession, but had left in place a blue collar structure. They criticised across the board increases because they took discretion away from management, and did not allow the service to reward particular groups of officers who were coming under pressure, nor individuals who deserved higher rewards, nor did it allow slackers to be penalised by withholding increments. They too wanted severe restrictions on payment for overtime, and the first two hours in each week of 'casual' overtime should not be compensated, with time-off only for other overtime. To round off a document which the Federation would have found extremely depressing reading, the Inspectorate described the payment of rent or housing allowance as 'largely indefensible'.

The Federation's 1993 Conference at Blackpool was held in the looming shadow of Sheehy. Clarke, who would within a few weeks be elevated to the Treasury following the exchange rate fiasco, concentrated on law and order issues in his address. Alan Eastwood, making his last Conference speech before retiring (along with Vee Neild) criticised the Home Secretary's decision to ban projected trials of new kinds of batons, for which the Federation had been pressing for some years. A series of shocking assaults on officers, including women, had highlighted the inadequacy of the traditional truncheon as a protection for officers faced with knife wielding assailants. The Federation was angered because the ban seemed to be related to a case in Los Angeles where police had been filmed using excessive violence towards an arrested man, and the modern batons had been employed in the beating.

Bearing in mind the anxieties felt by the service, the exchange between Eastwood and Clarke was curiously subdued. The feeling was inescapable that the real battle was just about to begin. However, the Conference made its feelings of disenchantment with the Conservative government clear enough by the warmth of its reception for the Shadow Home Secretary, Tony Blair. He was guarded about Sheehy, but his speech, which called for a new approach to crime, dealing toughly with the criminal but attacking the social causes, earned him a standing ovation from an audience that would not normally have applauded such an even handed approach.

The Sheehy Inquiry's report was published on the 31st July 1993. It confirmed the gloomiest expectations of the Federation, which immediately dubbed it 'a blueprint for disaster' and informed the new Home Secretary, Michael Howard, that it rejected the report in its entirety. This prompted the immediate criticism that the Federation was indulging in a knee jerk reaction, but Sheehy himself had made no other course available. On the day of publication he told a press conference that the report had to be accepted in its entirety, not as an *a la carte* menu to be selected or discarded at will. In any case, there was practically nothing in the report that the Federation could support.

Anticipating Federation opposition, the Home Office arranged for the executive summary of the report to be sent to every police officer. Either by accident or design, the summary missed out particulars of how the new pay system proposed by Sheehy would affect the membership, and this point was crucial to its reception by police officers. Within days of publication, the Federation had remedied this significant omission by sending the full recommendations to every member.

The introduction to the Sheehy report made it clear that this was a management, cost-efficiency exercise, not an updated version of predecessor inquiries from Willink to Edmund-Davies. The authors dismissed the notion that policing was a unique occupation;

> 'While there are features which apply only to the police and which need to be recognised, there has been

a tendency on occasion - some feel an exaggerated tendency - to claim special status for the police when this is not justified. This is particularly clear in the long held tradition of tenure (a job for life and restrictions on the ability to dismiss police officers).'

The report said that the service would be better run if clearer lines of accountability were established for chief officers. The Committee had seen in advance the Government's White Paper on Police Reform (published two days earlier) and the report dovetailed with the White Paper in proposing the replacement of existing police authorities with 'business driven' bodies;

'chief officers should be accountable to a competent body drawn from a group of suitably qualified individuals who are known to have financial, organisational and management experience.'

Sheehy began by recommending a reduced rank structure, abolishing the posts of chief inspector, chief superintendent, and deputy chief constable. He did not adopt the Federation's proposal that the chief inspectors should be assimilated into the superintendents.

Sheehy proposed reducing the minimum starting pay of a constable by close on £2,000. He also proposed the scrapping of the housing allowance for new entrants, thus reducing the value of the starting package by roughly 40 per cent. All recruits would join on fixed term appointments, initially for ten years, renewable at the chief officer's discretion for periods of five years, up to the age of sixty. The fixed term appointments would apply to officers who chose to be employed on these terms, and to those who took promotion. Such officers would, like recruits, not draw a full pension until they had completed 40 years' service.

Next, Sheehy called for the scrapping of the incremental scales and of uniformity of remuneration within ranks. He put forward what he beguilingly termed a 'simple matrix' to be applied to an evaluation of the roles, responsibilities and performance of police officers. It contained four key variables;

scope of the role: responsibilities, scale and specialist requirements associated with the job. This would take account of variations in the levels of responsibilities of the role and its scale in terms of manpower and resources;

policing circumstances: impact of the policing environment and related requirements, such as the role's relative risk of assault; the availability of support; its working pattern; disruption to family life; the nature of the environment in which the role was performed; any requirement to work long hours regularly without overtime payment; particular difficulties in filling the role;

experience and skills: proven track record and skills possessed by the individual and required by the job;

performance: an individual performance rating would be devised from the appraisal system.

Each of these key variables would earn points on the pay matrix. Sheehy claimed that his performance related pay proposals offered serving officers the opportunity to earn up to £8,000 a year extra, a point the press seized upon. Lyn Williams, the Metropolitan constable who had just taken over from Vee Neild as General Secretary of the Federation, told the membership that this was a confidence trick. The first thing that would happen to their pay would be a freeze. Any officer with 15 years service would be unable to earn an additional penny by performance related pay. The same would apply to top rate sergeants and inspectors. Williams said that only a small percentage of officers would ever benefit from the Sheehy plan, and an officer would have to be superhuman to score the maximum points on the matrix.

The Sheehy report gave some interesting examples of how officers in various posts would fare. A constable on foot or car patrol in Brixton, who had been doing that job for the past two years and was rated an average performer, would get two points for the scope of the job, three for the circumstances of the role, none for experience and two for performance. This would give him, at current rates, £17,135, some £2,600 less than the constable's maximum scale. A PC on foot patrol in less stressful Hampstead would fare even worse. He too would have two years experience in his current role, and even though an above average performer himself, his job circumstances would give him only one point. His pay would be only £15,608 a year.

On pay reviews, Sheehy said that future adjustments would be made by reference to the median of the non-manual private sector employee, which in a time of recession was bad news indeed. Moreover, only two thirds of the global sum accruing from the annual review would be used to increase core pay. The rest would be put in a pool from which to pay performance related bonuses to individuals and teams. An interesting feature was that chief officers would be able to earn up to 30 per cent of their salary in additional bonuses, a point to which Paul Condon, the Metropolitan Commissioner, took exception, saying that he could not in conscience take such a bonus at the cost of the pay increases due to junior officers. The bonus pool would be swelled by part of the savings Sheehy anticipated from the abolition of all payment for overtime, with the rest of this economy going to finance the performance payments.

More consternation was aroused when the manpower implications of Sheehy were spelt out. He proposed that the total number of police officers would be reduced by up to 5,000 up until 1999. If funds were available, the service could then begin to recruit up to 2,000 'extra' constables. The bulk of this reduction was occasioned by the need to make severance payments to redundant senior officers.

Other key proposals were that the framework of statutory regulations governing conditions of service should be swept away and left largely to local discretion and negotiation.

When the Joint Central Committee met to consider the report, it was unanimous in endorsing the instant rejection which Eastwood and Williams had given it. A new slogan was born. Out went the statesmanlike *Only our best will do*. In came a combative and uncompromising declaration;

The police service says 'No' to Sheehy.

THIRTY—EIGHT

We're on our way to Wembley

Within a few days of the appearance of the Sheehy Report, the JCC team deputed to run the Federation's campaign against it, decided to call an open meeting in London. It was realised at once that the usual venue, Central Hall, would not be large enough, and with some hesitation Wembley Arena, normally the site of mammoth pop concerts, was reserved for a meeting in two weeks' time. As soon as it was announced, the response told the organisers that this was going to be a huge meeting, but as the details of coaches booked by boards came in, it was decided to reserve one, and then both the exhibition halls at Wembley to cater for the overflow.

Michael Howard, who had inherited the Sheehy hot potato from Clarke, from the outset adopted a neutral approach to Sheehy. Clarke, the father of all the thoughts in Sheehy, would have endorsed its findings unreservedly. Howard saw that the initially favourable press reviews were quickly turning to criticism as the implications of the changes sunk in, and he soon became aware of the strong hostility of the service, not just the Federation but the other associations and the chief officers. He said that he would take the views of all interested parties before making up his mind, and stressed that 'Sheehy is not a Government report. It is a report to the Government'.

Eric Caines, a couple of days after the report was published, wrote a vitriolic article in *The Guardian*, entitled *Stop money with menaces*, in which he urged Michael Howard to 'take on the boys and girls in blue';

> The Police Federation will object to most of the recommendations ... ... in this it will be no different from

the Prison Officers Association, the Royal College of Nursing and the British Medical Association, three of the most reactionary and arrogant staff interest groups in the public sector ... ... they threaten death (in the case of doctors and nurses) and destruction (in the case of prison officers and policemen).

Chief officers, some of whom had given a guarded welcome to the report after reading only the edited summary or press reports, soon began to issue condemnatory statements. Paul Condon went so far as to hint that he would find it difficult to continue to be Commissioner under a Sheehy regime.

Two hours before the meeting was due to start the huge arena was full and by the time the JCC members and guests came on to a specially designed stage setting to a roar of support, the audience knew that some 23,000 police officers, who had come in their own time from all over England and Wales, were at Wembley, with several thousand more arriving too late to get into the halls. It was probably the largest indoor meeting ever held in England. Eastwood, in his last address as chairman, told the audience;

'We are here because a vainglorious politician decided that the police were fair game for a shake-up. We are here because this monumental blunder has thrust this service to the edge of a cliff. We will never accept this God-forsaken, deeply wounding, totally wrong analysis of our service.'

Michael Howard declined an invitation to attend and speak, but sent a message to say that he and his colleagues 'would have to consider very carefully before deciding whether implementation of all or any of the report will achieve the purposes we had in mind when the Committee was set up'.

One almost unknown politician, Robert Maclennan, the Liberal Democrat Home Affairs spokesman, stole the show. Regarded by his Parliamentary colleagues as a reticent speaker who lacked charisma, Maclennan unexpectedly caught the mood of the largest audience that he or any other politician in history had ever addressed, and brought the hall to its feet with a rousing address. The primary purpose of Sheehy, he declared, was not to improve policing, it was to cut the cost of policing.

In contrast, Tony Blair did not enthuse the audience with a speech that was more or less a rerun of his address to the Federation Conference two months earlier. He was critical of Sheehy but insisted that Labour would make up its mind about the Report after considering it in detail. Blair concentrated much of his attack on the White Paper on police reform, and said that the country wanted to see the Government and the police fighting crime, not each other.

The meeting closed with everyone standing rigidly to attention and singing the national anthem. It had been an emotional, stirring, and totally orderly gathering. Staging the rally had cost the Federation around £250,000, but the resultant publicity, and the boost it gave to the membership's morale, more than justified the expenditure. The JCC was to spend well over £1 million during the Sheehy operation, most of it on meetings, advertising, and consultancies.

After Wembley, the problem facing the JCC was to maintain the impetus of such a dramatic start to the anti-Sheehy campaign. It did not help that Parliament was just about to go into the long summer recess. It was decided to enlist the branch boards in a co-ordinated approach to as many Members of Parliament as possible during this period. The JCC, following the setting up of Sheehy, had enlisted the services of a lobbying firm, Westminster Strategy, which assisted with details of MPs backgrounds. The firm also arranged a number of meetings between the Federation officers and MPs with a special interest in Home Affairs. Armed with a series of detailed briefings prepared by the Federation, the branch boards went about their task in a professional manner which deeply impressed many Members of Parliament. Tory back benchers began telling Michael Howard that they could not support the Sheehy proposals. This reflected a major turn round in opinion at Westminster. A private poll of MPs taken immediately after Sheehy by Access Opinions had found Tories almost unanimous in supporting the Report, and a surprising number of Labour MPs in favour of relating pay to performance.

The Federation ensured that the membership was kept fully informed about the full implications of Sheehy on their incomes and career prospects, through a series of supplements to *POLICE* which were sent to every member. One of the problems was that many members felt that the worst proposals in Sheehy would only affect new members. The emphasis of the JCC information drive was to explain to serving officers how much they stood to lose. Another problem was that the Federation's public relations campaign was proving so successful that many members began to assume that the battle was won.

The Federation's exhibition stands at the party conferences, and the message which Dick Coyles emphasised at the fringe meetings held at each of them, was that the Federation was saying a resounding 'No' to Sheehy. On the morning that Michael Howard was due to make his Conference debut as Home Secretary, and announce his 27 point plan for beating crime, full page advertisements from the Federation, urging him to reject Sheehy, appeared in the serious papers. He was, however, saving his decision for the new Parliamentary session.

The Federation, in its detailed response on Sheehy to the Home Secretary, told Howard that it welcomed change where it was designed to enhance the quality of service to the public. The service was now at a pivotal point of its history. If Howard accepted Sheehy, it said, the resulting inflexibility, divisiveness, and substantial fall in the incomes of so many officers would lead to a progressive and irreversible decline in policing standards and quality of service, combined with a collapse of police morale.

On rank structure, the Federation condemned the Sheehy plan to reduce the number of sergeants by 9 per cent and of inspectors by 22 per cent. The abolition of three managerial levels was likely to require more officers in junior management posts, not less. The report of the Royal Commission on Criminal Justice, published during the summer, had emphasised the need for better training, improved administrative procedures, more scrupulous supervision and more effective interviewing techniques. None of this could be achieved with a drastic reduction in first and second line management.

Analysing the pay proposals, the Federation said that the sheer complexity of the pay matrix illustrated the Inquiry's failure to grasp the fundamentals of policing. It was impractical, bureaucratic, immensely costly and would never achieve its objectives. Front line policing was variable, multi-skilled and multi - tasked. Sheehy had failed to grasp the flexibility by which officers could perform one task on one day, and another the next, and that the service could not function without such omnicompetence. Research by Touche Ross had shown that many police officers performed three roles within a year, which made a nonsense of Sheehy's proposals.

Howard was told that the reality of Sheehy proposals was that basic salaries of constables would be £3,000 a year less and the basic salaries of sergeants would be cut by £2,000. More than half of the constables were being paid a basic salary above £18,000, whereas Sheehy offered this to only 5 per cent. Two thirds of sergeants were getting over £22,000 a year. Under Sheehy this proportion dropped to 10 per cent. The basic salaries of inspectors would be over £2,000 less, even though they would have assumed greater responsibilities. In addition, uniformed constables and sergeants would lose an average of £1,000 a year in overtime compensation, whilst still performing the additional duties. Overtime was essential to the service and should continue to be paid at premium rates. The Sheehy report would bring in variations in pay between forces and even between one force division and another. This would impede flexibility of deployment. The national rate of pay was a unifying influence, providing the service with a sense of common identity.

The Federation strongly defended incremental scales as the most efficient and effective means of establishing the basic rewards package. They rewarded developing skills and maturing judgement.

Performance related pay, said the Federation, would not work. Under Sheehy, three quarters of the constables would gain only one matrix point and only ten per cent would gain two. Just five per cent would qualify for three points. The rewards on offer were trivial when compared to the losses resulting from the abolition of the incremental scales. The

Federation reminded Howard that PRP had been largely discredited when tried elsewhere. Quantitative measures of police activity, it claimed, would destroy the scope for the use of discretion by officers and shift the focus of activity still further from traditional policing.

Housing emoluments were defended as an integral part of police pay. On fixed term appointments, the Federation said that policing was a vocation, not a job to be taken up for a few years before moving on. In other sectors, FTAs were used to manage short term fluctuations in the labour market. In the police, they would create uncertainty and instability. Particular objection was taken to the proposal that officers should be subjected to compulsory redundancy on structural grounds, such as a need to revise the age profile of the force. The Federation said it would be outrageous if an officer whose capability, conduct, health and performance were not in doubt, should be severed simply to reduce the age profile. Objection was also taken to the suggestion that partially disabled officers should be retired on structural grounds. This could mean officers being sent out of the job with no pension at all. The Federation ridiculed the Sheehy proposal that officers should have to serve until 60 for maximum pension.. Howard was told that Sheehy's proposals would reduce pension commutation payments by about £21,000 at current rates. The Federation counter proposed that officers should have the right to retire on a reduced pension after 22 and 25 years service.

Sheehy had called for extensive changes to the negotiating machinery, with the official side's councillors being replaced by chief officers and professional advisers. He had proposed a system of binding pendulum arbitration which meant 'winner take all'. The Federation pointed out that Sheehy had exceeded his terms of reference here, as he had with proposals to limit the duty time allowed to Federation officials for their representative work.

Sheehy and his colleagues were annoyed by the impact of the Federation's campaign and demanded that the Home Office should counter attack in support of the report. They found that Howard, unlike Clarke, was not going out on a precarious political limb for a plan that was beginning to lack all credibility. Sheehy did his best to keep the cause alive, but his efforts were naive and counter productive. Here was a man unused to being contradicted, and it showed. Addressing ACPO and police authority councillors at their 1993 Conference, he criticised the chief officers for their own attitude to the report. He told them that the Committee had tried to give them 'freedom to manage' and could not understand why they were not his most enthusiastic supporters.

In a document headed *The way forward* the Federation set out an alternative strategy. In summary, the Federation said;

> 'Rewards should be somewhat above those elsewhere in the public and private sector to acknowledge the unique stresses and risks of policing. The calculations of rewards should be simple, clear, and easy to apply; each rank should be regarded as a career in which there is clear scope for the recognition of both experience and performance; overtime should be paid and it should not be exposed to inefficient usage and abuse; uprating should be fair in comparison with all non manual overall increases. It should be consistently timed, evenly distributed and achieved with the least fuss.'

At the end of October, Howard told the House of Commons that he was rejecting substantial parts of the Sheehy Report. Fixed term appointments would apply only to ACPO posts, although it was possible they would be extended at a later date to Superintendents. The ranks of deputy chief constable, chief superintendent and chief inspector would be abolished in April 1995. Serving officers in these ranks would be regraded as their chief officers decided. Later, he decided to retain the chief inspector rank, at the request of ACPO.

Howard rejected the Sheehy pay 'matrix'. Instead, he was asking the Police Negotiating Board to consider the proposals on pay which had been put to him following the Sheehy Report, by the official side. These proposed appraisal related pay for all ranks, new salary scales, changes in overtime payments, and local discretion over payments of allowances.

Howard said that the PNB would be expected to make detailed proposals on pay to him in time for the September 1994 pay round. He stressed that he expected that these would make savings in the pay bill of the kind mentioned by the official side.

Pay would continue to be uprated, but by the median of private sector non-manual pay settlements instead of the movement of the underlying index of earnings. None of the product of pay reviews would be set aside for bonuses to individuals or teams. Serving officers would continue to receive rent or housing allowances, but there would be no further uprating. Officers recruited from 1st September 1994 would not be paid housing allowance.

Howard said that full pay entitlement during sickness would be set at a maximum of six months, with chief officers free to extend it in appropriate cases, such as illness or injury related to duty.

The Government, said Howard, would commission a full review of police pensions, including retirement on ill health grounds, the cost of which was causing so much concern to the Government and police authorities. Howard rejected Sheehy's proposals for extending the service for maximum pension to forty years.

On severance, Howard said that Government would bring in procedures for ridding the service of unsatisfactory officers. The disciplinary procedures would be changed to make it easier to get rid of officers deemed to have committed serious misconduct. There would be a reserve power to introduce severance on structural grounds, but only if and when the Home Secretary agreed, and it would operate only for a set period in the force concerned.

The Home Secretary said that the negotiating machinery would not be changed, except that chief officers would join the official side as full members instead of advisers. Federation duties would continue to qualify for duty time.

Howard, whose statement was received with approval on both sides of the House, said he was glad the period of uncertainty was over. He said he had listened to what individual police officers and the staff associations had said.

The new staff side negotiator, Lyn Williams, welcomed

Howard's decision to refer the pay and conditions package to the PNB, as the Federation had asked for from the outset. But he was concerned by Howard's stipulation that substantial cost savings must result from any agreement submitted to him for ratification. The Federation would be looking for a reasonable share of the savings accruing from the abolition of the chief inspector rank and the very large cuts in the housing aid bill. So much, the Federation thought, for Clarke's first promise that the levels of pay were not under attack. 'Fairness' and 'flexibility' had become a search for savings from the costs of policing.

Williams expressed his concern about the proposed review of pensions. It was not to be conducted within the PNB, but by the Home Departments. The staff associations would only be able to make submissions to the review, not take part in it. Howard had chosen to take an independent line on pensions, which ignored Sheehy, but also the service submissions.

Well aware that substantial parts of the current pay and conditions package were still at risk, Williams promised the membership; 'We have not fought Sheehy to a standstill in the open, only to lose behind closed doors in the PNB.' He expected that the negotiations on the official side's proposals would be long and difficult.

As it happened, the 1993 pay review was the first since 1978 not to be based on Edmund-Davies, but the cause was not Sheehy, it was the government, which had decreed that there must be a ceiling on public sector increases of 1.5 per cent. The Edmund-Davies formula would have produced an increase of 3.75 per cent. The negotiations took place in the PNB on the morning of the Wembley rally, and the staff side said it accepted that the country was facing a financial crisis, and was prepared on this occasion to accept the Government's ruling. It was a gesture which went virtually unnoticed by the media and the public. Starting pay went from £12,555 to £12,744 and top constables' pay from £20,952 to £21,267.

The negotiations on a new pay and conditions package, which began after Michael Howard's statement, were the most protracted and difficult since the Police Negotiating Board had been established fourteen years earlier. In fact, they were the first full blooded negotiations, covering every aspect of the package, for until then the Edmund-Davies pay formula had dominated annual reviews. There were many tense and angry moments in a succession of long meetings, several occupying whole weekends in a London hotel, when the staff side had cause to be grateful that someone as tough and uncompromising as Lyn Williams was heading the staff side team. He was determined to claw back as much as he could of the savings resulting from any changes, into the membership's pockets. The official side was equally determined to deliver the cuts in the police pay bill that Howard had called for, and for a long time there was little sign of give and take between the sides.

Eventually, towards the end of February 1994, a deal was reached. It gave both sides cause for satisfaction. The agreement retained the incremental scales. In future, and when an appraisal system was in place (which could take at least two years) incremental progression would be dependent on satisfactory appraisal as well as length of service. Constables who reached the eighth point on the scale would have the chance to acquire a non-pensionable supplement of £625 provided they were appraised as outstanding, and would retain it in future years so long as they continued to be so rated. When the fourteenth point was reached, officers already receiving the supplement could qualify for a further one, and the first would become pensionable. It thus became possible for an 'outstanding' constable to reach the maximum scale of £22,125 after 14 years, and have a non-pensionable supplement of £635 as well. When such a constable was promoted, he would start at the third point of the sergeants' scale. Corresponding arrangements were made for sergeants.

The total cost of this system, above the existing one, was put at £50 millions a year, and the money was found partly from assimilating some allowances, but mainly from the staff side conceding flexibility on working arrangements. In future, re-rostering with fourteen days notice or more would not entitle an officer to compensation. Previously this was twenty eight days. A change notified between eight and fourteen days would continue to be compensated at time and a half, but with less than eight days notice, the premium was increased to double time, but with no additional day off.

Overtime would continue to be paid for at premium rates, except that up to four periods of 'casual' overtime of half an hour each in any seven day period would not be compensated. Where overtime carried over to a scheduled rest day, the entitlement to a minimum of four hours at double time and a day off would cease. Management would compensate the first hour at double time, during which it would decide if the officer needed to be retained. If he was, double time would be paid for a minimum of four hours. It was agreed that officers serving at the 31st August 1994 would retain the right to a housing allowance, which was good news for officers in police accommodation who had feared they would not qualify for it.

The big stumbling block was the 'professional salary' for inspectors. The PNB decided to reach agreement on the conditions of sergeants and inspectors, and refer the dispute over inspectors to conciliation.

Commenting to branch boards on the agreement, Williams said;

> 'This agreement is better than any of us could have anticipated when the Sheehy report was published. It means that all the most objectionable features of Sheehy have been avoided. We have retained increments and avoided the damaging proposals for differentiation between officers in the same ranks in respect of posts. The pay scales will continue to be negotiated nationally, and we have held on to premium rates of payment for overtime. The new scales will provide additional benefits for our members, and because there was and will be no 'new' money available, we have done well in ensuring that the savings arising from greater flexibility have been used to finance the additional benefits.'

It still remained for Michael Howard to be satisfied about the cost of the deal and ratify the agreement, and the problem of the inspectors had to be solved. But at last the end of the Sheehy saga was in sight.

THIRTY-NINE

Whitelaw sinks the 'flagship'

The Sheehy Inquiry was just one part of Kenneth Clarke's plans for the police. The White Paper on police reform, published almost simultaneously with Sheehy, was a blueprint for the most fundamental reorganisation of the service since the Police Act 1919. It made little impact on first appearance, because Sheehy took all the press attention, but from the outset of that campaign, Federation spokesmen were careful to link the White Paper with Sheehy. The 'hidden agenda', the existence of which had long been suspected, had come into the open. It was widely reported that Clarke had wanted to drastically reduce the number of separate forces to about 20, but had run into opposition from the Environment Secretary, Michael Howard. Clarke was reported to have told his cabinet colleagues that getting the reforms through, in the face of inevitable opposition from the police and local authorities, would be harder than it had been for him with the teachers and the health service. As with Sheehy, it was to fall to Howard to fight that battle, while Clarke's political career was boosted with the Chancellor's post.

The White Paper asserted that the Government's purpose was to forge a 'new partnership between the police and the public against crime.' The reforms, said Howard, would 'put protecting the public and preventing and detecting crime at the top of the national agenda for policing.' Chief constables and local police commanders would be given more freedom to deliver the quality service local people wanted. This would be done by sweeping away all the existing police authorities, consisting of two thirds elected councillors and one third local magistrates, and replacing them with 'free standing' authorities. The chairmen of these would be appointed directly by the Home Secretary, who would also nominate five of the 16 members of each authority, the others would consist of eight councillors and three magistrates. Since 1974, combined police forces outside London had been controlled by police authorities representing the local authorities in the police area and magistrates, while the forces which policed just one county council area were under police committees of the county council, with appointed JPs. Now all would become corporate bodies.

The task of the new authorities would be to set local priorities and ensure that policing met both local and national needs. The white paper said that police management would be streamlined, with the object of putting more officers out on patrol. Kenneth Clarke had foreshadowed the general trend of the changes in an announcement to Parliament in April. He had sprung a major surprise by proposing a new police authority for London, on similar lines to the new provincial bodies. In the past, Tory governments had been strongly opposed to the idea of elected members of London councils being involved in running the Metropolitan. The idea infuriated the party's London MPs and Clarke's successor, Michael Howard, was soon persuaded to drop it in favour of a powerless 'consultative committee'.

The Federation was one of almost five hundred organisations and individuals who submitted their views on the White Paper to Howard. It transpired that all but a handful were opposed to the main thrust of the proposals. The Federation could find little to praise. It told Howard that it had applied three tests to the White Paper; would it create a more efficient police service; did it ensure that greater efficiency was not to be achieved at the cost of local democracy, and; did it retain the balance of power between local and central government and guarantee the operational independence of chief constables? The Federation's conclusion was, that while some proposals, such as more local discretion in how resources were spent, would improve matters, the cumulative effect of the plan was to weaken local control of the police.

The White Paper said that the main job of the police was to fight crime. The Federation retorted that protecting life was the first responsibility of policing, and preventing crime was better than detecting it. The Operational Policing Review had shown that the public wanted to see the police concentrating on 'non law enforcement' tasks, as well as crime. The White Paper's suggestion that the police should scale down 'non crime' activities was attacked. The Federation said the traffic role was of crucial importance. It disputed the Home Secretary's assertion that the tripartite system of governing the police, established by Willink, had been tested to the limit and was now creating confusion as to the roles of the Home Secretary, chief officers and police authorities.

The White Paper attacked police regulations as an inflexible burden that prevented managers from managing. While agreeing that the management style of some senior officers was detrimental to welfare and efficiency, the Federation said there could be no valid criticism of the professional ability and performance of police managers in delivering a high quality of service to the public.

The Federation expressed reservations about the abolition of authorised establishments, fearing that the size of police forces was going to be governed by a force's ability to pay for its manpower. The Home Secretary had stressed that chief officers would enjoy new financial freedom, but the Federation said that in reality Whitehall would keep its grip on the amount of money to be spent on policing. The White Paper said nothing about involving local communities in setting police objectives.

There was no case, the Federation said, for reorganising police authorities as proposed. It disagreed with the reduction of the elected element and the nomination of non-elected members by the Home Secretary. Too much power would be vested in the new chairman, a Home Secretary's placeman, and this would threaten the chief constable's independence.

The JCC decided that it should campaign against the White Paper, and the Police and Magistrates Courts Bill, which embodied the proposals and was published in December 1993. It was clear that the new police authorities would be powerful bodies, able to give directions on policing matters to chief officers. Moreover, there was every chance that some of the more objectionable features of Sheehy, having been defeated as a result of the Federation's resistance, could be introduced by local arrangement, especially if the statutory framework of police regulations were to be abolished.

The Federation was also angry because the Bill contained stringent new disciplinary procedures. The right of silence would be withdrawn from police officers under investigation and they would lose the right of legal representation at hearings where their jobs or ranks were in jeopardy, something secured only ten years earlier. The criminal standard of proof, another protection gained in the Police and Criminal Evidence Act, would go. There would be a new appeals board, and tribunals would no longer include a retired member of the appellant's staff association.

Kenneth Clarke had announced in December 1992 that he had found the disciplinary procedure 'unsatisfactory and unrealistic'. It was, he said, 'wholly out of proportion' that the Home Secretary should have to consider appeals against disciplinary punishments from police constables. In April 1993, the Home Office published a consultation paper, and gave the staff associations six weeks to respond. In addition to the changes mentioned above, it proposed to scrap the discipline code which set out the specific offences that a police officer could commit, and replace it with a single and loosely defined offence of 'discreditable conduct', something for which the Federation had been calling for years. An accused officer would lose the right to call witnesses at a disciplinary hearing, it would be up to the chief officer to decide whether the attendance of a witness was necessary. The 'double jeopardy' rule, which debarred disciplinary charges from being brought against an officer who had been acquitted of a criminal charge on the same facts, would go. The Federation took particular exception to the proposal that, in certain circumstances, an officer could be sacked on the spot.

This draconian package appeared to reflect growing exasperation among Ministers, the Home Office, and the Police Complaints Authority about the inability of the service to take effective action against officers who had been involved in well publicised cases, where complainants had alleged assault and false imprisonment, and had received substantial damages in the civil courts. In some cases, the Metropolitan and other forces had made large monetary settlements and did not defend the actions. The problem, said chief officers, the Crown Prosecutions Service and the PCA, was that the criminal standard of proof required to find an officer guilty of a disciplinary offence was much higher than the 'balance of probabilities' basis of civil decisions.

Even ACPO, which supported much of the consultation paper, was concerned about the package. The staff associations claimed it would alter the status of the constable from a crown servant to an employee. Because of the strength of the service objections, the Home Office said that a working party would be set up to finalise the long discussed incapability procedure and the proposals for changes in disciplinary procedure. It was, therefore, something of a shock when in September 1993, while the staff associations thought the consultation process was still ongoing, Howard told the Superintendents' Conference that he had decided to implement substantial areas of the reforms.

He announced that there would be a procedure for instant dismissal, which would be much shorter. In future, the PCA would only deal with allegations of crime or a breach of the PACE advisory codes. Allegations of unsatisfactory performance would be dealt with by a new procedure, designed to respond to complaints in accordance with the Citizen's Charter, the Government's mission statement on better public services.

The Federation told Howard that the proposals were unfair and unworkable; they were open to abuse and would undermine police discipline. As such they would be opposed and challenged at every stage. Meanwhile, the immediate issue was the changes in discipline outlined in the Police and Magistrates Courts Bill.

The government was faced with a timetable problem. The Bill was one of two Home Office Bills in the Queen's Speech, the other being the Criminal Justice Bill, which sought among other things to remedy some of the major mistakes of the 1991 Act. The Government saw the two measures as its flagship for the coming session of Parliament, putting its law and order credentials in the shop window. It was decided that the Criminal Justice Bill would start off in the Commons, and the Police Bill in the Lords. It was a fateful miscalculation, because as soon as the Committee Stages began, the hapless Earl Ferrers, who had been given the task of seeing it safely through the Lords, was the victim of a succession of ambushes, some from the Government side of the House.

The Government had anticipated a strong reaction from chief constables and the Federation. They had not foreseen that the Bill's accretion of power to the Home Secretary would enrage the Old Guard Tories, to whom the police were a part of the British way of life, not a political plaything of radical and ultra-ambitious 'new wave' Ministers.

The peer who found himself, much to his own surprise, leading the rebellion was Viscount Whitelaw, former Home Secretary and much revered Conservative elder. He had been briefed at some length on the Bill during a train journey from Carlisle to London by a Cumbrian, who happened to be the chairman of the Police Federation, Dick Coyles. What he heard made him inquire further, and as soon as he realised what was afoot, Whitelaw was incandescent. He warned Howard and the Tory whips that he would not support the Bill, and that many other like minded Tories were unlikely to, either. The Government's business managers chose to ignore the warnings, and similar advice from Lord Carr, a Home Secretary in the Heath government, and a succession of former Home Office ministers. Meanwhile, it was becoming clear that the Opposition parties in the Lords, the Law Lords (who were also furious about the Bill's plans for magistrates' courts), and most of the unaligned peers, were equally determined to oppose it.

The Federation's adviser in the Lords was Lord Bethell, who as a member of the European Parliament represented it in Brussels and Strasbourg. He was briefed on the Federation's antipathy to the Bill, and the JCC sponsored a reception in the House of Lords, at which a succession of distinguished peers of all parties and none, including Whitelaw, Carr, Harris of Greenwich and Merlyn-Rees emphasised that they were determined either to change the Bill or defeat it. Lord Callaghan, with the authority of a former Prime Minister and Home Secretary, was another powerful opponent.

The JCC worked closely with a broad alliance of peers, headed by Labour's Lord Macintosh of Haringey and the Liberal Democrat Lord Harris, once Roy Jenkins's Minister of State, and the local authority associations. One fierce opponent of the Bill was Lord Allen, a retired Permanent Secretary at the Home Office. A series of briefings was sent by the Federation to all the peers who were interested in the Bill.

Lord Whitelaw's speech in the House of Lords was a masterly and devastating destruction of the Bill's entire credibility. He said there was no justification for such an increase in the power of the Home Office over the service, and was blithely unimpressed by Earl Ferrers's protestations that the Government was seeking the exact opposite of this, and 'empowering' chief constables and the new police authorities. In a succession of votes, the Government was defeated, and was forced to make humiliating concessions on other clauses. There would be no Home Secretary appointed chairmen of the new authorities, they would be elected by the authority members. Local councillors would have one more seat than the magistrates and nominated members combined. The latter would be chosen from a Home Office approved short list by a panel of local people, not directly appointed by the Minister. Howard could not even get his way on this. He had suggested that the selection panel should involve the local Lord Lieutenant. The Lords decided it would consist of a councillor and a magistrate, who together would invite a third person to help them find suitable people to be nominated members. They would send twenty names to Howard and he would send back a shortened list for them to make the final choice. The significance of the changes was that all along the grand design had depended on 43 police authorities that could be relied upon to carry out the wishes of the Home Secretary. That concept now lay in tatters.

Lord Jenkins described the Bill as a classic example of how not to legislate. It had resulted in the government being 'humiliated by instalments'. These included some unexpected gains by the Federation. The clause deleting the right of legal representation in disciplinary hearings was defeated, as was the removal of a retired staff association member from the appeal tribunal. The Federation was unable to keep the 'double jeopardy' rule, to prevent officers from being charged with offences based on the same facts of a criminal charge of which they had been acquitted in courts. It did succeed in retaining a right of appeal for an officer who was reduced in rank. The Federation could congratulate itself over the success of its strategy on the Bill, although there was still the problem of contesting the Home Office proposals for other changes to the discipline procedures.

In December 1993, the Home Office revealed yet another 'initiative' in the Government's drive to create a dynamic and super-efficient police service for the start of the 21st century. It announced that a small team of three civil servants, an accountant and an economist, and a seconded chief inspector had been set up to review police core and ancillary tasks. It had been told to report to Howard by September 1994 on ways in which core functions could be carried out more cost-effectively and give options for relieving the police of ancillary tasks, together with a quick implementation programme. Dick Coyles responded to this information by writing to Howard to say that yet again the Home Office was identifying solutions before it had defined the problem. He expressed concern at the way the review team had been appointed, with the Home Office clearly in control of all its work. It was bound to lead to suspicion in the service of the government's intentions. Coyles asked why the Home Secretary had ignored the statutory Police Advisory Board, and reminded him of the successful examination of practically the same issues which the PAB carried out, at Roy Jenkins' request, in 1967. The Federation and other staff associations were being offered only minimal consultation, in the form of their written replies to a questionnaire prepared by the team.

The Federation believed that the Home Office wanted the core functions review completed and implemented in time for the start-up of the new police authorities in 1995. For some years, it had been clear that the government wanted to see parts of the police service hived off to other agencies, or privatised where possible. Forces had been obliged to accept compulsory competitive tendering and the market testing of some services, such as forensic science, catering, and vehicle maintenance. There was talk of an agency-run training operation. Forces had been driven to civilianise at a greater pace than most had wanted, a process which had been halted only by the adverse financial arrangements for paying government grants to police authorities for employing civilians, when compared with police officers. The privatisation of prisoner escorts had been introduced.Forces were not pleased to discover that the Home Office promptly deleted the number of posts previously engaged on prisoner escorts from authorised strengths. The Metropolitan 'lost' 300 officers in this way.

The review team's opening discussion paper talked about a growing role for the Special Constabulary, which the Government had been seeking to increase the size of, and an 'increasing interface' with the private sector.

In a detailed response to the core functions review, the Federation told the Home Office that it would not complete the questionnaire. It described the review as a 'cost cutting exercise, based on increasing civilian posts, greater use of Special and parish constables, and private security'.

The Federation knew that the core functions review had been set-up in response to Treasury insistence that the costs of policing should be thoroughly examined in order to identify savings.

At the 1994 Federation Conference, Dick Coyles summed up the anxieties that many police officers felt about the future of policing. He told Michael Howard;

'We are fearful that those who talk of a leaner, fitter and more effective police service really mean a service that concentrates on basic crime-fighting. That is not the police that you and I know, and it is not the police that the public know and want. If we have to get rid of all that social service, which is part and parcel of British policing, we will indeed be left with a force that concentrates on crime and public order, and is remote from ordinary people.'

In 1994, the 75th anniversary year of the Police Federation, the service was facing a future that contained many uncertainties. The organisation had come through all its trials. It was now a wholly professional body, offering a wide range of services to its members and, backed by substantial resources, able to mount campaigns with confidence. It claimed as of right its place in the consultative and negotiating process, and had established itself as able to speak with authority on behalf of its membership. But those members operated in a society that was infinitely more complex, questioning and dangerous than past generations of police officers had known. The economics of policing were being questioned and even the service's monopoly of the policing function was under investigation. The possibility of a much reduced number of police officers, assisted perhaps by auxiliaries, with a significant private sector involvement, was high on the current agenda. And in response to increasing risks, sentiment in the police service was beginning to turn away from unquestioning acceptance of the unarmed status of the British police officer. The police in future, with their new batons, would follow Teddy Roosevelt's advice, and walk softly, but carry a big stick.

There would be, as always for the Police Federation, work to be done.